Adolescents

Indiana University | **Gary M. Ingersoll**

Adolescents
IN SCHOOL AND SOCIETY

D. C. Heath and Company

LEXINGTON, MASSACHUSETTS   TORONTO

To Jules Fillips, Charles Lucas, and Francis J. Di Vesta, each of whom made a contribution to my personal development that had a significant impact on my life—and that I will never forget. To each I am eternally grateful.

International Standard Book Number: 0–669–02325–6

Library of Congress Catalog Card Number: 81–81598

Preface

Adolescents in School and Society focuses on the period of human development known as adolescence. It is meant primarily for use by those who expect to work with adolescents or those who are currently working with adolescents and wish to expand their knowledge in the area. My intention was, thus, to present a basic core of information about adolescents and adolescence, drawn from contemporary research in psychology, sociology, education, medicine, and allied disciplines, that would be useful to the practitioner. My selection of information was admittedly biased by my own experiences in working with adolescents and by the experiences of former students who have themselves worked with young people.

In writing this text, certain key ideas kept coming to the fore. First and foremost, adolescents are striving in a number of areas (psychological, social, vocational, and so forth) to get a sense of who they are. As adults working with young people, we need to help adolescents accomplish the task of developing a positive sense of self-worth. Second, in working with young people, we must consistently recognize the wide variety of differences that exist among adolescents. Finally, practitioners have to take a caring stance. Toward the end of the text I employ the phrase "Give a Damn," once used in a campaign by John Lindsay, then mayor of New York City. Most evidence suggests that it is *caring* people, whether they are parents, teachers, counselors, pastors, or others, who give an adolescent a sense that he or she is worthwhile. If you are able to convey that sense in working with young people, you will certainly have made a significant contribution.

Adolescents has been written at a level appropriate to the typical freshman or sophomore student. Insofar as possible, I have avoided using technical jargon. Only in cases in which specific labels of psychological, sociological, or medical phenomena are appropriate is technical language used. These technical terms are defined in the text and in the glossary at the end of the text. The reading level of the text was tested using standard readability formulas, which indicated that the level was low enough for students to understand but high enough to convey the ideas accurately.

The text includes certain features that are intended to improve the level of understanding of those who read it. First, material in each chapter is supplemented by the use of instructional "vignettes." These vignettes provide examples, drawn from nonacademic sources, of the concepts discussed by the text; they also provide interest and humor. The vignettes may also be used by the instructor as stimuli for class discussion.

Two short appendixes following the text are not necessarily central to the study of adolescence but are relevant to specific groups of people who might undertake such study. For students who may be required to engage in a research project, Appendix A provides an overview of the basic elements of research design, offers a general structure for evaluating existing studies, and makes some specific suggestions on how to get started. Appendix B provides a limited discussion of the nature of the job of teaching or counseling adolescents. It is intended to help students apply the information in this text to situations and conditions they will encounter in their work with adolescents.

The photos in *Adolescents* were selected to depict specific psychological or sociological concepts and to add another dimension to the discussion.

This book also includes a substantial glossary and an extensive bibliography. The glossary offers definitions of terms used in the text that might be troublesome for the introductory student. The bibliography lists all sources cited in the text and serves as a valuable resource for the student initiating a research study.

Finally, an *Instructor's Guide* is available to help professors to evaluate student performance. The *Guide* also includes some suggestions of films appropriate to a course of study about adolescents.

I would like to take this opportunity to thank a number of people who were instrumental in producing this text. First, Geoffrey Hughes, George Abbott, and Bryan Woodhouse at D.C. Heath and Company invested considerable effort in making the book a tangible reality.

Several colleagues, including Nicholas Anastasiow, Susan Eklund, Myrtle Scott, and David Gliessman, all contributed information or acted as sounding boards along the way. I would also like to thank Dr. John Love and the staff of the Adolescent Psychiatric Unit at Madison State Hospital for their assistance and ideas.

Mostly, I want to thank my wife, Helen. When I began work on this text, I did not fully appreciate the enormous amount of time and energy that would be required to complete it. Helen has been a major force in motivating me to keep at it. She has served as reader, critic, editor, and typist through the whole process. Any success that this text experiences is due in no small part to her.

G. M. I.

Contents

1 | Adolescence as a Period of Growth and Development

Adolescence is a period of development that adults tend to view with a combination of fear and fascination. Parents of elementary school children will often describe their dread of the coming catastrophe—their child being transformed into an adolescent, or "teenager." Many adults see adolescence as something like a disease, something both the child and the parent must live through. To describe someone's behavior as "adolescent" is generally meant as an insult, because it implies that the behavior is impulsive and immature.

On the other hand, adults view with envy the idealism and energy of youth and may voice their wish that they could recapture their "carefree days of youth." Somewhere between these extremes lies an accurate representation of the period of life we call adolescence. This book is about young people in that period.

Although there is a danger in viewing adolescence as a separate period of growth and development, there are also advantages. The major disadvantage is that viewing adolescence separately makes it appear overly different from other periods of growth. It tends to segregate adolescence too much. However, adolescence is unique, not so much in the fact that it is a distinct period of growth and development, but in the types of tasks and expected events that are part of the process of becoming an adult. It is precisely those differences, and the ways in which young people who are adolescents respond to the tasks, that frightens many adults. Most professional practitioners avoid working with adolescents because they are neither children nor adults, and the practitioners are unsure of how to relate to these young people. Practitioners are not the only ones who avoid adolescents. It would appear that social scientists have a similar aversion to the study of adolescents. You will find in your own studies that the proportion of research literature dealing with adolescents is small, compared to that dealing with, for example, infants and preschoolers.

DEFINING ADOLESCENCE

What is an adolescent? The question is not as simple as you might initially think. The most common and obvious feature of the adolescent transition is a sudden spurt in physical and sexual development. Although physical and sexual maturation are very important components of the adolescent's transition to adult status and responsibility, they are only part of the total process. The growth spurt must be viewed together with the less obvious but also important changes in intellectual ability and in the expectations that parents and society hold for the emerging adults. Adolescence is a period of personal development during which a young person must establish a sense of individual identity and self-worth, which includes not only an alteration of his or her body image, but also adaptation to improved intellectual ability, adjustment to society's demands for behavioral maturity, and preparation for adult roles.

Adolescence should not, however, be seen as a singular, inclusive period of development. There are many who prefer to view early adolescence as different from middle adolescence and middle adolescence as different from late adolescence. Some have even suggested that a period of postadolescent development, preceding formal acceptance of adult roles, be designated as ''youth'' (Keniston, 1970). The term *youth*, however, has traditionally had a broader connotation, to include young people who are still within the period that we refer to as adolescence. Thus it will be used in its more traditional, general way in this text. (For complete bibliographic information on works cited briefly in the text, see the References at the end of the book.)

If adolescence in general has suffered neglect by researchers, the study of early adolescence is even less developed (Lipsitz, 1978). During early adolescence young people make the first attempts to leave the dependent, secure role of a child and to establish themselves as unique individuals,

Adolescence is a period not only of turbulence and soul-searching but also of great creativity and fun. (© Margaret Thompson)

independent of their parents. Early adolescence is marked by rapid physical growth and maturation, which forces the young person to adjust to a new body image. Early adolescence is also a period of intense conformity to peers. "Getting along" and being accepted seem somehow more important to the early adolescent than any other problem. The worst thing that the early adolescent can consider is to be seen by peers as different.

Middle adolescence is marked by the emergence of new thinking skills. The intellectual world of the young person is suddenly greatly expanded. Although peers still play an important role in the life of middle-adolescents, they are increasingly self-directed. The middle-adolescent's energies are directed at preparing for adult roles and making preliminary decisions regarding vocational goals. Beyond a small degree of delinquent behavior, middle adolescence is a period during which young people are oriented toward what is right and proper. They are developing a sense of behavioral maturity and learning to control their impulsiveness.

Late adolescence is marked by the final preparations for adult roles. Young people during this period attempt to crystallize their vocational goals and establish a sense of personal identity. Their need for peer approval is diminished, and they are largely independent of their parents. The shift to the adult stage of development is completed, or at least nearly so. It may be a mistake to conclude that all the outcomes of the adolescent transition are necessarily complete as we enter adulthood. As one friend puts it, "When I was an adolescent, I thought that when I got to be an adult I would have it all together. Now I'm an adult and I sure don't have all the answers; I've got more questions."

THEORIES OF ADOLESCENCE

G. STANLEY HALL

The psychologist who is generally credited with establishing adolescence as a period of psychological and social development deserving of separate study is G. Stanley Hall. Hall, like many other social scientists at the turn of the century, was enamored of Charles Darwin's theory on the nature of evolution. Hall was especially impressed with the writings of Ernst Haekel, who proposed that as organisms develop they appear to repeat characteristics that mirror their evolutionary stages of development. Haekel referred to this process with the phrase "ontogeny recapitulates phylogeny."

In his two-volume work with the forbidding title *Adolescence: Its psychology and its relations to physiology, anthropology, sociology, sex, crime, religion and education* (1916), Hall depicted adolescence as a transitional period bridging the "savagery" of childhood with "civilized" adulthood. In Hall's view, personal development retraces the social evolution from a savage to a civilized society. As such, adolescence reflects the tumultuous history of humanity arriving at its current civilized state. Adolescents are thus in a state of flux, alternating between periods of high enthusiasm and utter despair, between energy and lethargy, between altruism and self-centeredness. These radical shifts of necessity make adolescence a period of turmoil, of "storm and stress."

In one form or another, Hall's concept of "storm and stress" continues to be a popular conception of adolescence. Parents who seek advice about their adolescents often give a description of their offspring that is not unlike Hall's. One moment their adolescent is friendly and cooperative, and the next he or she is hostile and belligerent. Parents find that the child who was a docile, pleasant and helpful preadolescent now refuses to help around the house, will not listen to reason, is generally antagonistic and selfish, and seems to resent being part of the family. Further, the idea of adolescence as a period of turmoil is intrinsic to several theories of adolescence.

The view of these troubled parents is not, for example, very different from a description provided by Anna Freud (1968):

> Adolescents are excessively egoistic, regarding themselves as the center of the universe and the sole object of interest, and yet at no time in later life are they capable of so much self-sacrifice and devotion. They form the most passionate love relations, only to break them as abruptly as they began them. On the one hand, they throw themselves enthusiastically into the life of the community and, on the other, they have an overpowering longing for solitude. They oscillate between blind submission to some self-chosen leader and defiant rebellion against any and every authority. (pp. 137–138)

Not all writers agree that normal adolescence is a period of storm and stress, however. In his research Bandura (1964) found that most young people with whom he had contact were *not* anxiety ridden and stressful. Bandura felt that the assumption of a tumultuous adolescence was a gross overstatement of fact. On the other hand, we must be careful not to run to the other conclusion—that is, that adolescence is conversely a period of calm and serenity. Bandura's principal point was that when society presumes adolescence to be a period of radical tension, it runs the risk of creating a self-fulfilling prophecy. If parents, teachers, and other significant adults *expect* adolescents to be hostile, anxious, and emotionally variable and begin to worry if their teenagers are not, then adolescents, in order to conform to these expectations, may become hostile, anxious, and emotionally variable.

Recent reviews of the storm-and-stress concept again concluded that normal adolescence is *not* characterized by turmoil (Adelson, 1979; Oldham, 1976). Repeatedly, researchers have found that the evidence simply does not justify the stereotype of adolescence as any more tumultuous than any other period in life. Why, then, does the myth of a tumultuous adolescence persist? Oldham feels that a combination of popular novels such as *Catcher in the Rye* and *Ordinary People,* images presented by television and films, and reports of clinicians who work mainly with disturbed youth, all help to keep the stereotype alive.

The point is that any overgeneralization about adolescents and adolescent development is certain to meet with exceptions and qualifications. We, as practitioners, are dealing with a highly variable population. For some adolescents the transition to adulthood *will* be stressful and tumultuous. For others the transition will be smooth and pleasant. Not all adolescents are the same. To impose a stereotype on people because of their age may be just as prejudicial as racism or sexism. Your task, as an adult working with young people, will be to help them work through this transition and help them to adapt to whatever stress they may face.

THE CROSS-CULTURAL VIEW

Several writers, especially anthropologists, rely upon evidence drawn from cross-cultural studies of development and conclude that adolescence is a phenomenon found primarily in western cultures. Those who hold this view point out that there are several societies in which there is no discernible adolescence. At some point, usually around puberty, young people are no longer considered children and are given adult status. If adolescence does exist, it is not necessarily similar to western adolescence. Drawing on studies such as Margaret Mead's *Coming of Age in Samoa* (1928), for example, authors will emphasize that adolescence in some cultures is largely carefree and without stress. In cultures in which sexual constraints are few, adolescents do not seem to experience the same sexual anxieties that western teenagers feel. This does not mean that young people in such cultures do not experience *any* transitional anxiety, but rather, that if a culture does not emphasize an aspect of the transition to adulthood, anxiety in that area is lessened.

There are, however, some who examine the same evidence and conclude that indeed adolescence *is* a universal phenomenon (Ausubel, Montemayor, and Svajian, 1977). In their view, some demarcation of adolescents as a separate group is characteristic of human societies everywhere. There is even some evidence of "adolescent" status among some species of primates, but it is a much shorter period than human adolescence. In western culture adolescence may extend to ten years or more.

Perhaps the keystone of most anthropological studies of adolescence is the initiation rite, or the "rites of passage." In many cultures the transition from childhood to adulthood is marked by a specific test of manhood or womanhood. At some point in development, usually associated with puberty, young boys and girls are isolated from the community and readied for a test that will determine their suitability to be an adult member of the society. The ritual of initiation varies from culture to culture and may be relatively mild or quite severe. Once the adolescent has satisfied the demands of the initiation rite, however, he or she is then given status as an adult. Consider, for example, the initiation rites for young girls in a remote tribe of northern South America (Brown, 1975*):

> Initiation rites vary greatly from society to society, but the following description of the initiation of girls among the Maroni River Caribs may serve as one illustration. When a girl first menstruates, she is confined to a special part of the house for eight days. She remains in seclusion particularly to avoid the spirits of

---

Source: Paraphrased from Kloos (see References).

the river and of the forest. These would be offended by her condition and they would cause her to sicken and die. The girl is dressed in old clothes in order to be unattractive to the spirits, and her diet is restricted rather severely. During these eight days, she is expected to spin cotton to be used in making a hammock for a member of her family. At the end of her seclusion, an elderly couple noted for industry arrives at the home of the girl before sunrise. The girl is bathed. Then a small tuft of cotton is placed in the palm of her hand, and fire is set to it. She must move the cotton rapidly from hand to hand to avoid getting burned. This ritual is done because her hands must always be busy. Next her hand is placed in a bowl of large, biting ants. She must not show pain. The ants are to remind her always to be industrious like the ant. Were a lazy person to attend this part of the ceremony, the girl would also become lazy. The girl is then dressed, painted and adorned with jewelry. Guests arrive and there is drinking, dancing and singing. When she has washed her hands in grated manioc, she is free once more to move about the village, to take her daily bath in the river, and to work in the household. (pp. 41–42)

Note that each element in the initiation rite has special symbolic and magical value to the members of the tribe, and each step of the process is followed rigidly. One of the hallmarks of initiation rites is that the ritual and the elements of the ritual are tied closely to the values and needs of the community as a whole.

In our culture there is no clearly defined point at which we can say a young man or woman is considered an adult. Whether such a rite would be of value in this culture is not the issue. Instead, as students of adolescence, we need to assess what society demands of today's adolescents, in order to consider them adults.

VIGNETTE 1-1
Of Adolescent Cultures and Subcultures

Although the Maroni River Caribs described in the text choose to convey some of their cultural values through an initiation rite, global society as a whole uses a variety of techniques to convey what is valued. Often values are seen in the writing and art that a culture produces.

Source: Excerpted from Anthony M. Deiulio, "Of Adolescent Cultures and Subcultures," *Educational Leadership* (April 1978), pp. 517–520. Reprinted with permission of the Association for Supervision and Curriculum Development and Anthony M. Deiulio. Copyright © 1978 by the Association for Supervision and Curriculum Development. All rights reserved.

From the most elaborate literature and ornate artwork to the furtive scribblings on walls, people try to communicate the ideas and values of their society. Graffiti, although it is not usually considered as a primary source of literary enlightenment, is nonetheless often artistic, humorous, and reflective of current social and political forces. Graffiti is certainly not new. Archaeologists have found graffiti on walls of long-buried cities. In this short piece, Anthony M. Deiulio of the State University of New York at Brockport suggests that graffiti is a valuable source of information about the values and attitudes of today's youth. What values do you see reflected in graffiti in your locale?

Graffiti have been with us since prehistoric times. The Oxford English Dictionary defines a graffito as, "A drawing or writing scratched on a wall or other surface; as at Pompeii or Rome." It mirrors the world of its own day, and it throws a broad beam of light on the preoccupations and fears, dreams and desires, feelings and hopes of the people whom the social scientists quantify and computerize. So too with the graffiti of adolescents. Graffiti gives adolescents a certain satisfaction also, for through it they can vent their hostilities, express their fantasies, communicate their triumphs, declare their rebellion, and promote their propaganda.

Characteristics of Adolescent Graffiti

Certain characteristics of the phenomenon of adolescent graffiti, based on a number of long-term research studies, should be noted:

- *It is universal.* The sprays, scrawls, and scratches appear in all the world's teenage cultures. According to recent reports from Moscow, the handwriting is on the wall even in Russia with its long-time reputation as a graffiti-free society.
- *It is costly.* The New York City Transit Authority recently spent $4 million to clean its 6,200 subway cars of spray paint graffiti. In San Francisco, secondary students were to be granted cash incentives by the Board of Education if they could reduce the graffiti in their schools. And in some states, laws have been passed making parents financially responsible for the graffiti their children paint on buildings, rest rooms, and other property.
- *It can take several forms.* Usually graffiti appear as statements, single words, or pictures, but often can include various symbols to which certain meanings are understood or have been attached.

- *It is difficult to differentiate graffiti on the basis of sex.* Graffiti written by girls—that found in the girls' lavatories in churches and schools, for example—is as strong, political, trite, or sexual as that written by boys. One slight difference: girls' graffiti may sometimes show faint signs of the traditional romanticism of the girl-loves-boy theme. One other possible distinction, according to a report by the Council of British Ceramic and Sanitary Manufacturers, is that the quality of art work is higher in the ladies' "loos" than they found in the gents' lavatories.
- *It is usually transitory.* Despite those found in the excavations of Pompeii, most do not last a very long time. A custodian's paintbrush, a teacher's washcloth, or a plasterer's trowel are all impending threats to the longevity of these inscriptions.
- *It is not all pornographic.* The correlation between pornography and graffiti is not as high as many would like to believe. In fact, in some of the long-term collections, one can see the increasing seriousness of purpose and the larger issues being dealt with as opposed to the mere epithets, obscene statements, and pornographic invitations one finds among the earlier evidence.

A more serious look at this aspect of our adolescent underculture can give us a clue as to who our future criminals might be. Some authorities believe that the adolescent graffiti artist eventually graduates into serious felony crime; that the graffiti problem is multidimensional and involves a subculture that produces tragic criminal behavior. A long-term study of youths who were arrested for graffiti crimes over a two-year period showed that 40 percent of them faced other, more serious criminal charges in subsequent years. In this study, 90 percent of the youngsters arrested on graffiti charges were between the ages of 11 and 15. A random sample of the 15-year-olds was then followed over the next three years. By the time these 750 youths were 18 years old, 29 percent had been rearrested on felony charges; 11

percent for misdemeanors. Eight of them were accused of murder.

It would be convenient to report that as we reach the end of the decade of the 1970s an analysis of the adolescent subculture from recent graffiti studies shows we are reaching the end of an era. But such is not the case. The graffiti written by them and analyzed by the graffiti researchers tend to reflect the same feelings as those uncovered in the formal studies of adolescents done by the sociologists, consulting firms, and pollsters. Perhaps in the first years of the seventies, when the return to normalcy from the turbulent sixties began, that may have been. But what's happening now seems to be neither the beginning nor the end of an era.

The greatest advantages of cross-cultural studies of adolescence are to be gained not so much from studying rites of initiation but from increasing our awareness of differences in the socialization process from population to population within our own multifaceted culture. Any discussion of adolescent development must be tempered by the recognition that adolescence for a black youth in the Bedford-Stuyvesant section of Brooklyn is hardly the same as adolescence for a young white person in Shelbyville, Indiana. Neither of these young people share the same adolescence as an American Indian youth on a Hopi reservation in Arizona, an adolescent from an affluent suburb of Los Angeles, or a Mexican-American for whom English is a second language. Any generalizations about adolescents must recognize that the form and structure of adolescence is not common to all and must be modified in light of our knowledge of the society in which a young person is raised.

THE PSYCHOANALYTIC VIEW

In the view of psychoanalytic theory, adolescence is dominated by a renewed struggle to control sexual impulses. Sigmund Freud's original formulation emphasized the development of an individual through a series of psychosexual stages starting at birth and continuing through adulthood. In infancy, sexual arousal is concentrated in the *oral* erogenous zone. The infant's primary source of pleasure and gratification occurs orally through sucking, biting, and eating. Satisfactory fulfillment of oral needs during infancy is seen as a prerequisite to adequate adult adjustment. Undergratification or over-gratification of these needs may lead to a *fixation* in this stage; hence dependency on cigarettes or food or a need to talk constantly reflects a fixation in the oral stage.

At around one and a half, the toddler age, the child moves into the second stage of development, in which gratification and stimulation are concentrated in the *anal* zone. The primary developmental task associated with the anal stage is toilet training. Children quickly learn that they have some control over their parents through their ability to release or hold back their excretions.

Our ideas of who we are and our feelings about ourselves have their roots in our earliest experiences. (© Joel Gordon 1979)

Once again, undergratification or overgratification of sexual impulses at this stage may lead to a fixation. Children who are fixated in the retentive character of the anal stage may, as adults, show anal-retentive characteristics, such as hoarding or unwillingness to cooperate with others. On the other hand, failure to control the expulsive character of the anal stage may lead to personality traits such as squandering of money and irresponsibility.

At about age three, the child moves into the *phallic* stage. Sexual gratification is now concentrated in the genital area. During this period masturbation is quite common and, according to Freud, the manner in which parents react to this early masturbation has an impact on the child's development of attitudes about his or her sexuality. Overreaction by parents leads the child to see his or her sexuality as "dirty" and repulsive.

Later in the phallic stage, the male child experiences what Freud described as the *Oedipal conflict*. In girls the comparable phenomenon is the Electra conflict. During this stage the young boy develops incestuous desires for his mother and wishes to replace his father. The boy may want to sleep in his mother's bed and tells his father, "You sleep in my bed." Soon the boy begins

Part of the adolescent's preparation for adult roles is the establishment of caring relationships with members of the opposite sex. (© George W. Gardner)

to recognize that his father is displeased with the boy's desires and has the power to punish the boy. The boy also fantasizes that the form of punishment may be castration. In order to avoid this punishment, the child suppresses his incestuous desires and identifies with the same-sexed parent. The result of the resolution of the Oedipal conflict is the emergence of the Superego, or conscience. Until this point the child has had little in the way of internal controls over sexual impulses. The Id, or the center of these impulses, has had largely free reign.

Following the phallic stage, sexual impulses go into a *latency* period, in which they remain dormant until early adolescence. During this time the Superego increases in strength, and sexual drives are released through heightened physical activity. By and large, girls prefer to be with girls and boys with boys. Girls, however, usually show interest in boys earlier than boys do in girls.

At puberty the young person starts to move toward *adult genital* sexuality. At this point Oedipal conflicts are reawakened by the rapid increase in the output of sexual hormones. Increasingly, sexual drives are redirected away from parents and toward other members of the opposite sex. Freud felt that frustration of these heightened sexual drives, which is inherent in our society, leads to delinquent behavior and aggression. In an attempt to achieve balance between the sexual impulses of the Id and the overcontrol of the Superego, the individual develops an Ego, which serves to moderate the opposing forces. The Ego is the center of personality. A strong Ego keeps the forces of the Id and Superego in appropriate balance. A weak Ego leads to the domination of one over the other.

The intricacies of psychoanalytic theory as it applies to adolescents was developed largely through the efforts of Freud's daughter Anna. In her view the renewed conflict from Oedipal impulses and increased sexual drives leads to anxiety, because the adolescent, unlike the small child, is expected to have control over such impulses. To maintain control, the adolescent draws upon a variety of defense mechanisms (see Chapter 14) that help to deal with or dissipate the anxiety. The two most common forms of internalized control of these impulses are *intellectualization* and *asceticism*. With their improved cognitive skills, adolescents may try to justify gratification of their sexual desires through arguments for free love, new marital life styles, freedom of thought, and adoption of antiestablishment philosophy (A. Freud, 1966). On the other hand, adolescents may assume an ascetic stance using the same intellectual powers and may refuse themselves any form of sexual gratification. Asceticism may also include extreme religiosity and preoccupation with thinking about abstractions.

Like her father, Anna Freud saw adolescence as a period of critical development of the ego. In her writings (especially 1966) she describes the functions of defense mechanisms in the organization and development of a strong or weak personality. Although Erik Erikson, a student of both Sigmund and Anna Freud, made significant alterations in psychoanalytic theory, the Freudian ancestry of his writings remains clear.

ERIK ERIKSON

Currently the theorist whose work in the study of adolescents probably attracts the most attention is Erik Erikson, especially his works *Identity and the Life Cycle* (1959) and *Identity: Youth and Crisis* (1968). Because he found the psychosexual emphasis of Freud lacking, Erikson developed and modified Freud's stages of development into eight stages of *psychosocial* development. The details of these eight stages will be described more fully in Chapter 5, but the basic idea is as follows:

As noted in the previous section, Freud emphasized that the individual's motives are to satisfy basic sexual needs—first oral, then anal, and finally genital gratification. Failure to satisfy those early motives adequately, or oversatisfaction of them, leads to a fixation at an earlier stage of development. Erikson alters the focus from sexual conflict to social conflict. At each stage of life, from infancy to old age, the individual must work through a critical set of problems. Like Freud, however, Erikson feels that failure to resolve conflicts adequately at one stage of development interferes with adjustment at the next and later stages of life.

The primary crisis of adolescence—and the crisis that is at the heart of Erikson's theory—is the need to establish a personal sense of identity. The adolescent must accept himself or herself as a unique person, with strengths and weaknesses. The adolescent's identity also includes a personal assessment of his or her own sexuality and an understanding that one has control of one's own destiny. As adolescents become more aware that they control their own destinies, self-control, accepting adult responsibilities, and forging a personal set of values and vocational goals follow.

The point at which the individual adolescent goes through the clarification of this identity is called the identity crisis. The term *identity crisis* has become highly popularized and, as with many overgeneralizations, misunderstood. Some assume that adolescents will inevitably go through a major turmoil in which they are concerned with the questions "Who am I?" or "What am I going to do with my life?" However, not all adolescents experience a crisis. Some never have the chance to ask the questions. Social or economic factors may interfere with the opportunity to seek out options. Some young people accept an intact, adult identity with little or no questioning. For example, a young boy may be convinced early that he will become a doctor because his father and grandfather were both doctors before him. He may consider no other alternative. In any case, whether an adolescent develops a sense of identity by himself or assumes an identity that is provided by others, a personal identity is necessary for moving into adulthood. Failure to establish a sense of identity interferes with life tasks that are part of adult personal development.

THE BEHAVIORAL VIEW

In a traditional behavioristic conception, the behavior of an individual is seen to be a result of learning. Learning is the result of reinforcement controlled by an outsider or coming from a beneficial (or hostile) environment. To alter one's behavior therefore requires altering the environment and the reinforcement derived from it. The primary behavioristic principle is simple. A person learns to behave in a specified fashion because the behavior is *reinforced*. Any behavior that is followed immediately by a reinforcer will be likely to occur again, especially under similar circumstances. Reinforcement is not merely reward in the usual sense. *Positive reinforcement* does imply the presentation of a reward, but *negative reinforcement*, the removal of an unpleasant stimulus, is also strongly reinforcing. If you behave in a way that leads to the removal of something unpleasant in your environment, you are likely to respond the same way the next time you run into a similar unpleasant situation.

Control of behavior by an outside agent is achieved through the control of reinforcers and reinforcement. In developing a desired behavor, the behavior modifier identifies appropriate reinforcers and applies them as the learner approaches some specific level of performance. In behavioral terms, the trained behavior is *shaped*. Reinforcers in this sense are not necessarily physical rewards but may be social approval or disapproval. For the behavioral theorist, then, the analysis of adolescent behavior becomes a case of identifying the nature and effect of reinforcers in an adolescent culture.

A friend of mine tells a story of a young teacher who, during the course of a lesson, began asking students questions about information they were expected to know. When the teacher called on one particular student, he responded with a horrified gasp and whine. Not wanting to upset the student unduly, the teacher went on to another student. The next time the teacher called on the student the reaction was the same, perhaps even more terrified. By the end of the week, the student responded with virtual hysteria when asked a question. In behavioral terms the student had learned that he could rid himself of an unpleasant circumstance (answering the teacher's question) by putting on this act. The teacher, on the other hand, was learning to avoid the unpleasant situation altogether. One of the interesting things about avoidance learning is that it has a way of becoming self-reinforcing. If you manage to avoid an unpleasant experience, you find that pleasant.

The teacher in this case soon recognized that the problem had gotten out of hand. She was advised to go back to the classroom with a new strategy. This time when she asked the student the question, the reaction was the same, the student went into his act. The teacher, however, waited until the student calmed down and said, "Let me rephrase the question." The student started in again, but the teacher continued to wait. When the student began to quiet down again, the teacher said, "Perhaps you would like a different question," with the clear implication that sooner or later he was going to have to answer a question. After some time (the teacher reported it felt like an eternity), the student did answer the question, whereupon the teacher thanked him and went on.

This episode illustrates the next important characteristic of the behaviorist model: One eliminates behavior through extinction rather than punishment. In *extinction* either no positive reinforcement is given or the unpleasant stimulus is not removed following a behavior. In punishment, on the other hand, something unpleasant is introduced *following* the behavior.

By and large, behaviorists do not see punishment as a preferred method of behavioral control. Unless punishment occurs in a context in which the student understands what is acceptable behavior and recognizes a reward for behaving in the preferred manner, it is likely to be ineffective. Further,

VIGNETTE 1-2
Letters from Home

Magazines and newspapers often include cartoons or features that poke humor at the unwillingness of young people to write home to parents for anything other than financial support. What about letters from parents? Are

Source: Linda Lewis, "Be Proud and Useful, Be Merry and Wise," *Harvard Magazine* (January/February 1980): 38–44. Copyright © 1980 Harvard Magazine, Inc. Reprinted by permission.

they any better? The writer of this article would have us believe that letters from parents to their young offspring are similarly predictable. Oliver Wendell Holmes, looking back on advice given to him by his father in letters, categorizes it as "twaddle." It is interesting to note that the advice from parents to their young students away from home doesn't seem to have changed very much over centuries.

Indeed one letter from an Egyptian nobleman to his son some three thousand years ago strangely resembles letters from home today.

Dear Son,

If we waited for you to answer our previous letters, all communication would, presumably, cease. How are you? What are you up to these days? Are you enjoying your photography course? Your film course? Your Origins of Jazz course? Do you honestly think this is what a college education is all about? What do you suppose you will be doing ten years from now? Ever read *The Odyssey* or *War and Peace*?

Naturally we worry about you. The few times we have seen you in the last year have been far from reassuring. It isn't just outward appearance (the tangled hair, the stubbly chin, the leather jacket, the mirrored sunglasses), but also your offhand attitude that dismisses our legitimate queries as meddlesome. We are bound to wonder at your choice of courses, your grades, your lack of a plan for a summer job, the example you seem to want to set for your sister and brother. The only reason we say all this is that we have your best interests at heart, and that...Etc., etc.

Alternate version A.

Dear Son,

Life is a bit dull without you. No one to push around or be pushed around by. I must say, you remind me of myself at your age— rebellious, tough-talking, badly organized, intolerant. I was really terrified of being on my own, didn't know what I would do or where I would fit in. I did a lot of stupid things.

If possible, don't hurt yourself by doing stupid things. Don't mess around with crazy kids. Don't spoil your chances to do what you want to do.

Please keep me in your heart, and please make me proud of you. If possible. At least be proud of yourself. Take it easy, son. Etc., etc.

Alternate version B.

Dear Son,
I beat your father at Scrabble last night. Thought you'd want to know. Cookies on the way. Press on!

Love,
Mother.

Which letter to send, that is the question; whether 'tis nobler in the mind to suffer the slings and arrows of outrageous children, or to take arms and by opposing risk the fragile truce; whether to admonish, confess, or reassure; whether to go for short- or long-term results. It is hard to know what line to take. If one analyzed motives and probable effects too much, however, it is possible that no letter would be sent at all. And no cookies.

There is something about writing to a child away at school that brings out the worst in many of us. Approaching redundancy, needing to justify our parental existence, we re-enact scenes from our own childhood, play the parts our parents played, say things we said we'd never say.

There may be a certain dubious consolation in the realization that for many centuries parents have been writing letters to their absent children: letters whose petulant, anxious, reproving, improving tones scarcely change over time. Shining examples and purposeful blindness, self-interest and self-punishment, loving support and subtle undercutting are woven into repeating patterns that document relations between parents and children. Mothers and fathers continue to urge young people to study seriously, to organize their time, to do the nastier jobs first, to improve their handwriting and spelling, to make friends with the right sort of people, to make the most of themselves. In literate societies, it seems an irresistible form.

Justice Oliver Wendell Holmes, writing to a friend, said he had discovered among his father's papers letters from his father's father "inculcating virtue in the same dull terms" that had been passed on to him. "If I had a son I wonder if I should yield to the temptation to twaddle in my turn." Bound to.

More than four thousand years ago an Egyptian father, Ptah-hotep, setting down a long list of useful precepts, called upon his son to deliver them unaltered to his son in turn. If the "good sayings" of the father were heeded, the children would surely testify that "doing what thou sayest works wonders." Those were the days.

Ptah-hotep talked sense, nevertheless. "Be not haughty because of thy knowledge; converse thou with the ignorant as with the scholar; for the barriers of art are never closed, no artist ever possessing that perfection to which he should aspire. Do not lose thy temper when disputing...Do not get in a passion...Avoid intrigues with women, especially in the house of a friend...Do not carry a sour face." And so on.

There is no evidence that children who lived in the third millennium B.C. asked for the advice they got any more often than children in the twentieth century; there is plenty of evidence that parents gave it. These fragments of social history tell only a small part of the story, of course. Letters that have been saved and published are likely to be the letters of a few famous people. They may or may not represent a true picture of what went on between that parent and that child. Pomposity on paper does not necessarily indicate an unapproachable parent, and vice versa; there have been demon mothers and devil fathers whose recorded communications seem to have been penned by angels. There have even been demon children. In recent years the telephone has often taken the place of the written document. No one saves letters these days....

Instructive Examples of Ten Basic Twaddles

1. *Keep in touch....*"Do write to me. You know that as long as I get letters from you I am cheerful about your safety." An anonymous Roman-Egyptian mother to her uncommunicative son.

"I certainly don't get all of those letters you keep telling me you write."

2. *Study hard....*In the second century A.D. one Cornelios wrote to his son Hierax, who was away at school: "Take care you do not annoy anyone in the house, but study and devote yourself wholly to your books, and you will derive profit from them."...

3. *Honor thy God, Obey thy mother, Do thy duty, Etc., etc....*On his seventeenth birthday, Prince Edward Albert, who seemed destined never to satisfy his parents, Queen Victoria and the Prince Consort, received the usual spritely letter from them:

"Life is composed of duties, and in the due, punctual and cheerful performance of them the true Christian, true soldier and true gentleman is recognized."

4. *Abhor vice and resist temptation/evil companions/gambling/smoking/flattery/over-indulgence, etc., etc., etc....*

Lorenzo de' Medici, writing to his son Giovanni upon his investiture as cardinal at the remarkable age of sixteen, warned him against those who were jealous of him and would try, once he moved to that "sink of iniquity, Rome," to cause him to "slide into the same ditch into which they have themselves fallen, counting on success because of your youth."

"Darling Winston," Lady Churchill wrote to her fifteen-year-old son at Eton, "I hope you will try and not smoke. If only you knew how foolish and how silly you look doing it you wd give it up...."

5. *Marry wisely....*In the fourth century B.C. a young girl wrote to her mother to say she

would not marry the boring man to whom she had been betrothed, but was prepared to insist upon a beautiful lad of her own choosing. Her mother wrote to her immediately:

"You are mad daughter dear, and entirely beside yourself. You need a dose of hellebore...Compose yourself and thrust from your mind this mischief. For, if your father should learn a word of this, he would without a moment's thought or hesitation throw you as food to the sea monsters."...

6. *Get ahead....*Rose Kennedy, in a round-robin letter to her children, instructed them on some points of etiquette she thought they might have missed—the ritual of calling cards, for example. "I am just giving you these few hints," she wrote. "Perhaps if you follow them you will be more of a success socially."

7. *Keep well....*Medicine, cod-liver oil, leeches, purges, fasts, "plain, nourishing food," steel braces for turned-in toes, periods of solitary confinement for the overactive, fresh air or changes of scene for the low in spirits, all have been recommended by well-meaning parents for the well-being of the young. Among the saddest of letters are those from parents to children suffering mental or emotional difficulties: James Joyce's to his daughter Lucia, Robert Frost's to his son Carol. Mark Twain, who should have known better, wrote uncomprehending, impatient, resentful, sometimes abusive letters to his daughters, one of whom was hypertense, one seriously depressed, and one an undiagnosed epileptic....

8. *Think of me as your friend....*"Do not think I mean to dictate as a parent," wrote Lord Chesterfield to his son. "I only mean to advise as a friend, and an indulgent one too...."

9. *But remember who pays the bills and do not disappoint.* Having posed as a friend, Lord Chesterfield went on: "I do not, therefore, so much as hint to you how absolutely dependent you are on me—that you neither have nor can have a shilling in the world but from me; and that as I have no womanish weakness for your person, your merit must, and will be the only

measure of my kindness...When I reflect upon the prodigious quantity of manure that has been laid upon you, I expect you should produce more at eighteen than uncultivated soils do at eight and twenty...and I promise myself so much from you, that I dread the least disappointment."...

10. *Be happy, or, at any rate, don't be unhappy....*When John Adams recommended "ice skating" to his son John Quincy, spending the winter in Holland, he meant him to appreciate it as a fine art and to "restrain that impetuous Ardour and violent Activity into which the Agitation of Spirits occasioned by this exercise is apt to hurry you, and which is inconsistent both with your Health and Pleasure....Everything in Life should be done with Reflection, and Judgement, even the most insignificant Amusement. They should all be arranged in subordination, to the great Plan of Happiness and Utility. That you may attend early to this Maxim is the wish of your affectionate father."...

Modern expectations, expressed by means of psychological buzz-words and with due regard for the forms of self-determination, are not necessarily easier to fulfill than are the familiar authoritarian maxims of Ptah-hotep.... Is it any better to be told one is "acting out" than to be called a "trifler"? How much more useful is it to blame academic failure on an "identity crisis" than on "lack of diligence"?

"I want you to be among the best of your race, and not waste yourself in trivial aims. To be useful and proud—is that too much to ask?" Scott Fitzgerald, writing to his daughter at school, saddled her with his own disappointments and, in the name of love—not unlike the Victorians—threatened and wheedled and poured out his heart. A parent of piercing intelligence, literary proclivities, and high expectations may be the worst kind for a kid to have.

There are no shortcuts to maturity; we know that. Despite perpetual determination to smooth out the rough places, to instill virtue and pride, the wisdom of certified sages is apt to seem irrelevant to sons and daughters. The luckiest young people are those who get a measure of both the standard stick and the classic carrot, exhortation and reassurance, creative criticism and cookies. Such was the way of an eighteenth-century woman, Lady Fox, who sent a pigeon pie to her two young sons at Eton. She hoped it would be "as good a guzzle as your loaves was," she wrote. Then, speaking perhaps for the many of us striving to say exactly the right thing, she added mildly, "Be merry and wise."

students punished by the teacher may at the same time gain approval and prestige from peers. Punishment may be effective in limited settings, but it should be used with caution. Also, although from a purely behavioristic view extinction may take its form in the failure to remove an unpleasant stimulus, the human learner may interpret such actions as punishing. Even in the situation described above, the teacher must be sensitive not to carry it too far.

Although rewards or reinforcers are important constructs in the study of human behavior, it does not follow that if we reinforce someone for behaving as we wish, they will automatically fall into line. Human behavior is the result of many forces, one of which may be external reinforcers (Bandura, 1974; McKeachie, 1976). Indeed, McKeachie (1976) indicates that excessive use of extrinsic reinforcers may lead to a decreased motive to learn. Although learning does depend on adequate feedback and reinforcement, there is a limit beyond which reinforcement is ineffective or perhaps detrimental to performance.

THE COGNITIVE VIEW

According to cognitive developmental theory, adolescence is dominated by a radical shift in one's ability to think and to solve problems. Other issues associated with adolescence, such as vocational development, social development, and personal development, are all subject to these newfound abilities to think abstractly and to consider the world as it might be.

Cognitive development theorists draw mainly on the writings of the late Jean Piaget and his followers. Piaget, whose theory will be given greater attention in Chapter 3, proposes that beginning in infancy the human being progresses through a regular series of patterns of thinking and problem solving. Of primary concern for students of the psychology of adolescence is the shift from what Piaget refers to as concrete operational thought to formal operational thought.

During childhood, thinking is restricted by the child's need to have concrete representations of a problem before it can be solved. Problem-solving strategies are not very systematic, and the child is not capable of speculating about what might be if the environment were suddenly altered. Thinking is primarily categorical, and the child finds "exceptions to the rule" hard to consider.

During adolescence most young people experience a profound shift in their ability to think about their world. Rather than being tied to concrete reality, the adolescent's conceptual world is expanded to include abstract reality and abstract possibility. Problem-solving strategies become sophisticated and efficient, based on the ability to formulate hypotheses and to test those hypotheses. Rather than being incapable of handling ambiguities or exceptions to rules, the adolescent may become fascinated by them. They may become argumentative solely for the sake of testing out the limits of their new abilities. An adolescent may spend considerable mental energy playing with a concept as though it were an intellectual toy. A fourteen-year-old girl once spent forty-five minutes explaining to me that there could be no such thing as "nothing," because as soon as we consider "nothing" it becomes "something," and "nothing" ceases to exist. Adolescents may also "think about thinking" or question the nature of reality and existence. This new ability dominates their interaction with their environment.

Because of their newfound ability to consider what *might* be, adolescents, especially late adolescents, are often highly idealistic. They are likely to see a utopian, idealized world as a real possibility and to be frustrated that others, especially adults, do not see the world in a similar fashion. Adolescents may see the adult world as cynical, too committed to the status quo, and insensitive to the needs of humanity. Not surprisingly, discussions between adolescents with this view and adults whom the adolescent regards as irrelevant (for example, their parents) are often explosive. This idealism is, however, an expected outgrowth of the substantial, new intellectual powers of the adolescent.

DEVELOPMENTAL GOALS

Some writers follow the lead of Robert Havighurst (1948, revised 1972), who suggests that adolescence can be defined by a set of *developmental tasks* that must be completed in preparation for adulthood. Havighurst, like Erikson, felt that each of the developmental tasks of adolescence is an extension of the earlier developmental tasks of childhood and is a basis for the later developmental tasks of adultood. Some tasks, such as those associated with interpersonal relations, become increasingly complex as a person moves through life. Other tasks—for example, certain psychomotor skills—may be associated with a given period of development. All tasks, however, fit into a lifelong process of psychological and social development.

By the end of adolescence the young adult should have achieved certain goals, including adult physical and sexual status, a personal identity, financial and psychological independence from parents, mature sexual relationships, and some career goals. I prefer to refer to these as goals rather than tasks, because the demands of each problem are often not clearly defined, and the form that they take may differ among adolescents. As a simple example, the career goals of lower-income adolescents and those of adolescents from wealthy families are likely to be quite different. Nonetheless, both sets of adolescents need to have a workable set of career goals with which to enter adulthood:

1. *The adolescent must adjust to a new body image.* At no other time in life does an individual undergo such rapid and profound physical change as during early adolescence. Preadolescence and early adolescence are marked by rapid growth in height and weight as well as the emergence and accentuation of sexual features. No longer does the young person look like a child. Rather, the young adolescent starts to display features of adult physical and sexual maturity. The result is that the adolescent must reconcile this new image seen in the mirror with the self-image of a child. This radical change in the adolescent's physical self may at times be the source of personal anxiety and a

In their attempt to establish a new body image, adolescents may spend a good deal of time just studying themselves. (© Margaret Thompson)

One of the tasks adolescents must learn is how to channel their aggression and rapidly developing physical strength into productive and socially acceptable behavior. (© Margaret W. Nelson)

fear of being different. It is during this period of development that young adolescents often complain to their physicians about being too tall or too short or too developed or not developed enough.

2. *The adolescent must adapt to increased cognitive powers.* In addition to a sudden spurt in physical growth, adolescents experience a sudden increase in their intellectual abilities. As they mature intellectually, adolescents are able to think not only about more things but also about their world with a new level of awareness. Prior to adolescence, children's thoughts are dominated by a need to have a concrete example for any problem they try to solve. The preadolescent is not able to solve problems that involve abstractions. Around the middle of the adolescent transition, young people find themselves able to think about problems on a whole new level. Inhelder and Piaget (1958) refer to this transition in thinking as the shift from concrete operational thought to formal operational thought. Beyond an improved ability to solve problems, the shift to formal thinking may also be accompanied by a fascination with this newfound intellectual prowess. It is common, for example, for adolescents to "think about thinking" or have "ideas about ideas." These new abilities, which include the ability to ask the question "What if?" often lead adolescents to commit themselves to concepts of utopia or to idealistic political and social movements. As Piaget (1967) notes, this idealism may lead the adolescent to be impatient with adults who are seen as unwilling, unable, or unmotivated to correct social wrongs. Adults, on the other hand, who are no longer enamored of this intellectual ability, may lose patience with such "cognitive wanderings."

3. *The adolescent must adjust to increased cognitive demands in school.* Adults tend to see high school as a place where adolescents can prepare for adult roles. Courses of study are created with the view that they will help the students acquire adult roles. In some cases the relevance to adult roles is quite direct. In others the relevance is indirect—that is, the courses train students in modes of thinking about problems. Often, perhaps too often, the responsibility of the high school is interpreted with the understanding that adolescents will pursue additional training in college. Thus school curricula are often dominated by an assumed need to meet the academic demands that are to come. Even vocational training in high school is often influenced by the assumption that students will get additional vocational skill training beyond high school. Thus through high school curricula become increasingly difficult and often more abstract, irrespective of whether students have made the transition to formal operational thought. Not all adolescents make the intellectual transition at the same rate; students who have not completed the transition may find adjusting to demands for abstract thought difficult or impossible.

4. *The adolescent must expand his verbal repertoire.* As adolescents mature intellectually and adjust to increased demands for academic and social competence, they must also acquire language skills for relating to more complex problems and tasks. Their limited language of childhood is no longer adequate. Often this language development lags behind intellectual growth, and adolescents are able to think at levels well above those reflected in their

language. Elkind (1967) refers to this inarticulate behavior as "pseudo-stupidity." Adolescents may *appear* incompetent because of their inability to express themselves meaningfully, but they may be far more capable than their language suggests.

5. *The adolescent must develop a personal sense of identity.* Erik Erikson (1959, 1968, among others) conceives of adolescence as a distinct period separating childhood from early adulthood. During adolescence individuals must begin to recognize their own uniqueness and form personal identities. This new identity is a synthesis and reorganization of previous identifications with parents, adults, and other authority figures. The individual integrates previous experience, including resolution of early developmental crises, into a personal conception of "Who am I?" and "What is my role in life?" At the point at which an individual identity is reformulated, the adolescent may suffer a crisis of identity.

During this period, peer groups serve an important purpose. Because adolescents no longer find their childhood identities adequate and have not yet formed their adult identities fully, they need a setting within which they can experiment with alternate roles. Peer groups provide that setting. But there is a price that they must pay for this privilege: conformity to the demands of the group. As adolescents' identities take form, they become less dependent on their peer group and assume more responsibility for their own behavior. This does not mean, however, that identity formation stops after adolescence; complete identity formation is a lifelong evolutionary process. But adolescence seems to be central to the reorganization of a dependent-child identity into a responsible-adult identity.

6. *The adolescent must establish adult vocational goals.* As part of the adolescent's process of establishing a personal identity, he or she must also develop some plan for achieving an adult vocational role. Adolescents need to identify, at least on a preliminary basis, what they plan to do as adults and how they plan to achieve their goals. As part of making these decisions, adolescents need to develop a realistic idea of their resources, both psychological and economic, for achieving their goals. This process requires that adolescents evaluate their strengths and weaknesses realistically as well as determine what social, psychological, and economic barriers might need to be overcome to achieve certain goals.

7. *The adolescent must establish emotional and psychological independence from his parents.* Perhaps one of the more stressful developmental goals of adolescence is the need to establish psychological and emotional separation from parents. To adequately create a personal identity, adolescents must recognize themselves as independent beings. However, adolescents may still wish to keep the secure, dependent relationships of childhood. The adolescent may thus vacillate between the desire for dependence and the need for independence. The need to assert one's individuality and adult independence may take the form of hostility and lack of cooperation with parents or other authority figures. The parents' dilemmas are when to exert control, how much control to exert, and when to release control. That balance between control and release changes with time and circumstances. Eventually this need for

Friends are very important during adolescence, especially in providing a sense of belonging. (© Eric Kroll 1980/Taurus Photos)

psychological separation from one's parents is replaced by an adult relationship with them, which includes respect and appreciation but not dependence.

8. *The adolescent must develop stable and productive peer relationships, including heterosexual relationships.* Although peer interaction is not unique to adolescence, peer interaction seems to hit a peak of importance during early and middle adolescence. The degree to which an adolescent is able to make friends and have an accepting peer group is a major indicator of how well the adolescent will successfully adjust in other areas of social and psychological development (Hartup, 1977). Peer groups serve an important role in the socialization of adolescents to adulthood. Rather than being a negative force, peers often provide standards against which adolescents may compare and evaluate themselves. Peers expose fellow adolescents to alternative values, attitudes, and behaviors and offer a protective setting within which the individual adolescent can evaluate current values and establish psychological independence from parents. Ultimately, however, the adolescent must also establish psychological independence from peers. Early heterosexual friendships set the stage for later intimate and mature relationships.

9. *The adolescent must learn to manage his or her own sexuality.* With their increased physical and sexual maturity, adolescents need to incorporate into their personal identity a set of attitudes about what it means to be male or female, as well as a set of values about their own sexual behavior.

Although traditional sex role stereotypes may be inappropriate and perhaps damaging to adequate psychological development, adolescents must recognize their own femininity or masculinity as an integral component of their self-concept. Contemporary media are much more openly sexual than in previous generations. Society as a whole tends to have a much more permissive attitude about premature sexual activity. Thus, as McCreary-Juhasz (1975) suggests, the responsibility for deciding whether or not to be sexually active has shifted from society to the individual. If an individual decides to engage in sexual intercourse, then another set of decisions regarding contraception, as well as children and possibly marriage, must be made. Premature commitment may interfere with the satisfactory resolution of other developmental tasks. In addition to a sexual identity, which may or may not include sexual intercourse, adolescents must establish some concept of their masculinity or femininity.

10. *The adolescent must adopt an effective value system.* During adolescence, as individuals develop increasingly complex knowledge systems, they also adopt an integrated set of values or morals. Early in moral development the child is provided with a structured set of rules of what is right and wrong, what is acceptable and unacceptable. Some of those values and attitudes are readily verbalized, whereas others are intrinsic but less well recognized. Eventually the set of values that is provided by parents and society may come into conflict with values expressed by peers and other segments of society. To reconcile such differences, the adolescent restructures all those beliefs into a personal ideology. As adolescents progress from concrete to formal thought, their awareness and ability to abstract expands as they begin to consider various alternatives and ideas and as they hypothesize what would happen in an idealized world.

11. *The adolescent must develop increased impulse control, or behavioral maturity.* As the individual moves from early to late adolescence, hedonic, self-serving behavior is replaced by mature, socially appropriate behavior. Early adolescence may be marked by a high degree of impulsiveness and "acting out," especially among young boys. Many of those behaviors that appear to adults to be irrational are results of a failure to control that impulsiveness. Gradually adolescents develop a set of self-controls through which they learn what behavior is acceptable and what is not. In working with disturbed adolescents, I often encounter the diagnosis "Unsocialized Aggressive Reaction of Adolescence." At first the label struck me as odd and actually a bit amusing. I asked myself whether there were *socialized* aggressive reactions. The more I thought about it, the more I realized that indeed there are socially acceptable aggressive reactions. Being aggressive in socially approved manners, such as on a football field or in other competitive settings, is acceptable. Being aggressive in ways that are disapproved, however, may lead to trouble. Some psychologists expect some socially unacceptable aggression, maybe even some delinquency, among most adolescents, as part of the process of establishing self-control is trying the limits of what is acceptable. As socialization toward adulthood moves along, adolescents find that some of society's rules are ill-defined and may even be incompatible with their own

ideas. Gradually, however, adolescents replace "unsocialized" behavior, first with "socialized" behavior and eventually with behavior intended for the general good of society.

It may go without saying that these developmental goals are not independent of one another. An adolescent does not tackle them one at a time. As one goal is advanced it may have an effect on the advancement of the other goals. Similarly, life goals or developmental tasks do not suddenly cease after adolescence.

Many of the developmental changes that are described within this textbook follow a common thread. There is a regular progression that may be seen in adolescents' intellectual, social, and emotional growth. There is a shift from a rather undifferentiated, self-centered view of one's world to a more complex, highly abstract view of the world. In Piaget's terms this shift is seen in the transition from concrete to formal thought (Chapter 3). In David Hunt's view there is a similar growth in social development (Chapter 4), and Lawrence Kohlberg's theory of moral development follows a similar pattern (Chapter 10), as does an adolescent's view of self (Chapter 5), vocational goals (Chapter 6), and relationships with parents (Chapter 7) and peers (Chapter 8). It would appear, then, that at least on some level there is a general trend of movement toward the satisfaction of developmental goals during adolescence.

We need to be cautious, however, before we jump to the conclusion that we now have a general theory of adolescence. The state of the field is not yet at that point. If anything, what this trend represents is the author's biases and an attempt to offer a general structure within which you the reader may read this text.

Further, although early-, middle-, and late-adolescents clearly differ in their ability to interact with their world, it does not automatically follow that all young people progress in the same, orderly fashion so that at some magic age, say twenty-one, they are suddenly fully functioning adults who have satisfied all developmental goals and have no growth left before them. As Lipsitz (1980) warns, there is a danger in labeling adolescence as a "transitional" period because it implies that adolescence is unique in that sense. Although there are transitions associated with the period of life we call adolescence, there are likewise transitions related to early adulthood, middle adulthood, and old age.

INDIVIDUAL DIFFERENCES

A common theme throughout this text is that the practitioner must be responsive to the differing characteristics of adolescents. Perhaps at no other time in development can such heterogeneity among individuals in a group be seen as in early and middle adolescents. To encourage the practitioner to be responsive to individual differences is no small request. As will be seen in subsequent chapters, adolescents differ on a large variety of dimensions—physical, social, and psychological—and on three different levels:

1. Most obviously, because there is such a progression from concrete to abstract thinking or from undifferentiation to complex differentiation of one's world, it is important for adults working with adolescents to recognize that wide differences *among age groups* may exist. The social responsibility, intellectual behaviors, and value judgments that we can reasonably expect from a college sophomore are quite different from those we expect from a high school freshman.

2. *Within age groups* there may be large differences among individuals. These differences may be related to disparities in stages of development that individuals have achieved or to dissimilarities in social or personal style. In a typical class of high school seniors there may be a group operating on the more advanced levels of conceptual and social development, whereas others are operating at the level expected of the average sixth grader. On the other hand, among those who are operating at the level of formal operational thinking, there may be wide variability in the manner in which individuals apply those abilities in solving problems.

3. There are additional differences *within individuals.* Too often, we expect individuals to behave with equal maturity in all settings. For example, we may expect a boy or girl who is physically mature early to act with a corresponding social maturity. Adolescents may operate with different levels of social maturity given the familiarity of the setting, how tired or refreshed they feel, how near their friends are, and so on.

Adolescence is a period of development marked by great individual differences in growth and appearance. (Courtesy, Cambridge Rindge & Latin High School, Cambridge, Massachusetts. Photograph by Peter Vandermark.)

Individual differences should be viewed in light of how they affect the way in which particular adolescents respond to their environment. The problem of responding to individual differences is increased by the fact that one environment may be beneficial for one group of adolescents, whereas the same setting may be not only *not* beneficial but actually harmful for others. On the other hand, another environment may have just the reverse effect. The role of the practitioner becomes one of optimizing the match between the personal characteristics of adolescents and their environments to facilitate some outcome. Given this role, the practitioner may operate on any or all of the three elements in the setting: the individual, the environment, or the desired outcomes.

Remedial Intervention. In remedial intervention the adolescent is presumed to have a deficit that needs to be raised to an acceptable, functional level. If, for example, an adolescent's academic achievement suffers because of low reading ability, the intervention is most obviously to raise the reading level. However, the instructional procedures for accomplishing this end are different for teens than for primary-school learners. One remediational approach may not be effective for all, even when the desired outcomes are essentially the same.

In a different case, a physician or nurse may recognize that an adolescent's chronic stomach problems are not a result of something inherently wrong with the stomach but the result of a mouthful of decayed teeth. The intervention in such a case is more clear: the practitioner arranges, either through parents or a welfare agency, to have the adolescent's teeth cleaned and filled, bringing the adolescent's oral hygiene up to an acceptable, normative level of good health.

Compensatory Intervention. In a compensatory model the individual's predisposition is taken as a given, one that is perhaps unchangeable. The athlete with weakened knee ligaments wears a brace or support to compensate for the deficiency. Some school-related problems may be reduced if a nearsighted student is provided with glasses. The intent in the compensatory model is not to alter individuals but rather to provide individuals with external devices or compensatory skills that allow them to interact more satisfactorily with their environment.

In both the remedial and compensatory frameworks the individual is seen as needing change or aid. In some circumstances, however, a practitioner may feel it more appropriate to establish different environments in order to facilitate the desired outcome.

Capitalization Strategy. In the third strategy for individualization, a practitioner capitalizes on some trait of the adolescent that has benefited by one treatment as compared to another. In one case an individual with trait X performs better under treatment 1 than under treatment 2. In contrast, individuals with trait Y perform better under treatment 2 than under treatment 1.

French (1958) reports a study in which learners who were group oriented were compared to learners who were success oriented. French looked at the performance of these two kinds of learners when feedback was task related versus group related. When success-oriented learners were given task-related feedback, especially with respect to individual achievement, they performed much better than when given feedback of how the group was getting along together. Group-oriented learners responded just the opposite; they did not want to be singled out.

The capitalization model is based on the premise that *different treatments* have *different effects* with *different people*. The object is to maximize the effectiveness of a treatment, be it educational, physical, medical, or psychological, by matching the treatment to the strengths of the individual.

Use of individualized treatment does not imply that the practitioner needs to create an infinite set of treatment modes. Individualization may mean selection of a treatment from a limited number of alternatives or it may mean variation within a specific treatment modality. Consider the following two cases: Both Arthur and Bill were epileptics. Epileptic seizures may be effectively controlled through alternative drugs. The short-term goal in both cases was similar: control of the seizures. Both Arthur and Bill were given the same anticonvulsant drug. Bill very quickly showed an allergic reaction to the drug. The intervention strategy was therefore altered and a different drug was used. Arthur, on the other hand, was not allergic to the drug, but the normal dosage sent him reeling. It was simply too strong. Lessening the dosage accomplished the goal. In both cases the goal was the same, but the practitioner altered the treatment to meet the individual characteristics of each patient. Furthermore, the progress toward that specific goal was documented, so that subsequent practitioners and others in the treatment team were aware of the progress and modifications in the treatment plan.

Individualization implies professional selection and application of treatment modes, given a knowledge of individual predispositions. The decision-making process must be continuous as new information is made available. Often that information is unavailable until a treatment is attempted. Although the medical analogy of an allergic reaction may seem obvious, other noncompatible reactions may be seen in educational, psychological, or social interventions. In such cases the treatment program should be modified.

SUMMARY

Adolescence is a period of development bridging childhood and adulthood. During adolescence individual adolescents establish a unique identity with which they enter adulthood. This identity is a composite of the satisfactory completion of a set of developmental goals. Adolescence is not simply an upward extension of childhood, nor is it a downward extension of adulthood. The adolescent must adjust to a unique set of physical, psychological, and social demands of adolescence. Adolescents do not act randomly or irrationally any more than adults do. Although their ground rules vary, adolescents act purposefully in order to handle normal developmental stress.

Adolescence is marked by wide variability among individuals in maturational status, social background, and psychological predispositions. The practitioner who works with adolescents should be prepared to offer multiple modes of treatment or instruction. Decisions as to the most appropriate form of intervention depend on the degree of flexibility available in defining acceptable outcomes and the variety of appropriate paths to those outcomes.

2 | Physical Growth and Development

Biological changes are probably the most profound and noticeable transformations in the adolescent. Only during infancy does a person undergo a comparable period of rapid and extensive change. The radical alteration in physical appearance and the approach of adult sexuality necessitate a major revision in an individual's self image. The result of these changes often takes its form in adolescents' increased awareness of their own bodies and a preoccupation with looking at themselves in the mirror. Sometimes to the consternation of other members of the adolescents' family, they may spend increased time in the bathroom primping.

The general name applied to this period of change is *puberty*. Puberty is the stage of physical development in which an individual begins to show secondary sexual characteristics such as pubic hair, breasts, and widened hips in girls, or facial hair, pubic hair, and lowered voice in boys. Primary sexual features also mature to their adult function. Strictly speaking, puberty ends when sexual maturation or the ability to reproduce is achieved, even though growth may continue beyond that point. What actually triggers puberty is not clear, but the primary glands in the process are the hypothalamus and the pituitary, which control the release of human growth hormone (HGH), the gonadotropins, and other hormones.

Prior to puberty, growth in height is stable, averaging about five to six centimeters (two and a half inches) per year. At about age eleven or twelve for girls and thirteen or fourteen for boys, there is a sudden increase in output of HGH leading to a growth spurt of eight to nine centimeters per year. Once an individual has passed through this growth spurt, further gains in height are small, and by age seventeen or eighteen in girls and eighteen or nineteen in boys most adolescents reach adult stature (Tanner, 1970; Katchadorian, 1977). (See Figure 2–1.) During this transition there is an increase in weight for both boys and girls. However, the source of the increased weight differs. Girls show an increasingly greater proportion of body fat, whereas boys show rapid increases in lean body mass (Forbes, 1976).

These trends, of course, are averages, and we can find considerable variability within age groups. Thus in a typical class of seventh graders, some

Concern with physical appearance takes on a new level of importance in adolescence, and teenagers may spend much time simply "primping." (© Kit Hedman/Jeroboam, Inc.)

Figure 2-1 AVERAGE RATES OF GROWTH

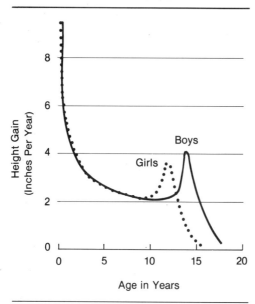

Source: Redrawn from Tanner, Whitehouse, and Takaishi, "Standards from Birth to Maturity for Height, Weight, Height Velocity and Weight Velocity: British Children," *Archives of Diseases of Childhood 41* (1966): 466. Reprinted by permission.

of the girls may be well into puberty, whereas others may not have begun their transition. Likewise, there may be differences in levels of physical maturation within the same individual. The growth spurt may not be quite as rapid or noticeable in some children as others. Those children who are late maturers, for example, do not show the exaggerated peak in growth that we see in early maturers (Faust, 1977).

HEIGHT AND WEIGHT

Height is a relatively reliable indicator of physical development during prepubescence and early adolescence. Because norms and standards for height and weight are often useful to practitioners who are involved with young people, the most recent height and weight norms for school-age children and youths compiled by the National Center for Health Statistics (Hammill et al., 1977) are reproduced as Figures 2–2 and 2–3. To find the relative standing of a boy or girl with respect to the national distribution, merely find the point of intersection of the person's age and height (or weight). The curved lines represent percentile ranks—that is, the percentage of the total population that is shorter (or lighter) at that specific height (or weight) for each age group. A boy of fourteen who is five feet five inches tall

Figure 2-2   WEIGHT GAIN BY PERCENTILES

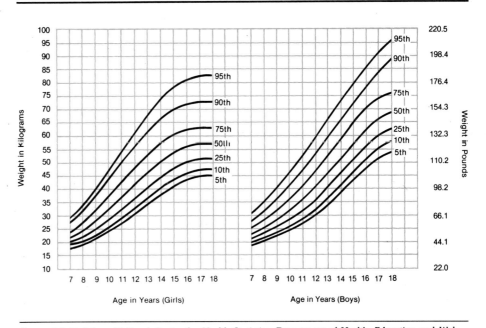

Source: Adapted from National Center for Health Statistics, Department of Health, Education and Welfare, *Vital and Health Statistics* (Washington, D.C.: U.S. Government Printing Office, 1977): 60–61.

Figure 2-3 HEIGHT GAIN BY PERCENTILES

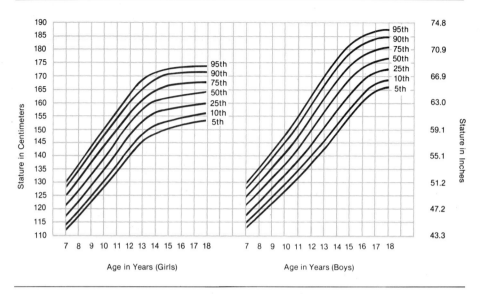

Source: Adapted from National Center for Health Statistics, Department of Health, Education and Welfare, *Vital and Health Statistics* (Washington, D.C.: U.S. Government Printing Office, 1977): 58–59.

lies somewhere between the fiftieth and twenty-fifth percentiles, which means that he is taller than at least 25 percent of fourteen-year-old boys but shorter than at least 50 percent.

Today's youths are taller than those in previous generations. If you were to compare the average heights of youths in 1902 (see Baldwin, 1916) to current norms for children and youths, you would find that from ages six to fifteen today's boys range from 7.9 to 12.9 cm. (centimeters—about three to five inches) taller than their 1902 peers. Girls are, on the average, between 4.7 and 12.4 cm. (about two to five inches) taller than their 1902 peers for the same age groups. At ages seventeen and eighteen, or at approximately adult height, the differences level out and males are about 5.2 cm. (about two inches) taller and females 3.7 cm. (one and a half inches) taller than their 1902 counterparts. In the 1890s, less than 5 percent of young men were over six feet tall (Gallagher, 1960). Today more than that percentage of fifteen-year-olds and nearly 25 percent of eighteen-year-olds exceed six feet (Hammill et al., 1977). This trend toward ever-taller generations, however, seems to be tapering off.

CHANGES IN FEMALES

For girls puberty is marked by increased size of the genitalia, the growth of breasts, and the appearance of pubic hair, which starts as downy, unpigmented hair that gradually becomes darker and coarser until it approaches adult quantity and texture. Perhaps the most significant change that marks the onset of physical maturity in young girls is menarche, their first menstrual period.

Menses is the normal expulsion of blood and the unfertilized ovum produced during the beginning of the menstrual cycle. The onset of menses does not, however, necessarily mean that a young girl is sexually mature or able to reproduce. There may be a period of one to two years following menarche when the girl is naturally sterile. Menarche typically occurs after the growth spurt and seems to be tied to a weight-to-height relationship (Frisch and McArthur, 1974). That is, for first menses to occur, the proportion of body fat must be 17 percent or more. Thus adolescent female athletes may experience a delayed menarche, and anorexic girls (described later in the chapter), who suffer rapid and massive weight loss, are also likely to suffer disruption of menses.

Irrespective of whether parents have talked to their daughter about menstruation before her first period (a large proportion of parents do not), the occurrence of menarche may be stressful, especially for early maturers whose peers have not also had their first menses. Thus parents and teachers should be prepared to be empathetic with a young girl who is upset by the event of menarche.

The average age of menarche in the United States is currently about 12.77 years, with 80 percent of girls having their first menses between ages 11.0 and 14.0 (MacMahon, 1973). Nevertheless, it is not uncommon to find girls having their menarche in the fourth or fifth grades. Further, like height, age of menarche has been shifting for the last several generations. The average age of menarche in 1870 was 16.5 years. By 1930, the average age of menarche had dropped to 14.5, and by 1950, it was 13.5. Given a 1970s estimate approaching

Figure 2-4 DIFFERENT DEGREES OF PUBERAL DEVELOPMENT

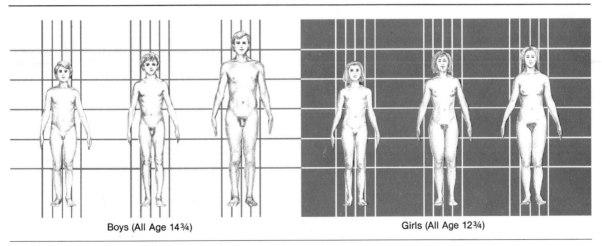

Boys (All Age 14¾)   Girls (All Age 12¾)

Source: J. M. Tanner, "Growth and Endocrinology of the Adolescent," in L. J. Gardner, ed., *Endocrine and Genetic Diseases of Childhood* (Philadelphia: Saunders, 1969). Reprinted by permission.

VIGNETTE 2-1

Are You There God?

Young adolescents have strong fears of being rejected by their peers for being physically different. Pediatricians report that the majority of physical complaints reported by adolescents are related to their advanced or delayed growth and their self-conscious fears that they are abnormal. A variety of physical problems, such as headaches and stomach cramps, can be caused by anxieties regarding advanced or delayed sexual maturation.

Judy Blume writes very popular books for adolescents (and adults). Perhaps the great appeal of her writing lies in her ability to see into the conflicts that young people experience. In this selection Judy Blume expresses the frustrations of a young girl who is waiting for her first menstrual period so that she will not be different from her friends. Can you recall examples of worries you had in your own growing up that are comparable?

When I went home I told my mother. "Gretchen Potter got her period."

"Did she really?" my mother asked.

"Yes," I said.

"I guess you'll begin soon too."

"How old were you Mom—when you got it?"

"Uh...I think I was fourteen."

"*Fourteen!* That's crazy. I'm not waiting until I'm fourteen."

"I'm afraid there's not much you can do about it, Margaret. Some girls menstruate earlier than others. I had a cousin who was sixteen before she started."

"Do you suppose that could happen to me? I'll die if it does!"

"If you don't start by the time you're fourteen I'll take you to the doctor. Now stop worrying!"

"How can I stop worrying when I don't know if I'm going to turn out normal?"

"I promise, you'll turn out normal."

Are you there God? It's me, Margaret. Gretchen, my friend, got her period. I'm so jealous God. I hate myself for being so jealous, but I am. I wish you'd help me just a little. Nancy's sure she's going to get it soon, too. And if I'm last I don't know what I'll do. Oh please God. I just want to be normal.

Nancy and her family went to Washington over Lincoln's birthday weekend. I got a postcard from her before she got back which means she must have mailed it the second she got there. It only had three words on it.

I GOT IT!!!

I ripped the card into tiny shreds and ran to my room. There was something wrong with me. I just knew it. And there wasn't a thing I could do about it. I flopped onto my bed and cried. Next week Nancy would want to tell me all about her period and about how grown up she was. Well, I didn't want to hear her good news!

Are you there God? It's me, Margaret. Life is getting worse every day. I'm going to be the only one who doesn't get it. I know it God. Just like I'm the only one without a religion. Why can't you help me? Haven't I always done what you wanted? Please...let me be like everybody else.

12.5, the age of menarche has been dropping one year every twenty years. The best guess is that the change in age of menarche, as in height, is due to improved nutrition (Cutright, 1971b). (One can project this trend to illogical extremes: carrying the trend backward to the year 100 would put the average age of menarche at 110, and projecting it into the future would anticipate girls in the year 2230 having their first menses *in utero*.) The trend, however, cannot continue indefinitely in both directions. In fact, there is recent evidence that it is leveling off in several parts of the world (Katchadorian, 1977).

The impact of the trend toward earlier sexual maturity must be recognized, especially in the social institutions most directly responsible to today's youths, that is, the schools. As Anastasiow and his colleagues (1975) have suggested, the change has important ramifications for school policy. Given a stable rate of sexual intercourse among teenagers across generations, the drop in the age of menarche and, as a result, the age of fertility, would lead to a net increase in teenage pregnancies. Given an increase in rate of unprotected sexual intercourse among contemporary teenagers, the likelihood of teenage pregnancies is even greater.

CHANGES IN MALES

For boys pubescence—arriving at puberty—is marked by increased sensitivity of the testes to pressure, as well as a reddening and change of texture of the scrotum. Testes increase to as much as seven times their prepubescent size (Barnes, 1975). The size of the penis and scrotum also increases, and pubic hair appears. As with girls, boys' initial pubic hair is downy and unpigmented. It begins to grow at the base of the penis and gradually gets darker and coarser, spreading upward along the trunk and downward along the thighs. Boys will also begin to show facial hair and a slight recession of the hair line. Their voices deepen by as much as an octave or more.

For boys, first ejaculation is not as significant an event as first menses is for girls. Its appearance does not lead to a significant change in life-style. Like menarche, however, it serves as an important marker in the adolescent transition. First ejaculation usually occurs during masturbation or as a nocturnal emission. Like menarche, first ejaculation is apparently occurring at earlier ages. Unlike menses, ejaculation does not occur without some psychosexual input (Eskin, 1977). Full adult sexual potency is not reached at first emission, but some degree of potency is present early, and that potency increases steadily (Steen and Price, 1977).

For both boys and girls, puberty brings an increase in axillary (armpit) sweating and axillary hair. Systolic blood pressure and heart rate increase to adult levels. One curious difference in development between adolescent males and females is seen in patterns of hemoglobin concentration in the blood. Boys show a steady increase in hemoglobin percentage, whereas the value remains quite constant in girls. Also, among black girls, not only is the average percentage stable across adolescence, it is well below the average for whites. Using typical norms, the values for black girls are hazardously close to anemia (Heald et al., 1974). It is not clear, however, whether the lower hemoglobin level indicates a tendency toward anemia among black girls or whether it represents a basic metabolic difference.

PSYCHOLOGICAL CORRELATES OF PHYSICAL GROWTH

Children and adolescents feel a variety of pressures not to be different from the physical norm. The extent to which an individual is different or does not fit the mold of most of his or her peers, because of gaps in maturation or physical handicaps, may lead parents, peers, and teachers to expect the adolescent to behave in ways that are thought to be related to those physical characteristics. That is, the fact that an individual is tall or short, heavy or thin, physically mature or immature, may lead others to expect that person to act like tall, short, fat, or skinny people. When peers and others see differences as undesirable, a young person may suffer ridicule or be excluded from social activities. On the other hand, when they regard the difference as desirable, positive reactions may occur; for example, one may be chosen as a leader. Adolescents who are different from the norm, or who view themselves as different from the norm, may fear being left out by peers or being singled out as odd. Those fears may, in turn, interfere with the adolescent's development of personal feelings of self-worth.

Although most people are anxious to one extent or another about their physical appearance, that worry may become particularly troublesome during puberty and adolescence. As Dwyer and Mayer (1969) note, demands by peers for physical sameness are greatest during adolescence, the period in which we see the greatest differences in development. Additionally, just the rapid physical growth and development alone associated with puberty and adolescence are likely to produce anxiety over body image (Conger, 1977).

SOMATOTYPES

Historically the best-known advocate of relationships between body type and personality was William Sheldon (for example, 1944). Sheldon classified physiques into three *somatotypes* and suggested that each body type was associated with a set of personality characteristics. Endomorphs are large torsoed, short, and fat, and were said to be outgoing, jovial, gregarious, and sociable. Mesomorphs are muscular and were said to be callous, noisy, assertive, and vigorous. Ectomorphs are tall and lean, and were said to be restrained, inhibited, neurotic, and shy. Sheldon saw the relationship between physique and personality as a direct one. That is, a woman was nervous and shy *because* she was a ectomorph. Although several writers have pointed out that Sheldon's original idea was unsound (see, for example, Hammond, 1957; Humphrey, 1957), a number of studies have shown stable relationships between somatotype, or physique, and behavioral patterns. Davidson, McInnes, and Parnell (1957), for example, showed that physique and certain psychiatric characteristics were related among children. Ectomorphic boys were, for example, more likely to be anxious and to score higher on a variety of measures of psychological stress or maladjustment.

You should be very cautious, however, in concluding that physique causes psychosocial adjustment. If a relationship does exist it is probably because of a form of social causality. Society has a set of cultural stereotypes for body types and personalities. A mesomorph is *expected* to be a leader and aggressive. These expectancies are communicated early in life and can be found even among preschool children (Staffieri, 1967). By the time boys or girls reach adolescence they easily identify cultural stereotypes relating physique to personality and will attribute those stereotypes to themselves in accordance with their self-perceptions (Sugarman and Haronian, 1964). That is, mesomorphs learn to behave like mesomorphs are *supposed* to behave. Further, there is some evidence that among junior high school students physique is related to classroom behavior and popularity (Hanley, 1951).

Although not a study of adolescents, Walker's (1962) study of the relationship between physique and school adjustment among nursery school children is relevant. Walker had photographs of nude preschool boys rated for the three dimensions of somatotype. He then had the teachers of those children rate their performance and adjustment in school. Recognizing that other factors might intervene between physique and behavior, Walker was nonetheless able to show regular relationships between teachers' ratings of a student's behavior and that student's physique. Walker found, for example, that endomorphic boys were rated as more assertive and revengeful, whereas mesomorphic boys were more apt to be labeled as easily angered or quarrelsome. Teachers were also more likely to rate the mesomorphic boys as leaders in play, ambitious, daring, chance taking, energetic, and self-confident. In general the teachers felt the mesomorphic boys were more "boyish." Ectomorphic boys, on the other hand, were more likely to be labeled as neurotic or timid. Although we cannot automatically assume that teachers' ratings and students' behaviors necessarily match, Walker's study gives us valuable evidence that there is a relationship between teachers' perceptions of a student's behavior and the physique of the student.

Staffieri (1967) had boys aged four to ten rate silhouettes of endomorphic, mesomorphic, and ectomorphic boys on a variety of psychological and social traits. The results of his study indicated that even the youngest boys had well-established social stereotypes for body types that they did not hesitate to attribute to the silhouettes. They typically rated endomorphs as socially offensive and delinquent, mesomorphs as aggressive, outgoing, assertive, and leaders, and ectomorphs as introverted or neurotic, nervous, retiring, and shy. Later Staffieri (1972) showed that slightly older boys not only have the same stereotypes but also clearly prefer to look like the mesomorph.

I often ask students and teachers in my classes to associate silhouettes of endomorphic, mesomorphic, and ectomorphic youths with a set of adjectives. They are told to choose the silhouette that is most likely to show a given trait. The results of that demonstration seldom vary. The same stereotypes that Staffieri found with preschoolers are found with undergraduate and graduate students and teachers. They attribute almost every negative social trait to the endomorph and attribute qualities of leadership and assertiveness to the mesomorph. They label ectomorphs as timid and studious.

In other studies physical attractiveness has been shown to be related to both perceived popularity and real demonstration of socially desirable behavior (Cavior and Dokecki, 1973; Kleck, Richardson, and Ronald, 1974). Physical height is also associated with positive and negative expectancies.

The point of all this is that, whether or not Sheldon was correct in his assumption that somatotypes cause personality, society has very strong stereotypes associated with given body builds and may selectively reinforce behaviors that conform to expectancies and thereby shape a personality to match a body type. When there is a mismatch between the behavioral predispositions of a young person and the behavioral expectancies of a person in power (for example, a teacher), conflict may arise.

EARLY AND LATE MATURATION

Discrepancies between one's own level of maturation and one's perceived ideal level of maturation may be a source of considerable anxiety. In the Oakland Growth Study, very early and very late maturers showed differential patterns of psychosocial adjustment that persisted into adulthood. Jones (1957) followed the status of early and late maturing adolescent boys from an earlier (Jones and Bayley, 1950) study. In the first study early maturers had substantial growth advantages over their late maturing cohorts. But by adulthood those earlier height and weight differences had been eliminated. However, differences remained between the two groups in psychosocial skills. The early maturers rated higher in general social ability including leadership and responsibility. Late maturers scored higher on indices of maladjustment and a need to be directed by others. Later Jones (1965) reported that early maturers are more likely to make a positive impression when meeting people for the first time.

In the case of the early maturer, the effects of the discrepancy may be either positive or negative. Early maturers, especially young girls who show very advanced physical development as compared to their age mates, may be tempted to identify with older youths, who may not reciprocate. On the other hand, teachers may see the precocious physical development as indicative of general advanced maturity and treat early maturers as if they were older by delegating more responsibility to them. Peers also respond differently to the early maturer. One study (Faust, 1960) showed that among sixth-grade girls, for example, a girl was more likely to be accepted if her level of physical development conformed to the rest of the class. The early maturing girl was rated lower in prestige. By junior high school, however, advanced physical development was an asset, and the early maturer had higher prestige.

Late maturers may suffer considerable anxiety associated with their body image. They do not show any outward signs of physical maturity. For example, late maturing boys do not have pubic hair or larger genitals, whereas late maturing girls lack pubic hair or noticeable breasts. Late maturers may be the object of teasing or ridicule, or they may *feel* that they are the object of ridicule. Thus the shower after gym may be a very threatening and anxiety-provoking experience.

The problem of late maturers developing a positive self-image is exaggerated in the case of the person with a hypoactive (underactive) pituitary gland. Normally the pituitary secretes sufficient HGH, human growth hormone, which stimulates two or more inches of growth per year until early adolescence, when there is a sharp increase in HGH output. In the person who has a hypoactive pituitary, the body fails to generate sufficient quantities of HGH and gonadotropins to initiate the prepubescent growth spurt and the appearance of secondary sex characteristics. The result is that these individuals are considerably shorter than their peers, and, more distressing, they fail to *look* grown up. Their physical development, *as perceived by others and by themselves,* is considerably younger than their chronological age. Because of this, others may expect that such individuals are also socially and intellectually immature.

Consider, for example, the following case of a young twenty-year-old man who suffered from a hypoactive pituitary (Money, 1973). His physical size and appearance were a source of considerable stress. He looked more like a fifth-grade child than a twenty-year-old man. His self-worth suffered considerably especially as it derived from the way others treated him. Potential employers, for example, assumed he was too juvenile to be responsibly employed. Further, his physical retardation had generalized to his sexual development, and although some sexual maturation had occurred, it was not very advanced. Again his self-image suffered: He wanted to be thought of and treated as an adult, but his peers, employers, and society as a whole viewed him as a child.

In the case of the hypoactive pituitary patient, hormonal injections can effect some improvement. For most late maturers, the problem is solved by time. Physicians, counselors, and school personnel, however, should be aware of the psychological stress that either the very early or very late maturer may experience. Physical education personnel should be particularly alert to the hazards of emphasizing those skills that place late maturers in a position where they cannot compete and thus become the focus of harassment from peers. Likewise, although most schools are sensitive to the need for privacy among young girls, especially in shower facilities, that privacy is not often afforded to young boys. For the late maturer whose physical and sexual development is delayed, the situation may be equally embarrassing.

PHYSICAL ATTRACTIVENESS

Society has a strong positive bias toward "good looks." Beauty and physical attractiveness are highly valued traits in our society. Our choice of friends, associates, lovers, and spouses is strongly influenced by their and our physical attractiveness. When university freshmen were randomly paired in a "computer dance," their attitudes toward their dates were largely determined by the date's physical attractiveness. Each person was asked to rate his or her date on a variety of characteristics. The more attractive the date, the more he or she was liked and the more likely the respondent wanted to date that partner again (Walster et al., 1966). Personality, intelligence, and social skills were viewed as insignificant. Further, Berscheid and Dion (1971) found that more physically attractive people expect to date more physically attractive partners.

Physical attractiveness is such a powerful factor in our interpersonal behavior that we have developed a bias that can be phrased "What is beautiful is good" (Dion, Berscheid, and Walster, 1976). That is, we automatically project a variety of positive attributes onto physically attractive people. Byrne (1971) found that when students are asked to rate strangers solely on the basis of a photograph, attractive females are rated as more intelligent and moral. Good-looking men and women are assumed to be more socially adept, more likely to achieve high-prestige occupations, and happier and better adjusted than their unattractive counterparts (Dion and Berscheid, 1974). The only area in which attractive people rate less well than their unattractive counterparts is as potential parents.

In another study male students were asked to complete the California Personality Inventory. They then received evaluative feedback on their performance from either an attractive or unattractive female graduate student. The male students were most pleased when the attractive female gave positive feedback and least pleased when she gave negative feedback. Whether the unattractive female gave positive or negative feedback made little difference (Sigal and Aronson, 1969). In a later study the males were given the chance to volunteer to help the female experimenter in another setting. Irrespective of whether the attractive female gave positive or negative

Physically attractive adolescents enjoy extra attention and popularity. (Rick Smolan/Stock, Boston)

feedback, the males wanted to help (Sigal and Michela, 1976). Apparently it made no difference that she had just given them negative feedback on their performance on a personality inventory; it was more important to the males to be close to her so that they might change her opinion.

Consistently, attractive people are favored along a variety of dimensions, whereas unattractive people are seen as less desirable. Not only do peers respond this way, but so also do professionals interacting with attractive and unattractive clients or students. It is not surprising, then, that young people want to be seen as attractive. Further, youths and society are inundated with images of what it means to be physically attractive and what physically attractive persons like and do. One has only to watch television commercials to see the simple (but erroneous) logic that people use, that is, "Beautiful people use this product. If I use the product, then I will be beautiful."

Advertisers capitalize on this basic belief by repeatedly assuring the teenage public that their product will lead to popularity, happiness, desirability, and success. One indication of the size of the teen cosmetic market is the fact that the annual market for acne preparations alone is in excess of $110 million (Weil, 1979). Whether or not the idea is valid, advertisements emphasize the message that "Attractive people have it made."

OBESITY

Among the variety of problems associated with body type and psychological adjustment, obesity holds a position of considerable current interest. Even the American government has warned that American society is, on the whole, overweight. The problem of weight control has become big business with considerable profit being made by catering to the desires of people who want to lose weight. Media advertising is a curious mix of encouragements to gorge oneself with high-calorie junk foods and to sign up for various weight-reduction plans.

Many physicians are concerned that excess weight is troublesome for more than aesthetic reasons. Obesity has repeatedly been linked to a variety of medical anomalies, including hypertension, cardiovascular disease, myocardial failure, and diabetes, as well as premature death. More recently, some evidence has been found that women who have been obese since adolescence run an increased risk of uterine cancer (Blitzer, Blitzer, and Rimm, 1976). Obesity is also associated with a general pattern of psychological distress. The combined effects of physical stress and social expectancies associated with obesity, reviewed earlier, could well lead to generalized anxieties and negative self-image, which in turn lead to inadequate social adjustment, including school adjustment.

Obese students are self-conscious about their body image and blame their body image for causing their interpersonal problems. When given open-ended questions about social interaction, obese girls will give many more weight-related responses than their normal counterparts (Canning and Mayer, 1968). Obese individuals often report hating their body, and they attribute past and present unhappiness to their physical appearance (McQueen, 1973). They are also likely to rate themselves as aggressive, socially isolated, self-conscious, hostile, phobic, and fearful (Crisp et al., 1970; Wunderlich and Johnson, 1973).

Categorizing someone as obese is not simply a matter of saying that a person is overweight, although a fairly common criterion for obesity is being more than 20 percent heavier than the average weight for their height. Such a criterion by itself may be misleading, however. For example, two men who are both six feet tall and weigh 215 pounds may be judged very differently if one is a football player whose weight is mostly muscle mass, whereas the other's weight is primarily body fat. What we need for a judgment is an index of body fat.

To obtain a truly accurate index of body fat is very difficult and expensive. Some contend that the use of skinfold thickness measured by a set of calipers offers a quick and reliable estimate of body fat. Selzer and Mayer (1965) suggest that the tricep skinfold, which is measured about midway on the upper arm, is the easiest and best single indicator of body fat. Before puberty, body-fat and lean-body-mass percentages are about the same for boys and girls. Following puberty, girls show a more rapid increase in body fat. Once the pattern stabilizes, accumulations of body fat are 2 to 3 percent higher for girls than boys. For adolescents the cutoff points for identifying obesity in girls are up to twelve millimeters thicker than for boys because of this difference. Although skinfold criteria are not without problems, they are much better than measures that depend on a ratio of height to weight (Ingersoll, 1979). The early identification of the obese child remains, however, an important problem, because the obese child is the precursor of the obese adolescent, who is in turn the precursor of the obese adult. The longer one is obese, the more difficult it is to lose the extra weight.

Treatment of obesity has been and remains a difficult problem. Weight reduction for the chronically obese adolescent is very difficult. It is not sufficient to assume that the cause of obesity is excessive eating and that reduction of calories will lead to weight loss. Although excess calories are the predominant cause of obesity, with less than 5 percent of the cases "glandular" (Barnes and Berger, 1975), it is not sufficient to assume that reduction of caloric intake will automatically lead to weight loss. Treatment is not that simple. Obesity for the 95 percent who do not have glandular problems is not the same and therefore cannot be treated the same way. Because there are a wide variety of factors that motivate the obese adolescent, one treatment is not going to work well for all.

Some recent research indicates that obese children and adolescents develop more adipose (fat) cells than their normal weight peers. Further, those adipose cells remain in the body even after considerable weight is lost. It is as though the cells shrink but remain ready to expand again. The common complaint of many chronically overweight people that even eating "normal" portions causes them to gain weight may have some truth.

It is not, however, simply the amount of food that the obese individual eats but the type of food and the patterns of eating that contribute to the problem.

Obese individuals not only eat more, they eat more more often (Leon and Roth, 1977). Further, as Schachter and Rodin (1975) suggest, chronically obese people are more likely to view themselves as unable to control their own behavior. They feel controlled by their environment.

Any program of weight reduction must combine dietary restriction with some alteration of eating habits. Thus some investigators have proposed that behavior modification techniques are most appropriate. In some way the therapist must shape new eating behaviors that will lead not only to weight reduction but also to maintenance of the weight loss (Leon, 1976). Therein lies the frustration of most weight-reduction programs. Although some programs are successful in helping obese individuals to lose weight, they often fail to help their clients maintain that weight loss for any period of time. A program of weight reduction should include an attempt to divorce eating from other activities—for example, watching television. A therapist may encourage the obese patient to eat only at the kitchen table and only at certain times of the day. An obese client should be trained to eat more slowly and to be able to leave food on the plate. The individual should also be given alternative behaviors to cope with emotional stress, boredom, and fatigue (Barnes and Berger, 1975). Obviously certain foods should not be available, and a reasonable dietary regimen should be followed. Crash and fad diets can be temporarily rewarding in the psychological benefit of rapid weight loss, but they run the risk of physiological damage that may have very serious ramifications. Further, crash dieting does not attend to the behavior patterns that led to the weight problem in the first place.

ANOREXIA NERVOSA

In contrast to obesity, practitioners increasingly report another problem related to eating. The problem, anorexia nervosa, is most often seen among white girls, but occasionally it is also seen among boys. Roughly translated, anorexia nervosa means "nervous loss of appetite," but that is a misnomer. More realistically, anorexic patients seem to have a food phobia, just as claustrophobics have a fear of enclosed spaces. An anorexic patient, although hungry, typically either refrains from eating or, if she eats, induces vomiting following a meal or uses laxatives excessively. Anorexia should not be thought of, however, as just being underweight or overzealous in dieting. In some cases anorexic patients become so emaciated that permanent physical harm results; some may actually starve themselves to death. In the past few years, the number of cases seen by physicians has skyrocketed until now roughly one girl in three hundred suffers from this disease.

Curiously the anorexic patient may view herself as fat. Sometimes anorexic patients report that they started by trying to take off a few pounds but just could not seem to stop. Feighner and his colleagues (1972) provide the following as criteria for classifying a person as anorexic:

1. The patient is typically younger than twenty-five, more commonly an early- or middle-adolescent.

This girl's appearance is typical of that of the growing number of American adolescents, mostly females, who suffer from anorexia nervosa. (Neal Boenzi/ NYT Pictures)

2. The patient shows a weight loss of at least 25 percent of original body weight.
3. The patient has a distorted attitude toward food and eating that is resistant to change despite admonitions and hunger.
4. The patient has no known medical condition that could cause the behavior.
5. The patient has no other identifiable psychiatric disorders.

In addition to the above, anorexic girls often cease having menses and develop a downy hair that covers their body. As the condition progresses, circulation may be affected, and the extremities may develop a bluish cast.

Like obesity, anorexia is particularly resistant to treatment, perhaps because of the avoidance characteristics of a phobia or perhaps because we really do not have an adequate understanding of what causes anorexia. Those programs of treatment that have had apparent success have typically been

VIGNETTE 2-2
Anorexia Nervosa

A young girl explained to me that she just wanted to lose a little weight. She was, as she put it, a bit "poochy" and wanted to try out for a cheerleading team in her high school. But after losing fifteen pounds, she just couldn't seem to stop. By the end of her senior year in college she was still trying hard to break the cycle of binge eating and starving that had become a part of her life. Her self-concept and feelings of self-worth suffered badly. This is the story of another young girl who developed similar symptoms of the disease called anorexia nervosa and the impact of that disease on her life.

At only 71 pounds, waif-like and emaciated, 23-year-old Rochelle Spangolett is slowly starving herself to death.

Eighteen months ago, Miss Spangolett, 4-foot 1-inch brunette, decided, like so many other young women, to diet. Her intention was to reduce her "nicely distributed," 128-pound frame to about 113 pounds. The diet succeeded and Miss Spangolett concedes that she was happy at a new weight of 107. But not "happy enough."

"So I went on another diet and got down to 100," Miss Spangolett said. "Then another diet until I got to about 90. At 90 pounds everyone said I was skinny and I loved it, but suddenly my eating habits began to get very strange and things got out of hand."

Unknowingly, during the dieting, Miss Spangolett lost her ability to determine and regulate what, when and how much she would (or could) eat. A psycho-physiological disease called anorexia nervosa took over, seizing control of her eating habits and, in a very real sense, her life.

98 Percent of Victims Females

Anorexia nervosa is appropriately described as a young woman's disease; 98 percent of its victims are female, usually aged 11 to 24, from upper and upper-middle class backgrounds.

Simply defined, anorexia nervosa is a loss of appetite from psychological causes. According to doctors, however, the disease should be defined as an avoidance of food because victims "dream about food, feel hunger and are often obsessed with food."

The disease's symptoms and their effects upon those it afflicts—called anorexics—are wide-ranging and often bizarre. Among the most dramatic symptoms are the following:

- Excessive weight losses—Resulting from willful starvation.
- Amenorrhea—The total cessation of menstruation.
- Distorted body image—Characterized by the victim's inability to perceive her deteriorated physical condition. Many anorexics, even when standing before mirrors, contend that they are pretty and healthy looking.
- Binging—Spells of compulsive eating, often followed by induced vomiting and/or days of starvation.
- Eventual muscle-wasting—In the disease's most active stages, the body, in a desperate search for protein, begins feeding upon itself, often eating away such vital organs as the heart and lungs.

"Anorexia Nervosa: A Diet Disease That Proves Thin Is Dangerous," *The New York Times* (May 11, 1978):39,45. ©1978 by The New York Times Company. Reprinted by permission.

• Continual constipation—Causing a reliance on enormous amounts of laxatives.

• Obsession with food—Many anorexics will prepare entire meals for their families, bake for their friends but never consume what they prepare.

Starvation Seems Goal

"Starvation seems to be the anorexic's ultimate goal," said a psychotherapist, Leslie Jane Maynard. "They want to gain complete control of their biological, physiological and emotional reasons to eat. So they go against nature, overriding the need to refuel and overriding the image of being drastically thin."

But according to Dr. Hilde Bruch, professor of psychiatry at Baylor College of Medicine in Houston and a highly respected authority on anorexia nervosa, "Starvation is merely a symptom and not the real problem."

"The main thing I've learned is that the worry about being skinny or fat is not the real problem," Dr. Bruch said. "It's just a smoke-screen and not the real illness. The real illness has to do with how you feel about yourself. There are many underlying personality conflicts."

Dr. Bruch believes that the anorexic's fundamental problem is the fear of being unable to live up to what's expected of her. The disease, according to Dr. Bruch, enables the anorexic to prove that she has control, that she "can do something nobody else can" and that she is, therefore, not ordinary, not average.

"Having the anorexia makes me kind of unique," said Miss Spangolett. "It gives me a special label, I'm not just the ordinary man in the street...I stand out in a crowd. It's not a positive special, but still it's special."

Miss Maynard, who treats anorexics at the Dieter's Counseling Service in mid-Manhattan, said that anorexics do not see themselves as being skinny.

Some patients actually believe they're getting fat. So they get locked into a very tight behavior of starvation and the diet becomes the most important thing in their lives."

Patient Agrees With Therapist

Rochelle Spangolett, whose battle with the disease has caused her to fall behind in her studies at Brooklyn College, where she is currently a third-year student, is now so thin that she is hardly able to walk from one campus building to another or climb a flight of stairs. She agrees with Miss Maynard's observation:

"The diet controls my life. It's taken over everything. I can't go anywhere or do anything. It rules me."

"It's like there are two of me," Miss Spangolett continued. "There's the intelligent Rochelle, who knows all about nutrition and what the proper things to eat are. But then there's the emotional Rochelle, who's dominating and won't let me take the upper hand and do the proper things.

"It's like she's saying, 'You are not going to weigh more than 70 pounds and if you do, you're going to lose that weight.' "

According to her doctors, Miss Spangolett has reached a dangerous level of deterioration. Unless she gains a minimum of 10 pounds, they say, she will be hospitalized and fed intravenously against her will. An even more ominous possibility, is death.

"Of course, the possibility of death terrifies me," she said with a sigh of remorse. "I'm not suicidal! I'm terrified of catching a cold because the doctors have said that I'd get pneumonia and it would kill me. But that doesn't make me eat more. It just doesn't seep in."

Though cognizant of what is likely to happen without additional weight gains, Miss Spangolett refuses to abandon her abnormal eating habits. At about 9:30 each night, after her parents have retired, she prepares her versions of breakfast, lunch and dinner.

Fearful that others will add calories and protein to her food, she insists upon preparing her own meals with "my own utensils and dinnerware that I don't let anyone touch."

Every Calorie Calculated

Her daily menu, which has remained unchanged for more than six months, consists of dried cottage cheese, low-calorie rice patties, eggplant, one apple (of a specific weight and calorie value), "Thinny Thin" (a dietetic gelatin product), low-calorie coffee and herbal teas.

"I calculate every single calorie," Miss Spangolett said. "I refuse to let my calorie exceed 776 ⅓. I measure everything, even the water for my tea. If it comes to too much, I discard it. I won't let it happen...won't have it."

The causes of anorexia nervosa are not easily determined or explained. There are varying opinions, even within the medical community, about what sets off the disorder. Many physicians and psychiatrists speculate that the disease is a rejection of adulthood, a refusal to accept the inevitability of becoming sexually mature.

All Patients Hospitalized

"All of our patients are hospitalized," Dr. Silverman said of his program at the Babies Hospital of Columbia Presbyterian Medical Center, where anorexia research and treatment has been conducted since 1967. "But we don't use behavior modification, medication, chemicals or supplements to get them back on their feet. We don't want them eating their way out of the hospital."

According to Dr. Bruch, who has written two books on the disease, there are no statistics to indicate the incidence of anorexia nervosa in the United States.

"Studies conducted in England, among 14- to 18-year-old girls in boarding schools, found that the incidence was one in 200. But there are no figures for the general population."

Dr. Bruch added that statistics on anorexia's mortality rate were also unavailable but were directly related to early detection and proper treatment.

Many young women develop anorexia during real or imagined breaks in familial ties— during the first year away at college, in summer camp or in the first months "on their own."

"The one real cause is basic emotional disorder," Dr. Silverman said. "Lots of people have been misguided into believing that normal, healthy young girls can be trapped into the disease by dieting. That's not true. There is always some underlying emotional pathology."

The methods of treating anorexia are almost as varied as the opinions about its causes. At the Stanford University Medical Center and University of Pennsylvania hospitals, patients are hospitalized and, through contractual arrangements, agree to gain specified amounts of weight while undergoing psychological therapy.

At the Philadelphia Child Guidance Clinic, patients are rarely hospitalized, except when their physical conditions prohibit them from sustaining a rigorous outpatient and family therapy program.

Such detection and treatment are the aims of the Anorexia Aid Society, a five-month-old nonprofit organization comprised of 30 pediatricians, psychotherapists, internists, recovered anorexics and lay people.

"We're an all-volunteer, self-help group for anorexics," said Estelle Miller, a psychotherapist and director of the society. "We've received about 400 calls, mostly from parents. We serve as an information and referral service.

"We can tell them where they should go and what they should do when their children aren't eating. We can recommend the professionals who know the symptoms."

The Anorexia Aid Society, which is based in Teaneck, N.J., operates only on funds donated by its members. With such limited funds, it is able to offer a speaker's bureau, publish a newsletter and manage a self-help group for parents.

Probably the most heartbreaking effect of anorexia nervosa is the frustration it brings to the families of its victims. What is a mother or father to do helplessly watching a daughter destroy herself? And who is to blame?

"It affects my family terribly," Rochelle Spangolett said. "They're hurt by it. They're my parents and they love me so much but there's nothing they can do for me...but suffer.

"I see them suffering and I want to do something, but then I get guilt feelings, which make it harder for me. So I eat less. It's a bitter, vicious cycle."

"It's just up to me. All the doctor and my parents can do is be there when I need them and to help me through each day."

some form of behavior-modification therapy. In such cases a therapist views anorexia as a phobic response. Phobic responses are notoriously resistant to extinction because the avoidance response is self-reinforcing. Thus the dilemma for the therapist becomes one of finding the appropriate rewards for the anorexic and withholding those rewards until she eats. A therapist may hospitalize a girl and prohibit any phone calls, visitors, reading material, or television unless she eats her meals. The patient views being confined to the hospital as aversive, so positive reinforcement in the form of privileges and negative reinforcement in the form of release from the hospital are made contingent on eating and weight gain (Bhanji and Thompson, 1974). A therapist who uses this technique has to watch patients carefully, because they have been known to hide their food and claim that they ate it.

Psychoanalytically oriented therapists often suggest that anorexia is primarily a rejection of one's femininity. The excessive loss of weight diminishes the external signs of femininity, especially breasts, and leaves the girl looking boyish. Treatment involves dealing with such psychodynamic factors as fear of oral pregnancy, parental conflict, and sexual anxieties. Some criticize the use of lengthy psychotherapy on the premise that the anorexic syndrome is potentially lethal. Also, Hilde Bruch (1962), an expert in the area, points out that the anorexic girl is often rebelling against parents who have repeatedly told her what she needs or feels, thereby making her feel helpless. The therapist, Bruch argues, often ends up duplicating the parental role. Bruch (1974) also criticizes the behavior modification approach on much the same grounds. That is, the patient is being controlled and may feel even more helpless or tricked.

Others point to the excessive emphasis in our society on thinness, especially in advertising. Being thin to the point of gauntness is portrayed as the main criterion for beauty and desirability. There is some interesting support to this concept in a report on health attitudes of young people in the United States (Scanlon, 1975). Teenagers were asked two questions relative to their body image. They were asked first whether they thought they were thinner than most of their peers, about the same size as their peers, or heavier than most of their peers. They were then asked whether they would prefer to be heavier or lighter or to stay about the same as they were. As you can see in Table 2-1, girls reported overwhelmingly that they wanted to be thinner than

Table 2-1 REPORTED SELF-PERCEPTION AND DESIRED BODY SIZE AMONG ADOLESCENTS AGED TWELVE TO SEVENTEEN*

Self-Perceptions	Want to Be: Thinner	The Same	Heavier	Total
Thinner than Most	Boys 1.4	24.5	74.5	17.9
	Girls 7.9	36.2	55.9	9.0
About the same as Most	Boys 10.7	70.2	19.2	69.7
	Girls 41.6	53.9	4.6	63.0
Heavier than Most	Boys 68.3	26.9	4.8	12.4
	Girls 93.7	6.0	0.4	28.0
Totals	Boys 17.9	55.0	27.1	
	Girls 48.4	40.8	10.8	

Source: National Center for Health Statistics, Department of Health, Education and Welfare, *Vital and Health Statistics* (Washington, D.C.: U.S. Government Printing Office, 1975):7.
*Adapted from Scanlon, 1975.

they were, and boys reported that they wanted to be heavier than they were. Even among those girls who rated themselves as thinner than most, over half reported that they wanted to be thinner still. Cultural stereotypes of desirable body styles seem to have a profound effect on adolescents' personal image.

ACNE

Among the more common problems facing adolescents is the appearance of blackheads and whiteheads, or *acne*. Acne vulgaris, the form of acne most common among teens, is usually a minor ailment requiring minimal medical intervention. The most effective treatment is time. Only in severe cases may radical intervention, such as cosmetic surgery, be required, but this is rare. Because acne is common, there may be a tendency on the part of teachers, counselors, and physicians to view it as unimportant unless it becomes severe. However, as Reisner (1975) warns, the psychological stress that a young person may suffer from fear of rejection or exclusion may be more important than the physical marring of the complexion. Schachter (1972) studied young people with and without acne and found that although there is no overall difference in the number of activities participated in by the two groups, acne sufferers enjoyed the activities less.

Because acne is associated with a variety of old wives' tales relating it to increased sexuality or masturbation, the adolescent who has acne may suffer unwarranted feelings of guilt. Most probably, acne is simply the result of increased androgen output (Gallagher, 1960) or a genetic propensity. The fact that acne is usually more severe in boys gives this theory some credence. Although girls are more likely to display signs of acne earlier—for example, 38 percent of twelve-year-old girls versus 21 percent of twelve-year-old boys

report acne—the trend reverses by age fourteen, and by age seventeen, 68 percent of boys versus 53 percent of girls report acne (Scanlon, 1975). Further, although girls are more likely to consult a dermatologist for treatment, boys usually suffer more severe cases of acne.

Acne vulgaris is different from other forms of acne and should not be confused with acne that is a result of drugs, both legal and illegal. Blackheads and pimples in acne vulgaris result from increased activity of the sebaceous, or oil-producing, glands located beneath the skin. If the oil in a pilosebaceous duct is exposed to the air, it will oxidize and become a blackhead. If, on the other hand, the oil is not exposed to the air, if a layer of skin covers the duct, the result is a whitehead.

The most effective treatment for mild cases of acne is frequent washings with antibacterial detergent soaps or skin cleansers (Reisner, 1973). In more severe cases, an acne sufferer should consult a dermatologist, who might prescribe antibiotics. Although some treatments of acne include topical applications of a vitamin A ointment, adding vitamin A to the diet will do nothing for acne, and in cases where too much vitamin A is added to the diet, liver damage may result. Very recently a new treatment for severe cases of acne, using a derivative of vitamin A, has had very good results (*Newsweek*, 1979). Other ointments or topical preparations typically include sulfur, resorcinol, or salicylic acid, or some combination of these (Reisner, 1973). "Medicated" cosmetics do nothing. Because acne often diminishes during the summer months, some case might be made for the use of sunlamps. On the other hand, summer may simply be a more relaxing time, which might also account for the change.

Although many caring parents nag their teenagers about diet as a cause of acne, there is no objective evidence to support this. Even chocolate, unless the individual is allergic to it, is not a culprit. A well-balanced diet, although beneficial to one's general well-being, does not seem terribly important in the control of acne. Parents should be advised against making unreasonable and unnecessary dietary restrictions that might prevent acne-suffering adolescents from participating with peers at a time when they fear being excluded because of their acne.

SUMMARY

It is not surprising that some writers, especially those with a medical orientation, key in on physical development as the critical feature of the adolescent transition. The large proportion of adolescent patients whose principal concern reported to physicians revolves around physical and sexual maturity reinforces that view. Further, the radical changes associated with puberty are so profound that they demand attention. However, it is a mistake to assume that adolescence is only a physical transition. As you will see in the next and subsequent chapters, adolescents must also adjust to other intellectual and social transitions. However, the appearance of secondary sexual characteristics and the rapid physical growth during early adolescence cause young people to reform their personal body image. When adolescents feel that their body image is different from the type of image valued by peers and society, they may suffer a great deal of anxiety.

3 | Intellectual and Cognitive Growth

There are two general ways of looking at the question of intellectual or cognitive growth in adolescence. The first is the more traditional view, which encompasses intellectual growth within the assessment of intellectual ability through formalized tests. The second draws on more recent theories of cognitive development, especially those of Piaget and Inhelder. Both approaches are relevant because they reflect the complex nature of cognitive development. The first remains important because standardized tests of intelligence continue to be a focus of social policy and controversy.

TESTS OF INTELLECTUAL ABILITY

Toward the end of the last century, Alfred Binet and Theodore Simon were commissioned by the French government to develop a test to screen "feeble-minded" students who would benefit from special training. It was felt that without a scientific assessment technique teachers might use such special classes as a way of eliminating troublemakers from the class. It was (and still is) not uncommon for a teacher to refer a rowdy but bright troublemaker and keep a quiet but intellectually retarded student. A more objective procedure was needed. To avoid teacher bias in the selection of students for special classes, Binet developed a screening device known commonly as the intelligence test.

THE BINET TEST

Binet and Simon studied the behavior of children in a wide variety of problem tasks. Through astute observation Binet and Simon found that the developmental characteristics of certain tasks made them useful in differentiating intellectually retarded or intellectually precocious children from average children. Later, relative intellectual status, as measured by the Binet-Simon Test, was indicated by an intelligence quotient (IQ), or the ratio of a child's mental age (MA) to his chronological age (CA) multiplied by one hundred. Chronological age was simply the age of the child in months, and mental age was the age at which an "average" child scores as the testee did. If, for example, a testee scored as high as an average child of twelve years three months, the testee's MA would be 147 months. If that testee was a girl whose CA was ten years three months, or 123 months, her IQ—equal to her MA (147 months) divided by her CA (123 months) times 100—would be 119. In such a case, the girl would be assumed to be intellectually above average. If, on the other hand, the same girl was found to have an MA of a child seven years six months, she would be labeled as intellectually below average, with an IQ of 73. If her MA equalled her CA, the result would be an IQ of 100, the index of average intelligence. The ratio is multiplied by one hundred solely to remove the decimal. Imagine having an IQ of 1.15.

The Binet tests were adapted for use in America by Lewis Terman and Maude Merrill at Stanford University. The result, the Stanford-Binet, is still one of the two predominant tests of individual intellectual ability. The other test, the Wechsler Intelligence Scale for Children (WISC), and its adult version, the Wechsler Adult Intelligence Scale (WAIS), use a somewhat different testing format, but the intent is the same: a variety of tasks of differing difficulty define a testee's relative intellectual performance. Although many still call the score from such a test an "IQ," that name is not really accurate. For a variety of reasons, the IQ per se was found to be an inadequate index of intellectual performance. The IQ has been replaced by a standardized index that reflects an individual's relative standing within a distribution of people of the same CA. Because the distribution of intelligence-test scores is essentially normal (with a small discrepancy in the lower end of the scale), we are able to tell approximately what percentage of the population lies above or below a given intelligence test score. Figure 3–1 shows the distribution of intelligence-test scores in the population as a whole. A little more than two-thirds of the people tested with the Stanford-Binet will have intelligence-test scores between 84 and 116. About two percent have scores higher than 132, and about two percent have scores lower than 68. Statistically, only one person in a thousand scores 148 or above, and only one scores 52 or below.

Figure 3-1 EXPECTED DISTRIBUTION OF 1,000 SCORES ON A STANDARD TEST OF INTELLIGENCE

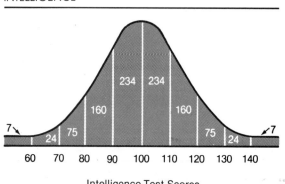

Intelligence-Test Scores

As students progress through high school, achievement tests and tests of intellectual ability are more likely to measure abstract knowledge. (Arthur Grace/Stock, Boston)

GROUP VERSUS INDIVIDUAL TESTS

Although most people have taken some form of intelligence test, they may not have taken an individual test. Rather, they have taken a group test, in which they were given a test booklet and a response sheet to complete, very likely in a large auditorium or classroom. The purpose of a group test is to approximate the scores obtained on individual tests. Group tests are considerably more efficient and less expensive than individual tests, but a practitioner should be very careful about equating the two. The individual examination provides considerably more diagnostic information. An individual test should be administered only by a qualified psychometrist who is able to provide more than a single number, the test score, at the end of the testing session. Sometimes, however, psychometrists do not provide additional information; in those cases the teacher or practitioner should feel free to ask for more information.

What is it that intelligence tests are supposed to measure? I have tried to refrain from equating intelligence with intelligence test scores. However, the famous psychological historian E. G. Boring (1923) is credited with saying that intelligence is what the intelligence test measures. What Boring meant was that we define a psychological trait in terms of the way we measure it. Unfortunately his definition avoids the question of what is being measured and what it means to be intelligent.

Perhaps the most widely used definition of intelligence is the one offered by Wechsler (1958):

Intelligence is the aggregate or global capacity of the individual to act purposefully, to think rationally and to deal effectively with his environment. It is global because it is composed of elements of abilities which, though not entirely independent, are qualitatively differentiable. By measurement of these abilities, we ultimately evaluate intelligence. (p. 7)

The assessment of intelligence would thus be accomplished by using a variety of measures intended to evaluate purposeful or adaptive thinking. Intelligence in this sense is seen as a composite of abilities, a general intellectual capacity.

In contrast, some theorists argue that intelligence must be defined in light of specific intellectual abilities. The theorist who paved the way for this point of view was L. L. Thurstone (1938), who proposed that there were seven "primary mental abilities" and that descriptions of intellectual ability should reflect relative standing in all forms of ability rather than in terms of a global ability.

J. P. Guilford extended the logic of the multifactor model of intelligence by proposing that intelligence is described by the intersection of the type of *content* of the problem posed, the *mental operation* required to solve the problem, and the *product*, or type of response demanded. Each dimension of the task was further divided into smaller units. By combining the three dimensions with each set of units, Guilford identified and labeled 120 separate intellectual abilities. He envisioned the "structure" of intellect as a box depicted in Figure 3–2.

Figure 3-2 GUILFORD'S STRUCTURE OF THE INTELLECT

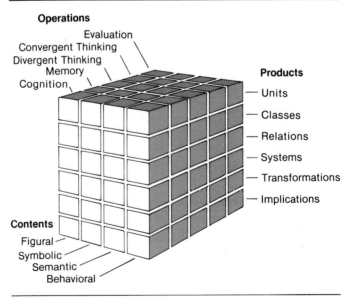

Source: J. P. Guilford, "Three Faces of Intellect," *American Psychologist 14* (1959): 470. Copyright 1959 by the American Psychological Association. Reprinted by permission.

Among Guilford's better-known distinctions was the difference between convergent and divergent thinking. According to Guilford, most educational and psychological tests demand convergent thinking, in which there is a single, clearly correct answer to a problem. (For example, What are the first three elements in the periodic chart?) However, very little testing is directed at divergent thinking, which allows and encourages multiple possibilities for the same question. (How many ways can you use a shoe?) Many writers believe that divergent thinking is basic to creative thinking and originality. We will give more attention to creative thinking later in the chapter.

CULTURAL BIAS

Some critics have argued that tests of intelligence are "culturally biased" and are questionable indicators of intellectual abilities, especially for minorities whose language and cultural base may be incompatible with the demands of the test. Such critics point to specific items as discriminatory or racist. One of the items on a WAIS subtest is "Who was Goethe?" It may be argued that this item is biased toward middle- or upper-class youths, who have a greater chance of hearing about Goethe. On the other hand, advocates of intelligence testing argue that the information is generally available and that the bright youth will encounter it regardless of social class. And the bright youth will likely recall it at a later time. Others point to specific items that reflect middle-class value systems. For example, one item from the Stanford-Binet test is "What is the thing to do when you are on your way to school and see that you are in danger of being late?" Although the item is intended to measure "comprehension," knowledge of the correct answer implies adherence to a value system that emphasizes punctuality.

The selection of one or two items from a test of mental ability to demonstrate cultural bias may be misleading. The tests are made up of a variety of items that are meant to sample intelligence across many areas. However, items for an intelligence test are deliberately chosen from those skills and abilities that are favored by the dominant culture. Because the tests are designed to sort those who will do well or poorly in that dominant culture, they are by definition culturally biased.

CULTURE-FAIR TESTS

Some test makers have tried to develop culture-fair tests of mental ability—that is, tests that assess intelligence with items that have little or no inherently culture-biased material. Typical items on these tests are mazes or figure problems that are said to require fewer language skills. The logic is that if differences in language based on ethnic background are eliminated, then the cultural bias will also be removed. Tests such as the Culture Fair Intelligence Test (Cattell and Cattell, 1959) and the Raven's Progressive Matrices (Raven, 1965) are said to measure general mental ability without bias stemming from cultural or language differences.

VIGNETTE 3-1
A Test of Intelligence

Every so often a popular magazine like Reader's Digest *prints a short test that they claim to be a test of intellectual ability. Whether these tests would stand up under scientific scrutiny is not the question. The tests are challenging and use items that are common to group tests of intelligence. Notice the types of questions that are asked, and as you try to answer the questions, consider how you solve the problems.*

You're smart, but are you brainy enough to qualify for Mensa, the international organization whose only requirement for membership is an I.Q. in the "genius" range? *The Reader's Digest* first asked that question in January 1974 with a quiz similar to the one that follows. Mensa subsequently received over 70,000 letters from Digest readers. Of those hopefuls, over two percent became eligible for membership. To see if *you* belong among the intellectual elite, take this test. Be sure to time yourself; there are bonus points for finishing in less than 15, 20 or 25 minutes.

1. Which of the lower boxes best completes the series on the top?

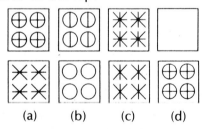

(a)   (b)   (c)   (d)

2. I am a man. If Larry's son is my son's father, what relationship am I to Larry?
(a) His grandfather   (d) His grandson
(b) His father   (e) I am Larry
(c) His son   (f) His uncle

Source: "Are You a Genius?" *Reader's Digest* 114 (April 1979): 96–98. Reprinted by permission of Mensa.

3. Which word does not belong in the following group?
(a) Knife   (d) Feather
(b) Swan   (e) Lovely
(c) Smile   (f) Thought

4. Which two shapes below represent mirror images of the same shape?

(a)   (b)   (c)   (d)   (e)

5. What number comes next in this series?

9, 16, 25, 36, . . .

6. Complete this analogy with a five-letter word ending with the letter "H." High is to low as sky is to ----H.

7. In the box below, a rule of arithmetic applies across and down the box so that two of the numbers in a line produce the third. What is the missing number?

$$
\begin{array}{ccc}
6 & 2 & 4 \\
2 & ? & 0 \\
4 & 0 & 4
\end{array}
$$

8. Complete this analogy with a seven-letter word ending with the letter "T." Potential is to actual as future is to ------T.

9. In the group below, find the two words whose meanings do not belong with the others.
(a) glue   (d) nail
(b) sieve   (e) string
(c) buzz saw   (f) paper clip

10. Mountain is to land as whirlpool is to:
(a) forest   (d) sky
(b) wet   (e) shower
(c) sea

11. Find the number that logically completes the series:

2, 3, 5, 9, 17, . . .

12. Two of the shapes below represent mirror images of the same shape. Which are they?

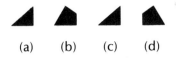

(a)   (b)   (c)   (d)

13. Statistics indicate that men drivers are involved in more accidents than women drivers. The only conclusion that can certainly be drawn is that:
(a) Male chauvinists are wrong, as usual, about women's abilities.
(b) Men are actually better drivers but drive more frequently.
(c) Men and women drive equally well, but men log more total mileage.
(d) Most truck drivers are men.
(e) There is not enough information to justify a conclusion.

14. In the box below, a rule of arithmetic applies across and down the box so that two of the numbers in a line produce the third. What is the missing number?

6	2	12
4	5	20
24	10	?

15. If A × B = 24, C × D = 32, B × D = 48 and B × C = 24, what does A × B × C × D equal?
(a) 480   (c) 744   (e) 824
(b) 576   (d) 768

16. Which of the four lower selections best completes the series on the top?

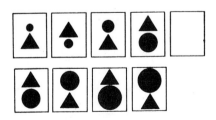

17. Which word does not belong in this group?
(a) microscope   (b) magnifying glass
(c) microphone   (d) telescope
(e) telegraph

18. Find the two words nearest in meaning to each other.
(a) beam   (d) ray
(b) lump   (e) collection
(c) giggle

19. If Jim turns right *or* left at the stop sign he will run out of gas before he reaches a service station. He has already gone too far past a service station to return before he runs out of gas. He does not see a service station ahead. Only one of the following statements can be positively deduced:
(a) He may run out of gas.
(b) He will run out of gas.
(c) He should not have taken this route.
(d) He is lost.
(e) He should turn right at the stop sign.
(f) He should turn left at the stop sign.

20. Complete the following analogy:

(a) + − 0 are to:
(a) + − 0   (c) − + 0   (e) + + 0
(b) 0 + −   (d) 0 − +

Answers

(1) C. Omit the horizontal line in the asterisk, as it was omitted in the circle. (2) C. (3) E. The other words are nouns. (4) D and E. (5) 49; 9 is 3 squared, 16 is 4 squared, 25 is 5 squared, and so on. Also, 9 + 7 = 16, 16 + 9 = 25, 25 + 11 = 36, and so on. (6) Earth. (7) 2. In each vertical and horizontal row, the second number is subtracted from the first. (8) Present. (9) B and C. All the others hold things together. (10) C. A whirlpool is part of the sea as a mountain is part of land. (11) 33. The difference between the numbers is progressively multiplied by 2. (12) B and D. (13) E. (14) 240. (24 × 10 and 12 ×

20 both equal 240). (15) 768. It is not necessary to determine the values of A, B, C, D. Simply multiply 24 × 32. (16) D. The ball gets larger in each box, while the triangle remains the same size, and the ball and the triangle keep alternating positions. (17) E. The others are all things that increase images or sounds. (18) A and D are synonyms. (19) A. Just the fact that Jim can't see a service station ahead doesn't mean there isn't one. (20) C. Positive and minus change positions; neutral stays in the same place.

Scoring

Give yourself one point for each correct answer. You receive an additional five points if you finished the test in less than 15 minutes, three points if you finished in less than 20 minutes, and two points if you finished in less than 25 minutes.

If you scored:

- 20–25 points: You are extremely intelligent—a perfect candidate for Mensa.
- 15–19 points: This should put you in the higher percentiles of the population— definitely a Mensa candidate.
- 10–14 points: Nothing to be ashamed of—a most respectable score. You should probably try the complete, standard Mensa test.
- Fewer than 15 points: forget about joining Mensa, but don't stew about it. You may just be having a bad day. Some of the most successful writers, businessmen, artists and other famous people don't have exceptionally high I.Q.'s, either.

What's the verdict? If you think you may be Mensa material, or you'd like to receive membership information, write to Mensa, Dept. DC, 1701 W. Third St., Brooklyn, N.Y. 11223.

THE GROWTH OF INTELLIGENCE

Prior to adolescence, scores on intelligence tests are highly variable. The earlier individuals are tested, the less stable are their scores. As children reach adolescence, however, their relative position in the intelligence test distribution begins to stabilize (Bayley, 1965). That is, although intellectual ability may continue to grow during and after adolescence, relative standing in the mental ability distribution will remain about the same. Selective individual cases may show dramatic change in intellectual growth during adolescence, but the overall pattern of cases does not.

One popular notion regarding intelligence is that intellectual growth peaks during late adolescence and from that point continually declines through adulthood. This idea has its roots in a study reported by Wechsler (1958). Wechsler reported data taken from a cross-sectional study of intelligence in which the best average performance at the time of testing was shown by testees aged twenty and twenty-one. However, although the data for the fifty-year-olds and the twenty-year-olds were from the same test, the differences in performance may have resulted from very different experiences. For example, assume that the tests were given in 1950. In 1950 nearly 60 percent of seventeen-year-olds graduated from high school, whereas in 1920 (when the forty-seven-year-olds were seventeen) only about 15 percent of seventeen-year-olds did so (Golladay, 1977). Thus the differences in performance were not necessarily a result of age. The same problem might occur in a contemporary study, because the twenty-year-olds of 1950 would be compared with students of the 1970s, who are even more likely to have completed high school. Curiously, though, a national study of youths in the late 1960s found that overall students were scoring somewhat lower on Wechsler tests of intelligence than their 1949 counterparts (Scanlon, 1973).

When data from cross-sectional studies are compared to those from longitudinal studies, very different interpretations emerge. In one study, for example, Owens (1953) retested a group of men who had taken an intelligence test in 1917 as college freshmen. He retested those same men again ten years later (Owens, 1966). Rather than showing the drop in intellectual performance anticipated by the Wechsler study, Owens's data showed a net increase in performance from age seventeen to age fifty. The largest gains were in general verbal ability and general reasoning. Performance in numerical ability showed a decline. Bayley (1965) also found a leveling off in intellectual growth after adolescence but did observe a steady increase over adulthood. Further clarification is offered by the study of Schaie and Strother (1965), who found that gain or decline in intellectual abilities, whether reviewed in longitudinal or cross-sectional studies, varies with the type of task used.

Although there is overall stability in patterns of intellectual growth, there are differences among individuals. Some adolescents will show much larger gains during their teen years than others. Those who show the larger increases often show higher levels of curiosity and higher motivation to achieve. Those who show a decrement in performance are more likely to be rated as passive (Kagen et al., 1958).

There is little doubt that the home environment in which a child or adolescent is raised has a significant impact on the development of intelligence. It is unclear, however, how much we are able to alter intellectual growth by programs of intervention. Some studies would lead us to believe that early and intensive intervention has a major impact on socially induced retardation (Heber et al., 1969), but the results of those studies are not well documented. Also, there is little research on attempts to alter intellectual development by programs of intervention during adolescence. Studies such as those by Heber indicate, however, that intellectual growth is not unchangeable or irredeemable.

ETHNIC DIFFERENCES

Perhaps the most inflammatory topic associated with the measurement and study of intelligence is the question of ethnic and socioeconomic differences in performance on traditional tests of intelligence. Researchers have repeatedly reported a difference of ten to twenty intelligence-test points between black and white Americans (Backman, 1972; Jensen, 1969, 1972; Scanlon, 1973). Similar differences are reported between lower-income and middle-income children and youths (Backman, 1972; Herrnstein, 1971; Scanlon, 1973). You should remember that the researchers are reporting *averages*. Because a person is black does not mean that his intelligence is fifteen points lower than a white person's. Nor does reporting such differences explain why they occur.

Arthur Jensen (1969, 1972) has proposed that 80 percent of the *variability* in intelligence is determined genetically and, further, that the difference in intellectual performance between whites and blacks is genetically determined. Jensen's arguments are based on (1) the premise that certain psychological characteristics can have genetic components and (2) the fact that differences in racial characteristics are genetic. Herrnstein (1971) offered a slightly modified version of this argument to account for intelligence score differences between lower- and middle-income populations. Herrnstein suggested that the genetic pool for the lower-income population has been depleted over generations as the more intelligent people move vertically through the social class structure and leave the lower-income group a genetically inferior pool.

Not all researchers agree with the genetic hypothesis. A variety of alternative explanations have been offered to explain the differences in performance on tests of intelligence. Some suggest that the differences are the result of bias in the testing situation, nutritional deficiencies, racist characteristics of the test, educational differences, ethnic attitudes, linguistic patterns, or some combination of these (Gordon, 1971). The evidence is simply not conclusively favorable to the genetic hypothesis.

The difference in the distribution of scores on tests of intelligence for ethnic groups has serious educational ramifications. Because the distribution of scores among black children and youths is below that of their white peers, they are six times more likely to be assigned to classes for the retarded (Shuey, 1966) if intelligence tests are used as the primary selection criterion. The problem is not resolved simply by dismissing the intelligence test as irrelevant or racist. Black youths must still be provided with a quality education, and, at this point at least, the characteristics of the predominant educational pattern are not compatible with their needs.

PIAGET'S THEORY OF COGNITIVE DEVELOPMENT

An alternate model of intellectual growth and development to that represented by standardized tests of intelligence is the model of conceptual development described by Jean Piaget. To Piaget, it is not enough to say that adolescents score higher on tests of intelligence than younger children simply because they have had more learning and experience. Not only do adolescents know *more*, their knowledge is qualitatively different than children's. In some sense this shift is represented in standard tests of intelligence by a qualitative shift in the types of questions asked as the individual matures. Advanced questions on these tests usually require abstract thinking.

To Piaget, however, the shift in thought was more than just coincidental. The shift from concrete thought to abstract thought is the hallmark of adolescent cognitive development. Piaget referred to the newfound intellectual ability of adolescence as *formal operational thinking* and believed it represented the culmination of stages of cognitive development that begin in infancy. With the change, the adolescent is able to think beyond the present, to consider the abstract, and to think of alternate possibilities beyond those immediately available.

Piaget's theory of cognitive development was built on certain assumptions of the nature and purpose of thinking. It is sometimes helpful to know that Piaget was trained as a biologist and that he drew on the basic adaptive principles of homeostasis—the body's tendency to return to stable equilibrium after a disruption—to represent human intellectual adaptability.

The central element in Piaget's theory of conceptual growth is the schema, or mental structure. A schema is a collection of bits of knowledge in an organized pattern that aids in our interpretation of our environment. As collections of knowledge, however, schema are not simply a conglomeration of facts. Rather, schema also contain strategies for analyzing and evaluating information. The backgammon player, for example, possesses not only a knowledge of basic rules of the game, but also flexible, adaptive strategies for playing the game. In the same way mental structures serve to guide our adaptive behavior when we encounter new problems. In Piaget's terms, mental development results from the individuals' interacting with and adapting to their environment. Although a strong genetic component of mental development influences the patterns of cognitive growth, intellectual growth is a result of both maturation *and* environment.

The child progresses through the course of developing mental structures by means of experiences that lead to imbalance in mental structures, or in Piaget's terms disequilibrium, and by the adaptive responses necessary to achieve balance or equilibrium. As the child has more adaptive experiences, the mental structures become more complex and more flexible. In adapting to disequilibrium, the individual draws on the processes of *accommodation* and *assimilation*. That is, when people recognize new information in their environment, their schema are unsettled. To resolve the imbalance, a learner may either alter the cognitive schema to be compatible with the new information (accommodation) or alter the perception to be compatible with already existing mental structures (assimilation).

Consider the following: Jack is an adolescent boy who has been raised in a Protestant household. He was asked by his Roman Catholic girlfriend to go to church with her one Sunday. Jack agreed, though with some anxiety, because he had never been to a Catholic church before and he was unsure about what would happen. The day arrived and Jack escorted his girlfriend to her church. As the service progressed Jack was surprised to find that, although there were differences, there were also common features between his own and his girlfriend's religious services. Finally, the service progressed to a prayer that Jack knew from his own religious training. The prayer is common to Christian religions. Jack joined in and felt reasonably comfortable in participating because, with the exception of the substitution of "trespasses" for "debts," the prayer seemed the same. Suddenly, however, Jack realized he was continuing with the prayer as he knew it while everyone else had stopped. Jack was noticeably embarrassed but his girlfriend told him not to worry.

What happened? In Piagetian terms, Jack was presented with a problem to which he needed to respond. As he assessed the problem he found common elements and applied a schema he already possessed. What Jack did not know was that the prayer ending he was familiar with did not occur immediately in the Catholic service. His experience, although momentarily embarrassing, led to an alteration and refinement of his schema. The application of his existing mental structures to the problem is an example of assimilation. The modification of the structure is an example of accommodation.

It is not necessary to actually experience an event to modify a cognitive schema. The act of reading about a problem and someone else's solution may alter your mental structure. That is, you accommodate your schema to incorporate new information by indirect or vicarious experience. By most definitions learning occurs only under conditions of accommodation. It would, however, be misleading for you to infer that all assimilation is bad. In many cases we assimilate new information in an attempt to keep things simple.

This is an important point in Piaget's theory. For accommodation to occur, something must cause disequilibrium in your current schema. As an adaptive learner you try to correct this imbalance. The entire course of cognitive growth is thus marked by a series of problems that cause disequilibrium and by attempts to reestablish equilibrium through assimilation and accommodation.

STAGES OF DEVELOPMENT

According to Piaget, intelligence progresses from infancy to adulthood through an *invariant* sequence of four cognitive stages. To say that we progress through stages of intellectual development means that to reach adult levels of functioning, we must first go through the earlier stages. The order of progression through the stages is invariant: each of us goes through them in the same order although we may go through them at a different rate.

At birth children operate with sensorimotor schema, which are knowledge systems based on sensations gained first by the infant's reflexive or random movements. The infant's world is composed of those things that can be sucked, smelled, seen, or touched. Knowledge of the environment is based on nonverbal responses and is linked to the immediate physical reality. The infant who shakes a rattle associates the physical movement with the noise of the rattle. If you observe babies, you will notice that initially their movements are not well differentiated. They move everything. As they mature, however, their schema become more refined and their behavior more precise. Knowledge, however, remains tied to the immediate physical reality of a setting. In Piaget's terms, if a stimulus is not in the immediate physical environment of an infant, it does not exist for that infant. "Out of sight, out of mind" defines sensorimotor thinking.

At around two years of age, the child begins to use preoperational, or *intuitive,* thought. By this stage children recognize that something exists even when it is not within sight or touch. However, if there is an alteration of the perceptual character of their environment, they presume the object has changed. The prime characteristic of this stage of cognitive development is the formation of images. Children's conception of the world around them is based largely on perceptual images. However, the child also develops language skills during this time. During the next few years children acquire an extraordinary vocabulary and ability to produce syntax. However, their schema are still relatively primitive.

Children at sensorimotor and preoperational levels of thinking are highly *egocentric*. As Piaget used the term, egocentrism refers to the child's assumption that his or her view of reality is the view that everyone shares. The child is unable to conceive of an alternate view of reality. If you ask an eighteen-month-old girl to show you a picture she has drawn, she is most likely to show you the back of the picture while she looks at the front (Flavell, 1977). The child assumes that if she can see it, so can you.

Egocentrism continues into the intuitive stage of thinking. The world of preoperational children is still perceptually bound. If their perception of an object is altered, they presume the object is altered. In perhaps the best-known task developed by Piaget, equal amounts of liquid are poured into two identical beakers. The liquid from one beaker is then transferred to a tall, thin beaker, and the child is asked whether the amounts are still the same or whether they are different. Preoperational children will answer that they are

Cognitive development is a lifelong developmental process. Even young children enjoy solving problems. (© Susan Lapides)

no longer the same, that the tall, thin beaker has "more." [Wadsworth (1978) describes a variety of such tasks for interested readers.]

As children pass to the next cognitive stage, they no longer respond that the tall, thin beaker has "more." Rather, they will recognize that, although the shape has been altered, the quantity has not. They are able to *conserve* their schema even when what they see changes form. However, they can manipulate schema only with concrete, hands-on referents. They are working with *concrete operational schema.*

Children typically make the transition at around ages six to eight, although some will not make it until somewhat later. During the concrete operational stage the learner is capable of solving problems as long as there is a concrete referent. This does not mean that the concrete operational person lacks flexibility. The individual is able to generalize operations across a wide variety of settings and through various alterations. The concrete operational person, however, *cannot* relate to problems that require abstract referents. They are unable to handle problems requiring formal, symbolic logic.

During the concrete stage the individual sees the world in literal, concrete terms. Given a problem in which a series of red and white liquids are mixed, the concrete operational child will consistently expect that the result will be pink. If, however, the result of one combination of red (iodine) and white (starch) liquids is blue liquid, the child is now faced with an exception to the rule. A concrete operational child, when asked how this could be, is apt to answer "magic." Their literal system does not have room for qualifiers such as "Red and white liquids *usually* yield pink, *but some* red and white liquids yield other colors."

During adolescence the individual shifts from depending on concrete operational schema to using *formal operational schema.* Formal operational thought represents the final stage of intellectual development in Piaget's terms. The formal operational thinker is able to conceive of problems on an abstract level, can handle propositional logic, and can engage in hypothetical thinking, considering "what might be" or "what would happen if...." Whereas the concrete operational child's thought is dominated by the "real" world, the physical world is only one aspect of the formal operational child's experience. Indeed, Inhelder and Piaget (1958) found that for the formal operational adolescent, "reality is now secondary to possibility." Formal operational thinking permits the adolescent to make hypotheses, to consider radical alterations of their conceptual world, and to think about the implications of those changes.

When faced with a problem situation, concrete operational thinkers need familiar objects or real examples to relate to so that they can use the concrete, tangible properties of the objects to organize their world. Formal operational thinkers, on the other hand, are able to incorporate abstract relationships into the organization of their conceptual world. They are not tied to the physical reality in their consideration of possibilities. They are also able to use symbols to represent their thoughts.

One sixteen-year-old girl was intrigued by the fact that while most other materials contract when changing from liquid to solid, water acts in the

The rapid growth of cognitive abilities during adolescence often leads to heightened interest in new concepts. (Owen Franken/Stock, Boston)

opposite fashion. That is, as water turns to ice, it expands. The more she thought about this, the more she began to consider the ramifications for the earth if water acted as other materials do. She was able to ask the question "What if water contracted and got more dense when it froze?" By doing so she was able to project how this would change the balance of nature.

This ability to conceive of *what might be* is an essential characteristic of formal operational thought. The formal thinking adolescent is not constrained by reality. Whereas concrete operational thinkers see only concrete reality, formal operational adolescents see reality as but one aspect of the total situation and are capable of assessing or predicting what would happen if reality were altered.

Adolescents who have reached a level of formal operational thinking are also able to understand the concept of "control." Suppose you ask an adolescent boy if he can demonstrate that water boils at 100° C. (Centigrade). The adolescent dutifully goes to the water faucet, gets a cup or so of water, puts the pan on a Bunsen burner, and sticks the thermometer into the water. When the water boils, he removes it and finds that the reading is 101.2° C. (You look over his shoulder to make sure that he does not "round off.") The young person tries again with a second pan of water, but this time he finds that the boiling point is 100.8° C. After five tries, he finds that the average is 100.9° C. He repeats the procedure with river water but finds that the boiling point is 101.4° C.

At this point, the adolescent is faced with a dilemma. The textbook says that water boils at 100° C., but his results do not agree. The reason for the discrepancy is that the young person is not taking into account the other variables that have an impact on the boiling temperature of water. A formal operational youth will recognize the problem and be able to create an experiment to demonstrate that, *other things being equal*, water boils at 100° C. That is, the student would use distilled water and test the boiling point at different levels of air pressure. A concrete operational youth, on the other hand, is unable to solve problems that require control of several variables. In looking at a problem, he is likely to use a trial-and-error approach or focus on the variable that he sees as important, ignoring all others.

Sieglar (1975) provides an interesting task that examines thinking style. Please take time now to try to solve the problem. Ideally a tester would set up an electric train with the characteristics described in the problem and let you solve it by trying various combinations of switches. The strategy that you use to solve the problem would be important. Formal thinkers tend to solve the problem systematically, not at random. The most important problem for the formal thinker is not identifying the correct combination but determining *how* it works. Although concrete operational learners may "solve" a formal operational problem, they solve it by using concrete operational means or by trial and error (Herron, 1975, 1977) and are typically unable to explain how or why their solution works. The formal operational thinker can do both and, further, is able to generalize a principle gained from solving the problem to other problems. If you were unable to solve the electric train problem, does that mean that you are not formal operational? Not necessarily. One problem does not assess the total domain of formal thought. Further, people may achieve formal thought in one domain and not in another. It is a mistake to assume that a young person fourteen or fifteen years old is consequently thinking on a formal level. It is reasonably clear that not all adolescents achieve formal thinking. Kohlberg and Gilligan (1971) found that only 45 percent of late adolescents were operating at that level, and Blasi and Hoeffel (1974) concluded that less than 50 percent of adolescents achieve formal operational thought. In addition, there is a sizeable group of adults who do not display formal thought (Tomlinson-Keasey, 1972).

It is an additional mistake to presume that a person who is formally operational in one area is formally operational in another. The young person who thinks abstractly in areas of math or science may think in concrete terms

SIEGLAR PROBLEM

Imagine that you are running an electric train that is hooked up to three switches in front of you. Two of the three switches determine how fast the train will go. The way these two important switches are set—down and down, up and down, down and up, or up and up—will determine the speed of the train. The various combinations of positions are given below. Your task is to determine which combination of switches is important and how they work.

Switch 1	Switch 2	Switch 3	Train Goes
Up	Down	Down	Slow
Up	Up	Up	Not at all
Down	Down	Down	Fast
Up	Down	Up	Slow
Down	Up	Up	Slow
Down	Down	Up	Fast
Down	Up	Down	Slow
Up	Up	Down	Not at all

Which switches were important?

1 & 2   2 & 3   1 & 3

The way they worked was:

Source: R. S. Sieglar and R. M. Liebert, "Acquisition of Formal Scientific Reasoning by 10- and 13-Year-Olds: Designing a Factorial Experiment," *Developmental Psychology 11* (1975): 401–402. Copyright 1975 by the American Psychological Association. Reprinted by permission of the publisher and author.

---

in history and literature. Another young person may operate in the opposite way. Even within an area we may find ourselves using formal thought in one situation and reverting to concrete thought in another, depending on our mood, the complexity of the situation, or some other factors.

Because adolescents may be operating on a formal level does not mean that they are immune to problems of egocentric thought. David Elkind (1967, 1978) notes that young people suffer from a new form of egocentrism. Although adolescents are more capable of understanding another's perception, they are still subject to assuming that the other person's perception is the same as their own. They are able to differentiate between their perceptions and others' perceptions of physical events, but they are less able to separate their perceptions of abstract features. For example, the adolescents assume that other people value certain features or items in the same way they do. They project any uncertainties that they hold about themselves to an *invisible audience* of others who feel the same way about them. Thus, if a young girl is nervous about a birthmark, she may feel that everyone notices it and thinks it (and she) is ugly. She may even refuse to believe that others do not care. Consider yourself. What would happen if you were in a grocery store and knocked over a dozen or so cans of soup. You probably would feel embarrassed, sure that everyone was thinking, "What a klutz!" You look around and find that very few people are paying any attention at all. You have just created a similar invisible audience. In the adolescent this amorphous "they" may have a profound impact. The plea that parents hear, "Everyone is doing it," may be another version of this phenomenon. Beyond the fact that these pleas are attempts to coerce parents into allowing them to conform, adolescents may see this "invisible crowd" as very real. They do not want to be isolated from others ("everyone") as different.

Sometimes adolescent egocentrism takes the form of zealous idealism. In their thoughts about society and a perfect world, adolescents may develop what they see as perfect answers to social injustice. They may be frustrated when they find that not everyone agrees with them or sees the possibility of same perfect reality.

This egocentrism of adolescence leads to a *personal fable*. In a personal fable an adolescent boy, for example, may see himself as unique and somehow immune from harm. In more dangerous cases this personal fable may lead to chance-taking behavior that is sometimes characteristic of young drivers. Basically the attitude reflected in the personal fable is "It can't happen to me!" Of course the adolescent does not have a corner on the personal fable market. Consider smokers who provide excuses for not quitting or auto drivers who fail to use seat belts. Egocentric behavior is seen at all ages, but this behavior emerges most profoundly during adolescence.

VIGNETTE 3-2
Thirteen and Gifted

What is it like to be a child or young adolescent seen by adults and educators as "gifted"? What does the term gifted *mean? Are we able to select people at young ages who have great potential? Writers as early as Plato speculated that early identification of the gifted would be a benefit to the state because they could be educated to their fullest potential. Certainly exceptional levels of creative achievement have been recognized in young people for centuries. Michaelangelo's talent was recognized and nurtured early by Lorenzo de' Medici, who was himself a gifted politician. Albert Einstein wrote out the rudiments of his theory of relativity at the age of twelve in a letter to his uncle. At fifteen Mozart had already completed eighteen symphonies, two operettas, an opera, and numerous concertos. On the other hand, the creative talent of some is not recognized early, and their giftedness does not emerge until later in life. How can we identify potentially gifted young people early and nurture their talents? What talents should be nurtured?*

I would never want to be a teacher. When you are a teacher, you're in front of an audience and you can't be yourself. I could give a speech for 20 minutes, but I would never do it day after day. I would lose too much of myself."

Chances are Frank has never heard of the educational jargon "role playing," but his as-

From "Thirteen and Gifted," by Marge Scherer. Reprinted from *School and Community* (November 1978): 27–29.

sessment of teaching is swift. Whether or not he is right about teaching or even right about himself, he is bringing out a startling idea for his age (13). That is one of the characteristics of the gifted child, and Frank is identified as such.

Statistics say that a teacher who has 30 students in his classroom each year will meet one gifted child a year. Although there is no easy way to identify gifted children, certain characteristics appear to set them apart from their peers. Five children from the junior high gifted program in a St. Louis County suburb exhibit a number of textbook characteristics and a number of characteristics that could only be called their own.

Tom, for instance, raises an eyebrow at the term "gifted." "Gifted in what? Now that's a good question." He admits he is "terrible" at handwriting, spelling and, quoting from categories from tests he has taken, at "clerical speed and accuracy." His baggy jeans, tousled hair and dozens of papers scrunched up in his load of books testify that he may have chosen the right word, "terrible," to describe his neatness.

Oddly enough, that too is one of the characteristics of gifted children. Dr. Barbara Losty, a psychology instructor at Stephens College in Columbia, says, "The gifted child may hate to do his workbook. He may write poorly because his thoughts run ahead of his motor skills. Also, his interests may be different. He might be deeply interested in a few subjects. For instance, multiplication tables may not fascinate him at all, but Egyptology, dinosaurs or science fiction might."

Had she met him, she might have been talking about Tom.

"Back in elementary school I was called Encyclopedia," Tom says, "because I knew stuff like what is the population of Missouri." On a trip to Europe, his advisor relates she discovered the guide reading papers on British politics so he could keep up with "your Tom-child." Tom just remembers, with a sidelong grin at his advisor who is across the room and not listening, that he didn't get to see the Greenwich Observatory because she wanted to see the British Museum.

Like Tom, the other children have unusual interests, too. Frank has a greatly developed interest in science fiction. He is editor of a science-fiction newsletter in which he reviews books and programs. The newsletter is detailed and in a straightforward style. He started out printing the first three issues by hand—very neatly. Later the typing of the newsletter was arranged. Frank also took a course in probability taught to him by a senior in the high school Probe program.

Another student, Mark, built an eight-foot-long rocket last year. Although the engine fell off 200 feet after blastoff, he considers the project "interesting." His effort at putting battery-powered windshield wipers on a pair of glasses worked more successfully. (Frank reviewed the latter project in the Probe newsletter with the comment. "(The glasses) have a lot of unnecessary wiring.")

John, a student at another school in the district, has finished his three-act play about—what else—the landing on another planet by earth people. Jamie is doing a genealogy project.

Their interests seem to verify another characteristic of the gifted—that of the ability to grasp concepts of future and past more easily than other children.

Another characteristic of gifted children is high IQ—usually above 130. Dr. Losty calls this a speed measure. "The gifted child learns more things in a shorter time. What the normal child needs to be presented three times to grasp, the gifted child will grasp, understand and memorize the first time."

A few of the children, but not all, speak of a feeling of frustration with the slowness of things. Jamie says about grade school, "They let you go ahead or let you do other things so you didn't get bored, but you got bored anyway."

Tom mentions that he gets tired of activities in which he doesn't learn anything, activities he describes as "repeat, repeat, repeat."

He says, "Yes, I get bored easily. It's hard for me to find anything to do. There's no one to play Monopoly with. Most of the time it seems I am bored."

"Gifted children have the same physical and emotional problems their average peers do," according to John Patterson, a consultant in special education for the State Department of Elementary and Secondary Education, "but they may need special assistance to overcome the frustration. They may be more sensitive to the problems."

Mark, who only considers himself "50–50 gifted, not in gym, but maybe in science and writing stories," says, "This year I've been so busy I didn't think about my problems." He acknowledges that "some of the kids in Probe have different kinds of problems than regular kids. It's the way they look at things differently."

Each child openly and matter-of-factly discusses personal problems of the age group: not having friends or wanting more or other friends; not being able to communicate with family or teachers; anxiety about high school.

Jamie put it this way: "I'm unpredictable, have bad moods, then start laughing.... I don't like having a reputation of being straight, perfect, good, always getting 100 percent. They expect you to be very, very dull.

"I am not looking forward to the high school I am going to. They say that teachers there don't want to get to know you," she says. "At least, here, there's one teacher who will always try to find out what's bugging you."

Frank, too, is concerned about high school. "Nobody expects a boy to be intelligent. To do well in high school, a boy has got to be good at football."

When asked to evaluate the program for the gifted that they were participating in, all the children weigh both the good and bad points carefully, showing what Dr. Losty called the "judgmental quality."

Frank, who has been in a "gifted school" previously, is the most critical. "There you worked about a year ahead. I was taking advanced math. Here I haven't taken geometry yet. I am a natural A student, and I don't have to work." Yet, he says, there are good and bad points about each program. "Some people (there) didn't know how to talk to normal people. This one has more field trips. On field trips you learn in an outside setting rather than in a classroom in 85 degree weather. It is probably better to learn something unique and different."

John, Jamie, Mark and Tom voice the opinion that the program is good because it allows them to work independently and learn interesting things. John and Jamie say they are straight A students most of the time, except for gym, Jamie adds. But Jamie and Mark sometimes feel bad about losing time in regular class. "Getting out of classes does bother me. I try to keep field trips as few as possible—but they are interesting," Mark says.

None of the children seems to have a snobbish attitude about his gifts. John says, "When you are in school with all kinds of kids, you don't think of yourself as different than any of the people in the school. They are all different."

Frank disagrees somewhat. "I'm different from everybody. I don't try to be like everybody else—well, just enough to survive."

Tom, who is in a self-deprecating mood, says, "Besides myself being chubby, I'm flat-footed and knock-kneed." Then, seriously considering whether he is better than other people in certain things he says, "I know I am gifted, but that's not to say 'I'm gifted, you're not.' It's probably hard to find those who are gifted by tests. Probably there are lots of people who deserve to be in Probe but teachers can't tell who they are."

The gifted child is not a poster child, not like the handicapped child who tugs at our heartstrings. "Our hearts do not always go out to them," Dr. Losty says, "but the gifted children depend on their teachers to recognize them."

The following are signs, other than test scores or achievement records, that a child may be gifted.

- Early use of advanced vocabulary
- Retention of a variety of information
- Periods of intense concentration
- Ability to understand abstract concepts
- A broad spectrum of interests or a devotion to one discipline
- Strong critical thinking and self criticism
- Leadership, sometimes challenging to authority
- Ability to judge, especially an interest in moral and ethical judgments
- Speed in understanding
- Self-direction
- Sensitivity to personal problems
- Surprising ideas for age

Children gifted in visual and performing arts or psychomotor skills will display many of the following characteristics.

- Demonstrations of their specific talent at an early age
- A reputation for having wild and silly ideas that are off the beaten track
- A sense of playfulness and relaxation
- A tendency to be a nonconformist and to think independently
- Sensitivity to emotions and problems

Other ideas to keep in mind about the gifted: It is possible to lose giftedness, or, at least to stop showing signs of gifted behavior if the environment is not stimulating.

Boys more than girls are identified as gifted, perhaps because girls are expected to do well in school and are not considered "gifted" when they do.

Gifted children often try "survival strategies" to test the classroom environment. Some answer all the questions the first few days, then settle down to reading library books the rest of the year. Some learn that finishing their work fast may get them some attention, but that not finishing will get them even more. Gifted children, as all children, are looking for recognition.

For more information about the gifted, write to the Office of Gifted and Talented, U.S. Office of Education, Donohoe Building, 400 6th St. S.W., Room 3835, Washington, D.C. 20202.

For information about programs for the gifted, write Assistant Commissioner of Education, Division of Instruction, Department of Elementary and Secondary Education, P.O. Box 480, Jefferson City, Mo. 65102. Telephone: (314) 751-4234.

INDIVIDUAL DIFFERENCES

GIFTED ADOLESCENTS

Gifted adolescents are individuals who display some exceptional talent or promise in one or more areas, such as the arts, science, math, or leadership. Although the gifted do not necessarily score high on an intelligence test, a large proportion of those labeled as gifted perform well above the average on traditional measures of intelligence (Vernon, Abramson, and Vernon, 1977). Not surprisingly, intellectually precocious youths typically excel on Piagetian measures of cognitive development (Keating, 1976). Intelligence, however, should not be the sole criterion by which we identify the gifted.

About 1921, Louis Terman identified 1500 children whose intelligence test scores were in the range labeled "genius." For every thousand people in the population, only five would perform as well. Whether or not intelligence should serve as the primary characteristic of giftedness these children were certainly unusual. Terman followed the progress of these gifted individuals through their adult years.

In the original sample there were more males than females (857 to 671), and the discrepancy in performance between sexes was more apparent as the children grew older. One way to explain the difference is to suggest that at the time the sample was taken (and even currently) girls were systematically encouraged *not* to display marked intelligence and peer pressure to conform increased with age. In a sense society regards high IQ as better in boys than in girls.

The data from the Terman study are invaluable in dispelling common stereotypes of genius children. As a group the children were taller, heavier, stronger, earlier in arriving at sexual maturity, and more healthy than their average counterparts. Further, the gifted children rated high on what some have called "behavioral" intelligence. They were rated as more trustworthy and more honest (Terman, 1925, 1930).

By their mid-forties, the group had compiled an impressive list of accomplishments. Although Terman is quick to note that many nongeniuses make such achievements, the group was still exceptional. Of the sample, 70 percent finished college and 40 percent earned advanced degrees. The latter group was again disproportionately composed of males. It is also of interest that the death rate, rate of criminal behavior, and rate of alcoholism were very low. Emotional maladjustment was no more rare in the gifted group than in the population as a whole, but women in the sample suffered more than men (Terman and Oden, 1959).

A major study of mathematically and, more recently, verbally precocious youths is now being conducted at Johns Hopkins University (Stanley, Keating, and Fox, 1974; Keating, 1976). Among the problems that such studies encounter is the adequate assessment of the gifted. Stanley (1976) reports a case of a sixth-grade girl who scored at the eleventh-grade level on a vocabulary test. She might have scored higher because she got every item on the test correct. Thus Stanley suggests we may need to assess the gifted youth with tests intended for adults.

Many of the intellectually precocious youths identified in the Johns Hopkins study are accelerated into college-level studies early. However, for those whose early college admission is inadvisable or not currently warranted, some curricular intervention is still indicated. Program planning for the intellectually precocious youth is necessary. Fox (1976) notes that, to be effective, individualized intervention requires both adequate assessment of individual strengths and development of programs that capitalize on and nourish those strengths. She suggests that although some educational bureaucracies may be reluctant to create unique educational experiences, the problems of assigning gifted children to advanced classes can be simplified if an individualized treatment plan (ITP) specifies what outcomes can be achieved by such intervention.

As in the Terman studies, the mathematically precocious youngsters are behaviorally more mature than their agemates. Psychologically they are confident and well adjusted, seeing themselves as intelligent, capable, adaptable, logical, honest, and clear thinking. The boys in the study are also more likely to see themselves as sarcastic, opinionated, and cynical (Haier and Denham, 1976). Many educators have negative attitudes toward the gifted, seeing them as argumentative, opinionated, and impatient. However, they are also likely to see the gifted as alert, clear thinking, and intelligent (Haier and Solano, 1976). Teachers who are unfamiliar with gifted children seem to hold more negative attitudes than those who are familiar with some.

CREATIVITY

Educators are increasingly interested in the domain of creativity. This is in part a response to increased dissatisfaction with standard tests of intelligence and a feeling among many that creative learners are neglected in the schools. However, those who have tried to give a clear definition of creativity have found it even more difficult to define than intelligence. Wallach (1970) has gone so far as to suggest that we cannot explain what has happened with other psychological models of thinking. Crockenberg (1972) adds that we know relatively little about the antecedents to the creative process, especially among children and adolescents, and that measures of creativity lack validity.

Adolescence may be a period of increased creative activity as the young person becomes capable of conceiving of new, untested patterns. (Jean-Claude Lejeune/ Stock, Boston)

Figure 3-3 CREATIVITY PROBLEM

•   •   •

•   •   •   **Problem:** Connect these nine points using four straight lines without lifting your pencil from the

•   •   •   paper and without retracing any line.

Most conceptions of creativity are built in one way or another on the premise that creative individuals show a high level of flexibility in their thinking (Cattell, 1971). Creative people seem to be able to change direction or perspective in thought with ease and view a problem or creative domain from multiple points equally well. They tend to think about problems from other than conventional positions. Most investigators concur with E. Paul Torrance (1966, 1972) that flexibility is the ability to "break mental sets." A mental set occurs when our pattern for thinking interferes with our solving a problem.

If you see the pattern of nine dots in Figure 3–3 as a square with implicit boundaries, you will have difficulty solving the problem. The ease with which you can "break set" reflects general flexibility in thought. The converse of flexibility is rigidity of thought or resistance to changing thought.

Torrance (1966) adds two more attributes of the creative person. In addition to flexibility, creative people tend to generate many ideas (fluency) and many unique and unusual ideas (originality). Some speculate that the ability to "break set" may be critical in the development of creativity. I would argue, however, that, irrespective of whether flexibility of thought leads to creative results, the ability to "break set" is a worthy educational goal in and of itself. To make "creativity" a criterion for school success may be equally as fallacious as making IQ gain a criterion for head-start programs. However, it may be more realistic to try to foster some behavior (for example, flexibility) that is related to creativity. Torrance has suggested that the teacher or parent who wishes to encourage creativity must create an environment that fosters positive feelings about flexible thinking. Torrance gives guidelines to foster those attitudes:

1. *Value creative thinking.* The adolescent should see that the parent or teacher values and appreciates creative thinking.
2. *Make children more sensitive to environmental stimuli.* To be fluent and flexible, the adolescent must have a wide range of responses available and must have skills to observe a wide variety of characteristics. By teaching adolescents to be sensitive to variations and changes in their surroundings, you also increase their ability to consider alternative aspects of a situation.
3. *Encourage manipulation of objects and ideas.* Adolescence is a time when young people normally engage in mental games and play with thoughts. Instructors need to encourage this tendency.

4. *Teach the adolescent how to evaluate each idea systematically.* As an individual begins to develop divergent thinking abilities, the patterns of intellectual thinking may be unorganized and unsystematic. Sometimes concept flexibility can be encouraged through the use of heuristic techniques. A *heuristic* is a systematic procedure that serves as an aid to problem solving and originality, such as brainstorming, synectics, and so on.

5. *Develop a tolerance of new ideas.* Adolescents and children tend to be intolerant of uncertainty. Tolerance of ambiguity and uncertainty is fundamental to originality. Often such tolerance involves holding off judgment about the value of ideas. Sometimes what initially strikes you as a wildly silly idea may develop into an original and creative solution to a problem. (It may also remain a silly idea.)

6. *Beware of forging a set pattern.* Creative and original thinking is hindered when people think there is *one* right way to go about solving a problem. Once again, to be flexible means to be able to "break set," to be able to think about a problem in alternative modes.

7. *Develop a creative classroom atmosphere.* Part of the learning process involves seeing how creative people act. Teachers should practice considering alternatives, withholding judgment on unusual ideas, and maintaining a tolerant attitude about uncertain areas, if adolescents are expected to behave similarly. (Practice what you preach!)

VIGNETTE 3-3
The Barometer Story

This story of the experience of one science student who grew tired of answering questions in the same old way brings up a variety of issues. Not only does the vignette relate to the confrontation between an obviously bright student and the "system." It raises more general questions about the dependence on convergent thinking as the dominant mode of testing. Although we are tempted to leap to the defense of this student, who is obviously able, the problem of how to adequately assess their students still remains for most teachers. How might you have handled this situation?

Source: Alexander Calandra, "The Barometer Story," *Current Science: Science and Math Weekly*, Bulletin no. 14 (January 6, 1974). Special permission granted by *Current Science*, published by Xerox Education Publications, © 1974, Xerox Corp.

Some time ago, I received a call from a colleague who asked if I would be the referee on the grading of an examination question. It seemed that he was about to give a student a zero for his answer to a physics question, while the student claimed he should receive a perfect score and would do so if the system were not set up against the student. The instructor and the student agreed to submit this to an impartial arbiter, and I was selected.

The Barometer Problem

I went to my colleague's office and read the examination question, which was, "Show how it is possible to determine the height of a tall building with the aid of a barometer."

The student's answer was, "Take the barometer to the top of the building, attach a long rope to it, lower the barometer to the street, and then bring it up, measuring the length of the rope. The length of the rope is the height of the building."

Now, this is a very interesting answer, but should the student get credit for it? I pointed out that the student really had a strong case for full credit, since he had answered the question completely and correctly. On the other hand, if full credit were given, it could well contribute to a high grade for the student in his physics course.

A high grade is supposed to certify that the student knows some physics, but the answer to the question did not confirm this. With this in mind, I suggested that the student have another try at answering the question. I was not surprised that my colleague agreed to this, but I was surprised that the student did.

Acting in terms of the agreement, I gave the student six minutes to answer the question, with the warning that the answer should show some knowledge of physics. At the end of five minutes, he had not written anything. I asked if he wished to give up, since I had another class to take care of, but he said no, he was not giving up. He had many answers to this problem; he was just thinking of the best one. I excused myself for interrupting him, and asked him to please go on. In the next minute, he dashed off his answer, which was:

"Take the barometer to the top of the building and lean over the edge of the roof. Drop the barometer, timing its fall with a stopwatch. Then, using the formula $S = \frac{1}{2}at^2$, calculate the height of the building."

At this point, I asked my colleague if he would give up. He conceded and I gave the student almost full credit. In leaving my colleague's office, I recalled that the student had said he had other answers to the problem, so I asked him what they were.

"Oh, yes," said the student, "There are many ways of getting the height of a tall building with the aid of a barometer. For example, you could take the barometer out on a sunny day and measure the height of the barometer, the length of its shadow, and the length of the shadow of the building, and by the use of a simple proportion, determine the height of the building."

"Fine," I said. "And the others?"

"Yes," said the student. "There is a very basic measurement method that you will like. In this method, you use the stairs. As you climb the stairs, you mark off the length of the barometer along the wall. You then count the number of marks, and this will give you the height of the building in barometer units. A very direct method.

"Of course, if you want a more sophisticated method, you can tie the barometer to the end of a string, swing it as a pendulum, and determine the value of 'g' at the street level and then at the top of the building. From the difference between the two values of 'g,' the height of the building can, in principle, be calculated."

Finally he concluded, "If you don't limit me to physics solutions to this problem, there are many other answers, such as taking the barometer to the basement and knocking on the superintendent's door. When the superintendent answers, you speak to him as follows: 'Dear Mr. Superintendent, here I have a very fine barometer. If you will tell me the height of this building, I will give you this barometer.'"

At this point, I asked the student if he really didn't know the answer to the problem. He admitted that he did, but that he was so fed up with college instructors trying to teach him how to think and to use critical thinking, instead of showing him the structure of the subject matter, that he decided to take off on what he regarded as mostly a sham....

Table 3-1 LEVELS OF RETARDATION

Level of Mental Retardation	IQ
Mild	52–67
Moderate	36–51
Severe	20–35
Profound	19 and below

Source: H. J. Grossman (Ed.), *Manual on Terminology and Classification in Mental Retardation,* 1973 revision. (Washington, D.C.: American Association on Mental Deficiency, 1973).

MENTAL RETARDATION

Retarded adolescents, like their gifted counterparts, are identified by their relative position in the normal distribution of intellectual functioning. Their performance is, however, significantly below average, and diagnoses may range from mild to serious impairment. Typical definitions of retardation include guideline cutoff points, such as those in Table 3-1.

Mentally retarded adolescents are individuals whose cognitive development has not kept pace with peers of their own age (Zigler, 1969). This formulation would characterize intellectually superior adolescents as those whose pace of cognitive development has exceeded their age peers'. As Zigler notes, this formulation implies that both types of exceptional individuals (excluding those with organically caused retardation) fall within the expected *normal* range of variability of the distribution of intelligence scores.

Mental retardation results from several factors, including metabolic and genetic disorders, birth traumas, malnutrition, drug and alcohol use by mothers during pregnancy, brain injury, and social stress. About three-fourths of all cases of mental retardation occur with no clearly identified organic cause (General Accounting Office, 1977) and are associated with economically and educationally deprived backgrounds.

Often the problem of the retarded learner must be viewed beyond the confines of the individual. It is not uncommon for parents and families of severely handicapped children to feel resentment toward the child, who may be disruptive to the family. In some areas groups of parents with retarded children meet to exchange ideas and provide emotional support.

MAINSTREAMING

Until recently, schools have responded to the educational needs of the educationally handicapped by placing them in special classes. However, under Public Law 94-142, handicapped students of all kinds are reentering the mainstream. PL 94-142 demands that handicapped youths be provided with the "least restrictive environment" necessary to meet their needs. In most cases the least restrictive environment is interpreted to be the normal classroom, either in lieu of or in coordination with special classrooms. In

Interactions such as this one between a junior high school student and a developmentally disabled child may benefit both. (Peter Vandermark)

some cases of profound handicap, the least restrictive environment may turn out to be a total special environment.

The general term for providing least restrictive environments is *mainstreaming*. As Caster (1975) indicates, mainstreaming does not mean that teachers of traditional classes are going to be responsible for providing specialized training for dozens of severely handicapped youths. Rather, the complete educational system must attempt to meet the educational needs of handicapped youths, part of which is their need to interact with nonhandicapped peers.

The core feature of PL 94-142 is the individualized education plan (IEP). An IEP is a statement compiled by an instructional team identifying:

1. the current level of a handicapped student's performance;
2. specific long-term and short-term educational needs of the learner;
3. specific strategies and resources for meeting those needs;
4. target dates for initiating and completing the services;
5. a program of participation in the regular classroom; and
6. appropriate behavioral criteria for assessing progress (Pasanella and Volkmor, 1977).

Parents of handicapped learners are expected to participate in the planning process, and the planning team must ensure that the handicapped students' individual rights are not violated. The law further requires the team to review each IEP annually and submit a written report of the individual's progress toward the IEP goals.

In many ways PL 94-142 is going to require an alteration of the thinking and planning of teachers, principals, and other school personnel. To ensure that schools (and states) conform to the demands of PL 94-142, the bill includes a provision that failure to comply leads to termination of federal funds.

Cochrane and Westling (1977) provide guidelines for implementing mainstreaming in the schools. School personnel must be made more aware of the characteristics of mildly handicapped children and adolescents. This can be accomplished through in-service training or additional course work. Because special education teachers have been trained specifically for working with the handicapped, they may be used both as roving aids and as instructors of school personnel. Nonhandicapped adolescents in the school need to be educated about the needs of handicapped students. Too often, the mainstreamed adolescent may face exclusion or taunting by normal peers (Gottlieb and Budoff, 1973; Gottlieb, Semmel, and Veldman, 1978). Schools should avail themselves of community resources to supplement the skills and resources available internally.

SUMMARY

Adolescent cognitive development is a continuance of normal intellectual growth. However, during adolescence there is a marked qualitative shift in the ability to think abstractly and logically. No longer is the individual conceptually bound to concrete referents. Instead, the adolescent is able to conceive of what might be and begins to consider alternatives to the seen world.

Some adolescents are exceptional in their cognitive development, being either intellectually precocious, creative, or retarded. These students and others require specific intervention strategies. In the case of handicapped youths, federal policy requires that they be provided a free public education in the least restrictive environment. As part of the process of ensuring that education, schools are required to develop individual educational plans to specify educational goals for the learner as well as procedures and methods to evaluate success.

4 | Achievement and the Schools

Not long ago, a somewhat startling legal case came to the attention of the American public. The case involved a suit filed by a young man against the San Francisco, California, Unified School District. According to lawyers for Peter Doe (a fictitious name), school records indicated that Peter's measured intelligence was in the average range. He had maintained an above-C grade point average through elementary, junior, and senior high school. Further, Peter had not been retained at any grade level nor had there been any apparent consideration of retaining him. Peter's mother had repeatedly been told by school officials that Peter needed no remedial instruction. However, upon graduation from high school, Peter was unable to read well enough to fill out a job application or to follow directions printed on other forms. Peter was functionally illiterate (Abel, 1974; Saretsky, 1973). Although the initial court ruling favored the San Francisco schools, the case is currently under appeal.

The Peter Doe case is probably unusual for a variety of reasons, but it raises the question of how often students complete twelve years of schooling without achieving some basic level of competence. One wonders how such a student could go from year to year with no intervention or how his mother could fail to see that a real problem existed, irrespective of the feedback from school officials. But more than that, consider the implications of completing high school and being unable to read well enough to fill out a job application. What employment is available to a person like Peter Doe? Should we hold schools responsible to guarantee some basic level of competence? If a school fails to bring a student to this basic competence, can the school be held legally responsible?

ILLITERACY

The Peter Doe case also raises the question of how widespread the problem of illiteracy is among today's adolescents. Definitions of illiteracy vary, but most studies estimate that the number of young people who are functionally illiterate is considerable. In one study illiteracy was defined as being able to read no higher than the level of a beginning fourth grader. Using that criterion, researchers found that 4.8 percent, or about one in twenty American youths between twelve and seventeen years of age were illiterate (Vogt, 1973). This translates into more than one million young people, not including those over eighteen who cannot read well enough to handle their basic needs.

Further study of the problem of illiteracy shows that boys are more likely than girls to be illiterate. Minority and lower-income adolescents are much more likely to be rated as illiterate than white, middle-class youths. To what degree these differences can be blamed on early school experiences versus the failure of high schools to remediate reading problems is not a meaningful question. *Both* elementary and secondary schools need to reassess their teaching procedures if any significant change is to occur.

In addition to being disturbed about deteriorating reading achievement, the American public and the professional community are becoming increasingly alarmed by lowered levels of general academic achievement among today's children and youth.

VIGNETTE 4-1
Science Skills Skidding

Can we really say with confidence that today's young people are not scoring as well as previous generations on tests of academic achievement, or is the current furor "much ado about nothing"? If the decline is real, whom should we blame? The immediate temptation of most people is to blame the decline on the schools. That, however, is not totally fair. Schools must be evaluated in the broader context of current social values and social forces that have an impact on education and on people's attitudes toward academic achievement. School systems have, in fact, exerted considerable effort toward reversing the trend. The continuing drop in levels of academic achievement should lead us to question whether schools should be expected to solve the problem quickly or

alone. In this article the decline in one area of achievement, science, is described. Speculate on why, in light of the development of such innovative science curricula as the Harvard Project Physics or the Biological Sciences Curriculum Study, science skills and knowledge continue to decline. What are the implications of such a decline for our nation and for individual students?

America's high-school graduates are increasingly ill-equipped to deal with modern technology.

That's the conclusion drawn from the third nationwide survey of science knowledge among 80,000 students by the National Assessment of Educational Progress, a federally funded testing group.

The study found that 17-year-olds today know less about science than high-school students in 1969–70 and 1972–73, when previous assessments were conducted. By asking some of the same questions from one assessment to the next, it is possible to compare results.

On the average, 2 percent fewer children got correct answers to a given question in 1977 than they did in 1973. Between 1970 and 1973, there was a 3 percent drop.

The results are a matter of grave concern to educators. Arthur Livermore, director of the office of science education for the American Association for the Advancement of Science, says that "if the trend continues, it will reduce the ability of the society to keep up with other countries."

On the Upswing?

Yet there is a hopeful sign amid the gloom. The scientific know-how of elementary and junior-high-school students, which dropped between the first and second assessments, has stopped declining in the area of biology, although capability in the physical sciences is down.

Over all, the study finds that 9 and 13-year-olds did about as well in the 1977 assessment as they did four years before. This may reflect a leveling out of scientific achievement, possibly pointing the way to eventual advances.

John M. Akey, past president of the National Science Teachers Association, finds that the results at the elementary and junior-high level are "remarkable in the face of across-the-board de-emphasis of science education from kindergarten through high school." All of the attention paid to basics has reduced the time available to teach science, Akey declares.

TEST YOURSELF

From questions asked 80,000 youngsters in latest test of science knowledge:

Asked of 9-year-olds—

1. *How do dewdrops form on a leaf?*

(a) They are formed from melted frost. (b) They are formed from water in the air. (c) They fall as melted snow and are caught on the leaf. (d) They fall like a light rain and are caught on the leaf.

Asked of 13-year-olds—

2. *If all green plants died, what would be the most important effect on man?*

(a) Sooner or later he would die of starvation. (b) He would have to eat meat only. (c) He would get a little sick because he couldn't get vitamins. (d) He couldn't build houses because there would be no lumber. (e) The land would be bare and not very pretty to look at.

Asked of 17-year-olds—

3. *Which one of the following animals probably appeared on earth before the others?*

(a) dinosaur (b) fish (c) horse (d) man (e) snake.

Answers: 1. b; *2.* a; *3.* b

A closer analysis of the tests found the following:

- Students did better in biology than in the physical sciences.
- Males did better than the national average, with females doing worse.
- Students in the Northeast generally performed better than their peers in other parts of the country.
- The education level of parents is related to performance. Students who have at least one parent with a post-high-school education did better than average.
- Young people living in suburbs or in well-to-do urban communities also had above-average test results.

Students in the Southeast or from big cities performed below the national average, as did blacks and students whose parents did not graduate from high school.

Youngsters from rural communities generally did about average, a marked improvement from the first study.

When the first survey in science was undertaken in 1969–70, America was still caught up in the post-Sputnik era. It was a time of dramatic strides in space exploration, with men landing on the moon.

In the mid-60s, there had been a great deal of emphasis placed on science education, with tens of millions in federal dollars spent to develop curricula and educate scientists.

In the view of educators, these developments, along with the attention that the news media gave scientific breakthroughs, account for the relatively high performance levels in the first assessment. Educators believe that as public interest in science waned and federal support decreased, student interest in science diminished, helping to explain why 17-year-olds did not do as well in the recent survey as they did in earlier ones.

Spending Cutbacks

The National Science Foundation's budget provides one measurement of the falloff in support for science education. In 1968, the organization had 135 million dollars to spend on science education—27 percent of its budget. But in 1978, that figure was reduced to 74 million dollars, only 9 percent of the agency's total budget.

The foundation's support for an important part of science education—programs designed to keep elementary and secondary-school teachers abreast of the latest scientific developments—dropped from 30 million dollars to 10 million over the past decade.

Educators say that teachers need periodic retraining in their rapidly changing scientific fields if they are to do their jobs properly. If teachers fall behind, school administrators maintain, so will students.

Other experts say the downturn among 17-year-olds is explained by reduced enrollments in physics and chemistry classes. According to the National Assessment, half of the high schools in the U.S. do not offer courses in physics.

Some educators feel that the tests used in the survey fail to reflect the changing nature of what is taught in science classes. Today's curriculum puts greater stress on values and concepts and less emphasis on factual knowledge, while the assessment questions emphasize facts.

The science results at the high-school level are part of a generally depressing picture painted by the National Assessment since it began testing youngsters in 1969.

With a few areas excepted, tests over the years show that high-school graduates know less and less about a wide variety of subjects.

ACHIEVEMENT

In an attempt to develop a clear picture of educational achievement patterns in the United States, the ambitious National Assessment of Educational Progress (NAEP) was established in 1969, with two goals: "1. To make available the first comprehensive data on the educational attainments of young Americans in ten learning areas; 2. To measure any growth or decline that takes place in young Americans'' (Vandermyn, 1974). The results of the NAEP surveys have only recently begun to be useful in providing information regarding the second problem, but in general, the studies show small but regular declines in achievement since the original NAEP assessments.

The NAEP studies have shown that achievement levels among youths differ across subject areas, sex, race, region of the country, level of parental education, and so on. The lowered levels of achievement among minority children are found by age nine, and those differences increase with age.

In summarizing reading achievement, for example, NAEP researchers report that students have little difficulty in literal comprehension but are limited in areas of reading comprehension that require inference and interpretation (NAEP, 1976). In comparing reading performance of children and youths in 1974–1975 with 1970–1971, nine-year-olds showed a moderate increase in reading skills, whereas thirteen-year-olds showed a decline. No group showed an increase in inferential skills (NAEP, 1976).

Fears of a general drop in levels of academic achievement may not be quite as justified as they initially seem. The decline is not nearly as steep as the public furor would indicate. The differences are statistical differences, and not all statistical differences reflect practical differences. For example, the average nine-year-old in 1971 answered 63.979 percent of the reading items correctly, whereas the average nine-year-old in 1975 answered 65.195 percent correctly. This amounts to an increase of 1.216 percentage points, which could be used to conclude that American children are reading better (Venesky, 1977). However, we would hardly conclude that we are on the eve of an educational renaissance. Some results of the NAEP survey are given in Figure 4-1, p. 88.

In another study student reading records from about 1870 to 1970 were studied to see if any overall trend in reading achievement could be observed. When viewed over one hundred years, the data show a steady increase in reading performance, despite a variety of school-related factors that might be expected to lead to lowered performance among today's students (Farr and Tuinman, 1974; Farr et al., 1978). Such trends as tending to promote students who are below acceptable levels of performance to the next grade and keeping students, even poorer students, in school longer, might have led to lower overall performance. However, they did not.

Another assessment (NAEP, 1976), found that students have mixed knowledge about the nature of the governmental process and the rights of individuals. Although the greatest proportion of students recognized the rights of an accused person to remain silent, to have legal counsel, and to be tried by a jury, less than half of seventeen-year-olds and less than one-quarter of fourteen-year-olds recognize that the Fifth Amendment also protects someone who is a communist. American youths are largely unaware of the functions and composition of the Senate and the House of Representatives and have even less understanding of the functions of local government or of the United Nations (NAEP, 1976, 1979). Comparing the performances of students in 1976 and 1979, revealed a net decrease in political awareness among nine-, fourteen-, and seventeen-year-olds.

Among the widely reported trends in academic achievement has been the

Figure 4-1 ACHIEVEMENT TRENDS OF AMERICAN ADOLESCENTS

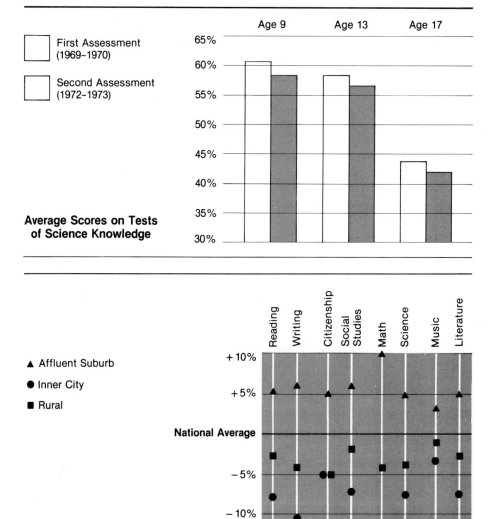

First Assessment (1969–1970)

Second Assessment (1972–1973)

Average Scores on Tests of Science Knowledge

▲ Affluent Suburb

● Inner City

■ Rural

National Average

Typical Educational Achievement by 17-Year-Olds

Source: National Assessment of Educational Progress, Denver, Colorado (Washington, D.C.: U.S. Government Printing Office, 1974).

general decline in performance on the Scholastic Aptitude Tests (SATs) over the past several years. (See Figure 4-2.) From 1952 to 1963, performance on the SATs remained fairly constant. However, from 1963 to the present, there has been a steady decline in performance. Not only has the overall average score declined, but also the number of students scoring over 700 on the SAT has also declined. A number of interacting factors could be contributing to this progressive decline; no single factor would be sufficient.

Figure 4-2 AVERAGE PERFORMANCE ON THE SCHOLASTIC APTITUDE TEST

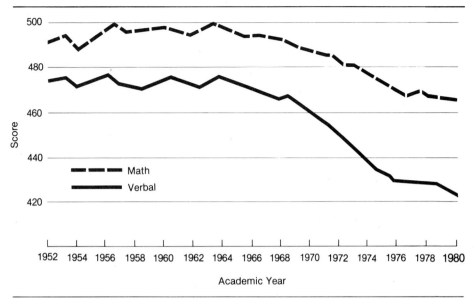

Source: College Entrance Examination Board, National Report on College-Bound Seniors, 1980 (Princeton, N.J.: Educational Testing Service, 1980).

VIGNETTE 4-2
Taking the SATs

Every year thousands of high school juniors and seniors take the Preliminary SATs or the SATs in hopes of being admitted to the college of their choice. Beyond the current publicity over lowered levels of achievement, there is a very real problem of anxiety and stress associated with taking the test. There is, as a result, a flourishing industry offering instruction in "How to Take the SATs." One school board member decided to see what the tests were like and to determine whether it was possible to improve students' performance. Read the following, *and try to recall your own experience with the SAT or a comparable exam. Do this person's conclusions make reasonable sense? (Consider them if you plan to take the Graduate Record Examinations.)*

Like blind men groping at an elephant, the much-discussed Scholastic Aptitude Tests (S.A.T.S) are many things to different people. But for many [adults] the tests seem to be confusing, alarming, and the subject of a great deal of...concern.

All of this concern led me—long after my formal education was completed—to a local high school one Saturday morning, No. 2 pencils and bifocals in hand, ready to sit down

Source: Anne Towne, "What One Board Member Learned from Taking the S.A.T.s." Reprinted, with permission from *The American School Board Journal* (August 1978):30–31. Copyright 1978, the National School Boards Association. All rights reserved.

and take the S.A.T. tests myself and discover some of what the debate is about.

What prompted me, a grown woman, to force myself to sit through the mind-numbing experience of taking a standardized test? The scenario goes something like this: At our local school board meeting, a general discussion took place over the much-reported national drop in S.A.T. scores. The familiar targets were paraded out and potshots taken. The problems, it seems, are many: television, the reported lack of rigor in the school system's English department, a general drop in the number of required subjects, a larger number of student test-takers, and the increased emphasis on technical rather than traditional academic courses.

While these may be comfortable whipping boys, parents at the meeting asked whether the drop in S.A.T. test scores meant the schools weren't doing the proper job. The superintendent then recited the now-familiar litany: The tests indicate only individual student achievement rather than the quality of education provided by a school system. This may be the traditional line of explanation, but it seemed to us that any student who steps into the crowded test room on a Saturday morning and nervously opens the test booklet is aware that the final score rests not only on individual performance, but on the training and preparation provided by the school system.

Then, in order to discover what the tests were all about, the school board members discussed the possibility of one of us taking the S.A.T.s. There was hardly a rush to the front. "I took the test in 1948 and that was enough," said one board member. Laughter. Silence. "I'll tell my scores if you tell yours." More laughter, more silence. "I couldn't take the math test, I can barely balance my checkbook."

Let me introduce myself. I'm the board member who said she couldn't always balance her checkbook.... I'm also the board member who double-checked the form so that no scores—repeat *No scores*—would be sent to

any local high school, the press, or even any college or university. I wasn't even going to tell my own teenagers that I took the test—unless, of course, I received brilliant scores.

So three weeks later I found myself at the local high school, looking for the room that contained my half of the alphabet. I presented myself to the test proctor, and hoped he didn't notice the rather obvious age difference between me and the teenagers in the room. He did. He looked at my admittance form and then asked for identification. Perhaps he thought I was an unscrupulous mother taking the test for her child. Reassuring him that I was indeed a candidate, and not my daughter, he handed me my test booklet, I found a seat and soon the test began.

Fill in all ovals, name, address, age. I winced at the last one. Age? I wondered, were I to ignore the age ovals, would that enrage the computer and invalidate the test. But that was the least of my worries. As I opened the test booklet, it struck me suddenly why so few adults take the S.A.T.s. All those columns of tiny ovals were long and blurry. Perhaps it's a fiendishly clever idea: It takes young eyes to see all those ovals, and even new bifocals don't help.

The proctor explained that the test was divided into six alternating sections, three verbal and three mathematics. This was a surprise; I had expected one whole section on mathematics, one whole section on verbal....

The reading comprehension portion was difficult, and I soon realized that as time was running out I began to hurry my answers. My panic over the loss of time caused me to skim the written material, so that I then found it difficult to answer questions without rereading the material to search for specific information. It soon became clear: I would have to use my time judiciously or fail to finish the test.

The mathematics section surprised me.... I discovered that many questions could be answered using simple logic....

I skipped around each math section and passed over areas I thought would take up too much precious time. I expected to spend most of my energy working on my strength—the verbal section. But each part of the test was carefully timed and monitored so that I could not return to any other section once time was finished.

After I completed filling in all the ovals, I turned in my test booklet and answer sheet to the proctor. As I left the room feeling relieved, I wondered about my school-aged compatriots. Many were still in the room (others had finished before me), but each person is given a test with the sections in different order (to minimize opportunities for cheating). Talking to some of the students following the test, I noticed an aura of accomplishment, but I wondered how many were worried about the impact of the test scores on their futures. We drifted off home; the test was finished and all that was left was for the computers in Princeton to spit out our scores.

While the content of the test didn't really surprise me, I now believe I am more informed about the S.A.T.s and what the scores indicate. From this experience, I also learned that there are several questions that school board members should ask their administrators in order to make sure kids are prepared for this academic hurdle:

1. Are all students who register for the test familiar with the *format* of the S.A.T.s? Do they know what to expect once they open the test booklet?
2. In English classes, is the proper emphasis placed on vocabulary, reading comprehension and standardized writing skills?
3. Are high school teachers familiar with the scope and requirements of the S.A.T., and should the school system emphasize the skills to cope with standardized tests?
4. As a matter of course, do students take lengthy examinations? Are students prepared for the pace and stress of long tests?
5. Are the school system's juniors and sophomores urged to take the P.S.A.T. (Preliminary Scholastic Aptitude Test)?
6. Would it be helpful if students rehearsed for the S.A.T.s by taking a locally designed test?

Oh yes, one last matter: My scores. I was reasonably hopeful that my vocabulary skills would enable me to score in the 600s. Fine, that was no problem. But I was sure that algebra and story problems in the mathematics portion of the test would petrify my brain. But as it turned out, I was able to score in the 400s. No Einstein to be sure, but better than I had hoped.

COMPETENCY-BASED EDUCATION

Partly in reaction to cases like that of Peter Doe and partly in recognition that a substantial number of college freshmen lack basic skills, there has been a movement toward identifying the minimum competencies necessary to complete high school satisfactorily. By mid-1978, two-thirds of the states had initiated mandates for minimal competency standards, and others are likely to follow suit in the near future.

In principle, the concept of competency-based education (CBE) is straightforward. Every learner should have a specific set of skills and concepts, in order to be certified as having graduated from high school. This set of outcomes would be understood to be minimal levels of performance for which a high school diploma or certificate would be awarded. Students who are below that level would not be certified until they achieved those basic competencies.

In practice, however, a variety of problems with the CBE approach have yet to be worked out (Brickell, 1978):

1. It is obvious that assessing competence at the end of high school is too late to allow for any meaningful remediation. Minimal levels of competence must also be identified at the elementary and middle school levels.

2. There is a lack of consensus on which skills are "minimal." For example, if the traditional basic skills of reading and math are used, how do we address other content areas, such as art, history, home economics, and so forth. There are also what might be termed "life skills," or knowledge necessary to get along in society. The question of which competencies are minimal has probably caused more difficulty than any other. To include competencies from all areas, however, might result in an unmanageable number of minimal competencies.

"Either this is a great moment, or we had better set some minimum standards for graduation from high school!"

3. It is not totally clear how to test for minimal achievement. If we use paper-and-pencil tests of the type used in most schools and by the NAEP, we may be unfairly discriminating against those who have poor test-taking skills. If we test in "real life" settings on the job, the costs become prohibitive. We are also left with the question of what constitutes minimal acceptable levels of performance. Can one set of minimal standards be fair or meaningful to all groups? If the same minimal standards were applied to all schools, we might find the standards too low for some and too high for others. On the other hand, such information might provide evidence by which *schools* could be judged for their level of "competency."

4. Finally, what is the school's obligation to those who fail to reach a minimal competency level?

The problems of CBE are numerous and unlikely to be solved overnight. It does appear at this time, however, that CBE is here to stay. Ultimately, it will be a positive step forward. But in the interim, schools and states will have to wrestle with many problems.

DROPOUTS

A problem closely related to lowered achievement is that of the school dropout. Each year over 750,000 young people leave high school before graduation. Although this number represents a significant decrease from previous years, the problem persists and deserves attention.

In one study by the South Carolina State Department of Education (1972), the "typical" school dropout was described as a seventeen-year-old, white male in the tenth grade who reads as about the seventh-grade level but has never failed a grade. His father had less than eleven years of education and his mother less than six. He did not participate in extracurricular activities and was absent for more than twenty-six days during the previous academic year. The most common reasons he gave for dropping out were that he disliked school and that he felt that nobody at school really cared about him, anyway.

Although the greater number of dropouts may be lower-income whites, we should recognize that the *rates* of dropouts among black and Spanish-speaking groups are substantially higher (U.S. Bureau of the Census, 1977). Further, there is some evidence that those who drop out are, on the average, of lower general ability as measured by tests of intelligence (Bachman et al., 1971; Voss et al., 1966).

Traditionally the school dropout is seen as an academic failure who is in turn doomed to a life of economic and social failure. This traditional view is an overstatement of fact, but it does reflect the greater likelihood that the dropout will continue to experience problems in society. In this sense, dropping out of school is not the *cause* of future problems, rather it is symptomatic of a more general set of problems. School dropouts have, for example, been linked with higher rates of unemployment, higher rates of delinquency, and higher rates of social problems as adults.

There is indeed considerable evidence that the school dropout is more likely to be unemployed (Bachman et al., 1971; U.S. Bureau of the Census,

1977). The dropout is at a disadvantage in the labor market and is usually a candidate for unskilled or semiskilled positions. On the average, a high school graduate can expect to earn 48 percent more wages in his lifetime than a dropout. A college graduate can expect to earn 98 percent more than a dropout (U.S. Bureau of the Census, 1977).

More generally, those who complete high school seem to show more signs of positive psychological adjustment than those who drop out. High school graduates in one study saw themselves in a more positive light on traits of social acceptance, such as sociability, self-confidence, and maturity (Combs and Cooley, 1968). Further, other studies have shown that dropouts are more likely to marry earlier, have more children, have marital problems, and die earlier (U.S. Bureau of the Census, 1977).

Some curious research goes against the traditional view linking delinquent behavior with school dropouts. Lower-income youths who ultimately dropped out of school did indeed show very high rates of delinquent behavior, which increased steadily until they finally dropped out. However, after they dropped out of school, their delinquent behavior declined steadily until, of all the groups studied, they had the lowest rates of delinquency (Elliott, 1966; Elliott and Voss, 1974). Among other groups of boys who

The high school dropout may suffer feelings of alienation because of lessened ability to get a useful job. (Owen Franken/Stock, Boston)

graduated from high school, there was no similar immediate decrease in delinquent behavior after completing school.

It would appear that dropping out of school reflects dissatisfaction, frustration, and alienation from the schools. Not uncommonly these young people have experienced repeated failure in the school and thus suffer a poor academic self-image. This frustration, in turn, leads to delinquency and rebellion (Elliott and Voss, 1974). When the source of frustration is eliminated, and the adolescent gains feelings of competence through employment and perhaps marriage, the delinquency rates drop (Jensen and Rojek, 1980).

As Gold and Petronio (1980) note, poor academic performance by a student strains the relationship between the teachers and the student as well as between the student and higher achieving peers. This psychological separation leads to alienation and frustration. For these estranged students, alternative schooling systems that provide for adolescents' needs for autonomy and that foster feelings of competence without dependence on traditional indices of achievement, are more apt to be beneficial.

ACADEMIC MERIT VERSUS SOCIAL CLASS

A long-standing controversy in the study of educational attainment is whether the primary variable underlying success is social status or academic ability (Rehberg and Rosenthal, 1978). One view claims that schools serve primarily to reinforce and solidify already existing social status in society. Success results not from any ability or motivation but from social class-related variables. Success for those of low social status is unlikely. The opposing view is that the American schools are based primarily on a model in which ability, not social status, is the variable of importance. Although able students from higher-income families may have greater long-range chances for further education and higher occupational status, the schools promote and encourage attainment among all students, irrespective of social status.

A longitudinal study of high school students found that, on the whole, contemporary schools respond more to ability than to social class. As early as ninth grade, assignment to the academic or college-bound curriculum had little to do with the social status of the student. Rather, ability and how the students perceived their parents' attitudes toward educational achievement were most important. Students from upwardly mobile families or low social status families who are motivated to achieve are not stifled by a rigidly stratified school system. School counselors, who might be expected to be influenced by social status if schools were so oriented, paid little attention to social status variables in their academic counseling. Advice or counseling was influenced more by academic ability (Rehberg and Rosenthal, 1978).

Another study showed that both academic ability and social status were significant contributors to status attainment fifteen years after high school. For males, however, academic ability had more impact than social class background. For females, social status variables seemed more important in long-range attainment. The only area in which ability seemed to play a more important role among women was in feelings of self-worth (Alexander and Eckland, 1975).

The increased cognitive abilities associated with adolescence are tied to increased academic demands. (© Elizabeth Crews)

The impact of teachers and counselors in encouraging lower-income students cannot be overstressed. Often lower-income and minority students view the schools as hostile and unresponsive to their needs. Teachers and counselors must be aware of these feelings and convey a positive attitude toward these students and their potential for success. Often adults in high-prestige occupations who come from lower-income backgrounds will report that two or three teachers or counselors really seemed to have faith in them and conveyed that attitude.

RESTRUCTURING THE SCHOOLS

In a recent report of a Presidential Commission on Youth entitled *Youth: Transition to Adulthood* (Coleman, 1975), James Coleman and his associates argue that schools are not capitalizing on the physical and creative energies of today's youths. In an attempt to become more efficient, schools have also become sterile and impersonal. The amount of time youths spend in school has increased, but the time is filled with curricula that have little relevance to the real world. This in turn has led to increased alienation of students including, but not limited to, school dropouts. What Coleman proposes is a radical change in the structure of American schooling with the goal of merging youths into society earlier. The Commission recommended the following changes in the structure of schooling:

1. *Reduce the size of the schools.* Smaller schools would facilitate the development of interpersonal relationships. Coleman and his colleagues say that large consolidated schools are impersonal. Their bureaucratic structure leads to an atmosphere akin to large university campuses. Smaller units would also reduce teacher specialization. Teaching would by necessity become interdisciplinary. On the other hand, large school districts are economically able to provide a broader spectrum of alternatives. Dividing large campuses into smaller units, the commission believes, offers the student the benefit of both worlds.

2. *Provide apprenticeship work experiences early.* The current structure of schools restricts interaction with adults and the "real world." Because instruction is isolated within the context of the classroom, its practicality is seldom seen. To change this, students could alternate between work and study. They would spend one-half of the school day in formal classes and the remaining half in an apprentice role on a job.

3. *Increase responsible participation by youths in the community.* The commission concluded that schools systematically reduce the decision-making responsibility of students. To be prepared to function in an adult community, students should have experience in meaningful responsibility beyond the very limited roles usually available in the schools. One might, for example, create internship roles in head-start agencies, political parties, election campaigns, or peer-counseling programs.

4. *Reexamine legal constraints on young people.* Laws aimed at the youth labor market were originally enacted to reduce economic exploitation of the young and their subjection to harsh working conditions. Those same restrictions ultimately limit the employment options available to young people. The current laws also protect the adult labor market from an influx of competitive, cheap labor. The commission proposed that the government provide tax or economic incentives for youth training programs.

5. *Introduce a voucher system.* Schools should allow young people the right to greater flexibility in job opportunities and provide for increased self-responsibility. The idea is to provide each young person a voucher equivalent to the average cost of a four-year college education. The young person could then cash the voucher in on any accredited training program. Such a system presumes a degree of maturity (or clarity of purpose) in young people, a presumption that may not be valid. Many college juniors and seniors are still unsure of their long-term career goals.

6. *Allow greater flexibility in completion of degree requirements.* Youths should be allowed greater latitude in leaving and reentering school. They should be able to leave school for a year or two, gain work experience, then reenter school, and complete their education with no penalty. Although college students can and do make use of such an option, similar fluidity among high school students is discouraged, directly or indirectly.

All in all, the overriding conclusion of the Coleman Commission was that the schools should be responsible for creating an environment that motivates students to learn, providing interesting and relevant curricula, increasing the options available to the students, and allowing increased responsible decision making among students.

Although few educators would argue with the general recommendations offered by the Coleman Commission, not all agree with the specific proposals that it offered. The report has met with hostile reaction from a variety of critics, including a former president of the National Education Association (Wise, 1971). The alternatives advocated in the report are built on presumptions about the workaday world that may not be totally accurate. It is not clear, for example, how the quality of apprenticeship training on the scale implied by the report would be monitored and controlled. Such a program would certainly require widespread government intervention to an even greater degree than is currently felt. Further, the report fails to differentiate between those students for whom the current system is unsatisfactory and those for whom the system works well.

Ebel (1973) argues for an alternative but more traditional view of the responsibility of the schools. In Ebel's view schools should help students acquire basic knowledge and competence that will be useful in later life. Knowledge is not, however, equated with pieces of information, but with those intellectual concepts that emerge out of using and applying the information. Intellectual skills and general ability to solve problems should emerge from knowledge acquisition. Also, Ebel feels that the schools should give up other roles that interfere with its primary function of developing intellectual skills. He points, for example, to the legal requirement to keep young people in school until some minimum age, usually sixteen. This makes the schools custodial institutions for delinquents and others who resent being there. Further, Ebel feels that schools should not be expected to provide interpersonal counseling, drug and alcohol education, and other extras that detract from its primary role.

In either view, Coleman's or Ebel's, there is clear dissatisfaction with the current structure of schooling. The nature and structure of schooling need to be reevaluated in light of the needs of the wide variety of students served by the schools.

MATCHING ENVIRONMENTS

The degree to which a school environment or atmosphere meets the individual needs of learners has an impact not only on higher academic performance but also on the personal satisfaction of students and their feelings of personal adequacy (Pervin, 1968). In school settings in which teachers fail to respond to the personal characteristics of learners, those learners demonstrate lowered performance and diminished feelings of personal adequacy.

Thelen (1967) has argued that classrooms should be organized so that there is an optimal match between learner and teacher characteristics. Thelen had teachers in junior and senior high school classrooms identify the types of students they felt benefited from their classes. He then had students rate the type of teacher from whom they felt they learned best. Thelen then created classes by matching students and teachers by their preferences. Other classes were established through ordinary procedures. The more teachable the students, in terms of the teachers' preferences, the better the outcomes for both students and teachers.

A variety of personal characteristics may interact with environmental features that lead to improved or impaired performance. Among the more promising work on generating matched learner–learning environment models in education is David Hunt's (1971, 1975; Hunt and Sullivan, 1974). Hunt describes the development of conceptual styles, combining Piaget's theory and his own earlier work in personality development (Harvey, Hunt, and Schroder, 1961).

Hunt outlines three general stages of conceptual style that are not dependent on age—as are Piaget's levels of cognitive development and Kohlberg's levels of moral development (see Chapter 10)—but that tend to develop across adolescence. Learners at Stage A are described as un-socialized, egotistic, and hedonic. Learners at this stage are motivated by what is personally gratifying. Stage A thinking dominates among preadolescents and early-adolescents. When asked to respond to the statement "What I think about rules," they give such answers as:

> I do not like them. They are no fun!
>
> Sixth-grade boy

> Rules sometimes can be a real trip! You are expected a lot of times to do things that don't even make any sense! Rules run you. I hate being ran (sic) around. Why can't we enjoy ourselves more? The reason is because of a lot of bummer rules!
>
> Twelfth-grade boy

Hunt describes learners at Stage A as impulsive and intolerant of ambiguity, with little self-control. Notice that even a twelfth-grader may still be at this stage. The optimal environment for Stage A learners is highly structured with emphasis on concrete examples and clear, immediate reinforcement for correct responses. Table 4-1 (p. 100) describes the learning styles and matching learning environments for Hunt's three cognitive stages.

The network of concepts that Stage A learners apply to the solution of problems lacks complexity. It is simple and categorical. In Figure 4-3 (p. 101), which describes the developmental matching model, Hunt tries to depict the low level of cognitive complexity of Stage A learners by the use of a simple, two-branched schema.

Stage B learners are highly socialized and depend on authority figures for guidance. Thinking among Stage B learners tends to consist of either/or, right/wrong categorical thinking and a high degree of conformity. Stage B conceptual development is associated with middle adolescence. When asked to respond to the statement "What I think about rules," they answer with such responses as

> I think rules are good. If we didn't have them, we wouldn't have a proper school, or know how to do anything.
>
> Sixth-grade girl

Table 4-1 CHARACTERISTICS OF COGNITIVE STYLE GROUPS

	Expected Characteristics of Stage Group	Observed Characteristics of Classroom Group
Stage A	Egocentric, very negative, impulsive, low tolerance for frustration	"Noisy, poorly disciplined, inattentive." "Easily confused, less self-control than others."
Stage B	Concerned with rules, dependent on authority, categorical thinking	"Orderly, quiet, attentive." "Questions asked to impress teacher." "Do not have faith in their convictions."
Stage C	Independent, inquiring, self-assertive, more alternatives available	"Did not rely on teacher's directions." "Interested in finding out information." "Stand up for their convictions."

Source: Adapted from D. E. Hunt, "Matching Models in Education: The Coordination of Teaching Methods with Student Characteristics" (Toronto: Ontario Institute for Studies in Education, 1971), p. 30.

You have to have them. But if you have them they should be used not for just a few but on all people that function with them.

Twelfth-grade boy

Hunt describes learners at Stage B as orderly and concerned with rules. The optimal environment for Stage B learners is moderately structured. Teachers should encourage independent thinking within relatively well-defined problem areas rather than assigning very unstructured tasks. Teachers of these learners do well to capitalize on their competitive tendencies.

Hunt describes learners at Stage C as autonomous thinkers who prefer working independently and maintain a high tolerance of ambiguity and uncertainty. Given the question about rules, Stage C learners may respond:

I think they have a place in society, or in the world, but many of them become oppressive and tend to restrict people from reacting in a natural way. I think this is bad. But they are good in school many times to keep order. In communities are all right too, if they are made for the good of the people.

Twelfth-grade girl

I think rules are necessary but shouldn't be taken in to extremes. A lot of people brake (sic) rules, but there are so many that you can't help it. If I had my way I'd live without them, but someone will always take advantage of a good thing.

Twelfth-grade boy

Hunt describes the optimal environment for Stage C learners as open with low structure and a wide variety of alternatives. Problem-based, discovery learning is best suited to Stage C learners, because they are self-motivated and prefer to work on their own. The network of concepts that Stage C learners apply to the solution of problems is highly complex. It is organized with many interrelations and qualifications. In Figure 4-3, the complexity of the concep-

Figure 4-3 HUNT'S DEVELOPMENTAL MATCHING MODEL

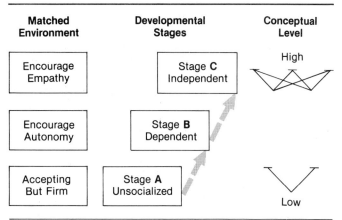

Source: D. E. Hunt, "Developmental Matching Model," *Review of Educational Research*, p. 223. Copyright 1975, American Educational Research Association, Washington, D.C.

tual level of Stage C learners is contrasted with that of Stage A learners by the use of multiple, interrelated schema with multiple branches.

Like Piaget's theory of cognitive development, Hunt's model is based on the presumption that the modes of cognitive style develop in sequential stages. To reach Stage C, learners must progress through Stages A and B. The teacher's or counselor's role becomes one of identifying the matching environment that best aids progress. If an environment is not optimal, the result is poorer performance. Hence, although an open environment with little structure is optimal for Stage C learners, when Stage A learners are placed in unstructured tasks, they are overwhelmed with the ambiguity and uncertainty. The result is frustration and poor performance. The opposite, however, does not seem to occur. Stage C learners are able to function quite well in highly structured tasks. They seem flexible enough to operate in most environments. If there are differences in the performance of Stage C learners in structured versus unstructured environments, they appear to be found in the students' attitudes toward the tasks. Thus, although they perform well on highly structured tasks, such as programmed instruction, they find them boring.

SUMMARY

Over the past several years, overall levels of academic achievement among high school students have gradually but steadily dropped. The drop has led college officials, business leaders, and government agencies to be alarmed at young people's lack of elementary reading and writing skills. In a move to counter this decline, many states are requiring that students demonstrate some minimal level of proficiency before high schools are allowed to award them diplomas. Although several problems still need to be ironed out, competency-based education seems here to stay and is probably a positive step forward.

Competency-based education by itself, however, is not enough. Schools must become more responsive to the differing needs of their learners. Simply moving students to a new school environment without regard to their unique needs is not likely to have any positive impact. Instead, schools need to provide alternative learning environments that respond to the characteristics of different groups of learners. In some cases it may be necessary to provide a totally different, alternative structure. When schools fail to respond to the different needs of learners, students exhibit lowered achievement and lowered feelings of personal worth.

Those who choose to work with adolescents as teachers most certainly face a major challenge. Understanding and relating to the adolescent student is no easy task. Although it is by no means a complete statement on the nature of teaching adolescents, an appendix to this text contains some general statements regarding the role of the teacher in the middle and secondary school.

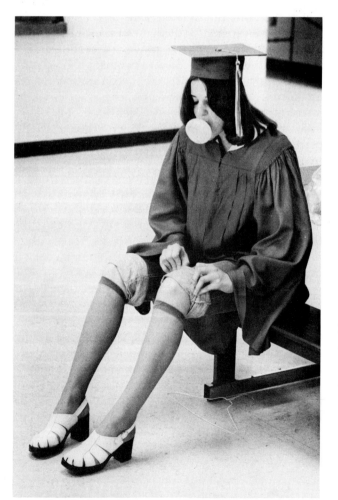

Adolescents are likely to exhibit an incongruous mixture of formality and casualness, maturity and immaturity. (Jim Richardson/Black Star)

5 | Affective Growth

During adolescence young people need to restructure their image of who they are. It is not simply a matter of knowing that they are no longer children and are now more like adults, but it is also a matter of working through the questions "Who am I? What is my role in life?" As such, adolescents form a new self-image and a personal sense of uniqueness that bring together their perceptions of their own sexuality, occupational plans and goals, value systems, and feelings of independence from parents. At its height, the process of answering those questions may be very unsettling, and the adolescent may experience anxiety or fear. Eventually, however, the self-image of childhood is altered and replaced by the more complex self-image with which the young person enters adulthood.

ERIK ERIKSON

Perhaps no other contemporary psychologist has had a greater impact on current thinking about personality development during adolescence than Erik Erikson. His "eight stages of man" described below have met with great public and professional interest, and his concept of the "identity crisis" has found its way into today's general language. Erikson was a student of both Sigmund and Anna Freud. Although Erikson was influenced by Freud, and his theory of personality has its roots in Freudian theory, Erikson shifted the focus from a set of inborn sexual motivations to social and environmental influences. One's personality is the result of how well one's social environment meets one's needs at each in a series of stages of development. Like Piaget, Erikson believes the sequence of stages is genetically determined but that their form is environmentally determined.

Erikson's writings have been immensely popular, and his psychological analysis of Mahatma Gandhi's militant nonviolence, *Gandhi's Truth* (1969), was awarded a Pulitzer Prize and the National Book Award for philosophy and religion. Likewise his psychological history of Martin Luther, *Young Man*

Figure 5-1 ERIKSON'S EIGHT STAGES OF MAN AND RELATED PERSONAL CONFLICTS

	1	2	3	4	5	6	7	8
VIII								INTEGRITY VERSUS DESPAIR
VII							GENERA-TIVITY VERSUS STAGNA-TION	
VI						INTIMACY VERSUS ISOLATION		
V	Temporal Perspective versus Time Confusion	Self-Certainty versus Self-Con-cious	Role Experi-mentation versus Role Fixation	Appentice-ship versus Work Paralysis	IDENTITY VERSUS IDENTITY CONFUSION	Sexual Polarization versus Bisexual Confusion	Leader- and Followership versus Authority Confusion.	Ideological Commitment versus Confusion of Values
IV				INDUSTRY VERSUS INFERI-ORITY	Task Identi-fication versus Sense of Futility			
III			INITIATIVE VERSUS GUILT		Anticipation of Roles versus Role Inhibition			
II		AUTONOMY VERSUS SHAME, DOUBT			Will to Be Oneself versus Self-Doubt			
I	TRUST VERSUS MISTRUST				Mutual Recognition versus Autiatic Isolation			

Source: Reproduced from *Identity, Youth and Crisis* by Erik H. Erikson, with the permission of W. W. Norton & Company, Inc. Copyright © 1968 by W. W. Norton & Company, Inc.

Luther (1968) makes fascinating reading and, as much as any of his other writings, gives the reader a picture of the dynamics of his theory.

Erik Erikson sees adolescence as a distinct period of development, separating yet bridging childhood and adulthood. Although Erikson focuses on the process of ego identity formation during adolescence, he sees ego formation as progressing throughout life.

In Erikson's view, a person develops a sense of identity as a result of working through a set of psychological and social tasks. The process of developing a sense of identity or a sense of self is a lifelong task. Although the stress associated with identity development in adolescence is of great importance, it must be seen as but one conflict in a series of conflicts that an individual must face throughout life. Thus, although the identity conflict of adolescence may be stormy, so might other developmental conflicts.

1. *Trust versus mistrust.* Like Freud, Erikson sees infancy as the first stage of personality development. During infancy the individual must develop a sense of *trust*. Parents provide affection and warmth and satisfy basic needs. Erikson feels that we never fully satisfy all our needs, but the infant from a healthy environment learns that others can be trusted. In contrast, infants who are raised in an environment of neglect and abuse, lacking in nurturance or love, develop a general attitude of *mistrust* of others.

2. *Autonomy versus shame and doubt.* In early childhood, about ages one to three, the child faces the second task. During this period the child must develop an initial sense of *autonomy*, or self-control. Children during this stage establish themselves as individuals and demonstrate that they can do things on their own. They are clearly still dependent upon their parents, but they begin to see themselves as individuals in their own right. During this stage parents need to exercise enough firm control to protect the child harm but allow the child to explore new areas independently. Failure to achieve a sense of autonomy or adequacy because belittling parents or overprotective parents do not allow experimentation during this period leads to a sense of *shame* and *doubts* about one's own abilities.

3. *Initiative versus guilt.* During preschool years, ages three to five, children begin to play with thoughts and are curious and imaginative. Through their imagination children test the limits of reality and fantasy. Their control over their own bodies is increased, and much of what they learn is through imitation of parents and other important adults. In a positive setting children develop a sense of *initiative* in which exploration and questioning are accepted parts of their identity. In nonconducive environments, in which parents are overly strict and discourage spontaneity, children develop a sense of *guilt*.

4. *Industry versus inferiority.* School-age children, about six to eleven years, are intent upon developing a sense of duty and accomplishment, or what Erikson calls a sense of *industry*. Children begin to set aside the fantasy and play of preschool and prefer to work with real things. During this period children develop social know-how and academic skills. Much of their thoughts are directed at clearly differentiating the real and the unreal. Children reach out to try new tasks and are increasingly competitive. Failures or mistakes, by themselves, should not be discouraged because they form the base for future learning. Repeated and excessive failure, however, may lead to a sense of *inferiority*. When children meet with repeated failure, they develop a self-image in which they see themselves as inadequate to take part in the working world.

5. *Identity versus identity diffusion.* During adolescence the previous elements of an individual's self-image are reassessed and reformulated into an image that includes what role the adolescent anticipates as an adult. The adolescent develops a sense of *personal identity*. Whereas adolescents at this period of development are likely to express a need for freedom from authority, especially parents' authority, they conform highly to the authority of the peer group. The peer group, rather than being a negative force, offers a protective setting that is alien to the adult world and allows the adolescent to experiment with alternative life roles and value systems.

VIGNETTE 5-1
The Fit in the Choir

The identity crisis is the keystone of Erikson's theory of personality development. Whether or not adolescents establish an adequate sense of personal identity is critical to their psychosocial adjustment during adult years. The process of answering the question "Who am I?" may be associated with some periods of considerable inner turmoil and rebellion. Such seems to have been the case with Martin Luther, who as a young Augustinian monk wrestled with the question of who or what he was and was not. Erikson studies the life of Luther as an archetypic example of a person going through the stages of personal development. The result of that study was his Young Man Luther. *Presented below is an abridged description of Luther's identity crisis, as represented in "the fit in the choir."*

Three of young Luther's contemporaries (none of them a later follower of his) report that sometime during his early or middle twenties, he suddenly fell to the ground in the choir of the monastery at Erfurt, "raved" like one possessed, and roared with the voice of a bull: *"Ich bin's nit! Ich bin's nit!"* or *"Non sum! Non sum!"* The German version is best translated with "It isn't me!" the Latin one with "I am not!"

It would be interesting to know whether at this moment Martin roared in Latin or in German; but the reporters agree only on the occasion which upset him so deeply: the reading of Christ's *ejecto a surdo et muto daemonio*—Christ's cure of a man possessed by a *dumb spirit.* This can only refer to Mark 9:17: "And one of the multitude answered and said, Master, I have brought unto thee my son, which hath a dumb spirit." The chroniclers considered that young Luther was possessed by demons—the religious and psychiatric borderline case of the middle ages—and that he showed himself possessed even as he tried most loudly to deny it. "I am *not,"* would then be the childlike protestation of somebody who has been called a name or has been characterized with loathsome adjectives: here, dumb, mute, possessed.

...[Luther's] days in the monastery were darkened by a suspicion, which Martin's father expressed loudly on the occasion of the young priest's first Mass, that the thunderstorm had really been the voice of a *Gespenst,* a ghost; thus Luther's vow was on the borderline of both pathology and demonology. Luther remained sensitive to this paternal suspicion, and continued to argue with himself and with his father long after his father had no other choice than to acknowledge his son as a spiritual leader and Europe's religious strong man. But in his twenties Martin was still a sorely troubled young man, not at all able to express either what inspired or what bothered him; his greatest wordly burden was certainly the fact that his father had only most reluctantly, and after much cursing, given his consent (which was legally dispensable, anyway) to the son's religious career.

It must have occurred to the reader that the story of the fit in the choir attracted me originally because I suspected that the words "I am *not!"* revealed the fit to be part of a most severe identity crisis—a crisis in which the young monk felt obliged to protest what he was *not* (possessed, sick, sinful) perhaps in

Source: Reprinted from *Young Man Luther* by Erik H. Erikson, with the permission of W. W. Norton & Company, Inc. Copyright © 1958, 1962 by Erik H. Erikson.

order to break through to what he was or was to be. I will now state what remains of my suspicion, and what I intend to make of it.

If we approach the episode from the psychiatric viewpoint, we can recognize in the described attack (and also in a variety of symptomatic scruples and anxieties to which Martin was subject at the time) an intrinsic ambivalence, an inner two-facedness, such as we find in all neurotic symptoms. The attack could be said to deny in its verbal part ("I am not") what Martin's father had said, namely, that his son was perhaps possessed rather than holy; but it also proves the father's point by its very occurrence in front of the same congregation who had previously heard the father express his anger and apprehension. The fit, then, is both unconscious obedience to the father and implied rebellion against the monastery; the words uttered both deny the father's assertion, and confirm the vow which Martin had made in that first known anxiety attack during a thunderstorm at the age of twenty-one, when he had exclaimed, "I want to be a monk." We find the young monk, then, at the crossroads of obedience to his father—an obedience of extraordinary tenacity and deviousness—and to the monastic vows which at the time he was straining to obey almost to the point of absurdity.

This general reformulation of personal identity takes place during the *identity crisis*, in which the adolescent actively breaks down and restructures the organization of his or her personality. The very complex and important nature of the decision-making process makes the period of transformation one of intense conflict. The adolescent may thus alternate between actively exploring new roles and stepping away from decision making.

In settings that provide too little structure for selection of alternative roles and values, the adolescent may be unable to decide on an alternative. In this case the adolescent has no clear personal identity and may suffer *role diffusion*. In the long run this alternative may be especially disruptive for the adolescent. Among disturbed and severely depressed adolescents, self-descriptions often include phrases such as "I'm nothing, a loser." Alternatively, the adolescent may choose a *negative identity*. In working with delinquent youths, one gets the impression, for example, that being "delinquent" is better than being nothing at all. Assuming the identity of delinquent offers a set of roles and values that give some direction to an adolescent's life, even though that direction is in opposition to the preferences of society.

Marcia (1966, 1980) has been able to measure differences among four states of transition in the movement toward identity achievement. When parents provide too little freedom for exploration of alternative roles, the adolescent may experience *identity foreclosure*. That is, the adolescent accepts as a personal identity a set of roles and values that have been specified by someone else. An adolescent boy who is expected to be a doctor or lawyer just like his father and grandfather before him may not see much room for divergence. Likewise, an adolescent girl who is led to expect a singular role as housewife and mother may not experience conflict, because no alternatives are seen as reasonable. Young people, both males and females, in a state of identity foreclosure tend to be dogmatic and willing to submit to authority. They lack self-directiveness (Marcia, 1980).

At the next level of development of a personal identity, Marcia sees *identity diffusion*, during which adolescents lack commitment to a set of values and goals. Their behavior is impulsive and self-centered.

Prior to achieving a functioning identity, adolescents enter a period of *moratorium*, during which they are actively in the identity crisis. Among the principle struggles that seem to be prevalent during this phase is the struggle to see oneself as free from parents and authority (Marcia, 1980).

Identity achievement occurs among those adolescents who have actually gone through the restructuring and decision-making process. Those who do achieve a sense of personal identity have a stronger sense of self-directedness and a feeling of satisfaction about personal beliefs and goals. In contrast, those adolescents in states of identity diffusion or moratorium are less likely to value or recognize their distinctiveness. In making the transition to an achieved identity, adolescents may need help in identifying their own strengths and limits and in recognizing their uniqueness and value as human beings. Counseling also requires aiding the adolescent in exploring and recognizing role and value choices. Ultimately, however, counselors need to ensure that the adolescents' decision-making activities are conducted in an atmosphere that is not restricted by arbitrary standards of what is and is not acceptable. On the other hand, neither should the process be conducted within a completely unstructured context.

Some cautions should be stated about the process as seen by Marcia, because it is not clear that the process of identity formation among females is comparable to that among males. Socialization toward adult identity formation is not the same, and it is not unlikely that the process of identity formation similarly differs. Identity foreclosure, for example, seems to have less negative impact among females than males.

Just as identity formation does not begin at adolescence, neither does it end with adolescence. An individual's sense of personal identity is continuously refined throughout life. But, just as the way the adolescent resolves the conflicts preceding identity formation—especially its immediate precursor, the struggle to achieve a sense of industry—affects the identity crisis, so does the adolescent's achievement of a sense of identity have an impact on subsequent conflicts. It has an especially strong relationship to the struggle to achieve a sense of intimacy in young adulthood.

6. *Intimacy versus isolation.* Following adolescence the young adult must establish a sense of *intimacy* with another person. Beyond the immediate, sexual intimacy which Erikson sees as essential to a relationship, there is a more general level of intimacy in which the individual's sense of identity becomes fused with the identity of another person. Close personal relationships with people of both sexes lead to a general feeling of acceptability in society. Failure to achieve a clear personal identity during adolescence interferes with establishing close relationships with others. If a young woman, for example, is unsure of who she is, then it is not possible for her to

Although adolescents need strong peer relationships, they also need time to be alone. (© Frances M. Cox 1981/Omni-Photo Communications, Inc.)

be open enough with another person to reveal herself enough to establish an intimate relationship. Failure to establish close intimate relationships leads to a sense of *isolation.*

7. *Generativity versus stagnation.* During middle adulthood a person develops a sense of *generativity,* which refers not only to parental status but also to a productive and creative role in the service of others. Generativity means feeling that what one does benefits successive generations. Failure to master this task leads to *stagnation* and self-indulgence.

8. *Integrity versus despair.* Finally, during old age, the individual needs to develop a sense of *integrity,* a sense of accomplishment and a feeling that

The interactions of young people with their grandparents and other senior citizens encourage a sense of the continuity of life. (Chris Brown/Stock, Boston)

one's life was worthwhile, that there was meaning to one's life. A feeling of integrity can emerge only when in retrospect an elderly man, for example, feels that he has been productive in work and in parenthood and that what he has done was of benefit to others. This does not mean that he looks back over his life "through rose-colored glasses." He sees his hardships and sufferings as a normal part of life, outweighed by the sense of accomplishment. Failure to develop this feeling leads to a sense of *despair*.

SELF-ESTEEM

At a more general level, the identity crisis can be seen as part of adolescents' formation of a self-concept and feelings of self-worth. It may be reasonably argued that the development of a positive self-concept is the most important developmental task of adolescence. A "concept" is a cluster of concrete and abstract attributes that allow a learner to group a variety of events into a common category. A self-concept may be thought of as an itemized listing of those characteristics you perceive in yourself.

As adolescents mature, their self-concepts are more likely to become more complex and to include abstract attributes. Early-adolescents and preadolescents, given the question "Who am I?" will respond with a list of physical features and things they like (Montemayor and Eisen, 1977). A typical nine-year-old boy, for example, responded:

My name is Bruce C. I have brown eyes. I have brown hair. I have brown eyebrows. I am nine years old. I love! sports. I have seven people in my family. I live on 1923 P. Dr. I am going to be 10 in September. I'm a boy. I have an uncle that is almost 7 feet tall. My school is P. My teacher is Mrs. V. I play Hockey! I am almost the smartest boy in the class. I *love!* food. I love fresh air. I *love* School. (p. 317)

Notice that the nine-year-old's answer consists almost completely of concrete attributes. By early adolescence, responses to the same question are still mostly concrete characteristics, but gradually reports begin to include references to interpersonal characteristics or abstract categories. One eleven-year-old girl wrote:

My name is A. I'm a human being. I'm a girl. I'm a truthful person. I'm not pretty. I do so-so in my studies. I'm a very good cellist. I'm a very good pianist. I'm a little bit tall for my age. I like several boys. I like several girls. I'm old-fashioned. I play tennis. I am a *very* good swimmer. I try to be helpful. I'm always ready to be friends with anybody. Mostly I'm well-liked by some girls and boys. I love sports and music. I don't know if I'm liked by boys or not. (pp. 317-318)

Although there are still many references to concrete characteristics, the girl also compares herself with respect to others and labels herself with such abstract terms as truthful, old-fashioned, and helpful; she also provides some assessment of her personality. By late adolescence, responses to the question are much more likely to include references to personal style. Concrete

Pranks and some limited delinquency are a normal part of the adolescent transition from childhood to responsible adulthood. (© Joel Gordon 1974)

attributes, although while still there, are not emphasized. A seventeen-year-old girl wrote:

> I am a human being. I am a girl. I am an individual. I don't know who I am. I am a Pisces. I am a moody person. I am an indecisive person. I am an ambitious person. I am a very curious person. I am a confused person. I am not an individual. I am a loner. I am an American (God help me). I am a Democrat. I am a liberal person. I am a radical. I am a conservative. I am a pseudo-liberal. I am an atheist. I am not a classifiable person (i.e.—I don't want to be). (p. 318)

The attributes that such an adolescent uses to describe herself may also reflect the value that she sees in herself as a person. Certain adjectives, such as friendly, pretty, or helpful, have a positive connotation and, when used, reflect a positive self-image. Other adjectives, such as ugly, sad, or dumb, have negative connotations and the person whose self-description includes such adjectives is said to have a negative self-image. Most people, however, see a combination of traits in themselves. Some of those traits are seen as positive, some are not. Whereas self-concept or self-image refers to those characteristics you see in yourself, self-worth or self-esteem reflects the overall value that you place on those characteristics. Not all characteristics are equally valuable to all adolescents. For some adolescents, body image may dominate feelings of self-worth, whereas for others some talent or lack of it may be most important.

Some psychologists prefer to look at both the adolescent's self-perceptions and those attributes that adolescents see as ideal. The greater the difference between the perceived self and the ideal self, the more likely an individual has negative feelings of self-worth. This is especially true if the self-perception is dominated by negatively laden descriptors and the ideal is the opposite.

In identifying an adolescent's self-concept, it does not matter whether the adolescent's self-perceptions are accurate from your or anyone else's point of view. The self-perception is the "reality" that dominates the adolescent's life. The anorexic girl who sees herself as fat even though she is emaciated has, as an integral part of her self-concept, the perception that she is somehow less than desirable. Likewise, the boy who sees himself as stupid even though teachers see him as potentially bright has, as an integral part of his self-image, the feeling that he lacks competence. Both will interact with others in ways that reflect that feeling, rather than in ways that reflect external reality.

The role of a practitioner working with a youngster with a misperceived self-attribute is not to confront the adolescent with the "truth." Most of us have seen a discouraged teacher look at a girl like the one described and say, "You have the brains to do well. Why don't you apply yourself?" That the technique is not effective is probably best shown in the expression on the girl's face after hearing this. The practitioner who wishes to alter this adolescent's self-image to a more realistic self-appraisal needs to do so gradually. The practitioner should also realize that it may not be possible to change an adolescent's self-image totally.

MEASURING SELF-WORTH

A variety of measures of self-concept and self-esteem are available to the practicing professional (for example, the Coopersmith Inventory and the Tennessee Self-Concept Inventory). One reasonably simple technique that many researchers and practitioners use is to have adolescents scan a checklist of several adjectives and mark those adjectives that they think describe themselves. The adolescents are then given a second copy of the list and are asked to check those adjectives that describe the way they would like to be seen. The closer the perceived self is to the ideal self, the stronger or more positive the individual's feelings of self-worth. If the two sets of adjectives are very divergent, then we can assume that the adolescent has lower feelings of self-worth. What a person sees and what he or she would like to see are too different.

Positive feelings of self-worth should not be confused with conceit. An adolescent boy, for example, who has positive feelings of self-worth, who has a feeling of respect for himself, is more likely to be at ease in stressful settings. As a society, we discourage individuals from saying, "I like myself" or "I am a really super person." We are encouraged to be humble and a bit self-effacing. For adolescents the pressures to conform to this demand are added to their own questions of whether they are worth much. A practitioner cannot help but be impressed to hear so many statements from young people like "I'm ugly," "I'm dumb," or "My feet are too big." It is often difficult to get early- or middle-adolescents to express their strengths.

The ability of an adolescent to work through the identity crisis satisfactorily and the type of self-image that emerges from that conflict differ as a result of any number of factors. The environment in which lower-income black adolescents develop a personal sense of identity is obviously much different than the environment of an upper-class, white adolescent. Further, the number of social and educational options available to the two groups are widely separated. Their freedom to consider alternate life-styles is simply not the same. Thus they will emerge from adolescence with very different self-images.

One study of affluent youths found, for example, that for a while they have to learn to live with an extraordinary number of choices. They grow up with the knowledge that they have the ability and the resources to do whatever they please. It is an attitude that stays with them throughout life (Coles, 1977).

Children's and adolescents' self-concepts and motives are strongly influenced by the environment of the neighborhood they live in. (*top*—© Frank Siteman MCMLXXX; *bottom*—© Eric Kroll 1978/Taurus Photos)

Lower-income youths do not see life as providing nearly as wide a range of choices. Adolescents from an inner-city, lower-income neighborhood or a poor rural farm do not see themselves as having many options. Their freedom to experiment is limited by lack of financial resources. Also, adolescents from lower-income families are less likely to see themselves as having much say in the control of their lives.

Middle-income adolescents fall somewhere between these extremes. Although their opportunities for choice are broader than for their lower-income peers, they have fewer options than the more affluent adolescents do. In each case, self-concept and identity are influenced by their families' level of income.

Not only the family but also the neighborhood from which an adolescent comes have an impact on self-perceptions. Adolescents who come from professional families are more likely to expect to go to college than those from blue-collar families. However, adolescents from blue-collar families are more likely to plan on college as the average family income of the neighborhood increases, and adolescents from professional families are less likely to plan on college as the average family income of the neighborhood decreases (Wilson, 1959).

Other factors also affect adolescent self-concept and feelings of self-worth. As adolescents' value systems differ from the majority of their neighborhood peers, the lower their feelings of confidence and self-worth. Youths from Catholic families who are raised in predominantly non-Catholic neighborhoods have lower self-esteem than those who grow up in predominantly Catholic neighborhoods. Similar patterns are found for Protestant and Jewish adolescents (Rosenberg, 1975). Apparently the discomfort of finding oneself with values or a relevant social-status variable that is different from that of the majority of peers is unsettling enough to lead many adolescents to question those values and therefore their own value.

Warm, caring, supportive parents play an important role in the development of positive self-esteem. (© Margaret Thompson)

Rosenberg (1965) also found that low self-esteem in adolescents was associated with parental indifference. That is, whereas positive, supportive interactions with parents were most associated with positive feelings of self-worth, low self-worth was not conversely related to negative, nonsupportive interactions. Rather, parental indifference or lack of parent-adolescent interactions seemed to lead to diminished feelings of self-esteem. Adolescents interpret their parents' lack of response as a lack of caring. In another study adolescents with low self-esteem viewed communication with their parents as nonconstructive (Flora, 1978).

SELF-ESTEEM AND SOCIAL ADJUSTMENT

Whether or not adolescents are able to accept the strengths and limits of others is directly related to their ability to accept their own strengths and limits (Swinn and Greger, 1965). Self-acceptance is basic to general social acceptance. Failure to accept yourself decreases the chances of others accepting you. Conversely, acceptance by others may increase your acceptance of your self. The two processes complement each other. When adolescents view themselves as different from their peers, they are likely to be seen the same way by peers and, because of that, be separated from them (Goslin, 1962). A healthy personality and positive feelings of self-worth are fundamental to positive social adjustment.

SELF-WORTH AND ACHIEVEMENT

Researchers have found that students' performance in school depends in part on how they feel about themselves (Covington and Beery, 1976). What an adolescent *thinks* about his ability may be more important than his actual level of ability. The more positively individuals feel about their ability to succeed, the more likely they are to exert effort and feel a sense of accomplishment when they finish a task. In the same fashion, the more negatively individuals evaluate their ability to succeed, the more likely they are to avoid tasks in which there is uncertainty of success, the less likely they are to exert effort, and the less likely they are to attribute any success or lack of it to themselves.

Persons with low feelings of self-worth tend to have a high fear of failure and high feelings of failure (Covington and Beery, 1976). Given a task in which they must set goals, those with low self-esteem are likely to set unrealistically difficult or overly easy goals. For example, in a ring-toss game in which students can toss the rings at the goal from any distance they desire, those with low self-esteem stand either right next to the peg or too far away. Those who stand right next to the peg avoid feelings of failure by assuring success. Those who stand too far away ensure failure but also provide themselves an excuse. Those with positive self-esteem are more likely to set goals of intermediate difficulty. In the ring-toss game, they are more likely to choose a distance that does not ensure success or failure but allows a reasonable chance of success. If, after one set of tries, the players are given

Success not only breeds more success but also leads to improved feelings of self-worth. (© Bill Stanton/Magnum Photos, Inc.)

the option of moving and trying again, the high self-esteem individuals will use the information from the first try and adjust the distance to make the task more reasonable (or a bit more difficult if the first try was too easy). Those with low self-esteem do not make use of that information.

In achievement-oriented settings like the school, the need to avoid failure may dominate a student's choice of activities and selection of courses. The student may either avoid participation in achievement-related activities altogether or participate just enough to get by but not enough to risk failure. Alternatively, the student may select tasks that are excessively difficult. The "blame" for failure is thus removed from the student and placed on the task (Covington and Beery, 1976).

Those students with high self-esteem, a motivation to achieve, and positive feelings of self-worth are more likely to select moderately difficult tasks and attribute the outcome to their own efforts. Although they do not desire failure, they do not have an overwhelming fear of it. They assume that any achievements are a result of a combination of their own efforts and talent.

The feeling that what one accomplishes results from personal effort and control of the situation is learned. By experience and training we learn to internalize responsibility and control. Further, the pattern is cyclical. Success breeds success and failure breeds failure. The motivation to achieve and successful achievement lead individuals to attribute the success to their own efforts. This builds feelings of pride in accomplishments, which in turn increases the likelihood that the individual will engage in achievement-related behaviors in the future with a willingness to continue to try to achieve. (See Figure 5-2.) Externalization of control, or assuming that what happens results from luck or from control by outsiders, is also learned. Adolescents who are low in the motive to achieve also see themselves as largely controlled rather

Figure 5-2 THE PATTERN OF DEVELOPMENT
OF THE ACHIEVEMENT MOTIVE

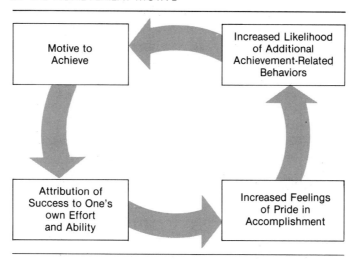

Source: B. Weiner, "Attribution Theory, Achievement Motivation and the
Educational Process," *Review of Educational Research 42,* (1972): 208. Copyright
1972, American Educational Research Association, Washington, D.C.

than in control of themselves. They are not only more likely to feel that effort
is not a primary characteristic of success but also that lack of success is
equated with lack of ability (Weiner, 1972).

Minority adolescents and adolescents from lower-income families are very
likely to display this attitude (Katz, 1967). They come from homes and
neighborhoods that not only do not reinforce the attitude that what people do
is a result of their efforts but instead reinforce the opposite. Middle-class
youths, on the other hand, have been instructed that to have ability and fail to
put out an effort is immoral; one is morally obligated to use one's talents
(Weiner, 1972).

In classrooms, when the teacher expects students to do well and the
students fail, the teacher is more likely to attribute the failure to lack of effort
or lack of motivation (Weiner and Kukla, 1970). Students low in achievement
motivation are apt to report, "I failed because I'm dumb." Teachers are apt to
answer, "You failed because you did not try." The highly achievement-
oriented teacher implies by this response that the student does have sufficient
ability (Weiner and Kukla, 1970). Similarly teachers give more praise and less
punishment to students who are seen as exerting effort (Lanzetta and
Hannah, 1969).

THE LOCUS OF CONTROL

People with a positive self-image usually feel in control of their own lives.
They feel that what they do makes a difference in whether they achieve some
outcome. On the other hand, individuals with a negative self-image are apt to
feel that what happens to them is mostly the result of luck or fate. The

tendency of people to attribute their success or lack of it to themselves or to luck has been labeled as the *locus of control* (Rotter, 1966).

Depending on their past experience, adolescents differ in their tendencies to see themselves as in control of their own lives. Teens from lower-income families and lower-income neighborhoods are less likely to feel such internal control. Rather, low-income adolescents are more likely to see their life as controlled by others. They see that they have little control over their livelihood. An adolescent who views major events as the result of luck, fate, or the whim of people in power, is said to have an external locus of control. Those who see such events as in their own control are internally motivated or have an internal locus of control. When asked how one gets into the college of one's choice, the externally motivated youth is likely to be convinced that it is all a matter of who you know. The internally motivated youth is likely to attribute such an outcome to individual effort or personal ability. Although it may be argued that the external perception is correct in some cases and probably correct in more cases if you are poor, the perception reflects a general attitude about who is in control.

Some studies show that, on the average, boys are more likely than girls to be internally motivated. In the same fashion, girls are less likely to picture themselves as leaders or as academically successful or as successful in traditionally male-dominated areas. One author described this tendency as a "fear of success" (Horner, 1970). When asked to consider the story of a woman who was at the top of her medical school class, a majority of women college students reported that the woman felt anxious and guilty and that success would lead to unpleasant consequences, such as loss of femininity or social rejection (Horner, 1970; Hoffman, 1974). The same projection of anxiety and guilt was not seen when the person being considered was male rather than female (Feather and Raphelson, 1974).

Among preadolescent and adolescent students it has been found that both boys and girls show a tendency to avoid success in the middle school years. By late high school, however, boys show an increased motive to succeed, whereas girls show an increased motive to avoid success (Romer, 1975). Further, the motive to avoid success was more noticeable among girls in coed schools than non-coed schools. The early dominance of a motive to avoid success may be related to typical peer pressure not to be "too brainy." The very strong needs of early-adolescents to be acceptable and accepted have a strong influence on willingness to be noncompetitive, and female achievement in male domains is discouraged. Thus if a young girl is successfully competing against her male peers, she receives negative feedback from friends and adults. Eventually she learns to avoid those settings in which she might succeed because they are anxiety provoking. She also learns to associate success with a loss of femininity. As an alternative, women may identify affiliation or getting along with others as a "safe" form of success (Bardwick and Douvan, 1971). More recently researchers have found that, rather than fearing success, women desire success but fear society's reactions toward women who compete against men and succeed (Tresemer, 1974; Olsen and Willemsen, 1978).

An integral part of the adolescent's self-concept is his or her sexual or gender identity. As part of their emerging personal identity, individuals need to incorporate those bodily features that make them male or female. To say that an individual needs to establish a sexual identity does not automatically imply that the identity incorporates society's traditional stereotypes of maleness and femaleness.

Western society identifies one well-defined set of personal attributes that are valued in men and a separate set for women. Autonomy, independence, dominance, aggression, and the inhibition of emotion are seen as valued traits in males, whereas females are expected to be warm, nurturant, passive, dependent, and emotional (Sears, Maccoby, and Levin, 1957). Occupational roles requiring administrative responsibility and strength are classified as "masculine" jobs, whereas roles of caring for others and being passive are "feminine."

To a large extent those stereotypes persist among children and adolescents. As early as first and second grades, children project maleness or femaleness to specific occupations (Siegal, 1973). Sex differences in vocational choice become more flexible as children approach adolescence, but in one study (Mitchell, 1977) the predominant expected adult role of adolescent girls was mother and homemaker with no outside occupation. This was true in spite of recent figures showing over half of today's married women hold jobs outside the home.

It is unlikely that gender roles are innately determined, although some tendency toward more aggressive behavior in males may be associated with higher levels of testosterone (Conger, 1977). Rather, it is more probable that specific gender roles are selectively shaped by society. One learns quickly what is acceptable for girls and conversely what is unacceptable. By late childhood and early adolescence, these stereotyped expectations are crystallized into rigid schema of maleness versus femaleness. If, however, Hunt (1971) is accurate in his assumption that adolescents must go through a stage of authoritarian adherence to society's rules, it may be necessary for young people to incorporate stereotypes before they can evaluate and modify them as they move to a level of independent thinking.

Society responds with approval when adolescents act in ways that conform to expectations and with disapproval when they do not. When asked to indicate what qualities among females make for a good student, junior high school teachers list the following (Sadker and Sadker, 1974, p. 58):

appreciative	sensitive
calm	dependable
conscientious	efficient
considerate	mature
cooperative	obliging
mannerly	thorough
poised	

On the other hand, those same teachers expect a good male student to be (p. 58):

active	energetic
adventurous	enterprising
aggressive	frank
assertive	independent
curious	inventive

These preferences parallel the traditional stereotypes of males and females and probably serve to influence how the teacher reacts to the adventurous, energetic girl or the appreciative, sensitive boy. It is not unlikely that these expected behaviors also generalize to subject matter areas. Thus girls are not expected to do well in math and science, whereas boys are. Conversely boys are not expected to do well in the arts or reading. Further, it is likely that curricula and textbooks are structured to preserve these expectations (Saario, Jacklin, and Tuttle, 1973). The adolescent boy or girl who deviates from these unwritten gender codes may be the subject of suspicion.

Although considerable attention has been focused on the inappropriateness of many traditional sex-role stereotypes, there is no reason to presume that society has relinquished them. Indeed, during adolescence, rather than ignoring sex roles, contemporary youths are very much concerned with being "masculine" or "feminine." As suggested before, some solidification of sex roles may be a necessary prerequisite to progression to higher levels of socialization. On the other hand, unilateral, unquestioning acceptance of traditional gender roles may disrupt the normal unfolding of an individual's personal identity.

VIGNETTE 5-2
Math Anxiety

One of the courses I teach regularly is in the area of statistics. It is apparent to me that the biggest stumbling block for most students is not *their lack of ability* to handle the material (most are quite capable), not *their lack of motivation*, but their very high level of anxiety about math in general and statistics in particular. They often suffer what we call "number shock" or "symbol shock." The causes for such anxiety are not always clear, but it seems that there is a socialization process in which one learns that being afraid of mathematics is acceptable and encouraged. This socialization is especially strong among girls and young women. Overcoming math anxiety is difficult but not impossible. How do you respond to math?

Source: Sheila Tobias, "Math anxiety," *Ms. Magazine 5* (Sept., 1976): 56–59. Copyright Ms. Foundation for Education & Communication, Inc. Reprinted with permission.

Do you "clutch up"? If so, are there ways that you can help yourself to relax? If not, are there other areas or situations that make you feel anxious? How do you try to cope with that anxiety?

The young instructor stood in front of the group of students, faculty, and administrators. "I'd like you to do a simple subtraction in your heads" he said. "A woman is thirty-eight, and this is 1976; in what year was she born?" The group was nervous. Was this a test? Were they going to have to compete with one another for the right answer? Should they raise their hands? He wanted none of this. "Just do the problem in your head; don't tell me the answer. But be prepared to tell me how you came up with it." Everyone relaxed. Somehow, if no "right answer" were being demanded, it was easier to comply. And so it began.

As each person told how she or he had subtracted 38 from 76, the mood of the group shifted from incredulousness to laughter. "I had that certain feeling I had to get to the nearest ten," admitted one adult man. "And so I subtracted seventy-six from eighty and thirty-eight from forty and then adjusted my answer to account for what I had done." "I took my own age," a woman in her thirties recounted, "and knowing when I was born, I subtracted the difference between the ages and had the answer." "I wrote the subtraction on a blackboard in my mind," said a third, "and then 'did' the problem the way I was taught in school." Around the room the instructor went. No two had done the problem quite the same way. People were stunned at the ingenuity of others' methods but each found her or his own perfectly reasonable. Mostly everyone laughed, first at the others, then at themselves.

"All these methods," the instructor finally commented, "represent perfectly good algorithms—systems for finding answers in a definite way. Few of you used the method you had been taught in school and most of you were ashamed that you did not. You think there's something wrong with having to get to the nearest ten. But there isn't. It's okay so long as it's correct and you're comfortable with it. And what's comfortable for you may not make the next person comfortable."

Everyone felt better.

The instructor went on to teach a number system, used by the Incas, which is based on five and involves many different ways of handling symbols. Later, he played some three-dimensional ticktacktoe. And he explained how confusing it is to learn arithmetic in elementary school when as a child in kindergarten you are told unequivocally that zero is "nothing"; in first grade that it is a "placeholder"; and in fifth grade that you can't divide by zero. No wonder you didn't learn arithmetic, he implied: you were too smart, too bothered by inconsistency, too creative, to ingest all this nonsense.

The "class" was an experimental demonstration and discussion of math anxiety, a condition that disproportionately affects females and racial minorities of both sexes; and the goal of the series was to find out more about math anxiety and to begin to search out ways of overcoming it.

Some of us teachers attending that first class had become intrigued with the problem of "math avoidance" during the previous year. We had been noticing great reluctance on the part of women college students to take courses that required or might require at a later stage either calculus or heavy use of algebra or rigorous statistics. Some of our students were even contemplating changing their majors to avoid math prerequisites. Adult women, too, who came for vocational counseling, were entirely unwilling to contemplate new careers having to do with data or with "things." They wanted to work with people, they said plaintively. At first we accepted this at face value, understanding that having been socialized as women, they felt at home in the helping professions. But when feminist sociologist Lucy Sells reported on the inadequate math preparation of entering Berkeley students, the pieces of the puzzle began to fit into place.

Of the entering class at Berkeley in 1973, Sells reported that 57 percent of the males brought with them four years of high school math, but only 8 percent of the entering females had the same preparation. Thus, 92 percent of the women in the first-year class were not even eligible to take any calculus or intermediate level statistics course. Moreover, all but five of the 20 majors at Berkeley in the early 1970s required either calculus or statistics. Women, then, were crowding themselves into the remaining five fields (the humanities, music, social work, elementary education, guidance and counseling), not only because of sex-role socialization but because of math avoidance.

If math avoidance were the result only of poor guidance counseling at the secondary school level, then the solution would be relatively simple: just get the word out that the social sciences have become "mathematized" over the past two decades, that business requires at least a familiarity with operations research, and that almost every administrative job will involve some work with budgets, financial statements, and comparisons of rates of change. Then girls and women would flock to remedial math classes and the problem would soon be solved. The problem was far more serious—growing out of a culture that makes math ability a masculine attribute, that punishes women for doing well in math, and that soothes the slower math learner by telling her she does not have a "mathematical mind." It all adds up to math anxiety, of which math avoidance is but a symptom.

Math anxiety is an "I can't" syndrome, and whenever it strikes—for some as early as sixth grade, with word problems; for others, with the first bite of algebra; for still others, not until calculus or linear algebra or statistics, after a high school record of achievement in mathematics—it creates the same symptoms and response. "I can't do this. No amount of practice or trying will make it work for me. I never really understood math. I always memorized and got away with it. Now I've hit the level I always knew was there. I can't do it."

Once a person has become frightened of math, she or he begins to fear all manner of computations, any quantitative data, and words like "proportion," "percentage," "variance," "curve," "exponential." Some students think that a simple table in a history textbook, showing, say, yields of a crop, by year, is "mathematics," and therefore inaccessible. Unless the same information is presented in a series of declarative sentences, they are uncomfortable with it.

Math anxiety is a serious handicap. It is handed down from mother to daughter with father's amused indulgence. ("Your mother never could balance a checkbook," he says fondly.) Then, when an employer or a colleague recognizes it in an employee, she can be barred from any endeavor or new assignment by the threat that the new job will involve some work with "data or tables or functions."

Whatever the causes of math anxiety may be, the cure presupposes a highly specific diagnosis of an individual's problem, including an attempt to do a kind of "cognitive map" of the person. Such a "map" could indicate whether she or he might better learn math through words (highly verbal, low spatial, medium numerical); through pictures (highly spatial, low verbal, low numerical); or through numbers, that is, through a method suited to her or his own personal cognitive strengths and weaknesses. Imagine numbers being introduced as either:

One, two, three, four, . . . ; or
1, 2, 3, 4, . . . ; or
- + -- + --- + ---- . . .

There is some risk that in focusing on math anxiety in women, feminist educators may unintentionally support the prejudice and discrimination against women mathematicians. It should be understood that currently about 10 percent of the Ph.D.s in mathematics are earned by women. But there is no question that math anxiety is a significant handicap for most women, since nearly every important issue of the day has a strong mathematical component. From a feminist perspective, mathematical literacy is a way to demystify the world. We feel that if we could develop a cure for math anxiety and "bottle" it for women engaged in self-help activities, these women would show increased self-reliance and with it increased self-esteem.

[*Note:* The original article in *Ms. Magazine* offered a more complete description of a program being conducted at Wesleyan University in Connecticut to combat math anxiety.]

DEVELOPING SELF-WORTH

In your role as practitioner, you will encounter many adolescents with negative feeling about themselves. As part of your dealings with these adolescents, you may try to nurture positive feelings of self-worth and a better self-image. Although there is no easy formula for accomplishing this goal, some guidelines may be useful:

1. *Help the adolescent learn to set goals.* Adolescents with low self-esteem typically set unrealistically high or low goals for themselves. As a person working with such adolescents, you will want to help them establish a realistic set of long-range and short-term goals. Further, it will be necessary to determine when the goals are achieved and what reward the adolescent may expect for completing the goals. You should state these goals and the plans for achieving them clearly and record them as an Individualized Treatment Plan (ITP).

2. *Guide the adolescent toward a realistic assessment of strengths and weaknesses.* For goals to be reasonable, they must be within reach but not overly easy. To be able to set goals, adolescents must recognize where they are starting from. Goals should capitalize on strengths and either compensate for or try to eliminate weaknesses. Evaluation of strengths and weakness should not be made by the practitioner and provided to the adolescent. The adolescent needs to exert honest effort in self-evaluation. The practitioner serves to augment and guide this process.

3. *Accept adolescents as individuals.* If adolescents with low feelings of self-worth are to accept themselves as individuals, then those who work with them must similarly recognize their individuality. Adolescents have special needs not only because of their developmental status but also because of their unique personal backgrounds.

4. *Encourage the adolescent to become involved and active.* Adolescents with low self-worth will often avoid participating in activities because they are afraid of failure. As a part of the ITP, specify plans for social activity and rewards for

participation. Because participation with others has been avoided, it may be necessary to increase demands for social interaction gradually.

5. *Listen to what the adolescent tells you.* Your conversations with adolescents will be filled with seemingly irrelevant wanderings. In the course of those wanderings, however, the adolescent may make vague reference to a problem with the hope that you will pursue it. To verbalize a problem openly may be too difficult for an adolescent with low self-worth. An offhand reference may be the adolescent's way of providing an opening for further discussion of a problem area without being too vulnerable.

6. *Encourage the adolescent to speak positively.* In talking with adolescents with low self-esteem, you will quickly see that the majority of their statements are negative. One strategy for change is to encourage the individuals to talk about themselves and about events in positive terms. One counselor tells his adolescent clients to stand in front of the mirror each morning and privately tell themselves, "I am the most important person in the world to me today." Because this is foreign to them, they look at him as though he were kidding. When he explains that he is not and that he would like them to try it for a week, they usually reluctantly agree. After a week they often come back and say, "Hey! That's not bad. It's really a nice way to start the day!"

7. *Include the adolescent in the decision-making process.* As decisions and goals are established, adolescents must see themselves as trusted and able to be part of that process. If the rebellion or maladaptive behavior that brought an adolescent to you results in part from a feeling that his parents will not allow him any decisions, it is critical that you do not replace one authoritarian relationship with another. For some adolescents the ability and willingness to participate may be greater than for others, but the opportunity must be there. Further, their role should be documented in the ITP. In some ways this may look like a contractual arrangement between the client and counselor—and in many ways it is.

8. *Allow the adolescent to make mistakes.* It is unreasonable to expect perfection. Many adolescents who come for counseling complain that they feel their parents expect them to be perfect, that they cannot make a mistake. Often an older brother or sister did very well, and the parents, teachers, and administrators all expect the same of them. Their feelings of self-worth suffer because they do not see themselves as perfect.

As a corollary to allowing adolescents to make mistakes, you may find it necessary to *allow the adolescent to save face.* Oriental cultures place a great emphasis on allowing a person to save face when he or she is humiliated. In a counseling role you may find that, especially during early interviews, you will have to ensure that the adolescent has the chance to avoid embarrassment over a mistake. Once rapport and trust are established this will become less necessary.

9. *Expect failures.* Although this does not sound terribly positive, it is realistic. As a counselor you should not become complacent when you make some progress with a client; it is still possible to have everything seem to fall apart. Such experiences are disheartening but common. For adolescents with lowered self-worth, however, failure may serve to confirm what they have

believed all along—that is, that they are losers. As a counselor you should be ready and willing to start over at some previous point in the progress. Remember, the client may have been establishing a low self-concept for fourteen years before coming to you.

10. *Be an effective model.* Much of what can be gained in the counselor-client relationship occurs because the adolescent sees how someone with positive feelings of self-worth acts. This does not mean that the counselor is a mindless Pollyanna. However, the counselor should exemplify the behaviors that adolescents see as desired.

SUMMARY

Like any inferred concept, self-esteem is difficult to define and assess. The manner in which practitioners try to measure an adolescent's self-concept or self-esteem will depend on their orientation and purpose. For purposes of this chapter, self-concept refers to an organized set of beliefs an individual holds about himself or herself. Self-worth or self-esteem refers to the value that the individual places on those beliefs.

Adolescents who have positive feelings of self-worth have a realistic appraisal of their strengths and weaknesses. They are more likely to be active, to initiate activities, to follow through even after meeting with some failure, and to attribute success to their own efforts and talents.

Adolescents who have negative feelings of self-worth are often oversensitive to criticism. Because they view themselves as inadequate, they take criticism as rejection. They are less likely to engage in activities, and, if they do, their participation is affected by fear of failure.

During adolescence the individual's self-concept is consolidated into a personal identity. It is with this identity of "Who am I?" that the adolescent enters adulthood. Failure to resolve the conflict of identity formation adequately may result in a diffused, unclear identity or the acceptance of a negative identity.

Early- and middle-adolescents place great importance on what others think. This concern is heightened by adolescents' assumption that an invisible audience is excessively concerned with everything that they do. For adolescents with low self-esteem, this concern may be nearly overpowering. They are convinced that others view them as losers and do not like them. To avoid the hurt of rejection, adolescents with low self-esteem may respond by maintaining a mask of hostility, contempt, or mistrust of others. If others see the hostility as unpleasant and avoid them, their feelings of inadequacy are reinforced.

The development of a positive self-concept may be the most important task of adolescence. Likewise, it may be the most important concept for you, as a practitioner, to keep in mind.

6 | Choosing a Vocation

Prior to the industrial revolution of the late eighteenth century, young men or women began their adult vocational roles as early as twelve or fourteen years old. Adolescents had little, if any, input into the decision-making process, because their vocational roles were largely dictated by their parents. When they reached an age at which parents and the local community expected them to start learning a trade, adolescents were assigned to some type of apprenticeship. In some cases this apprenticeship role was as simple as working with the father at his trade or, in the case of girls, assuming increasingly responsible roles around the home by working with the mother. In each case the adolescents' adult roles were assumed to be the same as their parents'. In urban areas a young boy might be apprenticed to a master craftsman. The agreement might be formalized in a written contract specifying that the boy would serve as an indentured servant for a given period of time, and in return the craftsman would provide room and board and train the young man in his trade (Kett, 1977).

By their late teens, young people were already well established in the working world. Even those who practiced law and medicine might be doing so by the age of twenty-one. Incidentally, those professions did not require a college degree—about the only profession that did at that time was ministry (Kett, 1977).

With the onset of the industrial centers and the need for large, cheap labor forces, the picture of youth employment changed somewhat. Although fewer youths were employed as apprentices, a large contingent of this new work force was young men still in their early teens. Young boys were hired to provide unskilled, manual labor in the mills or the mines. Once again, however, even this early occupation was assumed to approximate their adult vocational role. They learned their trades on the job. As the industrial revolution progressed and the need for cheap labor exceeded the available number of young boys and immigrants, young girls also began to work in the mills. (The need for cheap labor persists; the industry that currently makes use of youth labor most generally is the fast-food business. As Kett

Federal laws now prohibit the exploitation of children like this young coal miner from the early part of this century, but adolescents still form a large segment of the "cheap" labor force, especially in "fast food" restaurants. (*left*—Lewis W. Hine, George Eastman House; *below*—© Susan Lapides)

comments, only in commercials are the workers in fast-food restaurants over twenty-one.

As the strength of labor unions increased, and as social agencies became alarmed at the general exploitation of children and youths in industry, laws were enacted to restrict the employment of young people. By the 1930s, when the Great Depression was at its worst, jobs were so valuable that youth labor laws became even more restrictive and young people were forced into extended schooling (Borow, 1976). Thus the traditional apprenticeship and the introduction of young people into the labor market have been largely eliminated. The rationale has been, of course, that the additional schooling will better prepare young people for entering the labor market as adults.

Several writers agree with the President's Commission on Youth (Coleman, 1975) that there is a need to reevaluate both youth labor laws and the structure of education as it relates to future career opportunities. As you will recall from Chapter 4, the Coleman group advocated restructuring the schools to allow academic approval of apprenticeship roles. At present the structure of most schools often hinders the progression of youth toward skilled trades.

The purpose of this chapter is to provide an overview of the process contemporary adolescents go through in their selection of an adult vocational role and the factors that influence their decision. We will also look at the general picture of youth employment today.

VOCATIONAL CHOICE

The previous chapter noted that an essential part of an adolescent's personal identity is the adult vocational role that he or she expects to follow. Havighurst (1972) likewise sees preparation for a career as a primary developmental task of adolescence. The nature of that selection process depends on both general developmental characteristics of the adolescent and the realities of the working world. Further, those "realities" are constantly changing. Borow (1976) for example, has noted that in the years since the Second World War advances in technology continue to alter worker productivity. The purchasing power and standard of living for the average American has never been higher. Currently, however, vocational choice among young people is as likely to be influenced by what young people see as a necessary basis for a personally acceptable standard as by desires for material wealth. Increasingly, young Americans are entering large industrial organizations that are complex, highly structured, and impersonal. Decisions about how one's job will be done are often made at levels remote from the individual worker. Vocational choice is thus likely to be influenced not only by the realities of the working world but by one's own perceptions of and attitudes toward various choices.

ATTITUDES TOWARD VOCATIONS

The occupations young people aspire to are related to how they see the job fulfilling basic needs. However, those needs shift in priority as a young

Table 6-1 LEVEL OF PRESTIGE OF CERTAIN OCCUPATIONS

Top 10 (1 to 10)	*Middle 10 (41 to 50)*	*Low 11* (81 to 90)*
U.S. Supreme Court Justice	Owner-operator, Print shop	Restaurant waiter
Physician	Trained machinist	Taxi Driver
Nuclear Physicist	Farm owner and operator	Janitor
Scientist	Undertaker	Bartender
Government Scientist	Welfare worker, City	Clothes Presser in Laundry
State Governor	Newspaper columnist	Soda Fountain Clerk
Cabinet Member, Federal Government	Policeman	Sharecropper
College Professor	Reporter, Daily Paper	Garbage collector
U.S. Congressman	Radio announcer	Street sweeper
	Bookkeeper	Shoe shiner
		*Two were tied at 81.

Source: Reprinted from "Occupational Prestige in the United States, 1925–63," by R. W. Hodge, P. M. Siegal, and P. H. Rossi, *American Journal of Sociology, 70* (1964): 290–291, by permission of the University of Chicago Press.

person matures, and they continue to be altered at different stages in life. In one study, male and female students in the eighth, tenth, and twelfth grades were asked to tell what they valued in their future careers. The two most important characteristics were the same for both boys and girls across all levels: job satisfaction and personal interest in the job. Beyond that, however, boys were more likely to value salary and achievement of personal goals, whereas girls were more likely to value the chance to make personal contacts and the ability to help others. Both boys and girls rated whether a job is in demand and the opportunity for future advancement low in importance. Older boys and girls were both more likely to rank the relationship of an occupation to one's family life as highly important (Gribbons and Lohnes, 1965). Whether the same ordering would be found among high school students now, fifteen years later, may be questioned. However, the point is that the perception of what is valued in future vocations shifts with age and differs among groups as well as among individuals.

Vocational goals are also influenced by the level of prestige that is associated with various occupations. Studies have repeatedly shown that certain occupations are ranked as highly prestigious, whereas others are ranked very low. Table 6-1 shows the top, middle, and bottom rankings of ninety occupations used in one study (Hodge, Siegal, and Rossi, 1964). When prestige rankings are compared over long periods of time, there is a high degree of stability in relative standing (Hodge et al., 1964; Hakel et al., 1967). High-prestige occupations remain high and low-prestige occupations remain low. Further, the relative ranking of professions is stable across races and sexes (Braun and Bayer, 1973) as well as across national boundaries (Inkeles and Rossi, 1973; Mitchell, 1964).

Adolescents, like adults, are more likely to aspire to the high-prestige job of the physician than to that of the sanitation worker. (*top*—© Paul Fortin/Picture Group; *bottom*—Charles Gatewood)

SEX ROLES

Perhaps in no other area has the problem of sex-role stereotypes been addressed more fully than in the area of career opportunities. Historically women have been barred from a variety of occupations because of their sex. Even with many of the sexual barriers removed, women are still vastly underrepresented in some job categories and overrepresented in others. As was indicated in the previous chapter, sex-role stereotypes describe expected personality characteristics of men and women solely on the basis of their sex. Women were therefore expected to assume nurturant and passive roles with little opportunity to exert leadership and control.

Attitudes about women in the working world are changing; however, the changes in attitudes are not universal. There are some who, on the basis of their own personal and religious convictions, believe that the nurturant role should be the role of women. The degree to which attitudes among adolescents about work roles for men and women are changing is not totally clear. One study (Mitchell, 1977) found that most adolescent girls from the Midwest still expected to pursue only those careers that have been traditionally open to women, such as clerical work, teaching, and nursing. They were aware that a broader range of possible occupations existed. But if they did consider a male-dominated occupation, it was usually a high-prestige or glamorous job, such as doctor, lawyer, or airplane pilot.

A nationwide study of high school seniors found that although some young people still feel that a wife should not work at all and should assume total responsibility for child care, most thought that wives should work either part- or full-time and that responsibilities for child care should be shared. Males tended to be a little more traditional in their views, but the differences in expectations were minor (Herzog, Bachman, and Johnston, 1979).

Although many of the barriers to full employment of women have been eliminated, full equality is still to come. Many of the obstacles that remain are more subtle. For example, if a young woman chooses to enter the field of psychology, it is almost always presumed that she will pursue a career as a clinical psychologist rather than as a research or industrial psychologist. Such barriers, or at least stumbling blocks, are primarily attitudinal, not only in terms of men's attitudes toward women colleagues but also women's attitudes toward themselves. In one review of psychological barriers to occupational aspirations among women, O'Leary (1974) found that many of the attitudinal differences that might be expected on the basis of a traditional stereotyped view of women were not found. O'Leary reported that attitudinal problems were found in the areas of self-esteem, self-confidence, and role conflict. The last conflict results when what society traditionally expects from women is incompatible with expectations of an occupational role. O'Leary noted that part of the difficulty may lie in the lack of a clearly visible variety of women role models who demonstrate success at handling those demands.

VOCATIONAL APTITUDES

Much of the traditional research activity in vocational development has involved using aptitude tests to match individuals to the occupations most suited to their values or interests. Alternatively, similar instruments may be used to screen job applicants to see who is most suited for a given task.

Most adolescents have experience at one time or another with one of a variety of vocational interest inventories. The two most commonly used versions have been and remain the Kuder Occupational Interest Survey (1974) and the Strong Vocational Interest Blank (1943, 1955). In the typical survey, testees are asked to indicate their likes, dislikes, and values. On the basis of their responses, a profile of their interests is produced, which is then compared to interest profiles of those who hold a variety of occupations. Testees are then told which occupations seem to be most matched to their interest patterns.

Alternatively, an adolescent may be tested to determine particular areas of strength or weakness that make him or her suited for certain occupations but less suited for others. An adolescent who shows high verbal or high numerical aptitude but low aptitude in tasks that require dexterity and coordination would be encouraged to set career goals that build on the strengths and minimize the weaknesses.

That aptitudes influence one's success or failure in a given occupation is intuitively obvious. Further a person goes through a degree of automatic selectivity in recognizing his or her own strengths and weaknesses. The adolescent with poor math and spatial skills is not likely to have mechanical engineering as an occupational goal. Just how an individual develops this self-awareness and focuses in on career goals are a concern of a number of theorists, who have tried to make some order of the process.

THEORIES OF VOCATIONAL CHOICE AND DEVELOPMENT

Several attempts have been made to identify the process that adolescents go through in understanding the role of a career in their life and selecting a specific vocation. One view sees career development more broadly in light of the place a person's career holds in reference to more general personal adjustment and growth. The other view focuses attention on the selection of a specific set of vocational goals and plans to achieve those goals.

As with other characteristics of social and psychological growth during adolescence, vocational awareness becomes increasingly complex as young people approach adulthood. Thus it is necessary to account for both the breadth of awareness of alternative vocational roles paired with the increasing precision with which adolescents specify their expected vocational roles.

GINSBERG'S THEORY

Eli Ginsberg and his associates (1951) offered one of the first formulations of a theory of vocational choice. Their research focused on four variables that they saw as influencing adolescents' adult vocational *choice*. The first, the *reality factor*, includes economic, social, and environmental pressures that limit available options. As adolescents mature, they are increasingly likely to make compromises in career goals as a result of their recognition of these realities. The second factor, *education*, influences career development primarily in terms of its preparation for adult career choice. The higher the quality of education, the more options an individual has available. The last two factors, *emotional characteristics* and *personal values,* influence adolescents' career choice by their impact on the range of choices that are comfortable for the individual.

In Ginsberg's view vocational choice develops gradually from about age eleven to about age twenty-four. It does not occur suddenly or rapidly. Instead, adolescents progress through stages of increasingly realistic goal statements.

Ginsberg suggests that at the earliest level, up to about eleven years old, preadolescents' concepts of future occupational roles are largely based in *fantasy.* During that stage children imagine themselves in attractive adult roles with little regard to abilities or opportunity. The fantasy stage is, however, important because it creates a readiness to address the task of vocational choice during adolescence.

From age eleven to about eighteen, adolescents create *tentative* vocational goals that are altered as they progress toward a mature choice. Initially, tentative vocational goals are dominated by adolescents' interests—that is, what they like or dislike. Gradually, adolescents' choices are also influenced by their self-perceived abilities and their assessment of their potential for achieving certain goals. Finally, tentative goals are influenced by adolescents' value systems.

In late adolescence, individuals move into a stage where they make increasingly specific, realistic choices. This *realistic* stage of career choice is further broken into an *exploratory* phase, in which individuals try to implement career choices. As the individual enters a job or college training, the goal *crystallizes* and, gradually, as the goals become clearer and more stable, they become *specific.*

The early vocational fantasies of children are often influenced by people in jobs that children see as exciting, such as those of police officers and fire fighters. (© Beryl Goldberg)

The importance of the Ginsberg approach is that it recognizes the fluid nature of career choice during adolescence and begins to show that the adolescent's concept of career goals changes not only specifically but qualitatively with maturity. It also focuses attention on the decision-making characteristics of vocational choice, the need to compromise choices with a recognition of reality, and the need to capitalize on those characteristics that are likely to lead to success.

SUPER'S THEORY

Perhaps no other writer has had as much impact on our understanding of vocational development as Donald Super (1953, 1957; Super et al., 1963). Super combines aspects of developmental psychology and self-concept theory into a theory of vocational *development*. Vocational development includes both vocational choice and the orderly progression of the individual's view of himself and his relationship to a chosen vocation.

Super sees adolescence as a critical period in which individuals restructure their image of themselves. One's vocational goals and how one rates those goals in light of their indication of personal self-worth are important elements in one's total self-esteem. For example, two people choose truck driving as a possible occupation. One person sees it as "really exciting. I love the freedom of being on the road." The second sees the same job as one that "I can get because I am not able enough to do anything else." The values that they place on the occupation and therefore themselves are different. The more positive a person's feelings of adequacy, the more likely he or she is to have positive attitudes about a chosen occupation. Because the adolescent with a positive self-image is likely to have a valid assessment of personal strengths and weaknesses, the career choice is also likely to conform to pressures of reality. However, "reality" is also viewed as subject to change.

Like Ginsberg, Super sees vocational development progressing in a continuous, forward moving, orderly fashion through adolescence and into adulthood. However, Super more clearly specifies that vocational development continues through adult years. Super identifies five stages in the process of lifelong vocational development, beginning with *growth* (birth to early adolescence), *exploration* (early adolescence to young adulthood), *establishment* of a career (young adulthood to middle age), *maintenance* of a career (middle age to old age), and *decline* (old age.) These stages are further broken down into more specific, associated tasks.

During the exploration phase of adolescence, the young person must *crystallize* a vocational preference. By this, Super means that the adolescents' self-image gradually takes form as vocational options are evaluated. Eventually the adolescent makes some tentative choices. Next the adolescent must *specify* the choice. During late adolescence one is expected to convert general vocational goals into more specific occupational choices and to make a commitment. At that point the individual may recognize that additional training is necessary to achieve the more specific choice or that an entry job is a necessary step in achieving the goal. It is then the task of the late adolescent

to *implement* that choice. That is, the young person actively attempts to initiate the necessary sequence of events to achieve the specific goal.

During the establishment stage of early adulthood, when the young person has entered into the beginning stages of a career, he or she is then expected to stabilize and adjust to his or her role within the chosen vocation.

There may be during this stage a continued period of trial. That is, the individual may find that the initial concept of the job was unrealistic or that the specific employer was not compatible with personal values. Thus there may be some shifting in roles and positions. Gradually, however, this trial period is replaced by a commitment to a vocation and a desire to advance and improve.

Super's theory differs from Ginsburg's in that it contends that vocational development is a lifelong task extending beyond adolescence and young adulthood. In addition, Super calls attention to the fact that vocational development, although important in and of itself, is part of the more general process of self-concept development and must be viewed from this broader perspective.

HOLLAND'S THEORY

An alternative approach to vocational choice is found in John Holland's (1959, 1973) writings. Holland's approach is based on the assumption that choice of vocation is influenced primarily by the personality of the individual making the choice. His research has led him to conclude that there are six basic personality types related to vocational choice. The relationship among the six is seen in Figure 6-1.

Figure 6-1 HOLLAND'S HEXAGONAL MODEL

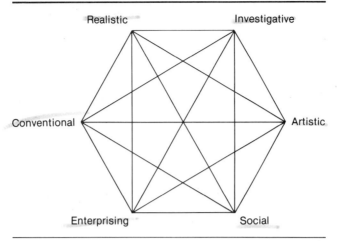

Source: ACT Research Report No. 29: J. L. Holland et al., An Empirical Occupation Classification Derived from a Theory of Personality and Intended for Practice and Research, (Iowa City, Ia.: The American College Testing Program, 1969). Reproduced with permission.

Holland defines the *realistic* person as favoring occupations built around objective, concrete tasks. Realistic people prefer jobs that require physical manipulation, such as agricultural or technical occupations. *Investigative* people, in contrast, prefer working with abstractions. These people are often found in scholarly or scientific roles. *Artistic* people tend to prefer creative careers in the arts, music, or drama. Artistic people view themselves as sensitive and more interested in subjective than objective reality. *Social* people prefer to deal with others and typically assume roles in counseling or religion. They are commonly seen as leaders. *Enterprising* people are highly self-confident and self-assertive and choose occupations in which they can accumulate recognition and power. These individuals often choose sales or supervisory occupations. Finally, *conventional* people choose vocations that lead to social approval but that are not likely to demand originality of thought. Clerical positions with accounting tasks that have clearly correct, acceptable answers are preferred by conventional individuals.

Holland goes on to say that one's choice of vocation is influenced by one's personality because each occupational environment has characteristics that correspond to the attributes of the personality types. Thus an individual gravitates to a work environment that provides the best fit with his or her personality.

Very rarely does an individual fall perfectly into one of the six categories. Rather, each individual has some combination of traits with certain facets more pronounced than others.

Holland's theory reflects a sophisticated extension of the traditional model in vocational counseling, in which a counselor attempts to guide individuals in career exploration on the basis of a personality or interest profile. However, in addition to the clearly applied character of such a model, Holland also provides evidence that the selection process is not capricious but predictable in light of individual preference.

SOME LIMITS ON VOCATIONAL THEORIES

Although each of the three theories described in this chapter, and other theories not covered, offer a perspective on vocational choice and development, they are not without problems. Osipon (1975) has shown that all the theories are based primarily on data on white males and that the validity of the models for describing vocational choice and career development among women and minorities is open to question. Further, the inherent danger in the misuse of models such as Holland's is that such categories will lead to oversimplified personality-occupational stereotypes.

YOUTH EMPLOYMENT

It is widely recognized that the rate of unemployment among youths is much higher than among adults. Further, the unemployment rate among black and other minority youths is nearly three times that of their white peers (Table 6-2). Moreover, youth labor is hardest hit by recession and economic instability because the young workers lack seniority or are employed as unskilled laborers.

Despite the figures in Table 6-2, the actual rate of youth unemployment is not altogether clear. Because of the way unemployment rates are computed, youth unemployment rates are very subject to error. Employment statistics are based *only* on those who are out of work *and* are looking for work. High school and college students who are looking for part-time employment are included in the figures, but school dropouts who are unemployed but who, in their frustration, have given up looking for work are not included. Even the rates of students who are employed or seeking part-time employment are not all the same. Those attending a two-year college, for example, are much more likely to work while going to school than those attending a four-year college (U.S. Department of Labor, 1976).

A variety of factors serve to keep unemployment rates among youths high. First, because they lack a skilled trade, young people are at a disadvantage in

Table 6-2 PERCENTAGES OF UNEMPLOYED YOUTHS AND ADULTS

	Whites	Blacks, and Other Minorities
Men, 20 years and older	5.1	8.3
Women, 20 years and older	3.5	10.2
Men, 16 to 19 years old	14.1	34.8
Women, 16 to 19 years old	13.9	35.9

Source: U.S. Department of Labor, Special Labor Force Report No. 218 (Washington, D.C.: U.S. Government Printing Office, 1979), p. 9.

An important part of the preparation for adult vocational roles is the acquisition of skills related to those roles. (© Billy E. Barnes)

competing for job openings. Also, some writers have argued that a high minimum wage works against early entrance into the job market. High costs for unskilled and semiskilled youths price them out. There is a period of training for most occupations, but young workers are seen as a poor investment because the chances of their long-range commitment to a job are low.

Thus a vicious cycle starts with the youths' need for training in skilled trades and the inability of youths, especially minority youths, to get that training. This, in turn, may lead to chronic high unemployment among the young and, among minority youths, to a feeling of alienation. It is not surprising that a recent Gallup Poll (1979) found that nonwhites were considerably more pessimistic than whites about chances of future employment.

The picture is not, however, totally bleak. From 1980 to 1990, there will be a drop of nearly 20 percent in the total number of sixteen- to twenty-four-year-olds in the national labor market. Thus, if the number of positions available to youths remains relatively stable, then there will be an automatic decline in the youth unemployment rate. The drop, however, will not likely represent a significant change in the principle problems of youth employment, especially early access to the skilled labor market.

ENTERING THE JOB MARKET

Many teens have a part-time job while in high school or college, but the time at which they leave school and attempt to find full-time employment still represents a major transition in their life. Achieving financial self-sufficiency represents the final stage of establishing independence from parents.

Although true financial independence may not occur immediately, the path is set. Further, full employment represents a principal element in one's personal identity. Finally, the first job seemingly plays some part in a person's long-term career goal.

Given all these characteristics, it would seem likely that young people would devote a great deal of time and thought to deciding about their first job. Actually, most young people select their first job after school in a very haphazard fashion (Singell, 1966; Orstein, 1975). Young people give little thought to the decision, and most simply take what is available. There is a certain pragmatic reality that any job may be better than none. But, although the first job may not bear *directly* on long-term career goals, the first job *is* related to later likelihood of unemployment and the level of wages one will earn (Stephanson, 1978). In addition, youths who are employed full-time or part-time while still in school are also at a career advantage over those who are not.

VIGNETTE 6-1
Teen Tycoons

When young people first start job hunting, they find that they are faced with what seems to be an unsolvable problem. Job notifications often sound appealing but usually insist that applicants must have experience. The young person is left with the unfortunate dilemma of needing experience to get a job and needing a job to get experience. This seeming "catch-22" can be very frustrating. One alternative that some young people have tried is to create their own business. Presented below are some examples of young entrepreneurs who have established themselves as businesspeople in their own right. Owning a small business does not necessarily mean that a young person will remain in that field for life. But being active shows initiative and motivation. When personnel managers in placement offices interview applicants, they often see "experience" more broadly than just direct experience in the job that they are filling. Almost any job experience is valuable. Young people should not be afraid to indicate that they have been employed in jobs only marginally related to the advertised one and that they show motivation to achieve and willingness to work. Presenting yourself to a personnel manager as a motivated, industrious individual may be more important than having directly relevant experience in the job area. In the meantime, consider the possibility of establishing your own business. Do the cases below give you any ideas?

Not everyone these days is suffering from what President Carter has called a "crisis of confidence." In fact, some young Americans are decidedly optimistic, because for them the American Dream is still very much alive.

Take, for example, Mike Glickman, who spells his name, "G, as in GREAT, L-I-C-K-M-A-

Source: Jessica Holland, "Teen Tycoons," *New York Times Magazine* (August 19, 1979): 44–49. © 1979 by the New York Times Company. Reprinted by permission.

N!" Mike says he led a "typical adolescent life" until the age of 16 when a friend of the family, a real-estate broker, asked him to deliver brochures of house listings to other realtors in the Los Angeles area. Soon after, he started his own business distributing listings throughout the real-estate community. Today, Mike is 19 years old and his firm, Brokers Specialized Services, has 30 employees who can be seen slipping in and out of greater Los Angeles real-estate offices, wearing T-shirts which say: "I'm Wendy, ask me about my service," or "Nothing beats the way we deliver your sheets."

Mike also became the youngest licensed real-estate broker with the San Fernando Valley Board of Realtors earlier this year and has so far sold over $1 million worth of property.

One of Mike's biggest obstacles as a teen-age entrepreneur was his family. According to Mike, his family wanted him to enter a profession. "My brother is entering U.C.L.A. law school this year. He was always a great student, and a varsity football player," says Mike. "But that stuff never appealed to me."

Mike says that he is "too busy to worry about the economy. Every day, I wake up with a new idea for business. I want to be a grand businessman, you know? I expect to make over $100,000 this year."

Thirteen-year-old Carson Levit, on the other hand, has given the economy a good bit of thought. What this Marin County, Calif., child has done in the stock market since March 1978 would turn many professional money managers green with envy. Without the advantage of being able to buy stock on margin (because he is a minor), he has parlayed an initial investment of $1,000, saved from paper routes, to over $8,000. When he grows up he hopes to be a combination professional basketball player and investment banker. Although his grandfather was California's director of finance under Gov. Edmund G. (Pat) Brown, Carson says that neither his father, a lawyer, nor his mother, who is active in local politics, has ever actively invested in the market. His own interest was spurred a year and a half ago when he read "The Stock Market Primer," by Claude N. Rosenberg Jr., while he was on vacation with his family.

After returning from his vacation, Carson visited the San Francisco offices of major stockbrokers to chat about what he had learned from the book. "No one paid much attention to me," he says. "I don't think they'd ever had a kid in there before and they just didn't know how to act."

The exception was Alan Baer of Kidder Peabody, who became Carson's broker. Carson speaks to Baer sometimes three times a day to check on the market and give buy and sell orders. For a long time the kids at his school thought he was joking when he told them he had to call his stockbroker.

Carson follows companies in most of the major business publications and also reads stock charts. "I have a theory," he says, "that you only have to be right in the market half the time if you know when to cut your losses. What I do is let my profits run and cut my losses. I put a 10 percent stop loss on all my stocks."

The first stocks he bought in March 1978 were Teledyne at $67 and Perrier at $8. In June 1978 he sold Teledyne for $116 and Perrier for $14. At current prices he thinks Amdahl, Brae Company and Verbatim Corporation are attractive buys. Reluctant to reveal too many of his secrets, Carson ends his interview with a giggle and a bizarre excuse among businessmen. "Sorry," he says, "I have to finish cleaning my room."

While Carson thinks that "oil is the only thing holding us back," Brad Pelo, a 16-year-old who lives in Orem, Utah, agrees with the President that some people are unnecessarily pessimistic. "If you've made up your mind and you have the potential," says Brad, "there won't be much to worry about in your life, no matter what the economy does." Brad, the third oldest child and the only entrepreneur in a family of 10 children, says, "I made up my mind in my preteen years that I was never going to be the normal middle-American person. I made up my mind I'd be everything from

President of the United States to a millionaire tycoon."

Though he is too young to run for elective office just yet, he is on his way to becoming a tycoon of sorts. After learning how to use audio-visual equipment in a class for eighth graders, he hit upon the notion that real-estate agents could save time, money and untold gallons of gasoline if they had videotapes of their listings to show clients in the office. He took the idea to the manager of a local real-estate office, Mildred Snow.

Mrs. Snow liked the idea and decided it should be broadened to include a wide range of services for builders, contractors, appraisers and other construction-related firms. She, along with four investors, formed a corporation, All Services Inc. Mrs. Snow is the president and Brad is a vice president in charge of audio and visual communications. By 1980 Brad projects his income at between $3,000 and $5,000 a month, 10 percent of which he will tithe to the Mormon Church.

"From the start," he says, "I've been treated like a person by everyone at the business, not like a kid." It hasn't been easy for him at school though. "At this point, the kids at school are a little uncomfortable around me. They ask 'What did you do last summer?' and you don't want to brag but you tell them and they feel intimidated because they just bagged groceries, so you lose some friends. But I feel comfortable with what I'm doing. I love the adult world. And I'll be O.K. when the kids have graduated from high school."

North and south, east and west, there are still plenty of young people who remain optists about their nation and its resiliency. Says Roger Conner, "People say, 'Oh, my, what's gonna happen with all this inflation?' but I know that we can handle any situation that comes along in this country. I'm very optimistic."

And based on the evidence in his life, he has every reason to be confident. In 1973, at age 13, Roger visited a flower shop as part of Career Day in Middletown, Ohio. In 1975, at age 15, he started selling flowers out of his basement. In 1977, at age 17, he bought his own flower shop for $12,000. Today, with two outlets, Flowers by Roger is the third largest shop in Middletown. Sales in 1978 were over $100,000.

Roger initially met some resistance to his business ventures. His father hoped his interest in flowers would pass and that, like him, Roger would become a carpenter. "When I started, everyone was perplexed. They couldn't understand why a kid would want to take on such a lot of responsibility. But I love to work and I've always loved flowers."

Perhaps the most famous child-operated business in the country is Kidco Ltd. Ventures, which was formed by the Cessna children— NeNe, 11, Bette, 13, Dickie, 14, and June, 16— in 1976 in Ramona, Calif. These four began by cleaning the streets and then started selling manure from their father's horse stable. Later on, they patented and sold a gopher exterminating kit. Most recently Kidco bought a 21-acre California coast town, Gorda, for $585,000. The town includes a general store, restaurant, gas station and seven houses. Warner Brothers is filming the story of Kidco.

According to Bette, all the children together "are close to being a millionaire." According to Dickie, who became president of the company at age 11, "If adults can do it, so can kids. There are 10 kids in the family and so by the time we were all fed, there wasn't much spending money left. And once we started Kidco we could help other kids by giving them jobs."

These are just a few of the teen-age tycoons who have found ways to prosper in what are seen by many parents to be "bad times." Who says youth is wasted on the young?

Perhaps the function that early employment serves is to improve an adolescent's vocational self-concept. Some have argued that the individual adolescent's attitudes about self and work may be the most important factors in career achievement (Coleman, 1971). When those attitudes are positive, the adolescent has less difficulty in adapting to the demands of the workaday world. When those attitudes are negative, the adolescent becomes alienated and views career opportunities as out of reach and therefore not worth striving for.

There is a higher likelihood of negative attitudes about self and work among poor black and poor white youths. In reviewing difficulties reported by managers of manpower agencies who had extensive experience with disadvantage youth, Kalachek (1969) found the principle problem to be one of attitude. Repeatedly counselors found young clients "alienated, discouraged, immature, lacking self-esteem and not conversant with accepted middle-class work values" (p. 7). On the other hand, high school youths who are internally motivated, who see career gains and rewards as resulting from their own initiative, experience higher rates of employment success and less unemployment than those who are externally motivated (Andrisani, 1978). As practitioners, therefore, the most beneficial intervention you may attempt in improving adolescents' career opportunities is to operate on their self-images. Changes in self-concept and self-esteem among minority and lower-income youths may do more to diminish employment disadvantages than any other factor.

It should, however, be emphasized that most young people do not have negative attitudes about work and employment. Indeed, their attitudes overall are strikingly similar to older workers' (Andrisani, 1978). If there are differences in attitudes, they lie in adolescents' perceptions that career development is *less central* to what constitutes personal fulfillment or personal satisfaction. Today's youth view work as more than simply a means to accumulate money and material goods. Instead, they see a career as having value only if it leads to personal growth and fulfillment. Youths are also likely to feel that their careers should not displace other intrinsically valued roles in their personal lives, such as their family or personal well-being. Overall, adolescents view a career as essential for personal growth and fulfillment but not primary (Havighurst and Gottlieb, 1975).

SUMMARY

Although adolescents' decisions regarding careers are an important part of the identity formation process, those decisions are not isolated from other decisions and processes inherent in the transition to adulthood. Neither is career development confined to adolescent development. It is a lifelong process. Educators and counselors should be aware that premature closure on a career choice may interfere with the adolescent's search for a personal identity by cutting off the exploration of alternative roles too soon. Conversely, prolonging the decision too long may result in a failure to achieve a stable identity before entering adulthood.

Career decisions during adolescence, although setting the stage for adult career development, should not be seen as forever unchangeable. Indeed, only a minority of high school seniors will be employed in jobs resembling their expected occupation. The development of a concept of oneself in an occupation is a continuous process. As adolescents mature conceptually and socially, their concepts of the role of work in their lives and their working roles become more complex. Further, those perceptions are balanced by an improved perception of reality. If self-esteem is low, those perceptions become distorted, and expectations become unrealistically high or low.

Career choice is an important element in identity formation. Schools should provide educational and guidance experiences that facilitate that process. Career development experiences should provide opportunities for adolescents to develop positive attitudes toward themselves and work, to acquire knowledge of alternative occupational roles, and to develop skills basic to the decision-making process. Career decisions should be considered an integral part of the adolescent's emerging self-concept. The types of career goals adolescents set are likely to reflect personality predispositions as well as general feelings of personal adequacy. In addition to acquiring the more general skills and abilities related to vocational choice, adolescents should be encouraged to develop needed job entry skills.

To be maximally responsive to career development needs during adolescence, schools may need some restructuring. Most schools are currently organized with college as the primary post-high school role toward which a student is oriented. To respond to career-oriented needs may require alternative experiences not now a part of the usual curriculum. This does not imply that we totally reject the current educational structure—it obviously works quite well for many students. It does not, however, work for all. Education that builds on experiences like apprenticeship may be more directly relevant to the long-term development of vocational skills.

7 | Parents and Adolescents

When I was a boy of fourteen my father was so ignorant I could hardly stand to have the old man around. But, when I got to be twenty-one I was astonished at how much he had learned in seven years.

MARK TWAIN

If there is a specifically turbulent part of adolescence, it is probably associated with adolescents' needs to establish psychological independence from their parents. Their dependent relationship of childhood must be altered as they near the independent status needed in adulthood. During this shift parents and adolescents are often at odds with one another. Parents still see the need to exert control over their children, whom they regard dependent and immature. Adolescents feel treated "like a child" and prefer to think of themselves as adults, worthy of adult trust and adult responsibilities. Some joke that adolescence *is* a period of storm and stress—*for the parents.*

Parents, when faced with this transition, may find themselves talking to a daughter or son who is suddenly argumentative and hostile. The teenager, on the other hand, views the parents as old-fashioned and, as Mark Twain puts it, ignorant. The problem for the adolescent is in part that the dependent relationship of childhood that is being abandoned is secure and they are not sure of the value of adult independence. For the adolescent both alternatives are thus attractive: although adult independence is enticing, the dependent relationship of childhood is secure. Parents may recognize intellectually that their adolescent must become independent in order to move out of the house and into adult maturity, but they may still relish the dependent relationship that their child has with them.

During late childhood and preadolescence, parents often see their child as cooperative and cheerful. Children see their parents in an idealized fashion: their mothers and fathers always right and all knowing. The child is thus motivated to cooperate and in general looks to parents and authority figures for guidance. Parents serve their children by providing for their basic needs and offering a secure home environment. Both parents and children become increasingly secure within this relationship.

As teens begin to see themselves as individuals and start to prepare for adult roles, then it becomes necessary for them to leave the dependent role of childhood behind. They strive to achieve emotional and psychological independence, particularly from parents. Adolescents' need to free themselves or, as Ausubel (Ausubel, Montemayor, and Svajian, 1977) describes it, emancipate themselves from their parents and childhood, may also be a source of fear and anxiety. The dependence of childhood is certain. The independence of adulthood is uncertain.

In their struggle to establish themselves as independent, adolescents may resort to a variety of maneuvers, including passive resistance, open hostility, or both. They may refuse to participate in activities with the family or to cooperate with parents. Arguments with parents may take the form, "You just don't understand," or "I'm the only one who can't do that." Parents at this point may become distressed that their adolescent is causing a major disruption in the household and may fear that this new behavior reflects the way the adolescent is going to go through life. In more tumultuous transitions, parents may become mutually hostile toward the adolescent.

Sometimes the adolescent *does* seriously disrupt the family, and the family may need professional help. In family counseling it is not uncommon to find that the parents are divided on issues concerning their adolescent and that the adolescent has seemingly tried to foster that division by pitting the parents against each other. In counseling families who have problems with their adolescents, it is very important not to take sides too quickly. The "fault" for the disruption rarely falls in one place.

Whether or not the emancipation process is tumultuous for a given family may depend in large part on the patterns of family interaction during childhood. If the transition is anticipated and if parents provide opportunities for increased responsibility, self-management, and independence throughout childhood and early and middle adolescence, then the need for greater independence during late adolescence will not be as sharply defined. The transition is less likely to be rocky. In families in which the teenager is not allowed to participate in the decision-making process, the transition may be more stormy.

The transition to adult independence is not a sudden one, and parents should not feel that they must "lose control" overnight. The adolescent's need to remain *dependent* dissipates gradually but continuously. Likewise, parents need to decrease the degree of control they exert over the adolescent and increase their expectations of self-control steadily. By late adolescence the shift to adult independence and responsibility should be nearly complete.

Establishing emotional and psychological independence from one's parents does not necessarily require physical separation. But some during late adolescence may need the added physical distance (such as being away at school) to solidify their psychological independence and form an identity with which to enter adulthood. Historically this was accomplished by sending the youth to another family to live and work as an apprentice. At the end of the apprenticeship, the adolescent was financially and psychologically independent of his parents (Kett, 1977). Among contemporary adolescents

that same process must be achieved while the young person is still financially dependent on his parent.

Other adults in positions of authority should also recognize that, as part of adolescents' emancipation efforts, they too may be the object of rebellion or hostility. They too must be responsive to the differing needs for dependence and independence within and among groups of adolescents.

When the struggle for emotional independence takes its form in hostility, belligerence, and perhaps some mild delinquency, the conflict may be very stressful for both parents and adolescents. Adolescents pleading not to be treated as children may act very childish. Parents driven to distraction may feel angry and resentful, which in turn leads to feeling guilty. Further, many professionals unwittingly place a heavy guilt burden on many caring parents by emphasizing the impact of neglectful or abusive parenting on psychological maladjustment. If parents see their adolescent as sullen, argumentative, and hostile, they are likely to blame themselves and try to determine what they did wrong. We need to reassure that the resistance and antagonism of middle adolescence are not necessarily their fault. We need to encourage parents to develop new modes of communication with their adolescents. On the other hand, parents should not presume that because the motive to establish emotional independence is a normal part of the adolescent transition, they should be benignly tolerant of their adolescent's outbursts. A balance that includes respect for the rights and needs of both the adolescent *and* the rest of the family needs to be achieved.

VIGNETTE 7-1
The Reluctant Companion

Can you remember the times when your family would visit an aunt or an old friend of your parents? Try to remember how you felt on those occasions, especially when you were about thirteen or fourteen years old. If you were like most young people, you were usually reluctant to go and probably voiced that reluctance. This vignette is directed toward helping parents cope with their feelings about those confrontations. What suggestions might you offer to a parent who consults you and says, "My teenager doesn't want to go anywhere with us as a family. What can we do?"

Somewhere between the beginning of the sixth grade and the end of junior high that most tiresome of creatures, the teenager, finds himself almost unable to bear being seen in the presence of his family, particularly, of his father and mother. This shrinking from being recognized as a member of a specific family stretches from an unwillingness to sit with them in the same pew at church to hurrying on ahead at the department stores or even to a flat-out refusal to do anything so wildly peculiar as going out to dinner with all or any of these embarrassing relatives with whom he lives. The teenager's unspoken "what if someone sees me?" attitude shows a reluctance as great as one might feel about being found to be consorting with known criminals.

The only place the average teenager will dine in public with his family is one of the fast food chains, and then he will feel called upon to sit separately from his nearest and dearest. They were, of course, the ones who paid for the three cheeseburgers with everything, the large chocolate milkshake, the big order of french fries, and the last-minute coke and pie ordered just before leaving in an effort to sustain life between this pitstop and home.

This phenomenon is so very common that anyone eating out or merely sitting in the waiting room of any large department store can quickly spot suffering parents and their mid-life offspring. There is always the Junior Miss who is willing to accept the new shoes and slacks suit that are exorbitant in price and found after two hours of trying on every possibility in the store, but who neither offers to carry the packages nor walks with the exhausted purchaser. Some parents feel especially hurt, almost betrayed, when this happens. This is almost always true of parents for whom this child is their first to enter puberty. Somehow the parents feel it isn't fair. They have been willing to pay to satisfy their child's every need and desire; they are eager to lavish time, effort, and love on him. Naturally, they are stunned to discover that Junior will accept any material gifts handed out but wants to share none of their companionship. The natural reaction is hurt and anger. Even case-hardened parents who have suffered and survived the turmoils of adolescence with another or several other children feel these pangs off and on.

Just as most remedies for the common cold only treat the symptoms, home remedies for surviving your adolescent without undue emotional stress also only treat the surface problems. Like the cold, the best solution is time. Meanwhile, the parents must live as comfortably as possible. The unwillingness of the teenager to accompany his parents anywhere is only one of the affronts with which the average

Source: Excerpted from Martha S. Shull, "Your Teenager as Reluctant Companion." © St. Meinrad Archabbey, St. Meinrad, Ind. 47577. Reprinted with permission from *Marriage and Family Living* magazine (August, 1978): 5–9.

parent must cope. As adults, parents must first examine the double-pronged nature of the teenager's feelings. As is the nature of the beast, the teenager is pulled two ways all the time: forward towards adulthood and independence and back to security and the dependent life within the family. Parents need to respond with a mixture of sensitivity, rooted in memories of their own adolescent feelings, and common sense.

Remembering is of vital importance in living with the teenager. How many parents remember hating to go every Sunday afternoon to visit dear, old Aunt Sally or having Sunday dinner with Grandma and Grandpa? Remember going to parties and shrinking inside every time your father told another corny story and then had the nerve to laugh at it? Remember having to go out to dinner with your parents rather than getting to go to the school basketball game and dance afterwards? Even worse, remember going to the school football games with your family and having to sit with them? Remember those horrible Sunday afternoon rides and those terrible vacations that were intended to show you America's beauties and to educate you?

When you dared to moan and groan a little, your mother was hurt. She was giving you the opportunities she had missed as a girl with the sole purpose of enriching you as an adult human being; your father was angry that they were wasting the money on such ingratitude. Looking back on all that misery now, the saddest thing is that both of your parents were right and you would be the first to agree with them. But that's because the tables are turned. Now you are the parent who has spent a staggering sum on two days for the family at Disneyworld and your weary teenagers are practically refusing to visit any other place with you, no matter what its historic interest or beauty.

There were always the families who took along a friend for their adolescent. This solution, of course, is frequently a good one, but it certainly doesn't work for all families, espe-cially those with more than one child. One would need a Greyhound Bus to accommodate my family doubled. One must always consider the plain fact that Mama or Papa might not want the burden of guest-effort every trip or the expense of another chow-hound even if all the family is going out for is an ice-cream cone. Two triple-scoop eaters in the family are enough.

Most adolescents are intensely self-conscious on social occasions and pose a real dilemma for parents. A teenager may feel uncomfortable socially since he is neither grown-up nor one of the little kids, but may desperately need to be exposed to such occasions in order to learn how to function at such gatherings. Junior needs the experience of helping with your dinner parties, going to First Communion breakfasts, wedding receptions, retirement dinners or any of the other formalities of life.

Some adolescents are self-conscious and nervous about making mistakes; they have not yet learned that other people are so concerned about themselves that they don't have time or the inclination to notice other people's behavior unless it is terribly beyond the acceptable. Teenagers tend to equate adulthood with seriousness and sobriety. They do not expect their parents to have a good time. I can remember being horrified by my parents' behavior at a wedding dinner. Why, they were having a splendid time!

My oldest son reminded me of my own teenage self the other night. We had been to see a movie and he had been embarrassed to hear me laughing at the funny lines. Even though he did not sit anywhere near me and had not acknowledged my presence, my laughing spoiled the whole movie for him. What if someone had heard me and known that the woman laughing was his mother?

Lots of teenagers, just like the one I once was, have trouble separating their parents' roles of mother and dad from their parents' reality as human beings. Everyone needs to remember and ask himself just when he realized that his mother and father were human beings with needs, preferences, ideas, and feelings instead of cardboard stereotypes. Learning that human beings play many roles and have many facets to their personality and that their parents and their parents' friends are genuine people with real feelings and emotions, in spite of their advanced years, are important realizations that every human being painfully arrives at as he struggles toward real adulthood....

Part of remembering your growing-up years in order to understand your child is remembering also how your parents handled the situation. After all, none of these situations are new. No one is putting an enormous burden of guilt on his child just because he is disappointed in his child's behavior and shows it. Use common sense here. If your spouse, sister, best friend or brother behaved that way, wouldn't you be surprised and not the least bit hesitant about saying so? If your child insists that he is now half-grown and nearly adult and deserves adult privileges, he deserves all the disapprobation meted out to rude and thoughtless adults. Your child who has been unpleasant and essentially childish had better decide which he really is: child or adult. If adulthood is what he is pushing for, he has to behave in conventional adult ways of courtesy and thoughtfulness....

There are many...family outings that definitely do not qualify for the "go or else" treatment. No one needs to take a rude, unwilling guest to dinner, to the movies, to the theatre, to a baseball game, to Disneyland, etc. In fact, anyone who was intolerably rude on the visit to Uncle Charlie ought not to be invited to go to Disneyland or dinner or wherever. He obviously has just demonstrated that he does not like family outings. This should be assumed by Mama. Here is where remembering how you hated some of those trips and meals out comes in handy. Say so; tell Junior Miss, "I remember how much I always hated Sunday dinner at Baker's restaurant with Grandma and Grandpa." Give her a big smile, a hug, and tell her cheerfully, "That's why I made reservations at the Gilded Fox for only the four of us. You know how the little kids adore steak." Then make your exit before she has anything to contribute.

Not taking ungrateful, unappreciative eaters to restaurants is just common sense. Did you ever go out again with the couple that embarrassed you at the Gilded Fox with their outrageously boorish behavior? Of course not, common sense told you not to throw good money after bad and never subject yourself to an evening with those boors again. Face it; Junior is a boor. He eats enormous amounts of food, but only food he really likes. He is gastronomic ignoramus, makes no effort to talk at the table or carry his weight as a guest, which is really the role he is in when Papa is treating. He may even have been hostile about wearing the appropriate clothing. Whatever made Junior think that his blue jeans and letter shirt would be appropriate when you had bludgeoned Papa into a tie and you had struggled into your tightest girdle so that you could wear your only long dress?

Surely Junior or Junior Miss does not really believe that he or she is so marvelous and wonderful that you'll lavish any amount of money on him or her just for the pleasure of that type of company? Either the poor dear is living in a dream world or he needs a dictionary to look up the meaning of pleasure, company, appropriate and guest.

Plan your outing. Get dressed and tell Junior to make a peanut butter and jelly sandwich if he gets hungry. Make it clear that you're not angry with him; you just don't want the pleasure of his type of company. Hopefully after several hassle-free evenings when he has stayed home and fixed his own supper, done his own dishes, and then had to endure his "dippy" brothers and sisters telling all about what a "super" time they had, Junior may change his tune.

Don't count those clichéd chickens too soon though. Some children do grow up and do acquire adult emotions and minds as well as adult bodies; unfortunately, there are many who never do. Remember your guests at the Gilded Fox. No one could accuse them of being under twenty, but no one could really assert that they are fully grown up if they remain unpleasant guests and spoil their friends' evenings. As adults, they get ignored and remain uninvited. If Junior Miss behaves like them, that will happen to her. She's got a better chance of growing up to be a charming woman if she is not coddled, catered to or her rudeness tolerated. Give your kid a chance; tell him to cook his own supper tonight; you're going dancing with Dad.

PARENTING STYLES

The general pattern of parents' interaction with their children and adolescents has an impact on the psychological and social development of their offspring. In their attempts to socialize their children, parents interact in ways that can be characterized, first, in terms of the degree of parental control they exert, and, second, in terms of the emotional support they provide (Thomas et al., 1974; Becker, 1964). The words *parental control* should not be confused with "overrestrictiveness." Parents who exercise firm control over their children may be just as warm and supportive as some who exert little control. Conversely, parents who use little control may be just as cold and rejecting as some high-control parents. Becker (1964) sees the relationship between these two dimensions of parenting style in the form shown in Figure 7-1.

Figure 7-1 BECKER'S MODEL OF PARENTING STYLES

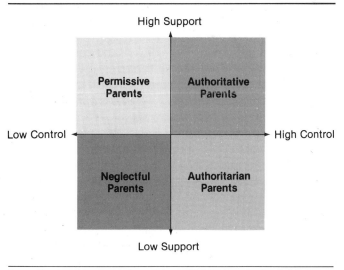

Source: Reprinted by permission of the publisher, from *Family Socialization and the Adolescent* by Darwin L. Thomas, Viktor Gecas, Andrew Weigert, Elizabeth Rooney (Lexington, Mass.: Lexington Books, 1974).

Baumrind (1968) describes four types of parenting styles that coincide roughly with the four combinations of control and support seen in Becker's diagram (Thomas et al., 1974). *Permissive* parents provide high emotional support but exert little parental control. Adolescents from permissive homes have the right to make their own decisions even if the decisions are in basic conflict with the parents' wishes. Baumrind suggests that the permissive style is associated with development of creative thinking, because the children are allowed and encouraged to try out a variety of ideas and life-styles. On the other hand, Baumrind also points out that although the parents may assume a permissive stance in a caring fashion, the child or adolescent may interpret their behavior as uncaring. The lack of assertive parental input may lead the adolescent to feel that the parents do not care what happens and may further result in feelings of insecurity.

Authoritarian parents provide low emotional support but high control. Authoritarian parents maintain absolute authority over what the child is to do, permitting little or no choice for the child. This type of parental style is often associated with adolescent delinquency, high aggression, low self-esteem, and low religiosity in the offspring (Thomas et al., 1974). Because adolescents from authoritarian homes are not allowed any input into decision making (even when decisions concern them), they may develop feelings of worthlessness. They feel incapable of making decisions. Adolescents from authoritarian homes will sometimes replace the parental decision maker with another equally autocratic substitute, who provides an attractive alternative. In some cases this decision maker may be a religious leader or it may be a peer group.

Authoritative parents also provide high control, but control is paired with warmth and strong emotional support. The authoritative parenting style is labeled by some researchers as democratic, although that label may be misleading. Although the child or adolescent has input in the decision-making process within the family, the final responsibility for decisions rests with the parents, who can overrule the child or children. As Baumrind notes, however, the balance of control and release of control in the authoritative household may need to shift during the adolescent transition to provide for an increased degree of independent decision making by the adolescent. Authoritative families tend to produce dependent and conforming offspring who do not engage in divergent or creative thinking, but there is some research to the contrary. Goertzel and Goertzel (1962), in a study of eminent and creative people, found that they often came from structured families with opinionated parents. However, even convergent thinking, perhaps more common among children of authoritative parents, is paired with high feelings of positive self-esteem and religiosity during adolescence and adulthood.

Baumrind's distinction between authoritative and authoritarian parents is a particularly important one: although both types of parents depend on high control, they differ in the amount of emotional support that accompanies their high control. The implicit assumption in the Baumrind position, as in others, is that discipline and control—when used firmly, fairly, and consistently in the context of a warm, supportive family environment—are positive components in effective childrearing.

Contrary to the popular image of mutual antagonism, most adolescents and their parents have generally positive feelings for each other. (Jean Shapiro)

Finally, Baumrind describes a subset of parents who are low in control and low in emotional support, whom she labels *neglectful*. Parents in such families see their children as burdens and essentially leave them to their own devices. As a result, children from these homes suffer lowered self-esteem and have poor social interaction skills (Thomas et al., 1974).

Elder's research led to a similar sorting of family interaction patterns, but Elder's analysis was concentrated more on the dynamics of interchange regarding the decision-making process, especially as that process had reference to the adolescent in the home. In those families that Elder described as *autocratic*, adolescents have no say at all in the decision-making process, even when the decisions directly affect them. The entire decision-making process rested with the parents, usually with one parent. In *authoritarian* families, adolescents have some input, but the authority and decisions were firmly fixed in the parents. *Democratic* families allow and encourage input from their adolescents regarding the decision-making process, but the ultimate authority for decision making still resides with the parents. *Equalitarian* parents, on the other hand, not only encourage input but also consider every member of the family as having an equal voice in family decision making. *Permissive* parents, as in Baumrind's description, prefer to let their adolescents exercise their own judgment in most or all major decisions. The permissive parent may help the adolescent by discussing a problem, but the decision-making responsibility ultimately rests with the adolescent. *Laissez faire* parents not only expect adolescents to be responsible for their own decisions, they also maintain a hands-off policy in the decision-making process. The adolescents are on their own. Finally, the *ignoring* parent, like the neglecting parent described above, leaves adolescents to their own devices. The parents impose no constraints because they do not attend to the adolescent's needs or care about the adolescent's needs. Notice that in Elder's scheme the shifts in parenting styles are somewhat subtle from one level to the next. Although warmth and caring are not immediately prominent as a sorting dimension, they are implicit.

Although such classifications are useful and important, you, as a reader, should be cautioned that not all parents can be neatly placed into little boxes. By splitting the descriptions into high and low control or high and low support, we ignore those parents who lie the middle range, whose styles may or may not have effects that fall between the extremes. It is not enough to split the difference. Also, parents use a variety of styles depending on their mood, their health, the problem area, the child, and so on. The typologies do, however, provide useful guidelines for classifying parenting styles. Moreover, they set the stage for demonstrating that the style with which parents interact with their children does have an effect on their children's social and psychological development.

PARENTING STYLE AND PERSONALITY DEVELOPMENT

The patterns in which parents exercise control and provide emotional support have a significant impact on the personality development of their children and adolescents. Although it is difficult to provide clear categories of family environments, the general consensus seems to be that children raised in warm, supportive families with firm but fair control are least likely to be identified as maladjusted during adolescence and adulthood. Children from cold, rejecting families that depend on harsh and often erratic control, are more likely to show problems in social and emotional adjustment.

Aggression and delinquency have repeatedly been related to the atmosphere in the home. Aggressive individuals are more likely to come from homes in which parents depend on severe and excessive physical punishment for discipline and control (Sears, Maccoby, and Levin, 1957; Bandura and Walters, 1959). Adolescents with psychiatric disorders are similarly more likely to come from homes with a higher degree of instability (Rutter, 1978).

A variety of factors influence the preferred parenting style within a given family. In a cross-cultural study of parent-child relationships, it was found that the degree to which parents emphasize "compliant" values (obedience, nurturance, responsibility to others) or "assertive" values (achievement, independence, self-reliance) was related to the economic stability of the culture (Barry, Child, and Bacon, 1959). As technology and economics provide greater ease of satisfying basic needs, then families are more likely to emphasize achievement-oriented behaviors. As cooperation among families becomes necessary for survival, then compliant behaviors are encouraged. However, when the economy is below some minimal subsistence level, cooperation among families is not reasonable. The result may be increased antisocial aggression and self-reliance.

Kohn (1959) has suggested that in our culture, white-collar, middle-income families tend to transmit values of self-reliance, achievement, and creative thinking, which are more in line with the traditional orientation of schools. Blue-collar families, on the other hand, have a different perception of social reality and are more likely to emphasize conformity to authority, dependence on others, and nonacademic achievement. White-collar parents are, for example, more likely to discipline their children on the basis of their interpretation of the children's motives, whereas blue-collar parents are more likely to respond solely to the behavior (Gecas and Nye, 1974).

Larger families are more likely than small families to depend on firm, authoritarian control (Holtzman and Moore, 1965). Older children in large families are, however, more likely to assume adult roles earlier. They often assume surrogate or "associate" parent roles in the care of younger brothers and sisters. Such parenting roles are more likely to be placed on older

Caring for younger siblings develops a sense of family and responsibility. (© Christopher Brown/Picture Group)

155

daughters than sons, because the role is largely a nurturant one. Because of this, the pursuit of independence and the establishment of a personal identity may be more difficult for girls than boys in large families. Girls from large families are more likely to be aware of family tension than boys, at least in the Holtzman study. They are also more likely than their small family counterparts to report family tension. Additionally, Holtzman found that the amount of tension reported in a family was negatively related to the amount of stress reported among adolescents. Large family size, low income, and little education are not *by themselves* significant contributors to tension and aggression within the family (Farrington, 1978). The impact of the total ecology of the family must be considered. Stress is related to a combination of factors.

In another important study by Glen Elder (1978), women and men who were adolescents during the Great Depression were studied as adults to see what impact that major economic upheaval had on their personality development. Elder found that the impact of the depression was mixed and was related to the social status and stability of the family prior to the catastrophe. Boys from middle-class families who suffered serious financial setbacks during the depression showed better psychological health and stronger drive as adults than boys who came from middle-class families who did not suffer a similar calamity. Boys from families that suffered financial setbacks achieved levels of educational achievement comparable to their more fortunate peers, but by age thirty-eight to forty they were actually employed in higher-status positions.

In contrast, the opposite seemed true for lower-class and working-class boys. Financial disaster had a very negative effect. Boys from working-class families who experienced financial setbacks were less likely than their peers who did not suffer setbacks to continue their education, and as adults they were employed in lower-status occupations.

Among girls from middle-class families, those who suffered financial setbacks were expected to assume household roles while their mothers went to work to help support the family. As adults they had less education and were more likely to prefer homemaking than their nondeprived counterparts. In general they had a much stronger commitment to traditional family life values. There was also some evidence that they, as with the males, had better psychological health as adults.

THE GENERATION GAP

A generally popular opinion holds that today's adolescents and youths are inalterably opposed to the attitudes and values expressed by their parents' generation and, conversely, that parents are antagonistic to adolescents' peers, who are viewed as antisocial or antiestablishment. This so-called generation gap leads to inevitable conflicts and hostility between parents and teenagers, because neither side understands the other.

The concept of a generation gap has been widely accepted by the popular media and by such notable social scientists as Margaret Mead (1970) and

VIGNETTE 7-2

"Teen-agese"

The "In" language and slang of adolescents and youth change regularly from year to year. What was once "neat!" became "groovy!" which became "bad!" which became "far out!" or "heavy!," and on and on. Parents and adults are rarely able to keep track of what new jargon is acceptable and what is out of date. Erma Bombeck, a nationally syndicated columnist and humorist, took a lighthearted look at this problem one day and, just for fun, the results of her ruminations are presented here.

There isn't one parent reading this column who is Sanforized. We all undergo a shrinking process the day our children reach the age of 12. Our brain diminishes, our vision is stunted, and we are virtually useless to society until the kid reaches the age of 20 or so.

As a parent who has just emerged from the Valley of the Ignorant, let me tell you it would have been far easier if someone had taught me how to understand "teen-agese."

"Awriiiiiiiiite!": This is a term of jubilation accompanied by one of those rare teen-age smiles usually directed at someone on the telephone. Worry a lot when you hear it.

"You know?": These two words are used in place of periods at the end of a sentence. They are not to be taken literally. "You know?" does not require an answer...or for that matter does it deserve one.

"Really!": One "Really!" is worth a thousand kisses. It's as close to civility as you get. It means they agree to something you have said.

"Who cares?": This is a mechanical retort that often comes out of their mouth even before you have said something.

"I hear you": Don't get your hopes built up on this one. It only means you are audible and that your request has been acknowledged. It does not mean anything will come of it.

"You going out tonight?": This phrase holds as much sentiment as Daniel when he was led out to the lion's den and asked, "You wanta go out for dinner?" It's a subtle way of asking you if the car is or is not available.

"Who used up all the hot water?": This is another rhetorical question. They know before they asked, but they are trying to make you feel guilty about rinsing your toothbrush in hot water when they, in effect, have just emptied a 30-gallon tank to rinse their hair.

"When do we eat?": Teen-agers do not consider this a question, but a salutation. It takes the place of "Hello, how are you? Was your surgery bad? Did anyone get hurt in the other car? You and Dad are getting a what?"

My favorite is "Everybody Else's Mother." A lot of parents interpret this saying as a collective group of liberal mothers who allow their kids to do as they please. Like Mary Poppins, Santa Claus, Tinkerbell and The Incredible Hulk, it's a convenient myth. If you don't believe me, ask for her phone number.

Well, parents, Hang Tough. That's Teen-agese for Good Luck!

Source: From *At Wit's End* by Erma Bombeck, © 1979 Field Enterprises, Inc. Courtesy of Field Newspaper Syndicate.

Theodore Roszak (1969). However, researchers who have attempted to demonstrate a general discontinuity in values and attitudes between the generations have not found any major rift. In fact, rather than discord, there seems to be a good deal of harmony between adolescents and their parents about what is valued (Douvan and Adelson, 1966; Feuer, 1969; Thomas, 1974; Yankelovitch, 1975).

One study asked parents and their teenagers to tell how they felt about "teenagers in general" and "adults in general," both from their own perspective and what they thought the others' perspective would be. That is, parents filled out the questionnaire from their own point of view and also from what they thought their teenager's point of view was. The teens were asked to do the opposite. The results indicated that both parents and teenagers had favorable views of adolescents. Parents, however, overestimated the ratings that teenagers would give themselves, and teenagers underestimated the ratings that parents would give to them (Hess and Goldblatt, 1957). The discrepancy was not so much in the real views but in the expected views.

In their study of conflicts between parents and youths over value structures, Douvan and Adelson (1966) found no major differences. Indeed they concluded:

> Parent-peer conflicts are less severe and general than they are reported to be. Some discrepancy of values is sure to be found since the two generations differ in perspectives, but for the most part, we believe, core values are shared by parents and peers, and conflicts center on peripheral or token issues. (p. 84)

Like the notion of storm and stress during adolescence, the idea of the generation gap may be the outcome of people projecting the behavior of a minority of adolescents onto the whole, and it may be reinforced by the emancipation efforts of middle adolescence. Baumrind (1975) suggests that the alienated, antiauthoritarian stance pictured in the generation gap is more likely to result in families whose parenting styles are either highly restrictive or very permissive. Keniston (1965) describes parents of alienated youths as themselves unfulfilled and trying to achieve fulfillment through their offspring.

Whether adolescents have positive or negative attitudes about their parents, and whether they accept their parents' ideals as valid, depend to a large degree on whether they see their parents as caring, responsible, and reliable (Smith 1970, 1976). By way of contrast, delinquent youths often describe their parents as inconsistent, unstable, and unreliable (Becker, 1964). As teenagers see their parents as less competent, they are more likely to see their peers as an attractive alternative. In a sense adolescents from unstable homes are "pushed" to their peers by parents who fail to provide adequate role models.

For the most part, however, the generation gap does not exist. Although we can observe some attitudinal differences between generations, depending on what questions we ask (Thomas, 1974; Chand, Crider, and Wiltis, 1975), we find no evidence of a massive rejection of parental ideals. Thus the adolescent may *behave* as though rejecting the parents' values, but inwardly there may be little difference in opinion.

PARENT-YOUTH CONFLICT

What then do we make of the parent-teen conflicts that are so typical in descriptions by both parents and adolescents? The arguments and tensions that often dominate family interactions are not figments of someone's imagination. The conflicts and arguments are real. But, rather than reflecting an outright rejection of parental values, the conflicts are part of the natural establishment of the adolescent's personal identity.

Adolescents often feel that their parents refuse to give them any responsibility and treat them like children. Parents, on the other hand, complain that they wish their teenagers *would* act responsibly and cooperate with the rest of the family. Both sides of the conflict usually include some truth and some fiction. Parents are often reluctant to give too much responsibility to adolescents, because they fear negative consequences. Teenagers may want additional responsibility, but they also want to enjoy the irresponsibility and freedom of childhood.

The parent's task is to provide the teenager with the chance to assume an increasingly responsible role in the family. This may be established in the form of contractual agreements—for example, "If you want the keys to the car, then you will mow the lawn." In other more general cases, adolescents should be expected to maintain a regimen of responsibility for their own affairs.

Adolescent reluctance to cooperate with parents or adult authorities should not automatically be interpreted as *refusal* to cooperate. A hostile, uncooperative stance may be necessary to protect the adolescent's feelings of self-worth by implying a rejection of a dependent relationship. If the parent's demands are in opposition to the peer group's desires, a lack of cooperation may serve to assert individuality. As the desires of parents and peers become increasingly incompatible, the chances for an explosive confrontation increase. Even still, the reluctance and hostility may be coping behaviors necessary to address the conflict. When parents assert control in opposition to peers, they often provide the adolescent with a workable rationalization for not participating with those peers: "I *have* to go with my parents," or "I can't do it. My *parents* won't let me."

The teen may really prefer to have the parent exercise control in these periods of conflict. Remember that at this point the adolescent vacillates between a desire for independent adult status and a need to maintain the secure, dependent status of a child. Thus, although their outward verbalizations are hostile and belligerent, adolescents may really want their parents to enforce control and assume responsibility.

One bewildered mother related an incident in which her fourteen-year-old daughter wanted to go with some friends on an unchaperoned weekend camping trip. The parents said no, they did not think it was a wise idea. After a highly argumentative and tearful session, their daughter called her friends to tell them, in caustic tones, "My parents won't let me go." Both parents expected a moody and hostile weekend. Instead, as their daughter hung up the telephone, she suddenly changed her mood and said, "Thanks, Mom and Dad," and calmly walked to her room. Her parents were baffled.

In fact, the daughter in this case may not have wanted to participate in the weekend, but she had not yet gained sufficient self-confidence to resist her peers. When her parents took responsibility for the decision, she was relieved of the problem of explaining herself to her peers.

Responsible parenthood implies, as Baumrind suggests, an authoritative role. But parents must achieve a delicate balance between controlling and releasing control of the adolescent. It is clear that part of the socialization process of adolescents approaching adulthood is their increased acceptance of adult responsibility. The balance, therefore, between control and release of control changes from early to middle to late adolescence. By late adolescence the transition to independence and release of control should be nearly complete, although strong emotional ties may still persist (Ausubel et al., 1977).

SINGLE-PARENT FAMILIES

With the steady increase in the number of families disrupted by either separation or divorce, many young people today must adjust to new roles that result from parental separation. It is not uncommon for young people to suffer anxiety and depression because of the crisis of separation in the family. Further, they may undergo additional adjustment problems if one or both of the parents remarries. Currently one child in six under the age of eighteen is being raised by a single parent.

In the past "broken homes" have been a convenient and ready target to blame for a variety of social and psychological maladjustments, especially delinquency. Even today, if we were to look at the backgrounds of teens who are in juvenile homes, it might seem that an extraordinary number come from broken or disrupted homes. We need to be cautious, however, not to jump to conclusions too quickly. It may be that juveniles who come from broken homes are more likely to become delinquent, *or* it may be that delinquents who come from broken homes are more likely to end up in penal institutions. Although divorce and broken homes are convenient scapegoats, there is little evidence to indicate that divorce will, by itself, produce delinquent children (Herzog and Sudia, 1973).

In a recent major review of the problems associated with adjustment following divorce, separation, or remarriage, Dr. Octave Baker, of the American Institutes for Research (1980), has found that many of the effects of divorce, separation, and remarriage on youth and their families are more directly related to the emotional crisis that precede and follow the separation more than to the actual separation itself. In Dr. Baker's view divorce is a crisis, and facilities for responding to this crisis should be available not only for the parents at the time of the separation, but also for the family unit both before and after the dissolution of the marriage.

Economic and family demands on children who grow up in poor, single-parent families may lessen their chances of experiencing the "luxury" of an identity crisis. (Bob Adelman/Magnum Photos, Inc.)

In counseling divorced, separated, or remarried parents and their children, a common set of problems seem to emerge that hinder the adjustment of children and youths in those families:

1. A turf problem is typically associated with custody of the children following separation. The whole question of who will now be responsible for the children is often the focal point of argument and misunderstanding.

2. Parents are often hesitant to discuss the coming separation with the children until it occurs or is imminent. Life between the parents up to the separation becomes a form of peaceful (or not so peaceful) coexistence, in which the parents assume that their children have no idea of what is happening. This attitude and behavior may have serious effects on the emotional well-being of the children. At certain levels of cognitive development, children may understand the concept of legal separation only superficially; they may fear that the parents may not only divorce each other but divorce the children as well.

3. Children and adolescents may misunderstand the causes of a separation and/or divorce and feel that they are somehow to blame. The children must be

assured that they are not the cause of the divorce and, once again, that the parents are divorcing each other and not the children. Parents need to explain to the children that they still love them and will continue to see them, even if they are not living together as a family.

Parents in families undergoing separation should encourage their children and adolescents to talk about their feelings about the crisis. Very often it is helpful to explain that most people, children and adults, suffer and feel depression when faced with such a crisis. That depression may take other forms besides despair and sadness—for example, apathy and lack of motivation to do schoolwork or to spend time with others. It may also be helpful to have a support group of other young people in similar circumstances. Such a group helps its members see that their feelings and fears are not unique and provides examples of the ways in which others have tried to solve their problems. This type of group can be particularly important because the suffering of the child or adolescent is often compounded by the fact that the parents—also undergoing an emotional crisis—simply do not have the time or energy or psychological resources to respond to their hurting children.

It is important, in the period following divorce, to encourage the parent who does not have primary custody to maintain contact with the children and adolescents. Too often the parent who is not living with the children feels that it would be better to disappear from the scene and not to interfere. That attitude, however, is not a realistic reaction to the problems involved. The physical separation of the parent may lead to the children feeling guilty and anxious. They may feel that they are at fault in some way. Although fathers are being granted custody more frequently, the father is still the parent most likely to be separated from the children. As you will see below, that absence of the father leads to specific kinds of problems. In either case, however, I cannot overstate the importance of the separated parent maintaining contact and communication with the offspring following the crisis.

Rather than single-parenthood, the family factor that is most likely to be associated with maladjustment and delinquency is a lack of stability and support at home. Sometimes the family is more stable *after* a divorce than before it. It may be the extra burden of single-parenthood added to an already unstable and stressful situation that contributes to the overall pattern of maladjustment among troubled youths.

That is not to say that the absence of a father or mother from the home does not create problems. There is some evidence that in father-absent homes, both boys and girls have difficulty establishing an adequate gender identity. Lacking a male role model, boys in fatherless homes may choose the mother or peers as their model. When boys select their peers as their role model, they may assume a stereotyped masculine, or *macho* role (Hannerz, 1969).

The effects of father absence on personal development depend on the reason for the absence and the age of the child when the absence begins. One study of adolescent girls found that girls from fatherless homes felt less secure around male peers and adult males than those from father-present homes. Girls whose father was absent because of divorce were more likely to try to gain the attention of adult males and females. Girls whose father had died, on the other hand, showed considerable anxiety in the presence of a male interviewer (Heatherington, 1972). Some writers suggest that fathers are important to both boys and girls in their development of gender roles and that, although mother absence may have an adverse effect on the personal development of girls, father absence has a negative impact on both boys and girls (Mischel, 1970).

At some point children of single parents may face an additional adjustment problem. If one or both of the parents decides to remarry, the children may need to learn to live with a new stepparent and perhaps stepbrothers and stepsisters. The adolescent who may have assumed increased responsibility in the absence of one of the parents may now be asked to give up that responsible role.

The displacement is additionally traumatic if the young person has assumed the role of a surrogate partner with shared roles in family decision making. Also, a young person who is fond of the new stepparent may suffer loyalty conflicts at remarriage. The young person may feel caught in the middle of obligations to both parents and in fact may hold on to some fantasies of reconciliation. These fantasies are egocentric in the sense that adolescents may feel that their behavior controls whether the parents reunite—if they can change, the parents will be reconciled. Remarriage, of course, puts a strain on those fantasies. (The fantasies are not unlike those of abused children, described in the next section, who feel that they have control over their parents' behavior and that, if they can alter their own behavior, the parent will stop being abusive.)

ABUSIVE PARENTS

An unfortunate reality that must be faced in a chapter on parent-adolescent relations is that a minority of parents physically, sexually, or psychologically abuse their children and adolescents. Although most reported cases of physical abuse are found in infants and young children, parental beatings of adolescents that lead to hospitalization are not unheard of (Young, 1964; Walters, 1975). John, a fourteen-year-old boy, threatened to kill his father after his father had hit him with a belt buckle hard enough to draw blood. John was placed on probation by the courts. After several instances of running away, following similar beatings, John was assigned by the courts to an adolescent psychiatric unit. John's father was not punished.

Sexual abuse is more common and typically takes the form of an adult male having sexual relations with an adolescent girl or boy. Cases in which an adult female abuses an adolescent boy are almost unheard of. In the great majority of cases, the sexually abusive adult is not a stranger but a member of the immediate or close family or a family friend.

Jane, a fifteen-year-old, was brought to the attention of a child-welfare agency by her older sister. Jane had been forced to have sexual intercourse with their stepfather several times over the previous six months. The stepfather had also been having sexual relations with the older sister until she had left home and was also sexually active with a younger, twelve-year-old sister. The two younger girls were removed from the home and placed in a foster home. In the meantime, the mother and stepfather blamed the three girls for causing all the trouble. "Besides," the stepfather argued, "it ain't nobody's damn business what I do with my daughters."

The nature of physical and sexual abuse is complicated by problems of definition and lack of public awareness. As Walters (1975) indicates:

> Persons not familiar with child abuse assume that the children desire to be removed permanently from the presence of the parents or adults abusing them and that "No one in his right mind" would ever harm a child ... Contrary to public opinion, most children who are abused do not feel victimized. They frequently feel worse about bringing adverse attention to the parents who have abused them than they do about being abused. (pp. 3–4)

In many cases abusing parents describe their own parents as having treated them the same way (Solomon, 1973; Steele and Pollock, 1968). People tend to "parent" their children in much the same way that their parents "parented" them. When a parent is abusive, succeeding generations are more likely to perpetuate the cycle.

Other factors appear in the picture of an abusive relationship. For example, the child is likely to have been conceived out of wedlock, forcing a marriage while one or both parents was still a teen. As parents, they are emotionally

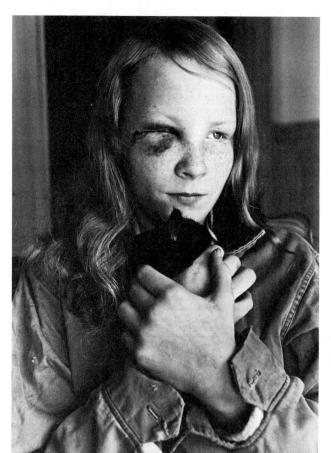

An unpleasant reality is that some children and adolescents are subject to physical or sexual abuse.
(© Eugene Richards/ Magnum Photos, Inc.)

immature and suffer general emotional and economic instability, which is accentuated by the presence of the baby (Solomon, 1973). In many cases abused children are unattractive or deformed (Elmer and Gregg, 1967).

One study followed the development of abused children in fifty abusive families (Elmer, 1967; Elmer and Gregg, 1967). Of those who had suffered physical abuse leading to broken bones, only 10 percent recovered fully. The remainder retained physical, mental, and emotional scars that seemed to become increasingly serious as the child approached adolescence.

Currently public agencies are demanding legislation providing them greater power in responding to cases of physical or sexual abuse. Treatment of abusive parents, however, is exceedingly difficult and varies with the type of abusers and the reasons for their abusive behavior.

SUMMARY

One of the primary elements in developing an individual identity during adolescence is the establishment of emotional and psychological independence from parents. The emancipation process may cause greater or lesser stress, depending on the patterns of parent-child interaction that have been established during early and middle childhood. Parents need to recognize that adolescents are attracted not only by the independence of adulthood but also by the secure relationship of childhood dependence. The task for parents, then, is to gradually shift responsibility from themselves to the adolescent. The moves toward independence are best facilitated in warm, supportive family environments in which structure and control are regularly replaced with demands for self-reliance.

Often practitioners who talk with parents about their teenagers, especially during those times when parent-adolescent communication is strained, will find that parents feel very guilty about their anger toward their adolescents. Resenting your own children is something that society says a "really caring" parent would never do. That attitude is indeed unfortunate, because we can all feel anger at someone we care for. Parents, however, often feel that their relationships with their children are somehow different. For example, when an infant screams all night, night after night, depriving one or both parents of needed sleep, the parents soon begin to resent the disruption. However, they also begin to feel guilty about resenting this "innocent child." The same thing holds for many parents of adolescents. If an adolescent uses hostility and lack of cooperation as mechanisms for establishing independence, the parents may start to have guilt feelings over their anger and resentment about these disruptions to the entire household. In addition, parents hear directly and indirectly that if their child has "problems," it is the parents' fault. Once again the parent may harbor considerable guilt.

Parents cannot ignore the needs of their adolescents to establish emotional independence. But neither should they ignore the needs of the remainder of the family while they attempt to facilitate the transition. Parents need to increase their demands for self-reliant and responsible behavior within and outside the family setting.

8 | Friends and Peers

One issue on which there is general consensus among those who work with, study, or raise adolescents, is the strong impact of the peer group on adolescent behavior. The need to "get along with" peers, be accepted by the group, and not be seen as different, may seem at times to totally dominate the adolescent's thoughts and actions. Few writers, however, would argue that this influence is automatically or necessarily negative. Indeed, peers and friends play a vital, positive role in developing social skills during adolescence.

If the impact of peers is negative at times, that impact is far outweighed by the ramifications of being excluded from the peer group. Failure to establish workable social ties with peers is a major predictor of social and emotional maladjustment during adolescence and adulthood (Hartup, 1977).

The relationships that adolescents establish with friends and peers, especially during early and middle adolescence, play an important role in aiding the adolescent to establish the social skills and feelings of personal competence that are necessary for adult functioning. As the adolescent works toward establishing a sense of personal identity and independence from family influences, peers and friends provide emotional support and a sense of security while the adolescent experiments with new roles. Thus the peer group serves as a kind of a buffer, providing a middle ground between the childish, dependent relationship with parents and adult independence. Among peers, adolescents are more free to experiment with alternate value systems and identities (Erikson, 1968). Friends and peers offer feedback on the acceptability or unacceptability of the experimental systems. In addition, they provide an adolescent with an interim identity as "one of the group." As the interim group identity is replaced by a personal identity, the need to conform to the demands of the peer group lessens.

Up to this point, I have used the terms *friends* and *peers* in sequence. The terms are not, however, interchangeable. The term *friendship* refers to close personal commitments among a small group of people with whom the adolescent is able to share feelings, plans, fears, and fantasies. Typically we think of friendship as a relationship that exists between two people. Of all peers, friends are the least demanding of rigid conformity.

Friends provide the most immediate source of peer influence. (© Frank Siteman MCMLXXX)

A small cluster of friends who closely identify with each other is called a *clique*. Cliques tend to be small groups of individuals who share common values and a common sense of purpose. In most cases a clique is usually homogeneous in terms of age and sex, and it is usually composed of individuals who live near each other and are of similar social standing.

Peers is a more general term referring both to close friends and to a broader, less clearly definable body of age mates or social mates who share common experience. At another level, more remote from the individual adolescent than the clique, is what we call a *crowd* (Coleman, 1980). A peer crowd is a conglomeration of cliques, larger and more diverse than cliques. As adolescents move into middle and late adolescence, crowds are made up of both sexes (Dunphy, 1963, 1969). The crowd sets up a dogmatic code of dress, language, and rules for acceptable behavior. The crowd is not nearly as

Cliques offer a sense of belonging but often at the price of conformity. (Tyrone Hall/ Stock, Boston)

sympathetic to the needs or feelings of the individual as the clique or a friend. Also, because the crowd lacks any clear boundaries, it may be most frightening to those adolescents who lack self-assurance. The demands from this group are less immediate than from the clique, but allegiance to the group may require some sacrifice of individuality.

Less clear and more remote, but apparently very powerful, peer influences come from an invisible "they" who are all wearing the latest fashion fad or who are all allowed by their parents to stay out late. This amorphous "they" is much like the invisible audience that the adolescent feels is preoccupied with his well-being (Elkind, 1967; 1977). In some cases the adolescent may even assume a defensive and protective posture for "them."

THE FUNCTION OF PEER GROUPS

Peers and friends seem to serve four areas of adolescents' personal development (Wagner, 1971):

1. Adolescents learn how to interact with others through peer groups. We are social beings and our ability to get along with others and be accepted by others is critical to adequate personal adjustment. Failure to develop these social skills is an antecedent to a variety of adolescent and adult mental health problems.
2. Peer groups provide a setting within which adolescents can establish and clarify their moral standards and value systems. Part of the process of establishing an adult ego identity is the exploration and evaluation of alternate value systems beyond their parents'. Peer groups thus offer a safe, supportive group within which to experiment with these systems.
3. At times of emotional stress, especially family-related stress, the peer group may offer emotional support.
4. The peer group serves an instructing and advising function. Adolescents are told what is "in" and what is not. Similarly, peers serve as a sounding board for questions and attitudes on sex, drugs, and social behavior.

Peer groups serve an additional important function for the adolescent in confirming the individual's acceptability. Early-adolescents' concerns about their value and worth and their fear of being left out are eased by belonging to a group. Belonging is very important for early-adolescents. They do not see the price of conformity as particularly large, rather they are usually sufficiently unsure of themselves to welcome the chance to depend on others for guidance. The price of allegiance to one group also implies the segregation and rejection of other groups.

With respect to the second of these functions, the peer group is often seen as replacing the parent. Although this may be true in part, adolescents do not turn to peers rather than parents in all cases. Whether adolescents turn to peers or to parents for guidance and support depends primarily on the quality of interaction between the adolescent and the parents at home. When the quality of parent-adolescent interaction is low, the attraction of the peer

The peer crowd has varying degrees of influence on the adolescent's need to conform. (Courtesy, Waltham High School, Waltham, Massachusetts. Photograph by Peter Vandemark)

groups for guidance is high, and consequently, dependence on peers and susceptibility to their demands also increase (Iacovetta, 1975). When adolescents regard the peer group as more stable, more supportive, and thus a more attractive alternative than parents, its influence increases. Conversely, when they see their parents as trusting and trustworthy, parental influence remains strong.

Even in those cases in which interactions with parents are positive, the desire for peer acceptance and approval is a powerful motive for the emerging adolescent. Some degree of conformity to the peer group is not only to be expected but is also a necessary part of the price young people have to pay to be accepted by the group. Adolescents may yield to demands for conformity ranging from common hair styles, clothes, and language, to pressures for some delinquent or antisocial behavior. If peer groups do have a clearly identified influence that is distinct from parents, it is in the area of negative, antisocial behavior (Burlingame, 1967; Siman, 1977; Kandel, 1978). Both boys and girls are more likely to engage in negative activities when those behaviors are encouraged and approved by their friends. If peer demands for conformity include some delinquent behavior, there are also strong social pressures to protect the group by not "squealing" or "ratting" on the others if one is caught. Both conformity to the group and demands to protect the group are solidified by the threat of exclusion. That is, the adolescent who does not comply may be left out. Because the adolescent—especially the younger adolescent—has a high fear of loss of acceptance, of unacceptability and exclusion, the threat is very effective.

THE STRUCTURE OF PEER GROUPS

Dunphy (1963, 1969) offers an important analysis and description of the nature of peer group organization among young people as they move through adolescence. Figure 8-1 shows the basics of this model. In preadolescence children tend to form same-age, same-sex cliques. These cliques are isolated from each other and operate roughly parallel to each other. As Dunphy (1969) notes, this age is sometimes called the "gang-age." But *gangs*, as the term is used here, does not refer to stable and formally organized youth gangs such as those found in urban areas. The gang has a common purpose only in the play activity it consumes. Early in this stage, the children may identify themselves as a "club," with secret passwords and special meeting places. Because the group is organized around play, it is not terribly stable, and it has no need to function in conjunction with other gangs.

At around age twelve, there is a change in the nature and function of the peer group. As Horrocks (1976) points out, during this time young people commonly talk about themselves with reference to "our crowd" or "our group." The clique in this sense has attained a certain integrity that makes it unique from other cliques. These cliques are largely unisexual, same-age groups, and the members usually come from similar social backgrounds and have similar values and interests. Unlike childhood gangs, these cliques are

Figure 8-1 STAGES OF GROUP DEVELOPMENT IN ADOLESCENCE

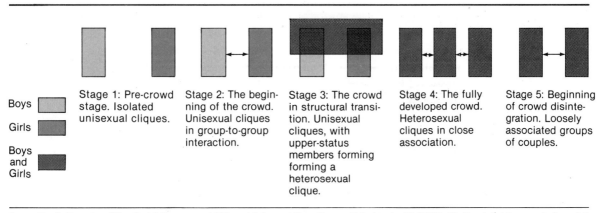

Boys

Girls

Boys and Girls

Stage 1: Pre-crowd stage. Isolated unisexual cliques.

Stage 2: The beginning of the crowd. Unisexual cliques in group-to-group interaction.

Stage 3: The crowd in structural transition. Unisexual cliques, with upper-status members forming forming a heterosexual clique.

Stage 4: The fully developed crowd. Heterosexual cliques in close association.

Stage 5: Beginning of crowd disintegration. Loosely associated groups of couples.

Source: D. C. Dunphy, "The Social Structure of Urban Adolescent Peer Groups," *Sociometry 26* (1963): 61. Reprinted by permission of the American Sociological Association.

more stable and function in conjunction with or in relation to other cliques. This interaction of cliques sets the stage for the emergence of the crowd. This "near-crowd," however, is still primarily unisexual.

During middle adolescence the increasing awareness of one's sexuality and the need to interact with young people of the opposite sex lead to another alteration of the structure of cliques. As the leaders of the cliques begin to interact with opposite-sex cliques, the pattern of organization becomes heterosexual, incorporating both boy and girl cliques. The emergence of the heterosexual crowd is in part necessitated by the onset of dating. As the male/female group becomes more firmly established, heterosexual cliques may emerge. The clique is still, however, largely homogeneous and close-knit.

During late adolescence the nature of the crowd becomes multidimensional, with heterosexual cliques operating in a highly interdependent manner. Membership in a clique is now based on patterns of heterosexual interaction. Gradually these patterns become even more stable as "steady" boy-girl couples join with other similar couples to form a loose association.

THE FORMATION OF PEER GROUPS

Peer groups do not form randomly. The old adage "Birds of a feather flock together" has some basis in reality when it describes adolescent peer group formation. Adolescents are likely to gravitate toward others who share similar values, who come from similar backgrounds, who are at about the same level of intellectual and social maturity, and who have similar interests (Douvan and Adelson, 1966; Kandel, 1978a,b). Usually preadolescents and early-adolescents form friendships with those who live nearby or, sometimes, with schoolmates. As a young person moves into high school, the school becomes increasingly the focal point for peer group activities (Coleman, 1960). Still the groups are formed selectively.

By middle adolescence friendships are increasingly based on common value systems. Not uncommonly, the central core of values of a peer group are more similar than dissimilar to parents' value systems. Common interests, hobbies, or even common choice of college have little to do with the choice of friends (Newcomb, 1966). Among girls there is a clearer transition in the factors that lead to the establishment of friendships as they move from early to middle adolescence. As personal maturity increases, the value that girls give to common value systems likewise increases, as well as their ability to explain the basis for forming friendships. Among boys, however, the transition was less well identified, and the boys were less clear in their explanations for the reasons their friendships were formed. That study also observed that friendships among girls were of shorter duration (Douvan and Adelson, 1966).

Living close to one another is an important aspect in the formation of groups, especially during preadolescence and early adolescence. But proximity does not cease to be a factor in friendships even during late adolescence. In a small college dormitory, residents are more likely to establish friendships with those on the same floor than with people on the next floor (Newcomb, 1966). Further, formal social groupings such as fraternities and sororities, which tend to draw individuals with similar values and social backgrounds, foster and solidify friendships by a common identifiable label and closeness in living arrangements.

Emphasizing the commonality factor in the formation of peer groups does not imply that peer groups are simply a gathering of individuals who think alike or that peer groups have no influence on behavior or developing values. However, it does imply that the effects of peer groups on value formation, though important, may be overstated. The peer group may influence the individual, but the individual also influences the group. Further, the values of the group are typically not widely divergent from what the individual holds in the first place.

AGE AND PEER GROUPS

As with aspects of personal and emotional development described in earlier chapters, the pattern of interpersonal development shows a shift not only in the form of the peer groups (Dunphy, 1963, 1969) but also in the functions and value that the adolescent attributes to friends and peers. As young people move through adolescence, they perceive that the roles played by peers and friends change from rather self-serving, nonmutual relationships during early adolescence to complex, mutual relationships during late adolescence (Douvan and Adelson, 1966).

During early adolescence young people do not appear to make any firm, lasting commitment to friends. Rather than seeing a friend as someone with whom one may share feelings, they see a friend as someone with whom you do things (Coleman, 1980). Early-adolescents fail to perceive any real reciprocal, mutually beneficial role of friendship.

By middle adolescence teens are more likely to see friendships as based on security and trust. They regard a friend as someone with whom they can share a confidence and who will be loyal even when they are not around (Douvan and Adelson, 1966; Coleman, 1980). The relationship among friends may still be rigid, because the need for trust and the anxiety over breach of trust or rejection keep the relationship uncertain.

As peer groups and friendships become more stable, the adolescent learns to place trust in other members of the group who, likewise, begin to trust one another. The sharing of secrets and fantasies serves as part of the testing process in establishing this trust. As group consensus of values and attitudes is achieved, individual adolescents place increased trust in the group judgment of what is acceptable and what is unacceptable (Newcomb, 1966).

As young people approach middle adolescence, their anxieties over rejection by peers increase and, likewise, so does their motive to conform. Figure 8-2 shows the results of one study of conformity among adolescent groups (Castanzo and Shaw, 1966). Notice that the tendency to conform to peer pressure increases dramatically during early and middle adolescence and then begins to taper off by late adolescence. The often-reported observation of eighth- and ninth-grade teachers that conformity to the group seems to be the dominant value in the lives of their students is not far from

Figure 8-2 CONFORMITY AMONG ADOLESCENT GROUPS

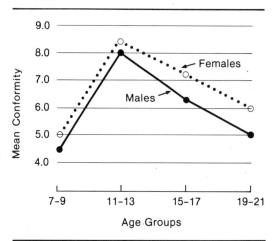

Source: P. R. Castanzo and M. E. Shaw, "Conformity As a Function of Age Level," *Child Development 37* (1966): 973. Copyright © 1966 by the Society for Research in Child Development, Inc. Reprinted by permission.

the truth. For middle school or junior high school students, acceptability by the group is paramount.

In another study, researchers found that early-adolescents were more likely to value friendships based on common activities, whether the friend was seen as a source of excitement or whether the friend lived nearby. Among adolescents in the age range associated with the shift from early to middle adolescence, there is an increase in the use of terms that refer to loyalty, admiration, and helping in the description of friendship.

During late adolescence young people see friendships less restrictive and less formal. They are more relaxed with less fear of a breach of trust or rejection. These mutually benefiting relationships are increasingly heterosexual and increasingly oriented toward a sense of adult intimacy.

You can also see in Figure 8-2 that girls were consistently more likely to conform than boys at all age levels. Girls are also more able than boys to articulate what constitutes good friendship (Douvan and Adelson, 1966).

There is, indeed, a consistent tendency for girls to place greater importance on friendships than boys (Coleman, 1980). Gold and Douvan (1969) suggest that this divergence reflects differences in patterns of socialization. Boys are encouraged early to be independent and self-reliant, whereas dependence is more likely to be fostered in girls.

PEERS AND ACHIEVEMENT

High school students currently and traditionally have displayed something of an anti-intellectual attitude. To be overly bright or to achieve too easily is seen not only as not positive but instead may be rated by peers as clearly negative. Classmates prefer the "competent plodder" to the highly intelligent, creative student (Liberty et al., 1963).

In a major analysis of high school students' attitudes, Coleman (1961) found that being intelligent was not valued nearly as much as being popular. In reporting what they felt were the most important characteristics of the "leading crowd" in high school, students felt that having a "good personality" and "being friendly" far outweighed any strivings for academic excellence.

Coleman concluded that adult society segregates adolescents into their own institutions and cuts them off from interacting with adults. Adolescents are thus forced to establish their own subculture, with its own rules and values. In that subculture, status among boys is tied to car ownership, athletic accomplishments, and extracurricular activities, whereas girls value social success, physical beauty, and nicer clothes. Neither sex sees academic success as important.

Other studies reinforce the view that academic success is not only *not* a prized attribute among high school students, but rather it may be a negative trait (Tannenbaum, 1962). Bright students may suffer conflicts between their ability and desire to achieve and their desire to be accepted. Although boys seem more able to reconcile those opposing needs and to strive toward higher achievement as they progress through adolescence, girls are apparently less

VIGNETTE 8-1
Lost at C

Some authors have a gift for seeing the humor in the things we do to "get along"—Mark Twain, for example. Among contemporary American authors, Jean Shepherd has this ability. One of the pressing concerns of young adolescents is not to be seen as different by their peers. What constitutes "different" is vague and unclear. That ambiguity may lead to even stronger motives to conform to the group norm. One aspect of the pressure not to be different involves not being too "brainy" or favored by the teacher. In this excerpt from a short story, Shepherd draws on his own experience of early adolescence and describes the convolutions of a young boy who just wants to get along. Can you draw on your own reservoir of experience and look back at some of your attempts to be acceptable to your peers? Do any of those attempts now seem humorous or even silly?

A wave of numbness surged through my body with stunning force. At last I knew what it felt like to be sitting with that brass hat on your skull with those straps around your ankles as the warden pulls the big switch. Out of the corner of my eye I caught the glint of Mr. Pittinger's horn-rims and the ice-blue ray from his left eye. As the giant baroque equation loomed on the blackboard, my life unreeled before my eyes in the classic manner of the final moments of mortal existence. I was finished. Done. It had all come to this. Somehow I had always known it would.

It all started in first grade at the Warren G. Harding School, where I was one among a rabble of sweaty, wrestling, peanut-butter-and-jelly-sandwich eaters. But it was not until the

end of the third month of school that I became dimly aware of a curse that would follow me throughout my life. Along with Martin Perlmutter Schwartz, Chester Woczniewski, Helen Weathers and poor Francis Xavier Zambarbieri, I was a member of the alphabetical ghetto that sat in the back of the classroom. Medical science is now beginning to realize that those of us at the end of the alphabet live shorter lives, sweat more and are far jumpier than those in the Bs and Es and even the Ms and Ls. People at the tail end of the alphabet grow up accepting the fact that everybody else comes first. The Warren G. Harding School had an almost mystic belief in the alphabet; if you were a P, you sat behind every O, regardless of myopia.

Me and Schwartz and Woczniewski sat so far back in the classroom that the blackboard was only a vague rumor to us. Miss Shields was a shifting figure in the haze on the distant horizon, her voice a faint but ominous drone punctuated by squeaking chalk. Within a short time I became adept at reading the inflection, if not the content, of those far-off sounds, sensing instantly when danger was looming. Danger meant simply being called on. Kids in the front of the classroom didn't know the meaning of danger. Ace test takers, they loved nothing more than to display their immense knowledge by waving their hands frantically even before questions were asked. Today, when I think of the classrooms of my youth, I see a forest of waving hands between me and the teacher. They were the smartasses who went on to become corporation presidents, TV talk-show guests and owners of cabin cruisers.

We in the back of the classroom followed a different path. Since we could neither hear nor see, we had only one course open if we were going to pass with reasonable grades. First of all, it was imperative never to be caught out in

Source: Excerpted from Jean Shepherd, "Lost at C." Originally appeared in *Playboy* magazine (May 1973): 143–144. Copyright © 1973 by Jean Shepherd.

the open; if possible, not to be seen at all. Each one of us evolved his own methods of survival. Helen Weathers was so fat, her expression so cowlike, her profuse perspiration under stress so pathetic that the teacher never had the heart to call on her. Woczniewski hid behind books, which worked all right until he hid behind *Plastic Man Meets the Thing* one morning. Perlmutter had the kind of face you can't remember even when you're looking at it, so he didn't *have* to hide. He was a born cost accountant.

One day during an oral quiz, however— always a dangerous time for all of us— Perlmutter displayed the true stuff of champions. Miss Kleinfeldt unaccountably called on him during an incomprehensible discussion of isosceles triangles. We thought Perlmutter was finished, but we had underestimated him. Without missing a beat, his face turned bright purple, his eyes bulged like a pair of overripe grapes, his neck throbbed and a spectacular geyser of blood gushed from both nostrils.

"This is terrible!" Miss Kleinfeldt shouted, scooping him up in her muscular hairy arms and rushing him to the nurse's office, where he was excused from school for the rest of the day. She never called on him again.

Zambarbieri, a devout Catholic, relied almost exclusively on prayer. But in his case it was academic, since he sat so far back in the classroom, deep among the galoshes, that even *we* couldn't see him clearly. Schwartz employed the simple but effective technique of slowly lowering himself in his seat until only his crewcut showed above the top of his desk during risky periods of interrogation. I made it a point to wear bland-colored clothes, the better to blend into the background. I learned to weave my body from side to side, dropping a shoulder here, shifting my neck a few degrees to the right there, with the crucial object in mind of always keeping a line of kids between me and the teacher's eagle eye.

For those rare but inevitable occasions—say, during a chicken-pox epidemic—when the ranks in the rows ahead were too thin to provide adequate cover, I practiced the vacant-eyeball ploy, which has since become a popular device for junior executives the world over who cannot afford to be nailed by their seniors in sales conferences and other perilous situations. The vacant eyeball appears to be looking attentively but, in fact, sees nothing. It is a blank mirror of anonymity. I learned early in the game that if they don't catch your eye, they don't call on you. Combined with a fixed facial expression of deadpan alertness—neither too deadpan nor too alert—this technique has been known to render its practitioner virtually invisible.

The third, and possibly most important, tactic of classroom survival is *thought control*. When danger looms, it is necessary to repeat silently, with intense concentration, the hypnotic command "You will *not* call on me, you will *not* call on me," sending out invisible waves of powerful thought energy until the teacher's mind is mysteriously clouded. After endless hours of rehearsal before the mirror in the bathroom, I had developed a fourth and final gambit—my cute look, a shy, boyish smile of such disarming cuddliness as to be lethal in its effectiveness. I flashed it, of course, only with great caution, during comparatively safe periods in the classroom—upon entering and leaving—and elsewhere in the school where one could afford to be seen and recognized with impunity.

Those of us in the back rows learned quickly that grades are handed out not on the basis of actual accomplishment but by intuitive feel. At that crucial moment when Miss Shields sat down to fill out my report card, I knew that my cute look would pop into her mind when my name appeared before her. Since she had nothing else to go on—other than catch-as-catch-can test answers gleaned from my shirt cuff or the bluebook of the kid ahead of me—it was only natural for her to put down a B, which is all I ever wanted out of life....

TABLE 8-1 PERCENTAGES WISHING TO GO TO COLLEGE

Father's Occupation	Neighborhood School Group		
	Upper White-Collar	Lower White-Collar	Industrial
Professional	93	77	64
White-Collar	79	59	46
Self-Employed	79	66	35
Manual	59	44	33
Overall	80	57	38

Source: A. B. Wilson, "Residential Segregation of Social Classes and Aspirations of High School Boys," *American Sociological Review*, 24 (1959): 839. Reprinted with permission of the author and the American Sociological Association.

able to resolve the conflict (Douvan and Adelson, 1966). Once again, it is possible that this difference results from the difference in general values transmitted to boys and girls by society as a whole. Girls, who are expected to be socially adept, may define success or achievement in those terms rather than through academic achievement (Bardwick and Douvan, 1971).

It is a bit unfair to point to the peer group as the primary source of the anti-intellectual attitude. We can easily argue that society devalues academic achievement in high school students and that peers merely reinforce that attitude. One has only to look, for example, at the newspaper coverage given to a National Merit Scholar versus a star athlete.

We need to note once again that friendships do not form at random. In large part, friends have highly similar educational expectations and goals (Duncan, Featherman, and Duncan, 1972). Further, they are considerably alike in their actual levels of academic performance (Kandel, 1978a).

In a more general view research demonstrates that the level of a student's educational aspirations is influenced by the overall pattern of educational aspirations of those around him. In the results of one study (see Table 8-1), both the occupational level of the father and the general socioeconomic level of the school had an influence on college aspirations (Wilson, 1959). A critical review of the impact of school peers on educational aspirations concluded that lower-income students who attend predominantly middle-class high schools are more likely to have higher educational aspirations because of the general level of school expectations. On the other hand, those same lower-income students are also likely to compare their performance to that of their middle-class peers and assess their own ability as low (Bain and Anderson, 1974). It is not simply enough to improve a student's motives. We must also provide the academic skills and behaviors necessary for success.

ADOLESCENT SOCIETY

One popular notion is that in some way adolescents are a social entity unto themselves, independent from and alien to adult society. The idea is not terribly different from the supposed generation gap discussed in the last chapter, but it goes beyond simply a difference in values.

The concept was given considerable credence by the publication of James

"Hanging out" and being seen by others is part of the process of maintaining adolescent social status.
(© Frank Siteman 1979)

Coleman's important study *The Adolescent Society* (1961). In that volume Coleman puts forth the view that because adolescents are neither children nor adults, adult society is unsure how to respond to them. Thus, historically, adolescents have been systematically isolated from both children and adults. To accomplish this end, society has created unique social institutions (for example, high schools, YMCAs, and so on) that are presumed to prepare adolescents for adult responsibility. In reality the institutions are often unrelated to adult roles and are seen by young people as irrelevant. Adults put adolescents into a social "holding pattern" until they are old enough and mature enough to be absorbed into adult society.

Because adolescents are cut off from adults and adult society, they are forced to turn to their peers for a set of values, for social support, and for learning social skills. Adolescents develop their own society complete with its own moral code, language, and fashions. The hallmark of this adolescent society is conformity to these behavioral codes. Peers enforce conformity to the adolescent society norms by including or excluding individuals as members of "the group." When young people are accepted as members of a group, they are expected to be loyal to the group and to reject adult society and any form of adult responsibility.

Although Coleman's description of an adolescent society has a certain intuitive appeal, not all writers agree that it exists in as extreme a form as originally thought. Adolescents do not form an anti-intellectual, antiestablishment population that conforms blindly to the wishes of peers (Weiner, 1976). Some researchers (for example, Douvan and Adelson, 1966) are concerned that adolescents do *not* have a significant period of separation from adults, that adolescents merge into the adult system of values too early and thereby miss out on a normal developmental progression. If adolescents are conforming, it is to the adult society, because they seem to buy into that system without question. Some differences in attitudes are certain to separate parents and teens, but the existence of a so-called "adolescent society" may be an overstatement of fact.

As with most arguments of this kind, the truth probably falls somewhere between the extremes. Today's adolescents are drawn to the support and acceptance of their peers. But rather than being forced to accept an entirely new set of values, adolescents tend to seek out friends who have values similar to their own. The result is an alliance with a peer group that may at times be in opposition to adult values, but which has, in balance, values very like those of adult society.

POPULARITY

The degree to which an individual adolescent is successful at establishing friendships or being seen as a desirable friend depends on a variety of factors. As Chapter 2 indicated, one of the important elements in being viewed as popular or unpopular is physical attractiveness. The more physically attractive an individual, the more likely he or she is to be seen as a person with whom others want to be associated. Other factors that lead to popularity or lack of it include social status, social skills, and personality attributes.

Consider the case of Dan. Dan is a fourteen-year-old boy who was referred for counseling after several episodes of "antisocial behavior" in the schools. During the counseling setting Dan complains that nobody likes him. As the counselor obtains more information, it seems that Dan is right—nobody does like him. Students seldom choose him to be part of a team, and they rebel about working with him. Even teachers see Dan as "a bit obnoxious." Students are less gentle and refer to Dan as a "nurd" or a "creep."

On the opposite side of the spectrum, consider Bill. Bill is seen by students and teachers alike as a leader. Bill is not especially athletic, but he is able to hold his own and is a welcomed member of a team in a "pick-up" game. He is also likely to be elected to some student political offices and is seen simply as a really important and popular person.

Dan and Bill represent the extremes in popularity: Dan, severely lacking in popularity, and Bill, having popularity to spare. Most adolescents fall between these extremes, and their popularity may range from high to low. In a typical classroom of adolescents, we can expect that individual popularity will be spread across the entire spectrum of "stars" who are highly popular to "isolates" who have few or no friends.

Although peer acceptance is not in and of itself the all-important determinant of behavior, the lack of peer interaction may lead to long-term difficulty in personal adjustment. The degree to which an adolescent or child is accepted by peers is highly predictive of social adjustment. Thus practitioners should be alert to problems or changes in the social acceptability of individual adolescents.

One method for measuring social prestige is the *sociogram*. A sociogram is a relatively simple assessment technique in which each person in the large group is asked a series of questions regarding choice of peers. Questions may

Figure 8-3 AN EXAMPLE OF A SOCIOGRAM

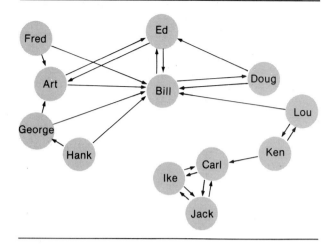

include "Name two people in the class you would like to work with on a project," or "Name two people in the class with whom you would *not* want to work." The results of the sociogram can be plotted in a figure in which each choice is represented by an arrow. (See Figure 8-3.) *Sociometric status* is reflected by the number of arrows pointing to each individual. Sociometric stars are the leaders and are most popular, as indicated by the number of times they are chosen. In Figure 8-3, Bill is chosen by seven of the twelve boys in the room. Fred, however, is chosen by none. Bill is a sociometric *star*, whereas Fred is a sociometric *isolate*. Further, because Jack, Carl, and Ike choose each other and no one else, they can be labeled as a *clique*.

An adolescent's sociometric status stays fairly constant across different settings and over time. Like intelligence test scores and achievement level, the later in personal development the measure is taken, the higher the stability. Also, the extremes of social status are more stable than the middle range. That is, those students who are stars in one setting are likely to be stars in others. One curious problem that this can create, however, occurs when a large group of stars converge into a single setting. For example, a freshman class at a prestigious college may include many young people who were leaders and stars in high school and who must now compete with one another for high status. For some this turns out to be a serious problem in adjusting to college life.

The consistency over different social settings, over different measures, and different ages suggests a generalized indication of social acceptability (Moreno, 1960). Sociometric results obtained from students are directly related to teachers' and adults' impressions of social acceptance. Sociometric status is also related to social and personal adjustment. Adolescents with high prestige show patterns of general positive feelings of self-esteem, whereas adolescent social isolates show very low feelings of self-worth. The isolate also comes across as socially inept. Social isolates seem to lack behavioral know-how.

Social isolates are a source of considerable social and psychological concern. The social isolate is more likely to drop out of school (Ullman, 1967), show problems in mental health as an adult (Cowan et al., 1970, 1971), and end up listed as a juvenile delinquent (Roff et al., 1972). The consequences of low peer acceptance may be more severe than low achievement. Social adjustment is basic to success in other domains. Social isolates who remain in school usually experience continued failure. Because part of the problem for social isolates is that they do not have the necessary social skills to make friends, one approach to the treatment of social isolates has been to train them in socially acceptable behavior.

A typical program of intervention involves providing the isolate with a fellow student who serves as a model and reinforces the isolate for socially appropriate behavior. In one study an isolate was paired with a peer model. Whenever the isolate behaved in socially approved fashion, the model would provide the isolate with a token. The token incidentally had no value beyond the fact that it represented recognition of achievement. Over time the number of inappropriate behaviors decreased, whereas socially appropriate behavior increased. Further, the number of appropriate behaviors continued to increase after the formal intervention program was terminated. Apparently the isolate learned the very effective strategy of modeling (Csapo and Marg, 1970; O'Connor, 1972).

SUMMARY

On the whole, peers complement rather than oppose the socializing influences of parents and society. Although peers may have divergent attitudes on some negative social behaviors, there is considerable harmony in attitudes of parents and peers. When family ties are weak and counterproductive, adolescents are more likely to depend on peers for support and approval. Conversely, when family ties are strong and parent-adolescent interactions are productive, adolescents are less likely to turn to peers in times of stress.

Although traditional social and psychological theories have sometimes stressed the pervasiveness of peer influences and the existence of a separately functioning adolescent society, that emphasis may have been overstated. There is a great deal of commonality in attitudes among peers who cluster together. On the other hand, the impact of peers, especially with respect to negative behaviors, should not be underemphasized. Peers and friends have an impact that is neither as great as some would believe nor as weak as others might prefer. In general peers provide a positive environment within which the individual adolescent is able to develop a personal sense of identity.

We can see perhaps the most profound impact of peers in those young people who are deprived of peer influences through social isolation. The absence of adequate social interaction during childhood and adolescence leads to social maladjustment during adulthood. Establishing appropriate interpersonal bonds during adolescence is a necessary prerequisite to developing feelings of intimacy as young adults (Erikson, 1968).

9 | Adolescent Sexual Behavior and Attitudes

The scientific study of adolescent sexual behavior is fraught with problems. In a recent review, Diepold and Young (1979) summarize and evaluate most of the existing studies of adolescent sexual behavior and conclude that our actual knowledge of normal adolescent sexual activity is disappointingly limited. Further, they contend that much of what we believed about a major sexual revolution during the 1960s was based on undocumented speculation by the mass media. What research has been done suffers from problems that force us to be skeptical about what we think we know. As Diepold and Young argue, the problems in studying human sexual behavior are difficult enough, but when the humans in question are adolescents, the problems are even more complex.

As an example, Robert Sorensen (1973) compiled what was expected to be a major analysis of adolescent sexual attitudes and behavior, *Adolescent Sexuality in Contemporary America*. The study, however, has not met with general acceptance. Among the reasons why reviewers are skeptical of his results is evidence that the youths who Sorensen interviewed were probably atypical (see, for example, Bell, Broderick and Goldsmith, 1973). Sorensen started his research by identifying a national sample of 839 teens who were scientifically selected to be representative of all teens in United States. To Sorensen's credit, he observed the ethical requirement of requesting the parents' permission to interview the teenagers (some studies have not). Only 508 of the parents agreed. Of these, only 393 of their teenagers agreed to respond to his questionnaire (which was almost forty pages long). Thus only 47 percent of the original sample ultimately participated in his study. Very serious questions remain over whether the 53 percent who would not or could not participate had attitudes and behaviors similar to the 47 percent who did. It has been shown, for example, that in the Kinsey studies (Kinsey et al., 1953) women volunteer participants were on the average higher in self-esteem and sexually more active (Maslow and Sakoda, 1953). Thus those who did participate in Sorensen's study may not be truly representative of all American teens. Nonetheless, Sorensen's study is not without merit. Most

Some cultures, such as the San Carlos Apaches of Arizona, have a formal "rite of passage" to mark the achievement of sexual maturity. (Martin Etter/Anthro-Photo)

studies of adolescent sexual behavior are much narrower in scope and use more restricted samples than Sorensen's.

Some questions about a young person's sexual attitudes may yield ambiguous responses. For example, 74 percent of Sorensen's young people answered "false" to this statement: "My parents and I sometimes talk about sex but it makes them very uncomfortable." What does "false" mean? That they never talk to their parents? That they often talk? That their parents don't feel uncomfortable? Using "proper" language may also lead to problems. In another study, Vener and Stewart (1974) reported that many preadolescents answered that they had engaged in sexual intercourse. When interviewers questioned further, they discovered that the youngsters thought that sexual intercourse was talking to someone of the opposite sex.

With these caveats in mind, let us turn our attention to adolescent sexuality.

VIGNETTE 9-1
The Games Teenagers Play

Today's young people are clearly more liberal than their parents in terms of attitudes and behaviors about sex and sexuality. This increased liberality has both positive and negative features. Although their more open attitudes as adolescents may lead to their healthier sexual identity as adults, the decisions about sexual behavior may be subjected to undue pressure by peers who make sexual activity a price of being accepted as part of the group. The authors of this article review some of the trends in current adolescent sexual behavior in contemporary America. Note that young people report strong peer pressures to conform to increased sexual activity. Conforming to belong, of course, removes the decision making about sexual behavior from the individual. When ill-informed decision making is tied with erratic or ineffective use of contraceptives, the risk of teenage pregnancy and venereal disease is sharply increased. Both pregnancy and venereal disease are skyrocketing.

Mary, a 15-year-old sophomore from Newton, Mass., recalls how she was swept up into the brave, sometimes bewildering, new world of adolescent hedonism. "I wasn't able to handle the pressure," she says. "I was part of a group in junior high that was into partying, hanging out and drinking. I started to have sex with my boyfriend and it was a real downer. It was totally against what I was, but it was important to be part of a group. Everybody was having sex."

Something has happened to those endearing young charmers who used to wobble around playing grownup in Mom's high heels. They are reaching puberty earlier, finding new freedom from parental restraints, taking cues from a pleasure-bent culture and playing precocious sex games in the bedroom—often while Mom and Dad are at work. The sexual revolution, spawned as a social protest on college campuses of the '60s, has filtered down to high schools and junior high schools.

For adolescent boys, sex has always been regarded as a rite of passage, like getting permission to drive the family car. In the past decade it appears to have become a ceremonial of young womanhood as well. While statistics on teen-age dating habits are still sketchy, they suggest that sexual adventurism among young girls has risen to an astonishing degree. The latest figures in a highly respected new study by Johns Hopkins University professors Melvin Zelnik and John F. Kantner indicate that nearly 50 percent of the nation's 10.3 million young women age 15 to 19 have had premarital sex. The percentage has nearly doubled since Zelnik and Kantner began their surveys in 1971. "Things that supported remaining a virgin in the past—the fear of getting pregnant, being labeled the 'town pump,' or whatever—have disappeared," observes Zelnik.

And teen-agers themselves report that the age of initiation is dropping. "I'd say half the girls in my graduating class are virgins," says 18-year-old Sharon Bernard, a high-school senior in New Iberia, La. "But you wouldn't believe those freshmen and sophomores. By the time they graduate there aren't going to be any virgins left."

One disturbing consequence of this advanced sexuality is that teen-age pregnancies are epidemic: 1 million teen-age girls—one out of every ten—get pregnant each year. Statistics in a 1977 study show that 600,000 unwed teen-agers were giving birth each year, with the sharpest increase among those under 14. Venereal disease is rampant among adolescents, accounting for 25 percent of the 1 million reported gonorrhea cases every year.

For all their carnal knowledge, in fact, teen-agers are surprisingly ignorant about the hazards of freebooting sex. Many girls find it less troubling to get into bed with a boy than to prepare for the act with a contraceptive. "If you come prepared, it appears that you're easy and available," observes Dr. Jackie Boles, a Georgia State University sociologist. An estimated 80 percent of the country's 5 million sexually active teen-agers fail to use birth control because of unwillingness, ignorance or the unavailability of contraceptive devices. Meanwhile, sex-education programs remain controversial and inadequate. "Fewer than 10 percent of all teen-agers are exposed to any valid sex education in the schools," says Syracuse University professor Sol Gordon, whose book, "You Would If You Loved Me," advises teen-age girls on how to say no. "Most plans for sex education are pathetic."

Though parents, educators and sociologists may be aghast at the reckless sybaritism of the young, some see it in retrospect as fallout from the decade's great social upheavals: women's liberation, the exploding divorce rate, the decline of parental and institutional authority, the widespread acceptance of "living together"—and the swift media reflection of those trends. The sexual revolution, they note, has also provided an unwitting new role model for teens. "There are a lot of divorced and single parents who are dating," says Judith Gorbach, director of family planning for Massachusetts' Department of Public Health. "The message everywhere is sex."

Guideposts

The media have been quick to relay that message. Sexual precocity is being packaged and promoted—and taken as the norm—throughout the popular culture. The Jordache jean company, for example, hypes its contour-explicit pants by picturing scantily clad teen-agers astride each other in such proper media as The New York Times Magazine. In teen music, such back-to-basics disco tunes as "Take Your Time (Do It Right)" and "Do That to Me One More Time" climb high on the charts. Provocative films like "Foxes," about four Los Angeles teen-agers blundering through a sexual initiation, and "Little Darlings," about two 15-year-old girls competing to lose their virginity at summer camp, pack movie theaters with agog adults and kids. TV has been no less exploitive of the trend. According to one group of Boston teen-agers, the only place where being "hard to get" is really admired these days is on "Laverne & Shirley."...

But beneath the wordly veneer there are adolescent doubts and conflicts. Many teen-agers are having sex as much because it is available and fashionable as because it is desirable. Once chastity was something to be guarded—or lied about when lost. Now an uncommonly virtuous teen-ager lies to protect the dirty little secret that she is still a virgin. There is more pressure than ever for a girl to "get it over with," as one teen-ager puts it. But for every girl who can carry it off with instinctual ease, there are many who cannot. For them the experience may turn out to be "a real downer"—something less than the lyrical, erotic awakening they had been led to expect by such soft-core film fantasies as "The Blue Lagoon," the story of two teen-agers on a desert island who gradually awaken to the joys of adolescent sex. And few can handle the emotional complications of the morning after. "I never expected the guy to marry me, but I never expected he would avoid me in school," says 14-year-old Susan of San Francisco, who lost her viginity—and her boyfriend—a few months ago and wound up in a deep depression.

Some experts worry about the potentially damaging effects of such sexual disillusionments—especially at tender ages when defense mechanisms are still fragile. "Sex before 16 or 17 is counterproductive emotionally," says Claudette Kunkes, a clinical psychologist at The Door, an adolescent treatment center in New York. "Younger kids haven't developed the ego functions which are crucial in making their own choices about sex. The younger girls I've interviewed never really enjoyed it."...

Childhood-development authorities also note the paradox that while adolescents are traditionally rebellious, within their own circles they tend to be fiercely conformist. Perhaps at no other stage of life is the behavior of one's peers so strong an influence. Experts believe that among teen-agers peer pressure is one of the most important reasons for taking the sexual plunge. Some girls manage to resist going over the brink. "A guy will say, 'Everybody's doing it, what's the matter with you?'" reports Dana, a 16-year-old San Francisco high-school junior. "You just tell him, 'Well, if everybody's doing it, find someone else to do it with.'" But not every girl will risk a flippant reply. "Think of a girl at 14 facing the pressures of rejecting her boyfriend," sighs Virginia Ghattas, a Newton, Mass., biology teacher, who says her younger students face sexual decisions today that older generations never had to contend with. And one 14-year-old at suburban Atlanta's Roswell High School has little doubt about the outcome. "All they think about is that they really want this guy to like them," she says, "and so they're going to do it."...

Denial

Birth control remains the greatest area of sexual ignorance. "Teen-agers commonly think they won't get pregnant the first time, or if the man doesn't ejaculate, or if they don't have an orgasm," notes Joe Friedman, of the Los Angeles Sex Information Help Line. But a knottier problem is teen-agers' refusal—or inability—to relate their conduct to its possible consequences. "It seems so improbable that

they would get pregnant because they cannot imagine themselves as women," says Harvard psychologist Carol Gilligan. Adds Claudette Kunkes, of New York's The Door: "It's the 'It won't happen to me' syndrome. They even deny to themselves they're having sex. Even after abortions they deny they were pregnant."

Unfortunately, sex-education courses often do little to address such confusion. The typical course in the schools is not much more than a protracted anatomy lesson, or what some teenagers consider overly graphic depictions of the ravages of venereal disease ("The Chiller Theater of Sex," one Sun Belt sophomore wryly calls them). Young people clearly want more information, especially on the "why" of sexual relationships rather than the "how."

Parents are equally confused about how to handle their adolescents' unseemly sexual stirrings; they vacillate between an enlightened view and viewing with alarm. Most parents are notoriously remiss in talking to their children about sex. Raised more restrictively, too many of them still suffer their own sexual hangups and are likely to transmit their conflicts when they do air the issue....

'Old School'

Adolescents find it no less awkward. "I'd rather pick a name out of a phone book and talk to a stranger than talk to my mother about sex," says Janice, a 13-year-old from Pleasant Hill, Calif. "It's too embarrassing." Many sons have just as much difficulty approaching their fathers. "I can't talk to my dad about sex," says James Williams, 18, of Los Angeles. "He's from the old school. I think he was a lady's man, but I also think he has a fear of talking about it with me. I think he fears I might get a girl pregnant. He was even hesitant about me taking sex ed in high school."...

Exploits

Despite such confusions, few teen-agers would turn the clock back to a more chaste era. They believe the new openness has made them more tolerant of their friends' sexual proclivities and more healthily disposed toward their own. Many are convinced their early sexual exploits will leave them better prepared for the vicissitudes of modern marriage, and some authorities bear them out. "There's a less frantic attitude toward sex because it's so available," says the Ackerman Institute's Bloch. "There's an opportunity for friendship to blossom, and it can open up a world of relationships, not just a prelude to genital sexuality. And that may well be a foundation for better marriages.". . .

But there is a midrange of some sadly troubled ones. Tender young things are sampling sex before its season—before they are out of dental braces—and then feeling the anguish of remorse. Many are less sexually liberated than they would like to think. "There's a danger of a kind of precocious sexuality that can lead to emptiness if there's no ongoing relationship," says Bloch. "I think the biggest emotional problem these teens have is loneliness—sex without connectedness instead of sex with significance." Adds University of Maryland's Dr. Kappelman: "A major part of sex education for teens must be that they have a right to say yes or no, based upon their own perceptions of self-identity. What's different from an earlier generation is that most kids today are straightforward with each other but not as honest with themselves. Too many of them can't say to themselves, 'I'm not ready'."

Society's mixed message to the young has left them with a mixed blessing. They have more choices than their elders ever had, but no guarantees that they will choose wisely. And that has left many of them with an equivocal appreciation of the benefits of sexual emancipation. As one reflective 16-year-old from Palo Alto, Calif., summed it up: "It must have been a lot easier when society set the standards for you. It can get awfully complicated. I guess that's the price we have to pay for freedom."

SEXUAL ATTITUDES

Whether or not there has been a sexual revolution, there has very certainly been a major shift in sexual attitudes among the young. In one study, sexual attitudes were assessed on similar groups over a period of ten years (King, Balswick, and Robinson, 1977). The results showed a significant liberalization of sexual attitudes, especially among college women. Table 9-1 presents an example of the change in attitudes. Note that in 1965, 35 percent of the male respondents and 56 percent of the female respondents felt that a promiscuous man was immoral. In 1975, only 19.5 percent of the males and 30.1 percent of the females felt the same way. When the same question was asked about a woman who had multiple sexual partners, 42 percent of the males and 91 percent of the females in 1965 felt that such a woman was immoral. In 1975, 28.5 percent of the males and 41 percent of the females responded similarly. We can observe at least two trends in these results. First, there was a substantial liberalization of attitudes over that time period for both males and females. Second, although the double standard, which allows greater sexual

Table 9-1 SEXUAL ATTITUDES OF COLLEGE STUDENTS

Statement		Males	Females
1. I feel that premarital	1965	33	70
sexual intercourse	1970	14	34
is immoral.	1975	19.5	20.7
2. A man who has had sexual	1965	35	56
intercourse with a great many	1970	15	22
women is immoral.	1975	19.5	30.1
3. A woman who has had sexual	1965	42	91
intercourse with a great many	1970	33	54
men is immoral.	1975	28.5	41

Source: K. King, J. O. Balswick, and I. E. Robinson, "Sexual Revolution Among College Females," *Journal of Marriage and the Family,* 39 (1977): 457. Copyrighted 1977 by the National Council on Family Relations. Reprinted by permission.

latitude for males, is greatly diminished, it has not altogether vanished. Both sexes were more likely to assess the woman who had sexual intercourse with multiple partners as immoral than they were to judge the man for similar behavior.

Although college students are more likely than their noncollege counterparts to have liberal sexual attitudes, the noncollege population is becoming increasingly tolerant of premarital sexual activity. Yankelovitch (1974) finds about a four-year lag in attitudes between college youths and their noncollege peers. In 1969, for example, Yankelovitch found that 57 percent of noncollege and 34 percent of college youths felt that premarital sexual relations were morally wrong. By 1973, 34 percent of the noncollege youths felt the same

Many people express worry over the high sexual suggestiveness of advertisements aimed at adolescents. (© Margaret Thompson)

way. In 1969, 72 percent of noncollege youths felt that sexual relations between consenting homosexuals were morally wrong, whereas only 43 percent of the college youths felt that way. By 1973, 47 percent of the noncollege youths held that attitude.

Although there has been a general trend in liberalization of sexual attitudes among youths, we should remember that wide diversity within and between age groups. Younger teens, on the whole, are more conservative in their attitudes and behavior. Likewise, the more religious a person is, the more likely he or she is to hold more conservative sexual values. As Table 9-1 showed, although much of the sexual double standard has dissipated, it has not been totally eliminated, and females still report more guilt feelings after premarital coitus than males (Schalmo and Levin, 1974).

A radical shift in sexual attitudes is not automatically accompanied by a similar shift in sexual behavior. We can trace a major alteration in sexual attitudes among youths from 1950 to the 1970s, but the increase in rates of premarital coitus has not been nearly as profound. Indeed the sexual revolution of the 1960s was apparently nonexistent (Conger, 1975). Some shift in behavior has been observed during the 1970s. Nonetheless, worries of a promiscuous generation may be largely unfounded.

MASTURBATION

Most educated people recognize that masturbation, or autoeroticism, is a normal sexual activity among adolescents. Many young people, however, still report guilt feelings about it. Available information about masturbatory activity indicates that by late adolescence virtually all males and the majority of females have engaged in masturbation (Kinsey et al., 1948, 1953). When guilt feelings are reported, they are often associated more with the fantasies accompanying the masturbation than with the activity itself. In a study of German youths, few reported that they preferred masturbation to sexual intercourse. Rather, masturbation was an alternative for sexual release when coitus was unavailable, or it served as a pleasurable alternative (Sigusch and Schmidt, 1973).

DATING, KISSING, AND PETTING

Dating, kissing and light petting, or petting above the waist, are nearly universal in the same behavior of late-adolescents. Douvan and Adelson (1966) reported that by age fourteen, 19 percent of girls were dating; by age sixteen, 72 percent; and by age eighteen, 91 percent. Saghir and Robins (1971) estimate that 90 to 100 percent of heterosexual youths and 85 percent of homosexual youths have experienced heterosexual dating by the age of nineteen. Kissing and light petting are as common as dating and probably serve to enhance feelings of sexual adequacy (Sorensen, 1973; Vener and Stewart, 1973; Vener et al., 1972). Genital petting, on the other hand, is much less common, but by age seventeen, 59 percent of females and 62 percent of males report genital petting as compared to 71 percent of both sexes reporting

Adolescence is marked by heightened awareness of sexuality and sexual feelings. (© Charles Gatewood)

light petting (Vener and Stewart, 1973). According to King and his colleagues (1977), however, genital petting has become increasingly common among college students.

HOMOSEXUAL BEHAVIOR

As a normal part of adolescents' attempts to clarify their sexual self-identity, many young boys and girls report homosexual feelings or experiences. It is not unusual, for example, for young adolescent or preadolescent boys to engage in group or mutual masturbation; such events are transitory and harmless. But if adults discover the activity and label the boys as homosexual, their unwarranted reaction might lead to unpleasant consequences. The event may be called a homosexual experience, but there is no evidence to suggest that such activity leads to adult homosexual preferences. Practitioners should bear in mind that a real difference exists between homosexual encounters and homosexual preference. Applying the label "homosexual" to a young person who is in the process of forming his or her sexual identity might act as a self-fulfilling prophesy. Many youths who are not homosexual may wonder if they are because of their past homosexual experiences; an adult who reacts by labeling them as homosexual may serve to confirm erroneously what they fear.

Elias and Gebhard (1969) report that 52 percent of males and 34 percent of females engage in sexual play with members of the same sex before puberty. Among males, 27 percent report a homosexual experience that led to orgasm during early adolescence, and 38 percent report similar experiences during

Not all adolescents choose heterosexual relationships; increasingly, gay couples are making their preferences public. (Rose Skytta/Jeroboam, Inc.)

late adolescence (Kinsey et al., 1948). Although homosexual encounters leading to orgasm are much less common among adolescent girls (Kinsey et al., 1953), homosexual encounters still occur.

Most adolescent homosexual acts are transitory and do not indicate a true homosexual preference, but the fact remains that some young people may opt for a homosexual preference. To do so, one runs the risk of strong negative social sanction, including social exclusion or rejection, even by parents. A recent survey found that although 68 percent of those questioned said what consenting adults do in private is their own business, 60 percent opposed laws that would permit homosexual acts (Hooker and Chance, 1975). In Sorensen's (1973) study, 75 percent of the adolescents felt that male or female homosexuality was disgusting, and 59 percent felt that we should have laws against homosexuality. Thus, although many gay groups plead for equal rights and encourage homosexuals to "come out of the closet," many homosexuals fear social disapproval and keep their preference silent. The question of whether a homosexual can or should be "cured" or whether he or she should be helped to adapt to living as a homosexual in a heterosexual society should be decided by the person involved. In many cases, counseling should include not only the homosexual youth but also his or her parents, because the parents' acceptance or nonacceptance of their child's homosexual preference may be a source of personal stress.

PREMARITAL COITUS

According to Sorensen (1973), by the age of fifteen, 44 percent of males and 30 percent of females are nonvirgins. By age seventeen, 59 percent of males and 45 percent of females have experienced premarital coitus. These rates are not terribly different for males in the Kinsey studies (Kinsey et al., 1948), but they are substantially higher than the rates for females in those early studies (Kinsey et al., 1953). Thus one might conclude that if a sexual revolution took place at all, it was among women. Other studies report somewhat lower rates of nonvirginity than Sorensen (Vener, Stewart, and Hager, 1973; Saghir and Robins, 1973), but the trends are still the same. On the average, males are much more likely to be sexually active during early teen years, but by later teen years the differences between the sexes are less. Of interest in the Sorensen study is his evidence that even among sexually active teens, the preference is for serial, monogamist relationships. That is, a sexually active teen has intercourse with only one partner, to whom he or she has a strong emotional commitment. When that relationship ends, the females tend to be sexually inactive until another monogamistic relationship develops.

Perhaps the most informative studies on premarital sexual intercourse among American youths are those conducted by Zelnick and Kantner (1972, 1977). In 1971, Zelnick and Kantner interviewed a national sample of unmarried women between fifteen and nineteen about their sexual behavior. They then repeated that study in 1976, covering areas like sexual history and contraceptive use. The principal finding reported by Zelnick and Kantner (1977) was that between 1971 and 1976, there was a 30 percent increase in the proportion of never-married teenage women who had engaged in sexual intercourse. By age nineteen, 55 percent of never-married women have experienced coitus. Although rates of premarital coitus are substantially higher among black than white teenage females, both in 1971 and 1976, the greater increase in sexual activity was among the whites.

Although Zelnick and Kantner's data show a general increase in sexual intercourse among unmarried teenage women, the data do not imply increased promiscuity per se. Nearly half of the sexually experienced girls reported no sexual intercourse in the month prior to the interview. This was an increase from 39.6 percent in 1971. However, the percent of unmarried females who reported sexual intercourse six or more times in the prior month had also increased, from 12.8 percent in 1971 to 15.3 percent in 1976.

The typical media image would have us believe that first premarital intercourse occurs in a parked car or in a hideaway motel. Actually, 79 percent of the sexually experienced girls in Zelnick and Kantner's (1977) study reported that their first coitus occurred either in their partner's home, their home, or a friend's home. Likewise, 86 percent of the incidences of most recent sexual intercourse (excluding those women who report only one coital experience) were in a home, either the partner's, her own, or a friend's. As Zelnick and Kantner (1977) concluded:

> The partner's home is the most likely place for the most recent intercourse to have occurred regardless of the girl's age at the time. The girl's home becomes increasingly important as the locale for her most recent intercourse as her age increases. Thus, for four out of five sexually experienced unmarried females who have had more than one encounter with sex, the choice seems to lie in the answer to "My place or your place," with his place having the edge. (p. 60)

TEENAGE PREGNANCY

Coordinate with increased sexual activity among adolescents has been a rapid increase in the number of teen pregnancies. From 1960 to 1975, there was a decline in the proportion of infants conceived and delivered out of wedlock for all groups of women over twenty years of age. However, during that same time period, such births among teenage mothers increased by 50 percent. Among very young mothers, the proportion of births out of wedlock was 85 percent. In numbers, there were 92,000 out-of-wedlock births to teenage mothers in 1960. By 1975, the number had risen to 223,500 (Baldwin, 1978). Further, whereas very few mothers under sixteen have had more than one live birth, a startling proportion of older teenage mothers are having their second or more births. This trend is viewed with alarm by a variety of agencies, because the teen mother and her infant are considered to be "at risk."

The teen mother is medically at risk because she runs an increased tendency toward premature labor, preeclampsia (high blood pressure and water retention), toxemia, and postdelivery infections. Although the likelihood of many of those complications is greatly reduced by adequate prenatal care (Zacker, Andelman, and Bauer, 1969; Rauh, Burket, and Brookman, 1975), the early teen mother is less likely to seek out early medical attention, and the increased tendency toward premature labor lessens the time available for potential care. Mortality rates for both mother and infant are higher among early teen mothers than among any other age group except women over forty. Infant deaths are 3.5 times greater among teen mothers than among mothers not at risk.

VIGNETTE 9-2
Teenage pregnancy: Whose fault?

An unplanned, unwanted teen pregnancy is a tragedy for a variety of social, economic, psychological, and educational reasons. But the stress of the pregnancy often yields hostility and blame from the boy, the girl, and, not unlikely, the adolescents' parents. An adage in psychology claims, "Frustration leads to aggression." The fears and frustrations caused by an unwanted pregnancy may lead to aggressive accusations of blame. The following article, taken from a magazine intended for adolescent girls, asks the question, "Whose fault?"

Source: Judith Wax, "Teen Pregnancy: Whose Fault?" *Seventeen* (October 1978): 132, 172–173. Reprinted from *Seventeen*® Magazine. Copyright © 1978 by Triangle Communications Inc. All rights reserved. Reprinted by permission of The Sterling Lord Agency, Inc., as agents for the estate of Judith Wax.

He was crying. That was something he hadn't done publicly since kindergarten, and his embarrassment about it made him doubly miserable. The other people (teen-age girls and worried-looking older women) in the cheerfully decorated waiting room eyed him uneasily. What they all had in common was that someone close to them—a friend, a sister, or a daughter—was in one of the rooms just down the corridor, ending an unwanted pregnancy.

So it was his gender, as well as his tears, that made sixteen-year-old Mark (who looks like a younger version of John Denver) conspicuous at the abortion clinic in Chicago that summer morning. And if some of the glances he got had an edge of hostility, you couldn't help suspecting that the anger was meant for another male—someone who, though he'd certainly been a partner to past action, wasn't on hand now to share in the anxiety.

It was red-haired Sandy, Mark's petite fifteen-year-old girl friend, who explained his tears (and her own swollen eyes) while she sat in the recovery area a few hours after her abortion. "A lot of people would probably say I'm lucky," she said, "because at least Mark cares; he came here with me today. Most guys act like strangers when they find out a girl is pregnant.

"But I can't help blaming Mark sometimes, because he kept insisting that we didn't have to use anything and that he knew the exact moment to stop. Well, forget it. When I told him I was pregnant, he cried that day too, and it was like a movie. Except when a movie's over, you get up and go home, and your life is the same. When the crying was over, I was still pregnant."

Later, Mark talked about his own feelings "I love Sandy," he said. "But I had this macho thing that made me act as though I'd had a lot of experience and insist that she should just trust me. Well, I found out I didn't really know that much and that it's not always possible to stop at the last second. And even if you do, a girl can get pregnant anyway. The worst thing I discovered is that even though I wanted to stand by Sandy afterward, what could I do? What kind of job could I get to support a wife and baby? I won't even have my high school diploma for another year. Sandy and I put all our money together to pay for the abortion. And things aren't the same between the two of us now."

Mark and Sandy's situation is one that has become depressingly familiar. The individual stories and details vary; teens may blame their partners or themselves, their parents, or society. But they all have in common the need to resolve who is responsible for what no one wanted. That word *responsibility* makes a lot of people yawn before the third syllable is out. Still, it's a more constructive word than *blame* or *fault*. And for couples like Mark and Sandy, it's important to reexamine the mistaken attitudes that can cause unhappy circumstances like theirs.

The 1970s have seen an epidemic of teen pregnancies in America. According to the most recent figures, there are 1,000,000 pregnancies each year among fifteen-to-nineteen-year-olds (two thirds are unmarried at the time of conception). In addition, each year, 30,000 girls younger than fifteen get pregnant. Of the yearly total, more than 600,000 teens give birth. What that means is that 10 percent of U.S. teenagers get pregnant each year and 6 percent give birth, and though the overall birthrate has declined in this country, out-of-wedlock births among younger teens have skyrocketed by 75 percent.

Opponents of abortion often blame its availability for the increase in teen pregnancies. But although some teens *do* mistakenly think of abortion as an alternative to using contraception, two recent studies indicate that among teens who opted for abortion, it was considered a backup in case of contraceptive failure, rather than a method of birth control in itself. (Of those 1,000,000 pregnancies among fifteen-to-nineteen-year-olds, 27 percent were terminated by induced abortion; the majority of the teens gave birth or miscarried.)

It is not the purpose of this article, however, to explore the pros and cons of abortion or to analyze the effectiveness of different methods of birth control; both issues were the subject of previous articles in *Seventeen*. What's important now is to find individual answers to such questions as: What should a sexually active girl expect from her partner in the way of accountability? What does she owe herself?

It's the unfortunate truth that many teen-age boys feel pregnancy is entirely a girl's responsibility. As one male teen counselor told me, "Very few boys are sensitive to what a girl has at stake; there's little emotional understanding on their part. Most of the guys I talk to say things like 'No matter how much I pressure a girl, she doesn't *have* to have sex with me.'

Some are concerned, but for many, the name of the game is scoring."

Gail Cantor, a Planned Parenthood social services specialist who counsels pregnant teens, says: "Studies show that the vast majority of teen-age boys today only pay lip service to responsibility. A lot of them are very good at telling a girl that they can be depended on if something goes wrong; they may even mean it when they say it. But it's the rare guy who sticks around once the girl gets pregnant."

There's hope, however, for changes in these attitudes. Planned Parenthood has inaugurated outreach programs in several cities not only to provide information about effective birth control but also to try to make teen-age boys more aware of the emotional aspects of sexual relationships. And this fall, the National Organization of Non-Parents (NON), whose headquarters are in Baltimore, Maryland, has planned workshops in seven cities that will bring teens of both sexes together with specialists in fields as diverse as sexual health care and career counseling. Dr. Peter Scales, teen projects director for NON, says, "It's important for teens to realize that pregnancy prevention is not a separate subject but part of a person's decision-making about the way to run his or her life."

Another effort to increase male awareness was a conference funded by the Department of Health, Education, and Welfare and held last spring in Rochester, New York. The program, called MAN '78 (for Male Adolescent Needs), was geared toward exploring male sexual roles and responsibilities. Surprisingly, it had as many female as male participants. The agenda included such topics as: "Am I ready for sex?", male lib, venereal disease, and dating and relating. Increased education and exchange— as in conferences like MAN '78—could turn the slight trend toward male involvement in preventing pregnancy into everyday reality.

Darryl Hale, program development specialist for males and adolescents for Planned Parenthood, in Chicago, recently conducted an informal study based on questionnaires that were filled out by more than one thousand males, aged fifteen to nineteen, 80 percent of them black, 7 percent Spanish-speaking, the remainder white. These percentages don't reflect the proportions of each group in the general population. But the percentage of teens of all races that are getting pregnant each year has risen alarmingly, and these boys' answers give some clue to male attitudes within the age group surveyed.

Here's how these boys responded on some key issues:

- *Birth control is for girls only.*
  True: 56 percent. False: 44 percent.
- *A guy should use birth control whenever possible.*
  True: 18 percent. False: 82 percent.
- *If I got a girl pregnant, I would want her to have an abortion.*
  True: 12 percent. False: 88 percent.
- *It's okay to tell a girl you love her so you can have sex with her.*
  True: 70 percent. False: 30 percent.

When making a decision about whether to begin a sexual relationship, few girls know how a potential partner would answer questions like these. But if the two of them either can't or don't speak openly enough to know each other's feelings and attitudes about such things, should they be considering the intimacy of sex? And if a girl knows that her boy friend doesn't believe in his using birth control, and that he would be against her having an abortion if she became pregnant, isn't it also important for her to know if his feelings about what she *should* do are the same as her own?

The problem of whether or not to engage in sex has become increasingly difficult because the sexual sales pitch now comes full force from many sources. There's the nightly TV blitz, for example; the trouble is, you rarely get to see an episode in which one of the glamorous stars has to apply for Aid to Dependent Children, or face an abortion with fear, no money, and no one to depend on. Although books, magazines, and television shows can't in themselves create a national pregnancy epidemic, they can turn up the pressure on both sexes and give a lot of teens the idea that "quality of life" means having provocative clothes, and a sexy wiggle.

That's as phony as the canned laughter on some of the same shows. Yet it's part of the reason that when a teen-age boy tells a girl, "Everybody's doing it," he may sincerely believe that everybody is. Statistics show, however, that although more teens are sexually active than ever before, more than half of America's teens have *not* had intercourse. The fact that millions of teens aren't "conforming" indicates that no one is confined to one way of living or being. So an important responsibility both sexes have is to assert their individuality and understand that people's needs are as unique as their fingerprints.

Ginny, a freshman at a midwestern college, told me. "A lot of us have misunderstood what liberation is all about. I mean, what's liberated about always being available? I finally realized that I didn't *owe* anything to anybody but myself."

Like Ginny, more and more young women are discovering the right to say no. It's a word that can be especially hard to say in your teens, mainly because many girls are concerned about being "different" or hurting someone's feelings or losing someone they really care about. Every yes, however, has a far-greater potential of risk: The possibility (however minimal) of side effects from the long-term use of some contraceptives, and the more-immediate dangers of teen pregnancy and childbirth. (The maternal death risk is highest for females under twenty, and teen-agers are much more likely than older women to lose their babies soon after birth.) Furthermore, if a teen becomes pregnant, she faces having to make painful decisions about whether or not to have an abortion or to have her baby and give it up for adoption. A decision to keep the baby even though she's not married means jeopardizing her education and career (which could result in lifetime financial dependency)

and taking on the hefty responsibility for another life for the next twenty years or so. If she chooses to marry, the future of her marriage—and her baby—is still precarious: Three out of five pregnant teen brides get divorced within six years.

Although the feelings of both partners are very important in any relationship, a turn-down needn't be hurtfully phrased or mean rejection of the other person as a human being. The Planned Parenthood booklet called "It's Okay To Say No Way" (available for 25¢ from Publications Section, Planned Parenthood Federation, 810 Seventh Ave., New York, N.Y. 10019) suggests some tactful phrases like "I'm just not ready to get involved" and "I've made up my mind to wait."

One of the ways a boy can be responsible is to try to understand that no and to respect it. After all, why should he feel threatened if his girl friend—no matter how much she loves him—is thoughtful about making her own choices? That very thoughtfulness makes it a compliment that she chose *him* in the first place. (If she isn't deeply involved with him, there's even greater reason for caution before beginning a sexual relationship.) And in practical terms, even a caring and well-intentioned teen-age boy is limited in his ability to bear the consequences of an unwanted pregnancy (as Mark discovered).

A responsible boy will act that way before, as well as during, a sexual relationship. He won't manipulate a girl by claiming feelings of love he doesn't have, he won't put pressure on her, and he'll be concerned about the risks she's taking and compare them honestly with his own.

A girl who is responsible will expect the same things of herself, and won't give one message when she really means another. She will recognize that it is essential to her well-being and that of her partner to have her feelings sorted out ahead of time—and of temptation.

Sol Gordon, director of the Institute for Family Research and Education, at Syracuse

University, said: "I don't think that teen-agers under eighteen should have sex. But nobody asked for my permission, so all I can really say is, at least use birth control."

A 1976 survey by Melvin Zelnick and John Kantner, of Johns Hopkins University, in Baltimore, Maryland, led them to the conclusion that although more sexually active teens are using contraceptives than before—based on a comparable survey done by the same research team five years earlier—teens still have a long way to go toward achieving responsible use of birth control. Among the teens surveyed, 11 percent of those who said they *always* used contraception became pregnant (but whether an effective method of contraception was correctly used was not determined). Of those who used contraception only occasionally, 24 percent became pregnant; of those who never used birth control at all, 58 percent became pregnant. The survey also suggested that access to birth control did not—as some adults fear—encourage sexual activity: 60 percent of unmarried teens became sexually active before they used any form of contraception at all.

It's interesting that the one safe and effective method of birth control that divides the responsibility between both partners—the male use of the condom at the same time a woman uses vaginal contraceptive foam—is often rejected by sexually active teens. "It's not spontaneous," some say—but then, neither is childbirth or abortion or raising a child.

Which brings us to what is perhaps most important of all—the understanding that the best sex comes out of concern, sharing, tenderness, and the kind of mutual trust that doesn't demand "proof" or endanger the well-being of either partner. Few teen-age girls are able to admit it to anyone when their sexual experiences turn out to be disappointing. They think, "Something must be wrong with me!" But what's wrong is that fear, haste, or the lack of a caring partner can take its toll on what ought to be a special experience. A truly healthy and enjoyable experience—one that grows out of genuine sharing—is worth waiting for. At the least, it's worth some honest self-evaluation.

Seeking outside advice can also help. Here's what Planned Parenthood suggests:

- Talk to people you trust and respect, at school, church, or club.
- If your parents have never talked about sex, they might be waiting for you to ask. Go ahead, and risk it.
- Some communities have discussion groups, hot lines, or peer counselors. Ask if your sex education program includes discussions of sexuality and relationships.

Rhonda Alter, from Winnetka, Illinois, who was a peer counselor at her high school youth health service last year, says, "Teens have to understand their own needs and values. One of the first responsibilities anyone has is to his or her growth as a person. There's a great deal of pressure on boys to perform sexually to supposedly prove their manhood, and girls can help show them that manhood can and does mean a lot of other things. Once a girl is pregnant, it's a little late for her to begin thinking about what she really wants out of life and relationships. I guess you could say that in a good relationship, responsibility begins the first time you say hello to each other.

Because the teen mother has an increased tendency toward premature labor, the likelihood of a high risk, low birthweight (less than 2500 grams, or 5½ pounds) baby is also increased. Low-birthweight infants display a high rate of early childhood anomalies and are disproportionately represented in the population of mental retardates (Ingersoll and Steger, 1979; Pasamanick

An increasing number of adolescent mothers are choosing to keep their babies. (Courtesy, Family Service Association of Greater Boston, South Shore Center. Photograph © Susan Lapides)

and Knobloch, 1961; Werner and Smith, 1976). However, once again, many of those risks are greatly reduced by positive hospital and home environments. There is some evidence that very young parents of low-birthweight infants are more likely to be physically abusive to the child (Elmer, 1967; Smith, 1975).

Teenage pregnancies also increase the likelihood of economic strain from interrupted education and limited employability of the mother. Some schools are encouraging teen mothers to complete their education by providing day care and special classes, but many schools still expel teenage mothers on a premise of morality. Such action increases the likelihood of both mother and child needing financial aid from welfare agencies.

If the father of the child is unavailable, the problem of teenage pregnancy becomes more complicated, because the birth is thereby illegitimate. With illegitimacy comes further economic stress: 60 percent of children born out of wedlock end up on welfare roles (Moore and Caldwell, 1977). Not only has the rate of teenage pregnancies been increasing, but the proportion of these births occurring out of wedlock is also increasing. Although unwed teenage mothers often choose to keep their infants, they may be economically or psychologically unprepared for the task of child rearing. Far too often the mother and child, or as the Reverend Jesse Jackson (1977) describes them, the child and child, return

> to homes where, because their mothers are immature, unprepared, too poorly educated to find meaningful employment, these children of children will experience enormous family insecurity and, all too often, be condemned to lives of material and mental poverty, physical and psychic deprivation. (p. C7)

Cutright (1971) offers a general scheme that describes the path toward out-of-wedlock births (Figure 9-1). He suggests that three factors determine the

Figure 9-1 STEPS TO UNWED MOTHERHOOD

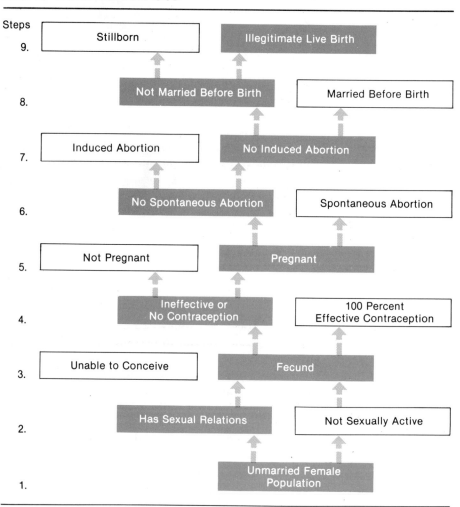

Source: Reprinted from K. Davis and J. Blake, "Social Structure and Fertility: An Analytic Framework," *Economic Development and Cultural Change* 4 (1956): 211, by permission of The University of Chicago Press. Copyright © 1956.

illegitimacy rate: (1) voluntary and involuntary controls over conception; (2) voluntary and involuntary controls over gestation; and (3) legitimization of out-of-wedlock conceptions by marriage prior to the birth of the infant.

CONTROLS OVER CONCEPTION

Clearly, the path toward an out-of-wedlock birth must begin with an unmarried woman engaging in sexual intercourse. Obviously, she must be sexually active *with* someone, and, although the diagram concentrates on the woman, the process implies both a male and a female. Except in involuntary cases such as rape or incest, most instances of premarital coitus are voluntary. In isolated cases a young girl may be motivated to become pregnant to escape an oppressive home or to ensure the commitment of a boyfriend, but such motives are the exception rather than the rule. In most cases teen pregnancy is unplanned and unpleasant.

If the young woman is not fecund (not able to conceive) or if the male is not able to impregnate, pregnancy is averted. The male or female may not be fecund for a variety of reasons. As mentioned in Chapter 2, a young woman who has passed her menarche is not necessarily fecund; there is a one- to two-year period of natural adolescent sterility folowing menarche. However, as Cutright (1972) has argued, the drop in age of the onset of menarche has had a significant effect on the rate of teenage pregnancies. If we assume an average year and a half period of natural adolescent sterility following menarche and an average age of onset of menarche of 12.5, about 50 percent of today's adolescent girls are fecund by the age of fourteen and 95 percent by age seventeen. By way of comparison, in 1870, when the average age of menarche was 16.5, less than 1 percent of girls were fecund by fourteen years old and only 50 percent by age eighteen. Thus, solely on the basis of increased proportion of fecund adolescent girls, we can expect a rise in the rate of teenage pregnancies. Tie this with an increased rate of premarital coitus, and you can begin to see the makings of a very serious problem.

A woman may not be fecund simply because it is not the correct time in her ovulatory cycle. However, using that factor as a method of contraception during teenage years may be a poor method, because her cycle may not have become stable enough to become reliable. Rhythm, as a form of contraception, depends not only on stable patterns of the release of ova during the menstrual cycle but also on understanding when pregnancy is most likely to occur. In Zelnick and Kantner's (1977) study, one-quarter of white teenage women and three-fifths of black teenage women who claimed to use rhythm as a form of birth control incorrectly specified the time of greatest risk. As Zelnick and Kantner (1977) note, "Rhythm is not highly regarded as an effective method of contraception, particularly when its use is combined with incorrect knowledge about the timing of ovulation" (p. 63). Having attended sex-education classes did not significantly improve the girls' knowledge of the ovulatory cycle.

A disturbingly large proportion of sexually active adolescents report little or no use of contraception (Sorensen, 1973; Zelnick and Kantner, 1977). When asked why they don't use contraception, adolescents report that they feel that contraception would debase the love relationship, or that contraceptives were unavailable, or that using contraceptives would be admitting that they need them. Most, however, don't use contraceptives because they do not think they will get pregnant (Shah, Zelnick, and Kantner, 1974; Sorensen, 1973). One team of writers describes this attitude as a form of adolescent egocentrism, reflecting a sense of omnipotence (Cvetkovich et al., 1975).

Zelnick and Kantner's study noted some increase in the numbers who reported having used contraception. If they use contraception at all, adolescents seem to be using more effective forms and using them with greater regularity. This may be a result of the greater availability of oral contraceptives; in 1971, only 27 percent of contracepting unmarried females aged fifteen to nineteen reported use of the pill, whereas 59 percent did so in 1976. Also, use of intrauterine devices (IUDs) nearly doubled among teenage women during those five years, whereas the use of withdrawal and condoms decreased. Although adolescent males often carry a condom in their wallet, mostly as a status symbol, over three-quarters of those who do reported not having used one during their last occasion of sexual intercourse (Arnold, 1972). Zelnick and Kantner also reported an increase in the number of women who claimed to use rhythm as a method of contraception, although the authors argued that the increase might be attributed to improved questioning procedures. Irrespective of the increased use of effective forms of contraception, Zelnick and Kantner reported no substantial decrease in the percent of never-married, sexually active females who never use contraception. If couples use effective contraception, they block the path toward teen pregnancy. However, regular contraceptive use among teens remains low

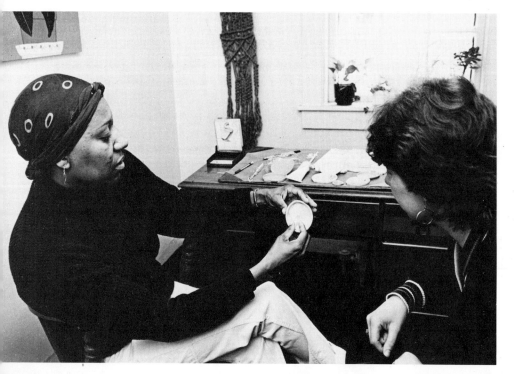

Today, many adolescents considering sexual activity are seeking contraception counseling. (Courtesy of the Crittenton Hasting House and Clinic, Boston. Photograph © Susan Lapides)

and haphazard. Although it is possible that a fecund, adolescent female can repeatedly engage in unprotected sexual intercourse and not become pregnant, such fortune presses the limits of Murphy's Law: If something bad can happen, it will.

CONTROLS OVER GESTATION

A pregnant woman may spontaneously abort the fetus, or miscarry. Although rates of spontaneous abortions among young women are high, improved nutrition and prenatal care have led to a decrease in those rates (Cutright, 1971). If, however, a girl does not spontaneously abort, she may then opt for an induced abortion. Prior to 1970, legal abortion was an option only in rare circumstances; thus many young women resorted to illegal abortions, which too often resulted in the mother's death. Since the 1970 decision by the U.S. Supreme Court allowing legal therapeutic abortions, the rate of abortions among teens and nonteens has risen steadily. By 1976, one-third of all abortions were for women under twenty years of age. Among girls under fifteen, abortions outnumbered live births, and among those fifteen to seventeen, the number of legal abortions was about two-thirds the number of live births (Kovar, 1979). In 1978, an estimated 434,000 women under twenty years of age in the Unted States obtained a legal abortion (Guttmacher Institute, 1981).

Actually, we know little about the psychological ramifications of an abortion on the mother. Adler (1975) reports that younger women are more likely to report guilt or depression following a therapeutic abortion. If the young woman comes from a background that views abortion as reprehensible for religious or moral reasons, she is more likely to report negative emotions. In any case, clinical counseling should be available both before and after an abortion to aid a young woman who opts for this alternative to adjust to those feelings. Because post abortion counseling may not be offered by abortion clinics that are not staffed for that service, the responsibility such for counseling may fall on other agencies.

LEGITIMATION BY MARRIAGE

Many young people elect to legitimate a baby conceived out of wedlock by marriage. About one-third of all babies conceived out of wedlock are now legitimated by marriage, although that percentage has dropped from over 50 percent in 1964 (Kovar, 1979). Teen marriages are notoriously unstable, but when that marriage is instigated by an unexpected pregnancy, the prognosis is even more dire. The rate of divorce is highest for marriages initiated before the age of twenty. Teen marriages in which the woman is pregnant at the time of marriage are nine times more likely to end in divorce. Further, among marriages that survive, those couples that were married as teens report higher rates of marital dissatisfaction, lower level of income, less satisfaction with their standard of living, and more tension (Lee, 1977).

Figure 9-2 ILLEGITIMATE BIRTHS AND ADOPTIONS IN THE UNITED STATES

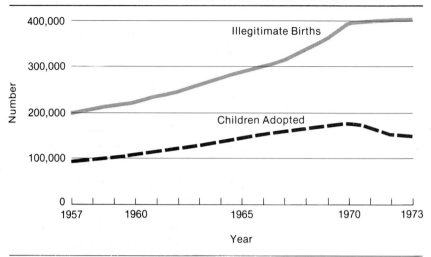

Source: Gordon S. Bonham, "Who Adopts: The Relationship of Adoption and Social-Demographic Characteristics of Women," Table 1, *Journal of Marriage and the Family* 39 (May 1977): 298. Reprinted by permission of the author.

KEEPING THE BABY

If the birth is not legitimated by marriage, the teenage mother faces the dilemma of whether to keep the baby or offer it for adoption. It is now estimated that 87 percent of all mothers who give birth to a baby out of wedlock, elect to keep the child (Guttmacher Institute, 1976). In Figure 9-2 you can see that, although the number of illegitimate births grew steadily from 1960 to 1970 and has remained at a high level despite the availability of legal abortions, the number of adopted children did not keep pace and in fact shows a decline since 1970 (Baldwin, 1976).

I want to make one final point on out-of-wedlock births. As Stickle and Ma (1975) point out, although many may deny it, people often view early pregnancy and illegitimacy as "racial" problems. It is true that illegitimacy rates are 8.5 times higher among lower-income blacks than among whites, but the impact of change in illegitimacy rate for blacks on the total illegitimacy rate for the country is negligible. Indeed, for some age groups of blacks, the illegitimacy rate is leveling off or declining. In 1960, the illegitimacy rate for white girls aged fifteen to nineteen was 6.9 births per 10,000 live births; in 1968, the rate was 9.9, an increase of 43 percent. For nonwhite girls in the same age bracket, the rate in 1960 was 78.5 versus 86.5 in 1968, an increase of 10 percent. During the same period, there was a 22 percent increase in the illegitimacy rate among white women twenty to twenty-four, whereas black women of the same age showed a 25 percent *decrease* (Cutright, 1973). Simply stated, because blacks compose less than 10 percent of the total population, their impact on the overall illegitimacy rate is small. Any major increase in the overall illegitimacy rate is the result of an increase in the rate among whites.

VENEREAL DISEASE

The second major hazard that the sexually active adolescent must face is venereal disease (VD). Both syphilis and gonorrhea are epidemic, and the spread of the diseases is particularly rampant among young people. Gonorrhea now ranks second behind the common cold as the most widespread infectious disease and first among reported communicable diseases in the United States (Center for Disease Control, 1977); syphilis ranks third. The number of reported cases of gonorrhea has tripled over the last ten years, with a 7 percent increase from 1975 to 1976. (See Figure 9-3.) Both diseases are, incidentally, vastly underreported.

Anyone who suspects that he or she has been infected with a form of VD should contact a physician or VD clinic immediately. The longer a person delays, the more serious the problem becomes. Most often a clinic will request the names of all the other sexual partners of an infected person. This procedure appears on the surface to be an infringement of a person's right to privacy. However, its purpose is to reduce the pool of VD bacteria and the chance of "ping-pong" infection—that is, the infection being passed back and forth. The best treatment is obviously prevention. Condoms offer a reasonable barrier to the transmission of VD, but the use of condoms has diminished. In fact, some point to that drop in use of condoms as one of the major causes of the increase in VD.

SYPHILIS

Syphilis (or "bad blood," "pox," "siff,") is transmitted by an infected carrier during acts of sexual intercourse, including coitus and anal or oral-genital intercourse. In very rare cases, syphilis may be transmitted by kissing. Because of the close intermixing of the male homosexual population, the risk of syphilis is ten times greater for them than for their heterosexual counterparts (Stern and MacKenzie, 1975). For both males and females, syphilis is most prevalent in the twenty- to twenty-four-year-old range, coordinate with the peak years of nonmarital sexual activity. Reported cases of syphilis are more common among males, but because women are more likely to show no symptoms, underreporting is greater among females.

A person who has contracted syphilis from an infected partner may display signs of the first stage of the disease, known as *primary syphilis*, within ten to ninety days after sexual contact. During this stage, a pimple-like sore called a *chancre* forms at the place where the bacteria initially entered the body. In males the chancre usually appears on the penis and is readily noticeable, but the chancre may also form on the mouth or rectum. In females the chancre may appear on the inside wall of the vagina; however, it may be far enough up on the walls of the vagina to go unnoticed. On the other hand, the chancre may not appear at all; hence the most obvious sign of syphilis may not be of help in some cases. Although syphilis can be detected by a blood test during the primary stage, unless a girl suspects infection, she has little reason to seek out such a test.

Because the symptoms of syphilis are not always detected, especially

Figure 9-3 REPORTED CASES OF GONORRHEA AND SYPHILIS

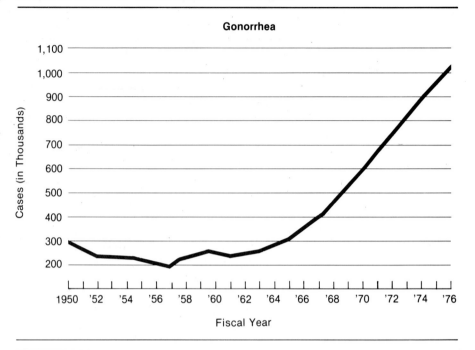

Gonorrhea

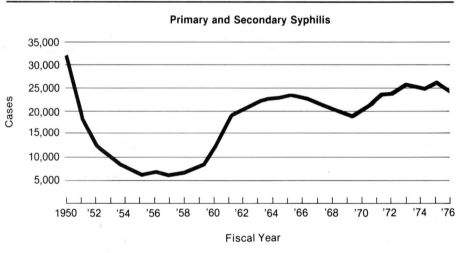

Primary and Secondary Syphilis

Source: Center for Disease Control, *VD Fact Sheet, 1976,* 23rd Edition. (Washington, D.C.: U.S. Government Printing Office, 1977), p. 9.

among women, the infection may not be discovered until it has moved into its secondary stage. The symptoms of *secondary syphilis* occur anywhere from six weeks to six months after the contraction of the disease and may show up as rashes or sores on other parts of the body, including the soles of the feet or the palms of the hand. The lesions of these rashes are highly infectious. Other symptoms of secondary syphilis are loss of hair, loss of eyebrows, headaches, sore throat, and loss of appetite. Except for the loss of hair and eyebrows, symptoms of secondary syphilis can be (and are) mistaken for a viral infection or flu. As with primary syphilis, the disease is insidious, because the symptoms are not obvious and, in some cases, disappear so quickly that they cause no alarm or fail to appear at all.

Untreated syphilis moves into a so-called *latent stage*, which lasts between five and twenty years. Actually, syphilis is anything but latent during this period. During this stage syphilitic bacteria attack and destroy healthy tissue and invade the central nervous system and the heart. Although a blood test can detect syphilis during its latency stage, most people do not suffer enough discomfort to warrant a test. Undetected, the disease progresses toward its final stage, *general paresis*, or *tertiary syphilis*, which is manifested by rapid, physical deterioration and eventual death.

A pregnant syphilitic woman has a high probability of transmitting her infection to the fetus, leading to brain damage, birth deformities, or death of the fetus. Fortunately, blood tests on pregnant women have led to the lowest rate of congenital syphilis since 1973 (Center for Disease Control, 1977).

GONORRHEA

Like syphilis, gonorrhea ("clap," "morning drip," "the dose") is transmitted during an act of sexual intercourse. A single contact by a male with an infected female involves a 22 percent risk of infection (Stern and MacKenzie, 1975). The gonococcus bacteria incubate on the inside skin of the ureter in males and on the inner wall of the vagina in females. Growth is particularly favored in females during menstruation. Unlike syphilis, no effective blood test is currently available for detection of gonorrhea, although some tests, as well as a vaccine, may be in the offing (Kolata, 1976). Treatment of gonorrhea with antibiotics is usually effective; however, a new strain of gonococcus, which resists all forms of penicillin treatment, has emerged (Center for Disease Control, 1977).

A male who has contracted gonorrhea from an infected partner may begin to show signs of the disease within two to six days, although in some instances the signs do not show up for a month, and in 10 percent of males there are no symptoms at all. Signs of gonorrhea in the male include a pus discharge from the penis and a burning sensation during urination. Most women show *no* symptoms except a slight vaginal discharge and a minor burning sensation, which can easily be misinterpreted as a urinary or bladder infection. Nonetheless, the Center of Disease Control (1977) estimates that each day, 5,750 girls will be absent from school because of gonorrhea.

Untreated gonorrhea can lead to sterility, heart disease, and arthritis. In the United States alone, 34,000 to 92,000 women are involuntarily sterilized annually from damage by gonorrhea (CDC, 1977). An infected mother may transmit the infection to an infant as it passes through the birth canal. Untreated, the gonococci may attack the infant's eyes, causing blindness. This blindness, however, can be prevented rather easily by a chemical solution (silver nitrate) placed in the baby's eyes immediately after birth. Such treatment is mandatory in all U.S. hospitals.

NONGONOCOCCAL URETHRITIS (NGU)

Professionals who work with the problem of sexually transmitted diseases warn of the increase of another infectious disease, which often follows gonorrhea infections but which may also occur in the absence of gonorrhea. Nongonococcal urethritis has been recognized since the late 1800s, when it was observed that some patients suffered gonococcal symptoms but did not exhibit gonorrhea infections. More recently the specific organism associated with this disease has been identified (chlamydia trachomatis), and proper methods of treatment have been identified. NGU is now considered the nation's most widespread venereal disease (*Urology Times*, 1977; Oriel, 1977). As in gonorrhea, males are more likely than females to show the symptoms of NGU, but the rates among both are very high.

HERPES VIRUS, TYPE II

Less generally known but increasingly a concern among those who treat and study VD is herpes simplex virus, type II. Herpes viruses are a class of viruses associated with such maladies as chicken pox, shingles, cold sores, and so on. One strain of herpes, however, is transmitted primarily through sexual contact. A person with genital herpes may suffer blisterlike sores, general fatigue, swelling and inflammation of the eyes, and difficulty in urination. Or, as is sometimes the case with gonorrhea and syphilis, one may not know one has genital herpes. Among women, genital herpes may be related to cervical cancer and does lead to high miscarriage rates. A fetus carried to full term by a mother who had a herpes infection during her pregnancy runs a high risk of being born dead or of suffering brain damage. At present, no generally recognized cure is available for genital herpes; the herpes sufferer has the condition indefinitely.

SEX EDUCATION

Much of the information in this chapter points toward the need for adequate sex education. The question is not really whether there should be sex education but where, how, and by whom it should be taught. Ideally parents should provide training and information about sex and sexuality. However, many parents are either ill equipped by lack of correct knowledge themselves or hampered by discomfort over discussing sex with their children. In Sorensen's (1973) study, parents were not a primary source of sex information. Only 16 percent of his interviewees reported that they often asked their parents for advice about sexual matters, and 23 percent felt that their parents got very uncomfortable talking to them about sex. One approach, therefore, might be an indirect one in which parents are trained to educate their own children.

Often, perhaps too often, the onus of sex education falls on the schools. The public sees the schools, as agents of society, as the vehicle for imparting knowledge in a variety of domains beyond the traditional curricula. Unfortunately, many segments of society also mistrust the schools; thus the likelihood of a general, well-conceived program of sex education is greatly reduced. Nonetheless, it is in the schools that some degree of control over the quality of sex education may be available.

Any program of sex education should be directed, first, at the self-perceived needs of those for whom the program is primarily intended. Some form of needs assessment is therefore a prerequisite for any successful program. In one such assessment (McCreary-Juhasz, 1975), teens reported needs in the domains of self-understanding and the physical and emotional changes that they were experiencing but did not understand and therefore found frightening. The content of a curriculum in sex education should also be based on needs defined by other sources, for example, experts and pretests on basic knowledge. Further, curriculum must respond to the differing cognitive levels and social backgrounds of the students, both within and between grade levels.

A successful program of sex education must fit the community within which it occurs. Innumerable sex education curricula have died before they began simply because the schools failed to gain community support. Although people who object to sex education are popularly portrayed as ignorant and reactionary, the fact remains that the schools serve the community and must recognize the differing attitudes within that community. In many cases, objections to the curricula can be appeased. Curriculum developers should realize that a good deal of fear is associated with relinquishing responsibility for sex education to the schools. Because sexuality and morality are so closely tied in many people's minds, some fear that the schools are going to provide moral training counter to the family's values. The limited available evidence suggests that those worries may be unfounded. The amount of *formal* sex education to which an adolescent is exposed does not appear to be related to increased premarital sexual activity, although *informal* sex education from peers does (Spanier, 1976). The validity or invalidity of such attitudes is almost irrelevant. The attitudes exist and any program of sex education must contend with them. In some cases many of the fears may be allayed by educating the parents before instituting the program in the schools. Nonetheless, topics such as homosexuality, abortion, and contraception, necessary in any comprehensive program of sex education, are likely to draw adverse reactions.

An additional question remains: Who should teach a course in sex education? Far too often the person selected is one who the principal thinks *should* be able to teach about sex—for example, a physical education teacher or a biology teacher. That person may be a good choice in some cases, but it does not always hold true. Any effective program of sex education requires that the instructor be able to reach to the students with factual information, be able to elicit responses from students about their sexual concerns, and allow the students to unravel their own solutions without imposing his or her own value system. McCreary-Juhasz (1975) concludes:

The adult best equipped to help the adolescent is one who: (1) is aware of the stages of heterosexual development through which the normal child passes from infancy to adolescence; (2) is cognizant of the pressures placed on individuals in a changing society; (3) recognizes the influence of the family and adults upon the child; (4) is himself secure about his own sexuality; and (5) is burdened with a minimum of problems related to interpersonal relations. (p. 345)

SUMMARY

A psychiatrist friend once explained to me that he was convinced that 95 percent of all adolescent thinking was sexual in nature—and he was not totally sure that it was not 100 percent. Whether he was unduly influenced by his most frequent clients, or whether he was exaggerating a bit to make a point, his comment describes the importance of sexuality in adolescent behavior and thought. Chapter 5 pointed out that our sexual identity is an intrinsic part of the personal identity with which we enter adult life. The adolescent's need to clarify what it means to be male or female is influenced not only by the alteration in body image but also by the emergence of sexual motives and the adult ability to respond sexually and to conceive children.

The past twenty years have witnessed a steady and significant change in sexual attitudes among teens and young adults. Both male and females are considerably more liberal in their views of what is acceptable sexual behavior. Those attitudes become more liberal as the adolescent gets older and reaches young adulthood. As a result, much of the traditional sexual double standard, which approved and encouraged premarital sexual intercourse for boys but disapproved of the same behavior for girls, has lessened. However, the double standard has not totally disappeared, although some adolescents believe that premarital sexual intercourse is all right for girls but only if love is involved. The change in sexual attitudes during the 1960s was followed by a change in sexual behavior during the 1970s. The percent of unmarried teenage girls—especially younger adolescents—who are sexually experienced has increased dramatically.

The changes in sexual behavior are not without risk. Adolescent pregnancy may be among our more serious continuing health problems, because the results of early pregnancy often lead to mothers and infants who are medically, psychologically, and socially "at risk." Likewise, increases in unprotected sexual intercourse have led to an increase in venereal disease to the point where syphilis and gonorrhea are at epidemic proportions.

Suggesting that the answer to problems associated with adolescent sexuality lies in comprehensive programs of sex education may be overly optimistic. Because sexuality is so intrinsically tied to religious and family value systems, it is likely that any program of sex education that responds to the needs of the students is certain to upset some groups of adults. And because parents are ultimately responsible for the well-being of their children, educators have a responsibility to include all groups in decision making regarding sex education curricula. Ultimately, this may mean that they must first educate the parents.

10 | Moral Development and Religion Among Adolescents

As adolescents develop more complex knowledge systems through formal operational thought, they also develop more complex value systems. As a result of their ability to consider abstractions, they are also able to question the validity of ideas that they had previously not questioned. For example, one fourteen-year-old girl wrote:

> Is there a God? It puzzles me. Some people say there is and some say there is not. There is no real proof. If we have never seen God or heard God or anything, how do we know he's there?

Too often such questions are met with adult fear and uncertainty. This girl's questions did not warn that she was rejecting all her parent's values; rather, the questions were part of a general reorganization of her value system. Questioning values is not only a normal part of moral development, it may also be necessary if a person's moral ideology is to be internalized.

Part of the personal sense of identity that an adolescent brings to adulthood is a value system or moral ideology. As with other characteristics of the emerging identity, adolescents must be able to explore and evaluate alternate value systems. At times during this process, the values of parents and society may come into conflict with values expressed by peers. During these periods adolescents may outwardly appear to be hostile and alienated. However, as noted earlier, the general value structure of adolescents remains more like their parents' than unlike it (see Adelson, 1979). Eventually adolescents merge appropriate aspects of alternative systems with the value system they learn from their parents. Only in rare instances do adolescents replace the value system of early adolescence with a completely new value system during late adolescence.

Three psychological models of moral development reflect the three major theoretical orientations in human development. In the psychoanalytic conception, moral development is incorporated within the broader context of individual ego development. Moral structures result from the resolution of ego conflict and adolescent's struggle to achieve independence from parents. Social learning theorists, on the other hand, see moral development as the result of social reinforcement. Morality results from what one has been taught to believe. Finally, in the cognitive developmental view, moral development

211

is seen as a step-by-step progression through a set of moral structures, which are increasingly abstract and which reflect the general morality of an individual.

THE PSYCHOANALYTIC THEORY

Although it is somewhat fashionable for nonpsychoanalytically trained writers to dismiss psychoanalytic theory, Freudian or neo-Freudian perspectives on moral development offer some insights into the character of the adolescent transition. Basically, psychoanalytic theory proposes that an individual's moral structures emerge from anxieties over conflict between an ideal moral code and a perceived reality. Adolescents develop a personal morality by resolving these conflicts. One such conflict is between the adolescent's need to establish emotional independence from parents and the desire to retain the secure, dependent relationship of childhood.

In the more traditional view, moral development is a continuous series of moves to balance the impact of the emerging superego (conscience). The superego began to take form following the resolution of the Oedipus conflict for boys and the Electra complex for girls, in which a child dealt with incestuous feelings toward the opposite-sex parent. In Freudian terms this conflict is the first in a series of struggles by which an individual gradually internalizes societal norms. In the case of a male, the boy wishes to marry and possess his mother. This leads to jealousy of the father who the child recognizes is sexually intimate with the mother. Eventually, however, this jealousy is replaced by fear of reprisal from the father and by guilt, because the boy recognizes both his incestuous feeling and his jealousy of his father. The boy may fear rejection or castration by his father, whom the boy sees as also jealous but more powerful. The way in which those Oedipal strivings are resolved sets the stage for moral development during adolescence, when the parents are forced into another role.

Following the resolution of the Oedipal conflict, the child starts to internalize the controls and guidelines that the parents establish. Indeed, the child becomes dogmatic in conceptions of right and wrong, good and bad, normal and abnormal. By preadolescence the perceived righteousness of the parents leads the child to idealize them and presume that they can do no wrong, that they are perfect. Unfortunately for the child (and the parents), the parents are soon recognized as imperfect. The child begins to see the parents' flaws and mistakes. Thus the child faces the first conflict of adolescence: their idealized model (the parents) is seen as both perfect and imperfect.

Adolescents' recognition of parental imperfections gradually leads to attempts to reject the parents as an ideal standard. The conflict increases through adolescence as a young person still tries to maintain the perception of an idealized parent and desires to be just like them and dependent on them. At the same time the adolescent wants to reject the parents and achieve independence. The yearning to reject the parents leads to anger and resentment, which in turn lead to guilt and frustration.

VIGNETTE 10-1
If Your Child Rejects Your Religion

Just as adolescents do not seem to want to participate in family activities in general, they may also be reluctant to participate in their parents' chosen religion. Parents see this resistance as a rejection of their values and beliefs. The more committed the parents are to a set of religious values and beliefs, the more disturbing this resistance is likely to be. When the resistance includes questions that go to the very heart of the parents' religious beliefs, the parents may feel especially anxious if they have never really adequately resolved those questions themselves. Perhaps the biggest problem is that the adolescent religious experience is seen as somehow isolated. Rather, religious development as well as moral development is a lifelong process, and people resolve certain value and belief questions several times in different fashions throughout their life span. Even recognizing this fact, most parents worry about the immediate problem of what to do when their adolescent seems to reject their religion. The following short piece provides some guidance for these parents.

Bob and Betty Lowe are upset because their 16-year-old son recently dropped out of the church choir and keeps finding new excuses to stay home from Sunday services.

Tom and Ellen Reilly's 18-year-old daughter refuses to join them at Sunday mass. When they insisted that she attend church last Easter, she showed up in blue jeans and an Army jacket.

Source: Alice Fleming, "If Your Child Rejects Your Religion," condensed in *Reader's Digest* 114 (February 1979): 35–40, from *Woman's Day* (March 1, 1978). Reprinted with permission from the February 1979 *Reader's Digest* and by permission of *Woman's Day* Magazine, Alice Fleming, and her agents Raines & Raines. Copyright © 1978 by CBS Publications, Inc.

Ron and Sheila Cohen are disturbed by their son's disregard for his faith. He went to a rock concert on Yom Kippur and vacationed in Florida with some college friends during Passover.

In the past few years, more and more parents have been hurt, baffled or angered to discover that their high-school- and college-age children have little or no interest in, or respect for, the religion in which they were reared.

"In our day," one mother sighs, "there weren't any arguments. If your parents expected you to go to religious services, you did; that was the end of it."

This doesn't mean that today's young people are any less religious than their parents. They are just quicker to question established ways of doing things and to reject those that don't appeal to them. "In an era when young people are challenging all the sacred cows—from the virtues of marriage to the value of higher education," says a college chaplain, "it's not surprising that traditional religions are being reexamined."

When teen-agers measure the family's faith and find it wanting, their parents are often at a loss. The first response for many is to issue an order. Bob and Betty Lowe, for example, tersely informed their son that unless he went to church more often, his allowance would be stopped and his use of the car curtailed. Unfortunately, the Lowes' approach didn't work; their son continued to stay home from church. When they followed through on their threats, the boy found a job to make up for his lost allowance and began hitching rides with friends.

Parents who try to lay down the law lose sight of one important fact: You can force a youngster to go through the motions of religious practice; but, as Dr. Harvey Tompkins, a psychiatrist at St. Vincent's Hospital in New York City, points out, "That won't guarantee—and may even work against—a deeper commitment."

Parents who realize that it's futile to force religion on children often make the mistake of accepting a youngster's decision without further discussion. When Jeff Cohen refused to observe the Jewish holidays, for instance, his parents concluded that Jeff was merely trying to assert his independence. They ignored his behavior, trusting that eventually he would return to his faith.

"The Cohens' conclusion was pretty much on the mark," says a psychologist who knows the family, "but they surrendered so meekly that Jeff's rebellion was a flop. Now he'll have to choose a new battleground; this time it may be something more destructive, like drinking, drugs or dropping out of school."

"Youngsters want and need something to push against," says Dr. Robert Simon, clinical director of the Ackerman Institute for Family Therapy in New York. "If there's no struggle, they have no sense of accomplishment when they win." Dr. Simon's advice to parents in this predicament is to take a firm stand, but be prepared to lose. "Just say that you stand by your beliefs, but that you respect your youngster's right to make up his own mind."

Experts agree that rebellion against parental influence and authority is a predictable and, for the most part, healthy crisis of adolescence. "At this stage," says Vladimir de Lissovoy, professor of child development and family relations at Pennsylvania State University, "young people are trying to define their own identities. Frequently this involves rejecting, at least temporarily, their parents' life-style, religious and/or political views."

This does not mean, however, that every youngster who rejects the family religion, or adopts a different one, is fulfilling a need to rebel. Sometimes the son or daughter has a legitimate complaint, like Cindy, a 15-year-old who disliked going to church because she felt out of place there. Her parents thought they heard the rumblings of a religious revolt—until they took a closer look at their parish and realized that most of the members were middle-aged or older, and the sermons and activities had little appeal to a teen-ager. They changed to a parish with a younger congregation and an extensive program of activities for teen-agers, and Cindy became the family's most enthusiastic churchgoer.

There are other, equally valid, reasons behind the reluctance of some young people to attend religious services. Some Sunday schools are poorly run, and some clergymen are well meaning but inept. In addition, even young children can often sense the contradictions between what is preached in church and what is practiced at home.

"Many boys and girls feel uncomfortable listening to words like 'Love thy neighbor' or 'Thou shalt not covet thy neighbors' goods' when their parents are obviously not living up to these ideals," says Dr. Tompkins. While many adults profess strong feelings for their faith, their attendance at religious services is sometimes more a matter of habit or social form than anything else.

Parents who hope to change the minds of children reluctant to practice the family religion must be prepared for a serious discussion of its values and its importance in their own lives. When parents can't offer either one, they are likely to confirm what the young people have already decided—that formal religion has little meaning and is "just for show."

Sometimes a youngster uses religion as a way of loosening an emotional tie with a parent. Jack Barry, for instance, had always been his mother's favorite. They went to church together when Jack was in grammar school and often talked about his plans to become a priest. As Jack grew into adolescence, however, he changed his mind about becoming a priest, started criticizing his religion and stopped going to church.

"Breaking away from religion was Jack's way of breaking away from an overly possessive parent," says a psychiatrist familiar with the case. "Jack had to let his mother know he wanted to be his own person and would no longer allow her to control his life."

If there are reasons to suspect that a young person's revolt against religion centers on an emotional conflict with one parent, the authorities recommended that—contrary to the usual advice on parent-child conflicts—the parents *not* present a united front.

"The parent who is less identified with religion should remain neutral," says Dr. Simon. "He or she should offer sympathy and support to both spouse and child, but let them work out their differences." If one parent goes to the defense of the other, explains Dr. Simon, the youngster will then be opposing both parents at the same time. "This," he says, "can be extremely difficult for a young person to handle."

Deeply religious parents are usually saddened and sometimes angry to discover that they have failed to pass their convictions on to their children. "Admitting their disappointment and talking it over with each other can go a long way toward helping them come to terms with their feelings," says a psychiatrist. "Trying to dismiss or conceal their distress will only lead to further bad feelings, many of which will inevitably be directed against their child."

If parents live a moral life, children will probably live up to their standards. "Youngsters may reject the outward observances of religion," says Professor de Lissovoy, "but the values that have been instilled in them since childhood are likely to remain with them for the rest of their lives."

One couple who consulted their clergyman when their daughter refused to go to church were advised to study the girl's behavior. When they did, the parents realized that she was considerate of her family and friends, and went out of her way to be helpful to others. One of her extracurricular activities was organizing a team of volunteers to work in a school for retarded children. "Your daughter may not go to church," the minister said, "but she *lives* Christianity."

Rebellion against religion is often a temporary phenomenon that disappears with time and maturity. But even if it doesn't, parents should try to make it clear that no matter how far their child strays from the family's faith, their affection for the youngster will remain unchanged. As Dr. Tompkins points out, "The essence of every religion is love and human understanding. Parents must not let religious differences destroy these two vital aspects of their relationship with their children."

Peter Blos (1972, 1974) suggests that when the adolescent's demands for perfection in the parents are not met, the adolescent suffers disillusionment. In a sense the adolescent is left with two alternatives: alter the ideal or alter the perception of the parent. Blos suggests that the ideals are so firmly established that altering or modifying them is nearly impossible. Thus adolescents must change their perception of the parent. The internalized ideals of childhood are consolidated into what Blos (1972) describes as an *ego ideal,* or the "externalization of the lost parental ideal" (p. 51). As they see their parents as increasingly divergent from the ego ideal, adolescents have a greater need to reject the parents. But to reject your parents is to reject a large part of yourself.

Moral development during adolescence thus becomes a progressive struggle to establish "new absolutes" or perfections intended to replace the parents. When adolescents are in the throes of this moral upheaval, they are particularly vulnerable to arbitrary moral systems. An alternative system, especially a religious or social system, may be adopted intact to replace the parental ego ideal. Occurrences like sudden conversion experiences are examples of this phenomenon.

THE SOCIAL LEARNING THEORY

Social learning theorists (for example, Bandura and McDonald, 1970; Bandura and Walters, 1963) see moral development as the result of learning much the same as other types of learning. The moral values you display result from your expectation of what will lead to reinforcement. In this case, reinforcement typically takes the form of social approval—that is, people will tell you what a good (and acceptable) person you are. The social learning theorist is talking of social reinforcement not only in the mainstream moral culture but also in alternative cultures. Those people with whom you wish to associate establish norms of acceptable behavior, which they selectively reinforce. In the social learning theorists' view, even the nonconformist yields to group expectations to achieve acceptance and reinforcement.

The learning of socially appropriate or acceptable behaviors starts early in life. Consider the value *sharing*. Parents encourage their very young children to share toys with friends or siblings. Sharing is not an innate virtue—if anything, children often embarrass their parents by refusing to share with children of visiting friends. When children balk at sharing, the parents usually encourage them to do so and if they give in, provide verbal approval and perhaps a hug or two. Over several trials, the child recognizes that sharing leads to social approval, and the behavior of sharing is gradually shaped. (Children sometimes overgeneralize the sharing principle and offer to share a half-eaten, sticky lollipop with their parents or the family pet.) Similar reinforcement is applied to other values. On the other hand, parents and adults try to eliminate socially undesirable behaviors through disapproval or withdrawal of approval. Eventually children develop a body of values; that is, they know which behaviors lead to social approval and which to social disapproval.

MODELING

People also learn socially appropriate behavior indirectly through modeling and imitation. When we enter an unfamiliar setting, we try to get some cues from those around us as to how we are expected to act. If you have ever gone to a formal dinner or banquet, you may have felt ill at ease with the array of dishes and silverware in front of you. Unless you have had some training in the etiquette appropriate to such occasions, you may wonder where to start. If you are like me, you would look at someone who seems to know what to do—perhaps the host or hostess—and model your own behavior after that person's. Your modeling, or imitating, is a highly adaptive response. Further, in cognitive terms, you begin to establish a schema for other similar settings.

In the same fashion children and youths model older adolescents in an attempt to learn the "rules of the game." One of the intervention strategies for social isolates described in Chapter 8 capitalizes on the ability to monitor and model another's behavior to develop social skills.

MODELING AND TELEVISION

In some instances the process of modeling may be the cause of some concern. Although the examples described above encourage socially approved behavior, the same modeling may be used for socially disapproved behavior. Specifically, society is becoming increasingly concerned with the potential for youths modeling violent behavior depicted on television and other media.

Under what circumstances does violence on television incite violence in viewers? In one case, four days following the airing of the television film *Born Innocent*, in which a young girl in a juvenile home is forcibly "raped" by other inmates with a broom handle, three girls and a boy similarly "raped" a nine-year-old girl with a beer bottle. In another case, a young man named Ronnie Zamora, on trial for murder, used as a defense that he had been driven insane by overexposure to violence on television. In still another case, television stations have been asked to refrain from airing the film "Doomsday Flight," because it depicts a skyjacking pattern that occurs frequently every time the film is shown.

For modeling of a televised or filmed behavior to occur, the viewer must see the model in the film as attractive and as achieving some reward for the violent behavior. It is unwise to infer that television violence "causes" violent behavior in the viewer; however, some individuals are clearly more susceptible to suggestion than others.

A recent British study concluded that repeated, continuous exposure to violence on television does lead to increased violence among delinquent boys (Belson, as cited in Munson, 1978). Whether the increase can be attributed solely to imitation, or to reduced inhibitions toward violence, is unclear. The results are, however, provocative.

THE COGNITIVE DEVELOPMENTAL THEORY

The third model of moral development is the cognitive developmental theory. This model was first outlined by Jean Piaget in his classic volume *The Moral Judgment of the Child* (1932). As with most aspects of cognitive developmental theory, the foundations were laid out by Piaget. The cognitive developmental view of moral development, however, has been refined to its current more well-known version by Lawrence Kohlberg (1964, 1975; Kohlberg and Gilligan, 1971). The cognitive model differs from previous models in that it is oriented toward the intellectual structures that an individual child or adolescent uses in determining moral behavior. Further, the cognitive model is a maturational model. Just as adolescents' intellectual structures change from preoperational to concrete operational to formal operational structures, the quality of moral structures changes as the individual matures, to permit more complex moral judgments concerning the surrounding world. In contrast to the behavioral view, the essential ingredients in moral development in the cognitive view are not moral behaviors but moral judgments (Kohlberg, 1964). Moral judgments precede moral behaviors but do not always lead to them. That is, an individual may analyze a situation and make a moral judgment, but then behave in a way that is not in accord with that judgment.

In Piaget's view moral development moves from other-oriented moral judgments (heteronomous) to self-oriented moral judgments (autonomous). Early in cognitive development moral judgments are based on an understanding of what parents or those in authority see as moral. The moral structures are not based on any inherent understanding of morality but on a set of external demands to conform to what is right and acceptable. Moral structures in this early stage of moral development are oriented toward obedience to authority and are seen as rigid and inalterable.

As children mature, Piaget claimed that their moral structures become more flexible and internally defined (autonomous). Right and wrong are defined in light of a more general moral sense. In Piaget's terms, this second level of moral reasoning is a natural outgrowth of intellectual maturation, and in an environment that permits social growth, the child will normally make the transition to this level of moral thinking.

While Piaget's model provided a general theoretical scheme for viewing shifts in moral judgments, it failed to discriminate adequately among the qualitative changes in moral judgment that occur between the morality of childhood and the more sophisticated morality of late adolescence and adulthood. Lawrence Kohlberg (1964) reworked and extended Piaget's initial idea into a more complete model of moral development. Kohlberg's model is currently, the more widely recognized and is having the more profound impact on social thought.

Kohlberg uses a clinical interview procedure similar to the technique originally used by Piaget. The child or adolescent reads or is told a story built around an ethical dilemma. (See Vignette 10–2.) After hearing the story, the

VIGNETTE 10-2
Kohlberg's Moral Dilemma

Presented below is an example of a moral dilemma used to attempt to measure an individual's level of moral development. Note that, regardless of the "answer" given to the first

question, the interviewer asks the person to elaborate on the answer. Beyond the value of this method for assessing moral development, it is useful on a more general level as an interviewing and teaching technique. If you decide to administer the problem to a friend, you need to explain that this is part of a set of problems that is used by psychologists to

Source: Extracted from Lawrence Kohlberg, "Stories, Stage Descriptions, and Example Answers," Harvard University Project on Moral Development. Reprinted by permission of the author.

assess moral reasoning. There are no right or wrong answers to these dilemmas. Rather, the questions are intended to press the limits of moral beliefs. You should allow the person to feel free not to participate. What my own students often find is that they expect everyone to answer the questions as they would, or they think they know how a friend will answer. If you use this structured interview technique, assess its value in more general terms for your role as a professional practitioner working with adolescents or others.

In Europe, a woman was near death from a special kind of cancer. There was one drug that the doctors thought might save her. It was a form of radium that a druggist in the same town had recently discovered. The drug was expensive to make, but the druggist was charging ten times what the drug cost him to make. He paid $200 for the radium and charged $2,000 for a small dose of the drug. The sick woman's husband, Heinz, went to everyone he knew to borrow the money, but he could only get together about $1,000, which is half of what it cost. He told the druggist that his wife was dying and asked him to sell it cheaper or let him pay later. But the druggist said, "No, I discovered the drug and I'm going to make money from it." So Heinz got desperate and broke into the man's store to steal the drug for his wife.

1. Should Heinz have done that? Was it actually wrong or right? Why?

2. Is it a husband's duty to steal the drug for his wife if he can get it no other way? Would a good husband do it?
3. Did the druggist have the right to charge that much when there was no law actually setting a limit to the price? Why?

Answer questions 4(a) and (b) only if you think Heniz should steal the drug.

4. (a) If the husband does not feel very close or affectionate to his wife, should he still steal the drug?
   (b) Suppose it wasn't Heinz's wife who was dying of cancer but it was Heinz's best friend. His friend didn't have any money and there was no one in his family willing to steal the drug. Should Heinz steal the drug for his friend in that case? Why?

Answer questions 5(a) and (b) only if you think Heinz should not steal the drug.

5. (a) Would you steal the drug to save your wife's life?
   (b) If you were dying of cancer but were strong enough, would you steal the drug to save our own life?
6. Heinz broke into the store and stole the drug and gave it to his wife. He was caught and brought before the judge. Should the judge send Heinz to jail for stealing or should he let him go free? Why?

person is asked to respond to a specific question about the story. No matter what answer the adolescent gives, the interviewer probes the boundaries of the answer to determine why the person answered as he or she did and what level of judgment he or she used. Eventually the interviewer analyzes the testee's responses in light of a set of criteria that classify the answers into Kohlberg's stages of moral development.

Kohlberg describes moral development as moving regularly through six stages, from a basically hedonic, egocentric morality to a principled morality based on respect for the dignity of human beings. In stage 1, the *punishment-obedience orientation*, moral judgment is motivated by a desire to avoid punishment or possible unpleasant consequences. Adolescents may avoid sexual intercourse because of a fear of pregnancy or a fear of "getting caught." Stage 1 judgments are not oriented toward the inherent morality of an event; rather, decisions are based on the fear of possibly unpleasant consequence if those in power are offended. Conversely, stage 1 morality justifies nearly any behavior as long as threat of punishment is removed or is not a possibility.

Later in childhood, moral judgments shift toward a slightly higher level. In stage 2, the *instrumental-relativist orientation*, moral judgments are directed not at avoiding punishment but at gaining favor or a material outcome. Stage 2

Concepts of right and wrong, of what constitutes acceptable and unacceptable behavior, are usually learned at home. (Peter Vandermark)

might be called the "What's-in-it-for-me?" level of morality. An adolescent's primary motivation is the satisfaction of personal, social, or physical needs. Stage 2 individuals, like their stage 1 counterparts, are not bothered by shoplifting, joyriding, cheating on income taxes, or fixing traffic tickets—as long as they do not get caught. When they interact with others, their moral judgments are based on a trade-off model. Any service or favor that a stage 2 adolescent does for another person is done with the expectation of payoff. Loyalty, gratitude, and a sense of justice are outside the realm of their thought. In Kohlberg's model, both stages 1 and 2 are seen as representing *preconventional* levels of moral judgment. In neither case do adolescents think of the rightness or wrongness of an act. Rather, they are motivated toward serving themselves. Morality has little role in their lives.

Stage 3 morality, the *good-boy/nice girl orientation*, represents a significant shift in moral thinking, because it reflects the first sense of morality of behavior. Adolescents at this level of moral development judge morality in light of the basic moral standards of society. Their interpretation of those standards, however, is rigid and inflexible. They are not motivated by the expectation of immediate payoff but instead by the expectation that what they do is *approved* by society. Being "nice," helping others, doing "what is right" are important at this stage. Adolescents at this level respond to problems in terms of fixed, literal interpretations of rules. Things are right or they are wrong. There is little ambivalence. Their commitment to authority and to others for approval, however, may create conflicts. In their desire to conform to those in control for approval, they may be forced to choose between pleasing either the crowd or the adult authorities. Decisions are influenced by the immediacy of the approving group. The nearer the peer crowd, the parents, or the authorities, the more effect they have. The individual has, however, begun to internalize the conventional morality of the dominant society and for the first time responds to the morality of a situation.

Toward early adolescence many individuals make a somewhat subtle shift in moral structures. At stage 4, the *law and order orientation*, individuals still respond in categorical right-wrong fashion, but they also recognize that moral beliefs require a context that assures social order. Both stage 3 and stage 4 morality reflect what Kohlberg calls *conventional* morality. By this Kohlberg means that the individual has internalized the conventions, the explicit values, of a society. Adolescents at the conventional level of development have a strong orientation toward authority figures. These authorities may be traditional authority institutions; however, because an individual claims to reject traditional institutions does not automatically imply that he or she is operating above or below a conventional level. Rather, the person may be oriented toward an alternate figure or authority system that offers another set of "absolutes."

During late adolescence or during adulthood, some individuals progress to a level of moral development that Kohlberg refers to as *postconventional*, or *principled morality*. At stage 5, the *social contract orientation*, individuals see morality in terms of individual rights and agree to the general standards provided by society. Stage 5 people have not only internalized these values

but have also evaluated them in terms of some logical standards. Because of this, Stage 5 people are more likely to see exceptions to rules and to assess morality in relative terms. They no longer see values as absolutes.

A very few individuals achieve the highest level of postconventional thought. At stage 6, the *universal ethical principle orientation*, individuals view morality in terms of a fundamental respect for human beings based on general ethical principles. For some at stage 6 (for example, Thomas Aquinas, Martin Luther King, Malcolm X, or Mahatma Gandhi), the ethical scheme may conflict with the predominant, conventional moral structures of their society.

Consider, if you will, how those at preconventional and postconventional levels of moral development would respond to a discussion of the 55-mile-per-hour speed limit. Those at a preconventional level would say they go 55 mph only if there is a police officer in the area. They may even describe elaborate devices that they use to avoid getting caught speeding. Those at a conventional level respond first and foremost that the 55 mph limit is the law and that they believe those who tell them that it saves gasoline. Those at a postconventional level may also respond further, that there is a good reason for the law because it has led to a reduction in traffic deaths. Their motivation to maintain the speed limit is the knowledge that their behavior affects the lives of others.

It does not follow that a person who is at a postconventional level of cognitive moral development will always behave in a manner that reflects that level. Although postconventional individuals are more likely to behave in ways that reflect advanced moral development, they may at times act in purely hedonic, self-gratifying terms.

Consider how you react to a stop sign when there is clearly no one else around at 3 A.M., 8 A.M., 12 noon, and 8 P.M. Most people, including me, react to the stop sign differently at different times of day.

THE UNIVERSALITY OF MORAL DEVELOPMENT

Kohlberg believes there is a *universality* in moral development—not in specific mores or values but in the sequential development of increasingly complex moral structures from preconventional through conventional to postconventional thought. Kohlberg supports this premise with data from several cultures. You can see in Figure 10-1 that in early adolescence, stage 1 and 2 morality dominate in both the United States and Taiwan. By middle adolescence the emergence of conventional thinking is evident. You can infer the degree to which conventional or postconventional thinking is differentially encouraged or fostered within the two societies.

Kohlberg's model of moral development bears strong resemblance to David Hunt's model of conceptual development, described in Chapter 4.

Figure 10-1 LEVELS OF MORAL JUDGMENT IN TAIWAN AND THE UNITED STATES

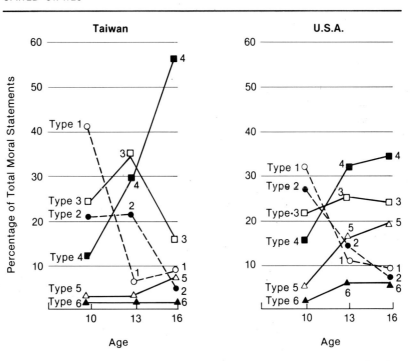

Source: Reprinted from "Moral Education in the Schools: A Developmental View," *School Review* 74 (1966): 10, by L. Kohlberg, by permission of the University of Chicago Press. Copyright © 1966.

Hunt's model is more broadly defined than Kohlberg's; however, many of the essential characteristics of a step-by-step developmental model are the same. For example, to achieve a level of postconventional thought, a person *must* first go through the levels of preconventional and conventional thought. As with other progressions, we assume that an individual does not fall back to lower levels of development.

You might infer from some of Kohlberg's writings that a person is clearly at one stage of development or another. It is more likely that moral development, as with other domains of cognitive development, is fluid, and a person may be in multiple levels of development depending on the environmental conditions and the ethical issues involved (Rest, Davison, and Robbins, 1978).

VIGNETTE 10-3
The Book Burners

The scene is not Nazi Germany in the 1930s but the United States in the 1970s and 1980s. Crowds of people are throwing "objectionable" books into a bonfire—books such as 1984, Catcher in the Rye, *and* Tom Sawyer. *In Hammond, Indiana, the* American Heritage Dictionary *was removed from the library for containing "objectionable" language, and review committees now analyze textbooks to see if they contain material they consider obscene or offensive. Many point to these activities and argue that such censorship violates the fundamental human rights guaranteed in the First Amendment to the U.S. Constitution. On the other hand, procensorship groups argue that, as concerned parents, they have the right and responsibility to review materials made available to or required of their children. Where do you stand on the issue? Is there validity on both sides? Does one set of "rights" override another set of "rights"?*

On the face of it, Ridgefield, Conn., is an unlikely setting for a pitched battle over academic freedom. Its stately colonial-style homes, rolling woodlands and quaint stone walls create a bucolic atmosphere that is surprising for a community of 20,000 people only 50 miles from New York City. But for three years now, Ridgefield has been seething over an effort to ban several controversial books used by the 6,000-pupil public school system. The dispute has pitted neighbor against neighbor, and has resulted in the abrupt dismissal of the town's moderately liberal school superintendent.

Book banning is not as much a thing of the past as most Americans might like to believe. The American Library Association reports more than 100 attempts to ban books from school libraries or curriculums last year in communities ranging from Dallas, Texas, to Hollidaysburg, Pa. "The general situation today is much worse than just five years ago," says ALA official Judith F. Krug. "People are worrying about things like drugs and crime. They are looking for easy solutions, and they think that if we can just get rid of this 'dirty' book or that 'subversive' book, our problems will go away."

"Catcher"

Books are banned for nearly as many reasons as they are written. The most suppressed book in the country is J.D. Salinger's "Catcher in the Rye," a favorite of high-school English teachers that has been attacked for twenty years because of its four-letter words and disrespect for parental authority. Right behind "Catcher" on last year's censorship list was "The Inner City Mother Goose," which retells nursery rhymes in a bitter urban vernacular. Conservative whites have sought to ban Eldridge Cleaver's "Soul on Ice," while black activists have set out after "Huckleberry Finn." Other books frequently assailed include "1984," "Grapes of Wrath" and even "Gulliver's Travels."

Ridgefield typifies the stresses that have made scapegoats of schoolbooks in so many American communities. Despite its affluent setting, the town contains many lower-middle-class wage earners, as well as struggling young executives and hard-pressed older folks. Many residents are appalled at the town's pell-mell growth (the population has increased 150 per cent since 1960) and at the rising tax rate and the encroachment of "big-city problems." One early sign of political unrest was the fact that Ridgefield hired and fired four school superintendents in the six years that preceded the arrival of superintendent David Weingast from Newark, N.J., in 1966.

"When I came here," Weingast told Newsweek's Phyllis Malamud last week, "I found a traditional school system that had grown cobwebby." But when Weingast tried to update the curriculum with courses in sex and drug education, he ran into strong opposition, notably from a conservative group called Concerned Parents, headed by an airline pilot named Norman Little. In 1970, Concerned Parents launched its first attack on books used in the schools, and early last year, school-board member Leo F. Carroll, 72, a retired state trooper, joined the fray. An old-fashioned liberal strongly in favor of the police and against obscene language, Carroll denounced "Boss," Mike Royko's stinging portrait of Chicago Mayor Richard Daley and his city's police force. The book was duly dropped from the recommended reading list of a high school politics course.

The long debate over books and the curriculum has left deep scars in Ridgefield. Norman Little charges that his children have been harassed in school. The local teachers' association complains of harassment from Little's allies and declares: "Fear is our constant companion in Ridgefield." One teacher claims that her family has been threatened. Last month, the feud came to a boil again when conservatives tried to ban "Soul on Ice" and another anti-Establishment book called "Police, Courts and the Ghetto." In a stormy meeting, the school board voted to retain the books. Then, when most of the audience had left, the board voted to withdraw the courses in which the books are used.

The bloodletting did not end there. At a subsequent meeting, the board decided not to renew Weingast's contract. A rumor soon spread that he had been fired for refusing to dismiss the high-school principal and the chairman of the social-studies department, both of whom had been branded as "too permissive." The leader of the conservative faction on the school board, Samuel DiMuzio, insists, "The decision about Dr. Weingast was made on the basis of his performance as an executive." But many other townspeople fear that the battle of Ridgefield has now turned from banning books to banning people.

Although the behavioral theorists tend to view the issues of moral behaviors without looking at the level of moral judgments, and cognitive theorists seem similarly disinclined to view the impact of levels of judgment on behavior, some research has crossed this artificial division. Quite obviously, the two theories are not independent.

As early as the classic Hartshorne and May *Studies in Deceit* (1928), evidence has shown that commitment to a set of moral values is related to behavior in other settings that require a moral choice. In a reanalysis of that data, Burton (1963) found that consistency between moral values and moral behavior increased with age across adolescence. Similarly, Bloom (1964) found that as personal maturity, including a commitment to a set of values, increased, impulsiveness decreased.

In a major study of the relationship between the level of moral judgment and behavior among college students and Peace Corps volunteers, those who displayed postconventional, principled moral judgments were more likely to be politically active, to live independently, and to describe themselves as idealistic (Haan, Smith, and Block, 1968). Those students at the conventional level of moral development were unlikely to be politically committed and were more likely to describe themselves as ambitious. Young people at the conventional level of moral development were less likely than either their preconventional or postconventional peers to have conflict with their parents. Youths at the postconventional level of development were more likely to rate themselves as not religious, but they were also more likely to have been raised in nonreligious families.

RELIGION AND ADOLESCENTS

There has long been interest in the attitudes of young people toward religion. The earliest studies of the psychology of religion focused on adolescence as a time of intense religious awakening. Starbuck, one of the first writers in the psychology of religion, went as far as to conclude, "If conversion has not occurred before twenty, the chances are small that it will ever be experienced" (1899, p. 28). Other early psychologists, including G. Stanley Hall and William James, were similarly convinced that adolescence was a critical period in religious development. Hall, for example, pointed to historical evidence that the religious fervor of the saints reached a peak during adolescence. Although we would question today the type of evidence that some of those early investigators used, we must still recognize the depth of concern about religion and spirituality among adolescence. Young people often develop strong commitment to or strong opposition to institutional churches and/or religion. As with other aspects of personal development, looking at religious or moral development in isolation from the lifelong process of acquiring a sense of values may be misleading. Actually, the process of religious development is a lifelong process, and as with other conceptual schemes, it is subject to shifts throughout life.

Some religions select early adolescence as the time for formal initiation into the adult community; the Jewish Bar Mitzvah is an example of such a ceremony. (Paul S. Conklin)

Currently, there is a renewed interest in the topic. The rekindling of evangelical movements among college-age and high school students, and the attraction that a variety of cults holds for many young people, have brought the question into the public eye once more.

Most explanations as to why adolescence is such a critical period in the development of more permanent religious attitudes have focused on two factors. On one hand, many see the adolescent religious concern in the context of the identity crisis. The adolescent's need to internalize a personal system of values is a part of the more general striving to establish a personal identity. Alternatively, some focus on the intellectual transition of adolescence and put the changes in religious beliefs within the broader perspective of general cognitive development.

IDENTITY DEVELOPMENT

Because an important element in developing a personal sense of identity is the internalizing of a personal value system, some writers see the characteristic interest in religion as a part of the general identity-formation process. Adolescents need to establish a firm, internalized concept of what is right and wrong, what is acceptable and unacceptable. Further, they wrestle with the question that most religions address: "What am I to do with my life?" "How did life begin?" "What is my responsibility to my fellow human beings?" "Is this all there is to life?"

As adolescents work through these issues they are brought to other questions about their relationship with a divine Being or about whether there is a God at all. It is important for adolescents to clarify and answer these questions in a personal fashion in order for subsequent, personal, moral development to occur.

In a similar view, Ruth Strang (1957) saw the development of a set of religious beliefs as part of the establishment of adolescents' feelings of self-worth. Teens' feelings of adequacy and self-worth may be inferred from the way they think God views them. Adolescents with negative self-worth see themselves as unworthy of God's love, or as being punished, or as unacceptable to those around them because of past sins. Those with positive self-worth are more likely to see themselves as loved by God, to see God as a help in times of stress, and to see God as a source of strength and courage in general.

INTELLECTUAL DEVELOPMENT

The second view of adolescents' relationship to religion focuses on Piaget's stages of intellectual development and Kohlberg's stages of moral development. Religious conviction is part of the general pattern of cognitive moral development. As Piaget (1967) explains, middle and late adolescence is a time when emerging formal thought leads to intense idealism. As abstract thought develops, adolescents are able to consider utopian schemes and are impatient with what they see as a lack of adult or church responsiveness to pressing social problems.

As adolescents shift from concrete to formal thought, their ideas about the teachings of their faith follow the same progression. Just as they think about science and math on abstract levels, they also examine their

People in religious roles frequently play an important part in helping adolescents clarify their value systems. (Peter Vandermark)

228

Table 10-1 CHANGES IN ADOLESCENTS' RELIGIOUS BELIEFS

Statement	Age:	"Believe" 12	15	18	"Wonder About" 12	15	18
God is a strange power working for good, rather than a person.		46	49	57	20	14	15
God is someone who watches you to see that you behave yourself, and who punishes you if you are not good.		70	49	33	11	13	18
I know there is a God.		94	80	79	2	14	16
Catholics, Jews and Protestants are equally good.		67	79	86	24	11	7
There is a heaven.		82	78	74	13	16	20
Only good people go to heaven.		72	45	33	13	27	34
Hell is a place where you are punished for your sins on earth.		70	49	35	13	27	34
Heaven is here on earth.		12	13	14	18	28	32
People who go to church are better than people who do not go to church.		46	26	15	17	21	11
Young people should belong to the same church as their parents.		77	56	43	10	11	11
The main reason for going to church is to worship God.		88	80	79	4	7	6
It is not necessary to attend church to be a Christian.		42	62	67	18	15	8
Only our soul lives after death.		72	63	61	18	25	31
Good people say prayers regularly.		78	57	47	13	13	27
Prayers are answered.		76	69	65	21	25	27
Prayers are a source of help in times of trouble.		74	80	83	15	10	9
Prayers are to make up for something that you have done that is wrong.		47	24	21	18	17	9
Every word in the Bible is true.		79	51	34	15	31	43
It is sinful to doubt the Bible.		62	42	27	20	26	28

Source: R. G. Kuhlen and M. Arnold, "Age Differences in Religious Beliefs and Problems in Adolescence," *Journal of Genetic Psychology* 65 (1944): 293.

religious beliefs on the same level. The simplistic beliefs of childhood are replaced by internal and personal understandings of the same concept (Kuhlln and Arnold, 1944). Concepts of God become more abstract and less literal (Conger, 1977). There is also evidence that they become less dogmatic and rigid. Note, for example, in Table 10-1 that there is a regular decrease in concrete beliefs and a regular increase in abstract beliefs and in questioning from ages twelve to eighteen.

Religious educators and clergy often find adolescents very hard to work with. When adolescents are not totally unresponsive, they ask endless questions about the meaning of life, immortality or the lack of it, the existence of God, and the value or truth of the religion in which they have been raised. Their emerging idealism may lead to confusion and anger about seeming inconsistencies between church doctrine and social policy. As they read history, they may become distressed at the politicization of religions and the justification of persecution of minorities by dominant religions. Too often those in charge regard such questions or concerns as indications of an emerging atheism, and they feel compelled to cut the question off with a dogmatic "truth." More than likely the young person who asks a knotty question does not really expect an answer. In the course of trying to clarify values, those questions naturally emerge. Rather than closing the questions off, adults should encourage them and allow the adolescent to expand on the question—and why it is a question.

PEERS

A third factor operates on the religious attitudes that a young person is willing to express. In much the same way that peers discourage appearing too academic, peers also influence young people to not be too religious. Cynicism about religion and religiosity is often expected among adolescents, and young people feel pressures to conform to that expectation. Thus parents may find that their son no longer wants to be an altar boy, not because he is suddenly antireligious, but because he fears ridicule and "hassles" from his peers.

STAGES IN FAITH DEVELOPMENT

To try to separate the development of a religious identity from religious cognitive development may be misleading. The views of Erikson, Piaget, and Kohlberg are not antagonistic to each other but are complementary. James W. Fowler (1978) has combined the approaches into a series of stages of faith development. According to Fowler's six stages of development of faith concepts, an individual's scheme of faith progresses from simple, narrowly defined concepts of faith to highly complex, multifaceted concepts. Like Kohlberg's conception, these stages are sequential—that is, to reach the higher levels of development implies progression through the lower levels. Table 10-2 presents the stages and their position relative to the stages of development defined by Piaget, Kohlberg, and Erikson.

Stage 1: Intuitive-Projective Faith. The lowest level of development is based on an intuitive and imitative knowledge of faith. Beliefs are focused primarily on an omniscient but magical God. The child sees such natural phenomena as lightning, thunder, and northern lights as rewards or punishment for their own behavior; for example, "God made the sun shine for my birthday," or "Why did God make me sick on the day I was to go to the dance?" The child's conception is highly egocentric. As adults, we are not immune to stage 1 feelings. When we are driving to an appointment and are in danger of being late, and every traffic light is green, we are likely to think something like "I must have done something right," implying that some magical power has caused the lights to be green as a favor to us.

Table 10-2 EXPECTED PARALLELS AMONG DEVELOPMENTAL THEORIES

Piaget (Cognitive)	Kohlberg (Moral)	Fowler (Faith)	Erikson (Psychosocial)
(0–2)—Sensory-Motor		0—Undifferentiated	1—Trust versus Mistrust
(2–6)—Intuitive or Prelogical [Preoperational]	0—The good is what I want and like	1—Intuitive-Projective	2—Autonomy versus Shame and Doubt
(7–11)—Concrete Operations	1—Punishment and obedience orientation		3—Initiative versus Guilt
	2—Instrumental hedonism and concrete reciprocity	2—Mythic-Literal	4—Industry versus Inferiority
(12-) Formal Operations	3—Orientation to interpersonal relations of mutuality	3—Synthetic-Conventional	5—Identity versus Role-Confusion
	4—Maintenance of social order, fixed rules and authority	4—Individuating-Reflexive	
	5—Social contract, utilitarian, law-making perspective	5—Paradoxical-Consolidative	6—Intimacy versus Isolation
(Piagetian stages are taken to be necessary but not sufficient for corresponding stages of moral and faith development)	6—Universal ethical principle orientation	6—Universalizing	7—Generativity versus Stagnation
			8—Integrity versus Despair

Source: Reprinted from "Stages in Faith: The Structural-Developmental Approach" by James W. Fowler, pp. 188–189, in *Values and Moral Development*, ed. by T. C. Hennessy. © 1976 by The Missionary Society of St. Paul the Apostle in the State of New York. Used by permission of Paulist Press.

Stage 2: Mythic-Literal Faith.   The next stage, most common to childhood and preadolescence, is a faith dominated by a literal acceptance of the dogma of a religion and a strict adherence to the concreteness of its symbols. That is, the child regards the symbol as important not because it *represents* something but because it has concrete reality. Not uncommonly, this concrete reality may also acquire stage 1, magical characteristics, as in a good-luck charm. Rules and guidelines are inviolable and absolute. Once again, adherence to the rules leads to rewards by God, disobedience to punishment.

Stage 3: Synthetic-Conventional Faith. At stage 3, faith provides a social structure within which to handle the complexities of daily living. Religious rules are interpreted rigidly, and members of the faith community are all expected to adhere to the rules. The strict interpretation is often extended to imply, sometimes implicitly and somtimes explicitly, that the rules are the *only* true ones.

Stage 4: Individuating-Reflexive Faith. During late adolescence young people find themselves in a struggle between loyalty to the community and a quest for individuality, between concrete objectivity and abstract subjectivity, between feeling obligated to serve others and a desiring to fulfill themselves. Those struggles may and do generalize to the adolescents' relationship to religion. Stage 4 requires a personalizing of religion and a recognition of personal responsibility to a faith community.

Stage 5: Paradoxical-Consolidative Faith. During this later stage of faith development, individuals recognize and appreciate the integrity and validity of positions other than their own. Recognizing the value of other faith forms, and exploring their extra dimensions, expands the individual's personal faith development.

Stage 6: Universalizing Faith. The rare person who achieves this level is able to live in harmony with all people. The feeling of oneness does not interfere with the person's sense of individuality, because the oneness with humanity is transcendent.

Older adolescents are considerably less likely than younger adolescents to attend church regularly. This phenomenon is not new and has been recognized for some time (Kuhlen and Allen, 1944). Does this mean that higher levels of cognitive moral development interfere with religious commitment? That is unclear. However, the reluctance to attend church does not necessarily mean an alienation from religion in general or even from the church in particular. Some young people reject institutional religion but maintain a personal set of beliefs that are very much like those of the church they rejected.

Adolescents reject the institutional church because they feel that the conventional church is unresponsive to personal and social needs (Beit-Hallahmic, 1974). They regard church attendance as superficial and uninteresting. Once again, the abstract value of a personal ideology may be incompatible with the more concrete value of attending church because of an imposed rule. As one young person declared, "God is not dead, the church is dead" (Babin, 1969).

Religiosity. This brings us to the interesting question of what we mean by the term *religious*. Quite clearly, "being religious" means something very different to adolescents at different stages of moral or faith development. Dittes (1969) notes that arguments about whether religiousness is observed in steadfast adherence to rules of the institutional church or in a personal knowledge of God can be found in the writings of the Old Testament prophets.

Dittes prefers to distinguish between *consensual* and *committed* religiosity. The distinction (based on earlier work of Allen and Spilka, 1967) is between the type of religious conviction an individual maintains. Consensual religion refers to a commitment to the formal, institutional church and adherence to its formal structure and rules. Committed religion refers to a subjective, personal set of beliefs that may or may not include a commitment to the institutional church.

In most studies reviewed by Dittes, evidence consistently showed that the greater the adherence to a purely consensual religion, the more likely individuals are to profess rigidly and dogmatically the unacceptability of those who adhere to another set of beliefs. As a corollary, their unwillingness to allow diversity and to recognize complexity may lead to antisemitism and racism (Dittes, 1969).

Given the distinction between consensual and committed religiosity, and the findings that older adolescents are more likely to see God or religion in abstractions, it is unclear whether trends such as the one reported by Yankelovitch (1974) in Figure 10-2 refer to a decline in the value placed on religion or a shift toward more committed but less consensual beliefs.

Figure 10-2 ADOLESCENTS WHO SEE RELIGION AS A VERY IMPORTANT VALUE

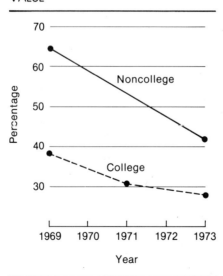

Source: From *The New Morality: A Profile of American Youth in the 70's*, pp. 14 and 26, by D. Yankelovitch. Copyright © 1974 McGraw-Hill Book Company. Used with permission of McGraw-Hill Book Company.

CONVERSIONS

Although conversion experiences are not uncommon among adolescents, conversions are not all the same. We can describe at least four different types of experiences, all of which refer to the deepening of a personal commitment to a set of religious beliefs or a supreme being (Glock and Stark, 1965).

By far the most common type of conversion is a *confirming* experience in which some event or series of events serve to confirm what an individual already believed to be true. Adolescents who undergo a confirming experience report no radical shift in their views. Rather, these young people report they have a more general sense of a divine being and that their knowledge is intensified.

In recent years the "born again" movement has been given much attention by the popular media. Being "reborn" is an example of what Glock and Stark refer to as a *responsive* experience. In a responsive conversion experience, individuals feel that not only have they come to know God better but also that God has suddenly taken a personal interest in them. This conversion may occur following a perceived "miracle" or some other event that an individual sees as a divine intervention or an answer to prayer. There is a strong bias toward this form of conversion experience among some denominations and a strong bias against it in others. Among Southern Baptists, for example, 93 percent reported a responsive conversion experience, whereas only 26 percent of Roman Catholics and 9 percent of Congregationalists did so.

Two other types of conversion experiences presumably include the former two but are deeper in intensity. In the *ecstatic* experience the relationship between God and the converted person becomes deeply emotional. Individuals report charismatic or ecstatic experiences in which they speak in tongues or have uncontrolled body movements and uncontrolled praising. In certain sects the ecstatic experiences are quite clearly sexual in content and symbol. The last form of conversion experience is the *revelational* experience, in which individuals believe they have achieved such a close relationship with God that he has chosen them to reveal a divine plan or message. They see themselves as prophets.

Whether adolescents experience one or another of these conversion experiences depends on a variety of factors. Because conversion experiences are common to certain denominations, and because historically adolescence has been seen as the prime time for conversions, we have the elements of a self-fulfilling prophesy. That is, adolescents are expected to have conversion experiences, thus they may feel motivated to seek such experiences.

CULTS

Any discussion of religious attitudes and behavior inevitably leads to the issue of cults. Many believe with a great deal of fear and uncertainty that young cultists are "brainwashed" or "programmed." These fears were crystallized by the 1978 mass suicides at Jonestown, Guyana. However, not

As part of their search for a personal value system, some adolescents explore alternative value structures. (© Susan Lapides)

all cults are as extreme as the Jonestown group; indeed, several cults have stood the test of time and are now recognized as religions.

Among the groups that continue to receive wide public attention are the Unification Church of Sun Myung Moon (the Moonies), the Divine Light Mission of Maharaj Ji, the Institute for Krishna Consciousness, the Children of God, the Church of Scientology, and the Way. Although these groups are the ones most often headlined, they are by no means the only such groups. If we include splinter Bible or gospel groups, one in ten Americans are affiliated with fringe religious groups (Zaretsky, 1977).

Criticisms of cults proceed along two lines. First, noncultists suspect that the leaders of the cults are hypocritical and are exploiting cult members to enhance their own personal wealth. Typically, such critics point to the lavish life-style of the Maharaj Ji or the financial power amassed by Sun Myung Moon, while their followers live at near-poverty levels and panhandle to support their church. It was reported, for example, that in its first full year of operation in the United States, the Unification Church cleared $10 million after expenses (Cornwell, 1973). Members of the cults, however, may see that same wealth as evidence of the truth of the leader's message. That is, if the leader has been lying, why has he been so successful?

The second major criticism leveled at cults is that they have "hypnotic" control over their members—that members are programmed and brainwashed. This accusation of mind-control is tied with allegations of kidnapping and deprivation to accomplish the brainwashing. Cults may have training sessions in which members are isolated in groups in which the teachings of the church are learned and memorized. Members may be

VIGNETTE 10-4
Europe's Rising Cults

What is a cult? During the past few years, many individuals and churches have become alarmed about the increasing number of young people associating themselves with splinter religious groups whose codes diverge from the mainstream religions. Worries about cultism, however, are not new. At the turn of the century, one author pointed to Mormonism and Jehovah's Witnesses as the two major cults. Today writers point to other groups, but their fears are much the same. The fears are typically built around distress over the adolescent's rejection of the family's religion and acceptance of a nonstandard church. As you can see in the selection below, questions and concerns about cults are not limited to America. In the context of religious and moral development, as described in the text, is it predictable that some young people will reject the religion (or lack of it) of their parents and select an alternative ideology?

The Earl of Rosebery once played billiards in the long, imposing hall, where high ceilings rise above the marble fireplace and stately windows frame the emerald lawn. Now the lord's billiard tables have been replaced by 25 foam mattresses, and the 50 young men who occupy Mentmore Towers, north of London, claim they engage in activities far more elevating than those favored by the earl. They are members of the Age of Enlightenment sect, followers of the Maharishi Mahesh Yogi, and their day literally reaches its high point during meditation exercises. "At each session, we levitate twice, rising to 1½ to 2 feet and moving forward about 2 feet," says the Right Honorable Stephen D. Benson, 27, the group's chief minister. "The foam mattresses are so we don't get hurt when we land."

The Age of Enlightenment has arrived in Europe—and so have a variety of other spiritual splinter groups that call themselves authentic religious organizations. Authorities and anxious parents contend that many of the outfits are mind-twisting and even dangerous cults that prey upon young people searching for simple solutions to complex problems. But the groups are growing—particularly in France and Germany—and not even the suicides of more than 900 cult members in Jonestown, Guyana, last fall has hurt their drawing power. "A spiritual supermarket now exists for people seeking spiritual fitness the way they seek physical fitness," says British researcher Carol Williams. "Cults are now a very, very big business."

Many European cults are American exports. "In the nineteenth century, the Jehovah's Witnesses, Seventh-day Adventists and Mormons came here from America," says James Beckford, a sociologist at Durham University in England. "Now it's the Rev. Sun Myung Moon's Unification Church and the Family of Love. America is a 'looser' society with freer relations in family community. This makes it easier for religious movements to develop."

Experts feel the success of cults in Europe, as in America, represents an attempt to plug some cultural leak. "In Great Britain, work, the family, the economy, politics, are all in a state of disintegration," explains the Rev. Barry Morrison, an Anglican priest in London. "There is a vacuum of hope and belonging." Father Gaston Zananiri, a Dominican who heads the

Center of Documentation of Churches and Cults in Paris, believes that organized religion has overlooked the needs of young people. "Traditional religion was so sure of its influence that it didn't realize all these movements fomenting underground are offering something quite similar," he says.

Aggressive

Although sects are not new in Europe—Scientology has been operating in England for twenty years, and the Children of God (also known as the Family of Love) established their German base in the early '70s—rarely have the groups seemed so aggressive in their recruitment or so upfront in their pitchmaking. They strongly resent attempts to link their goals and techniques to those of Jim Jones, the messianic leader who forced his followers to search for salvation in a vat of poisoned punch; nevertheless, the connection is made. After Jonestown, Alan Vivien, a Socialist deputy in the French Legislature, asked his colleagues: "Who's to say it can't happen here?" The Legislature answered by appointing a committee to investigate cult activities in France, where 250 groups operate.

Although most cults are protected by freedom-of-expression statutes, governments are trying to limit the scope of sects through legal means. Britain has put restrictions on the number of Scientologists who can enter the country (the group claims that 250,000 live in Britain now), and refused entry to the group's founder, L. Ron Hubbard. Official denunciations of the group as a "pseudo-philosophical cult" anger Scientologists, who are also involved in drug rehabilitation. "We are suing the government for libel," says Paul Spencer-Smith, a spokesman for the organization. "We have been harassed."

UFO'S

Families of cult members often believe *they* are the ones who have been victimized. As in the U.S., some parents seek the help of "de-programmers," antisect specialists who use psychological techniques to neutralize the effects of cult indoctrination, and others turn to organizations like Family Action Information Rescue, a three-year-old agency that monitors the activity of sects in Britain. "We have had a growing number of complaints," says Morrison, FAIR's codirector. "Most have been over the Moonies."

Some of the members become disillusioned on their own. Deborah Burdette, 27, a former Moonie now living in Frankfurt, said the restrictions on life-style and the exhausting work schedule caused her to quit. Burdette recalls that, when she allowed her hair to grow, the Moonies questioned her motives. "They thought I was stirring up sexual desires," she says.

Members of the groups say that the suspicions are founded in ignorance, but some of their behavior is undeniably extreme. Devotees of the mysterious Ananda Marga sect have burned themselves to death in public and attempted to hijack a passenger plane bound to Stockholm from Oslo. David (Moses) Berg, leader of the Children of God, instructs women converts in West Germany to overwhelm men sexually—in the name of Jesus—and some members of Iso Zen worship UFO's and practice homosexual lovemaking in public.

FLYING

Officials at the Age of Enlightenment, who claim 94,000 followers in Britain, say they issue no exotic imperatives. But at a recent "Cabinet meeting" all the leaders, who have renounced smoking, drinking and sex, were dressed in pinstripe suits. Enlightenment members insist that their levitation exercises—"flying together"—create an explosion of psycho-social energy that has reduced crime, unemployment and sickness. "The coherence of atoms reaches a maximum at the moment of liftoff and is so powerful the effect can reach London and influence the government," says Benson, who has offered to solve Ireland's religious strife by this method.

Like many religious sects, the Age of Enlightenment is in divine financial shape. The group bought Mentmore Towers for $480,000 and maintains it with proceeds from classes (levitation lessons cost up to $2,400). The Children of God turn their savings over to the group and hustle up more money by running a disco in Berlin. Ananda Marga members teach yoga, and Moonies operate a costume-jewelry factory in France and ginseng shops in Germany. Business has been good enough that Moon has bought an estate, reportedly for $400,000, in a fashionable section of Frankfurt.

So far, the sects have demonstrated considerable staying power. But can it last? "Cults will be big for a few years and then will disappear like drugs and hippies," says Father Zananiri. "These are whims in our society but I don't think they are stronger than the wisdom of humanity." Some sect leaders are philosophical on this point. "Life is temporary and so is everything else," sighs Succonda, a 30-year-old Hare Krishna devotee in Germany. "We must rely on faith and Krishna." Given the aggressive expansion of Europe's religious sects, many believe young people would be wiser to rely on themselves.

encouraged to associate with (and marry) only other members of the cult. They may be required to abandon personal wealth and turn it over to the cult.

A number of deprogramming groups have emerged in response. Often these groups resort to precisely the same tactics of which they accuse the cults. That is, kidnapping, isolation, and intensive teaching sessions. In one case, Daniel Eyink, a member of an Ashram in Cincinnati, was abducted by such a group, who had been hired by Eyink's parents. After a rather heated court fight, Eyink's cult was able to gain a court order for Eyink's return.

Those who justify deprogramming argue that because cult members have been brainwashed and because they are no longer in full control of their faculties, they should not be afforded the civil liberties of "normal" people. The tactic then is to have the cult member ruled "mentally incompetent" by the courts and to have the parents appointed as "conservators." (This maneuver was designed to provide for the care of elderly people who were no longer able to handle their own affairs [Robbins, 1977].) A serious question remains over whether such procedures deprive cult members of their civil liberties.

Finally, although some of the allegations against some cults may be true, there is no reason to assume that all cults operate in the same fashion. Likewise, it is an error to assume that all cult followers are impossible dreamers, unthinking robots, or mental freaks. Zaretsky and Leone (1975) found that, rather than being destructive to the primary moral codes of society, the major groups were very pragmatic and advocated highly moral doctrines.

MORAL EDUCATION

What should be the role of the schools in fostering and developing values in today's children and youths? Should the schools be involved at all? Some would argue that the second alternative is not an alternative at all, because value structures are inherent in the educational curricula in the form of explicit or implicit expectations. Silberman (1970) reports the extreme example of an elementary school principal who, after visiting a school for the deaf and mute, told his students, "The silence was just wonderful." The principal went on to praise the fact that those students could get their work done without being bothered by noise. Silberman concluded, "The goal was explicit: to turn normal children into youngsters behaving as though they were missing two of their faculties" (p. 128).

Schools, in this sense, relate values by making it clear what is valued. This "hidden curriculum" in the schools is composed of school rules and regulations, the racial and social attitudes of the teachers, administrators and peers, as well as the implied values that emerge from observing who is favored in the schools. Johnston and Bachman (1976) report data in which school personnel articulate a primary role of the schools as keeping the students busy and "out of trouble." Schools should ideally value scholastic achievement more than athletic achievement, but in a national survey teachers reported that athletics received more of their attention than scholastics.

Moral education may also take its form in what is *not* taught or what is not *allowed* to be taught. School libraries are often under pressure from public groups to remove materials they judge to be "immoral." Although that pressure is typically directed at books that contain sexually explicit scenes or objectionable language, pressure to censor books on the bases of racist or sexist descriptions may also be encountered. Even well-meaning English teachers who want to remove "low-level" novels because they are not intellectually challenging are engaging in censorship.

Given the fact that adolescents often pursue their exploration of alternative value systems through reading, such restrictions may be counterproductive. If Adelson (1979) and others are right, investigating alternative value systems through books is not going to radically alter an adolescent's basic value system. Indeed, such vicarious assessment of alternatives may help to solidify the adolescent's current values.

On the positive side, when teachers are valued and viewed as fair, students may acquire in the classroom such attitudes as compassion, tolerance of people with different beliefs, a love of learning, and so on. When rules are not enforced capriciously or arbitrarily, students are more likely to view fairness as a valued trait. Not incidentally, in schools with much vandalism, discipline and control are often seen by students as uneven and unfair (Bayh, 1975).

Kohlberg (1976) maintains that teachers should have an active role in the moral education of their students. By this, Kohlberg does not mean that teachers should moralize or present their personal value system. Rather, teachers should stimulate development of learners' moral structures by discussing moral and ethical dilemmas. To be effective in this mode, teachers should probe the limits of the students' understanding of an ethical conflict and allow the students to evaluate the rightness or wrongness of various alternatives. By opening the discussion of ethical issues, the teacher provides a context in which students can encounter and evaluate positions other than their own. As students face information new to their existing cognitive moral structure, they must respond not simply by assimilating the new information in a verbatim, rote fashion, but also by evaluating the information. Further, they may need to modify the existing schema in order to accommodate the new information. Facilitating moral development in Kohlberg's terms requires a transitional period of disorganization or disequilibrium so that reorganization may take place. Challenging beliefs through questioning, debating or role playing, generates such disharmony, but the teacher should also *provide time for the learner to reorganize* the schema before too much disharmony settles in. This reorganization may take as simple a form as a presentation or a project.

To be effective, instruction in this mode should maintain many of those characteristics of teaching for productive thinking in other domains. That is, it must occur in a positive, constructive setting in which alternative views are not dismissed out of hand. Teachers who engage in these interchanges must recognize that students may not resolve ethical dilemmas in precisely the fashion that those in authority would prefer. In fact, a student may evaluate the dilemma in ways dramatically opposite to what the teacher expects. This does not mean that Kohlberg is calling for total neutrality or moral relativism on the part of the teacher. Indeed, he believes that, as individuals progress through the stages of moral development, they gain broader, more pervasive concepts of right and wrong.

Bereiter (1978) asks the question, "Can the schools teach morality without covertly or overtly teaching a moral doctrine?" (p. 20). Kohlberg feels that moral education can occur within the context of traditional religious and moral systems—that they are not mutually exclusive. However, as Bereiter notes, the question of keeping the two separate may not be as simple as advocates of moral education presume.

SUMMARY

Young people develop increasingly complex moral structures and value systems during adolescence. During early adolescence, values are simplistic and dogmatic. As teens move through middle to late adolescence, their values become increasingly flexible, and they incorporate their multifaceted views of morality and their more complex ideologies into their personal identity. In a similar vein their political ideologies become more generalized and reflect their increased awareness of the complex nature of human interaction.

Adolescents' reactions to religion may range from mild discomfort and uncertainty to zealous adherence to a dogmatic position. It is not uncommon for adolescents to reject institutional religions temporarily or permanently in favor of personal convictions. Perhaps the relevance of religious conviction to an adolescent's personal identity is best indicated by the individual need to clarify a stand toward religion.

Adults and institutions may have a positive or negative impact on an adolescent's personal identity. The use of ethical or moral dilemmas is one way to promote moral growth. The problem for adults is to decide how best to guide young people in selecting or developing their own personal value system, rather than to try to force their own ideology on them.

11 | Drugs and Alcohol

Of all the problem areas in the study of adolescent development in contemporary society, few raise as much concern among parents and practitioners as the widespread use of drugs among today's young people. Not only has the rate of use of drugs like marijuana, barbiturates, amphetamines, and hallucinogens increased over the past two decades, the use of alcohol, long a popular drug among teens, has also increased. How widespread is alcohol and drug use? The answer depends in part on how we ask the question. If we ask adolescents whether they use a drug daily, we might conclude that marijuana is the most popular drug among today's young people (see Figure 11-1). If we ask them whether they have used a drug at all in the past month, we would conclude instead that alcohol remains the preferred drug of young people. Dangerous drugs such as heroin and LSD have not been and are not currently widely used by teens.

Interestingly enough, when teens are asked to rate drugs in terms of danger, the drugs they see as most dangerous are the ones they use least, whereas the drugs they see as less dangerous are the ones they use more frequently. There are two exceptions, however. Alcohol, which teens see as somewhat dangerous, continues to be widely used. Marijuana, which teens rate as a relatively harmless drug, is not used as widely as we might expect. (See Figure 11-2.)

The problem of drug use among today's adolescents is complicated by a variety of factors. Students find drugs readily available in school and out of school. Peer approval and tolerance of drug use has become very liberal. Only a minority of youths view drug use, including alcohol use, as unacceptable. Attempts by schools to respond to the problem are often disorganized and uncertain. Some schools seem to prefer to ignore the problem in a vague hope that the problem will disappear by itself. School administrators and principals may prefer to ignore problems of alcohol and drug use among students rather than try to handle the legal and social complexities of attending to the problem.

We will discuss four general classes of drugs in this chapter. *Stimulants* are drugs that excite or stimulate the central nervous system. Use of stimulants,

Figure 11-1 DAILY USE OF VARIOUS DRUGS BY THE CLASS OF 1977

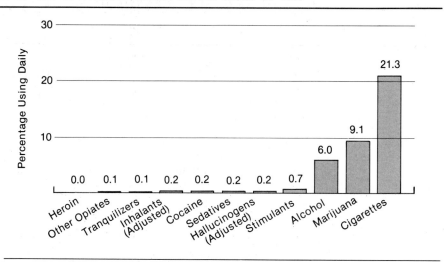

Source: L. D. Johnston, J. G. Bachman, and P. M. O'Malley, *Highlights from Student Drug Use in America,* *1975–1980*, National Institute on Drug Abuse, DHHS Pub. No. (ADM) 81–1066 (Washington, D.C.: Superintendent of Documents, U.S. Government Printing Office, 1980), p. 18.

Figure 11-2 RATINGS BY HIGH SCHOOL STUDENTS OF THE USE AND DANGEROUSNESS OF VARIOUS DRUGS

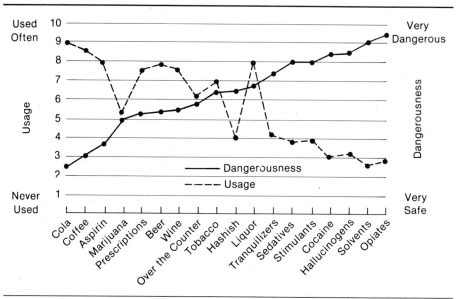

Source: M. R. Wong and T. Allen, "A Three-Dimensional Structure of Drug Attitudes," *Journal of Drug* *Education 6* (1976): 187. Copyright © 1976 by Baywood Publishing Company, Inc. Reprinted by permission.

Children learn attitudes about drugs from their parents, especially from their parents' *behavior.* (© Elizabeth Crews)

or uppers, is associated with increased levels of activity and the ability to go without sleep for extended periods of time. Amphetamines, cocaine, and even caffeine are all stimulants. *Depressants,* on the other hand, slow down or depress central nervous system activity. Use of depressants, or downers, is associated with feelings of drunkenness or intoxication. Barbiturates, sedatives, alcohol, and methylqualone (quaaludes) are all depressants. *Hallucinogens* are drugs that alter an individual's perception of reality by altering perceptions or by inducing hallucinations. Lysergic acid diethylamide (LSD), marijuana, hashish, and psilocybin are all classified as hallucinogens. *Opiates* are drugs that are synthetic or natural derivatives of opium. Officially, opiates are medically designated to reduce pain; however, they also have hallucinogenic qualities and promote feelings of euphoria.

What leads a young person to try drugs in the first place? Adolescents often volunteer that they initially try a drug out of curiosity, boredom, or pressure from friends. Whether or not their use continues after the initial experiment depends on a variety of factors. Jessor and Jessor (1977) found that continued regular use of drugs and alcohol is related to other attitudes considered as deviant by adult society.

Most analyses of variables that lead to continued use of alcohol by adolescents point to the level of parents' use of alcohol as a primary predictor. The more the parents drink, the more their offspring are likely to drink (Bracht et al., 1973). Other studies have found that peers play a significant role in reinforcing and encouraging drinking among high school adolescents (Jessor, Collins, and Jessor, 1972) and college students (Rogers, 1970).

VIGNETTE 11-1
Drink, Drank, Drunk

In simplest terms not only does an average teenager get drunk more quickly than an adult, but also the damaging effects of chronic, excessive drinking—including liver damage, stomach problems, and brain injury—occur more rapidly among teenagers. Whereas the impact of heavy drinking on an adult's liver or stomach may take ten years, the same effect can occur in teens in two or three years. The point is not that teenagers, or adults, should not drink, but instead that many people develop serious drinking problems before they are aware of it. The growing body of an adolescent who drinks heavily seems particularly susceptible to harm. By most estimates the number of early- and middle-adolescents who are already problem drinkers has reached alarming proportions.

The good news: teenage alcoholism is rare. The bad news: drinking, including plenty of outright drunkenness, is the norm among teens today in most parts of the country. The latest national picture shows that at least three out of four teenagers today drink beer, wine or liquor. One-third of the young people who drink get into trouble—partly because they get drunk easily, and partly because they are prone to flaunt their drinking—but there's no indication that young people are getting into more serious trouble today than teenagers did a generation ago.

It may seem that teenagers are drinking more than ever because there are 25 percent more teenagers today than there were a dozen years ago; six million more young people are probably drinking today. Their visibility has been heightened, too, in more than twenty states where the legal age for drinking has been dropped from twenty-one to eighteen or nineteen.

Dr. John Weir, director of a program to help teenagers overcome alcohol-related problems in Marin County, Calif., believes that most teenagers who drink do so moderately and "handle their liquor well." He is concerned, however, about the problems when teenage drinking becomes an important part of their social scene. For although teenagers drink less frequently than adults, those who do get drunk more often than adults. In the past, the majority of teenagers said they drank to feel more adult. Today, almost half say they drink to have a good time. The dramatic new finding about today's teenagers is that more than twice as many as in 1965 say they get drunk. Some say they don't stop drinking until the supply runs out or they pass out.

The latest national survey of teenage drinking, involving 13,000 students, . . . estimates that 24 million high school students drink; two-thirds take small amounts of alcohol from once a week to once a month and have no serious alcohol-related problems. Another eight percent drink more heavily at least once a week. But aside from getting drunk very often, they manage to stay out of serious trouble. Three percent of the young people across the nation drink heavily and get into a lot of trouble. Many teenagers now get together specifically to get drunk.

Youngsters do not seem to be aware of the dangers of drinking. The risk that a teenager will get into an auto accident triples after two or three beers. Few teenagers realize that one can of beer—their favorite alcoholic bever-

Source: Shirley Sirota Rosenberg, "Drink, Drank, Drunk," *Parents'* magazine 41 (July 1978):80–81. Reprinted by permission of the author.

age—contains as much as one glass of wine or a cocktail, or that light beer contains as much alcohol as regular beer. A recent study by the U.S. National Highway Safety Traffic Administration reports that two-thirds of the teenagers surveyed said they could drink up to four beers and still drive safely. Some think they can drive even better after drinking, and fifteen percent believe they can put down at least eight beers without effect.

Over the years, many theories have been advanced explaining why young people drink. In a National Institute on Alcohol Abuse and Alcoholism study, one finding occurred repeatedly: Although friends play a major role in what and how much teenagers drink, parents set the stage for whether or not their children will drink at all. In fact, 81 percent of families who drink have children who drink; 72 percent of families who abstain have children who abstain.

Learning what it feels like to drink is part of the mystical adult culture that most young people try on for size. The first drink is typically taken at age thirteen in the home, according to Dr. Howard T. Blane, Professor of Psychology and Education at the University of Pittsburgh, who analyzed over 30 years of teenage drinking for the National Institute.

Some of the most intriguing information from the Research Triangle study is a breakdown of youthful drinking by ethnic group and geography. The South consistently has the highest proportion of non-drinkers and infrequent drinkers; more than half the teenagers there have never had a drink. Black youths drink less than any other group, and have the lowest rate of heavy drinkers. White youths drink twice as much as blacks, and more than Spanish Americans and Asian Americans. American Indian youth show high rates of drinking and large numbers of heavy drinkers.

Boys outnumber girls two-to-one as heavy drinkers, and run into twice as much trouble. In a school district with 10,000 junior and senior high school students, about 300 young people—200 boys and 100 girls—probably will

have considerable difficulty because of alcohol.

In most studies, researchers ask students to report whether or not they have ever been drunk in the past year, experienced problems because of drinking, have been in a car while drinking or drunk, or have been picked up by the police for drinking. (Trouble with police varies widely, from being arrested for drinking at a school dance to driving while drunk.)

The incidence of serious trouble with alcohol—being intoxicated more than four times or running into other trouble at least three times a year—is placed at 2.5 percent by the students, not much less than the researchers' estimate. These problem drinkers manage to put down six times as much alcohol as their drinking classmates. They get drunk at least once a month, compared with problem drinkers who become intoxicated two or three times a year. Use of marijuana and other drugs is reported more often by students who have been intoxicated than students who don't drink to excess.

Police and parents report that drinking problems become more severe during vacations when young people stay up later. Drunken behavior starts to rise at graduation time and continues during the summer as young people have more free time.

Fights and vandalism go up fourfold when teenagers drink. Richard A. King, police chief of Fairfax County, Va., says, "After a big beer party, I saw a street that looked as though it had been struck by a hailstorm because some young people ran up and down the block knocking out auto and house windows with boards." Two years ago, he joined School Superintendent S. John Davis in an open letter asking parents and teenagers to make certain things didn't get out of hand at graduation. He credits that letter with lessening alcohol-related problems that summer.

Young people with the least number of drinking problems come from opposite ends of the spectrum. Jewish teenagers start to drink early in life and drink often, but only take moderate amounts and have a low rate of alcohol abuse. Only the children from Protestant sects which preach abstention have less trouble; they are at least eight times less likely to take even one drink or drink frequently than all others. However, according to Dr. Thomas C. Harford of the National Institute, problem drinking is sometimes disproportionately high among youths from temperance communities. Some specialists believe that for these children, drinking is an obvious form of teenage rebellion.

The heaviest drinking and the greatest problems take place in children of families with a drinking double standard. In the Research Triangle survey, parents of more than half the boys and three-fourths of the girls who drink excessively disapprove of teenage drinking, but drink themselves.

Most teenagers are interested in learning how to drink responsibly, not how to abstain. Alcohol education programs with this approach are growing in schools and community organizations across the country. Dr. Weir points out that when many teenagers first come to his program in Marin County they do not see their problems as being alcohol-related; they tend to blame their troubles on "being hassled by the authorities." Once they have information on how alcohol works, many teenagers realize that their drinking causes problems, says Dr. Weir. Changes in drinking behavior come about rapidly, before drinking itself becomes the problem.

Changes in regional drinking practices are taking place. Dr. Patricia O'Gorman, who heads the Prevention and Education Program of the National Council on Alcoholism, says she gets calls for help from communities in the West and the South concerned about such new developments as girls breaking out a bottle of wine at a pajama party. In the Boston area, Dr. Henry Wechsler found that drinking to intoxication among high school students was higher than the national average; by the time they are seniors, Boston girls drink about as much as boys, with 70 percent of both sexes drinking to intoxication. Dr. Blane of Pittsburgh predicts that "with the homogenization of American culture, more young people in the South will start to drink."

Some people shouldn't drink at all. If a pregnant woman, for example, consumes more than two drinks a day there will be a definite danger to her unborn baby. A teenage mother, whose pregnancy is already risky because of her age, should not take alcohol at all. People on medication, particularly any which affects the central nervous system, and people with any ailment, especially metabolic or liver disorders, should check with their doctor before they drink.

Although religious preference and commitment to religious values are predictors of drinking behavior among adolescents, the relationship is not a simple one. Those who are raised in religion in which alcohol consumption is permitted are more likely to drink than those raised in fundamentalist religions; but a curious phenomenon occurs when the second group does drink. Those who have been prohibited and then start drinking often fail to have any degree of control and are more likely to be problem drinkers (Bracht et al., 1973).

Family factors also are related to drug use. Chronic use of drugs is often related to unstable or erratic family environments. The more stable and

"Thank heaven! Maybe now he'll
stay away from pot."

Source: By permission of Bill Mauldin and Wil-Jo
Associates, Inc.

supportive the family, the less likely the adolescent will try drugs, and, if
tried, the less likely the adolescent will continue using them (Blum, 1976).

By and large, drug use among teens is concentrated within a few types of
drugs. Use of other drugs may occur in sporadic fashion, but it does not
usually last long. What is curious is that the most widely used drug, alcohol,
is often viewed with the least alarm by adults.

DRUG USE AND ABUSE

The question of when we can call drug *use* drug *abuse* is not an easy one to
answer. In the strictest sense, any use of an illegal drug can be called abuse
because the user has broken the law. Such a definition is thus not very useful.
Experimental use of drugs, although it might reasonably be discouraged,
often goes no further than experimentation, and no long-term or short-term,
negative impact occurs. Although we cannot consider all drug use to be drug
abuse, clearly certain kinds of use create problems for the individual and
society. I will define *abuse* for purposes of this chapter as any drug use that
interferes with an individual's performance at school, home, or work, or in
society.

Drug dependence may take two forms—*physical dependence* and *psychological
dependence*. Physical dependence occurs when an individual's biological
balance is altered and the drug is needed to avoid serious withdrawal

symptoms. Psychological dependence occurs when an individual has a preoccupation with the altered states of consciousness brought on by drugs or feels unable to cope with stress in the absence of drugs. Not all drugs lead to physical dependence, but all drugs may lead to psychological dependence. Not all drug abusers are drug dependent.

Dr. Joseph Zabik, a researcher in alcoholism and pharmacology at Purdue University, describes the progression toward drug dependence in the following manner (personal interview): Initially an individual may experiment with a drug out of curiosity or to be part of the crowd. An adolescent who continues to use the drug regularly over an extended period of time develops a tolerance to the drug. That is, at first a small dose creates the desired state of mind. Gradually, however, larger and larger amounts of the drug are required to achieve the same impact. Individuals who continue to use these increased dosages may develop a physical or psychological dependence on the drug. Although some drugs have no known physically addictive characteristics, all may have psychologically addictive characteristics. Dependence is most obvious when an adolescent goes through a period of withdrawal, in which the drug of dependence is no longer available. Withdrawal symptoms may be mild—including minor physical discomfort and anxiety or irritability—or, in cases of strong dependence on certain drugs, it may be *very* stressful, with severe pain and paranoid hallucinations. Although while not all drug users develop a physical or psychological dependence, it is, nonetheless, a very real possibility. The common notion that addicts were once "experimenters" has a good deal of truth in it.

Kenniston (1968) describes three groups of drug users on college campuses: tasters, seekers, and heads. By far the largest group are those he calls *tasters*. Tasters' use of drugs is usually casual or experimental. The second group are called *seekers*. Their use of drugs is occasional but regular. They try to achieve heightened awareness, relief from boredom or depression, or just plain "an experience." Finally, the most regular users of drugs are the *heads*. They are a small but highly visible minority who use drugs with frequent regularity. As Kenniston says, however, even heads are not necessarily drug addicted, although addicted youths would fall into this category. The important point is that, even with the general upswing in drug use, the percent of regular drug users among the college population is relatively small and varies with the type of college campus and the section of the country.

DEPRESSANTS

ALCOHOL

We can easily argue that drinking alcohol is an American institution. When the Puritans set sail for America, their cargo included fourteen tons of water. It also included forty-two tons of beer and ten thousand gallons of wine (Miles, 1974). Today, alcohol consumption supports a multibillion dollar business in the United States alone. Further, as a drug, alcohol continues to be the most widely abused substance among both adolescents and adults. (The most widely used drug is probably caffeine.)

Whether alcohol or marijuana is more widely used among today's teens depends on the way *use* is defined and which group of teens is being studied. However, 93 percent of high school seniors in 1978 reported having used alcohol, and more than 70 percent of seniors reported using alcohol in the previous month (Johnston, Bachman, and O'Malley, 1979). On the other hand, 59 percent reported ever having used marijuana, and nearly 40 percent reported using it in the previous month. If, however, the question is asked in terms of daily use, marijuana use exceeds alcohol use 10.7 percent to 5.7 percent.

Before proceeding, you might want to classify your own drinking behavior on a scale that has been used in several recent studies of alcohol use and abuse (from Rachel et al., 1975):

CATEGORIES OF DRINKERS

Abstainers: Do not drink or drink less than once a year.

Infrequent Drinkers: Drink once a month at most and drink small amounts per typical drinking occasion.

Light Drinkers: Drink once per month at most and drink medium amounts per typical drinking occasion *or* drink no more than 3–4 times per month and drink small amounts per typical drinking occasion.

Moderate Drinkers: Drink at least once a week and small amounts per typical drinking occasion *or* 3–4 times a month and medium amounts per typical drinking occasion *or* no more than once a month and large amounts per typical drinking occasion.

Moderate/Heavy Drinkers: Drink at least once a week and medium amounts per typical drinking occasion *or* 3–4 times a month and large amounts per typical drinking occasion.

Heavy Drinkers: Drink at least once a week and large amounts per typical drinking occasion.

Alcohol, or more accurately, ethanol, is a depressant. When we drink alcohol, 20 percent is processed immediately from the stomach into the bloodstream. The term *depressant* refers to a drug's effect on the brain and the central nervous system, not to the emotion of depression. In small quantities, alcohol may seem to have the opposite effect—that is, energizing a person and reducing inhibitions. The reason for this is that small quantities of alcohol depress brain activity in the area related to emotional arousal. However, as the level of alcohol in the bloodstream increases, the depressant action of ethanol becomes more profound.

Blood-Alcohol Levels. Blood-alcohol level (BAL) refers to the percent of alcohol found in a person's bloodstream. A BAL of .05 indicates that an individual has .05 parts alcohol to 100 parts blood, or 1 part per 2000. Although .05 does not sound like much, it is a potential factor in auto

Figure 11-3 STAGES OF ALCOHOLIC INTOXICATION

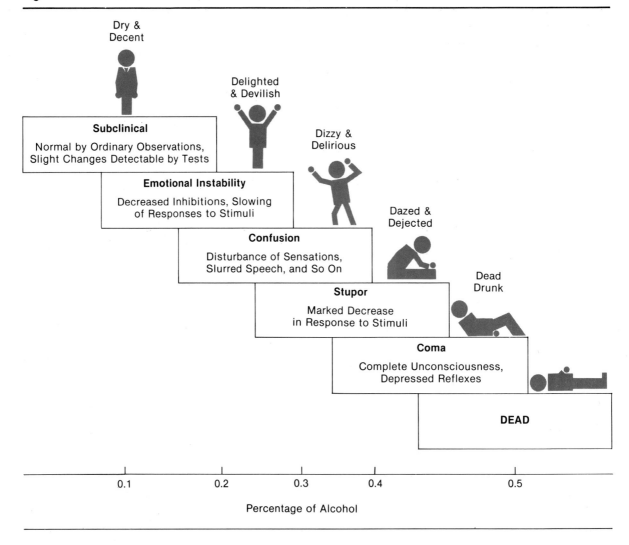

accidents, because at that level activity in the front of the brain is slowed down. A BAL of .05 is roughly the blood-alcohol level of an average 160-pound person who has drunk three ounces of whiskey within two hours *after* eating a meal. That same amount of whiskey would affect some 160-pound people more quickly and would have a stronger effect on people weighing less than 160 pounds and on those who have not eaten a meal in the previous two hours. Because teens are likely to weigh less than adults, they are likely to be affected by alcohol more quickly.

A BAL of .10 is usually the legal limit that defines drunkenness. At .10 people become clumsy and awkward, their speech may be slurred, their senses are dulled and distorted, and their ability to do skilled tasks is impaired.

By the time a person reaches a BAL of .20, coordination is severely affected, and the person is likely to stagger and reel. Emotional outbursts involving crying and raging are common. A BAL of .30 is very serious. The ethanol is affecting the deeper parts of the brain, and the person may become confused and disoriented. At BALs of .40 and .50 the inner brain is profoundly affected, and the person will fall into unconsciousness. The depressant activity may lead to stoppage of the heart or lungs and death. Figure 11-3 traces the progression of intoxication at increasing blood-alcohol levels.

Teenagers' Drinking Patterns.   Alcohol remains the number one drug used by teenagers. By the end of high school nearly all have sampled alcohol, and the majority drink with some regularity. Although most adolescents—like most adult drinkers—drink only occasionally, one in nine is considered to be a problem drinker, but there are an estimated 500,000 teenage alcoholics.

A nationwide survey of junior and senior high school students found that, using the scale presented earlier in this chapter, about 11 percent

Alcohol remains a highly popular drug among teenagers, many of whom view drinking as a symbol of adult status. (© Susan Lapides)

could be rated as heavy drinkers, and another 14 percent were classified as moderate-to-heavy drinkers. On the other side, 27 percent of teens described themselves as abstainers. However, if we study those percentages more closely by age (Table 11-1), we see that although 38 percent of thirteen-year-olds were abstainers, only 20 percent of eighteen-year-olds were. Twelve percent of thirteen-year-olds were listed as moderate-to-heavy drinkers. By age eighteen that percentage almost quadruples to 41 percent (Rachel et al., 1975). Among adults 32 percent rate themselves as abstainers (Callahan, 1975).

In a ten-year study of drug use in San Mateo County, California, high school students were asked how often they used certain drugs. The results are recorded in Figure 11-4. From 1968 to 1977, there was an increase among all groups in the percent of students who admitted to having used alcohol during the preceding year. However, most of that increase occurred between 1968 and 1973. During years 1973 to 1977, there was an apparent leveling off of percentages. This trend has also been observed in other studies.

Adolescents are more likely to be adversely affected by alcohol than adults for several reasons:

1. On the average adolescents weigh less than adults; thus comparable amounts of alcohol are less effectively metabolized.
2. Adolescents lack experience with alcohol and have not developed a set of internal standards by which to govern their drinking.
3. Adolescents are more likely to try to demonstrate they can handle alcohol by "chugging."
4. Adolescents lack emotional maturity and are more susceptible to the psychological impact of intoxication.

Why do young people start drinking? Although the answers are not totally clear, it seems that parents, more than peers, seem to be involved in early drinking experiences. The first use of alcohol usually occurs at home with the

Table 11-1 DRINKING LEVELS OF TEENAGERS

Drinking Level	Age					
	13	14	15	16	17	18
Abstainer	37.8%	27.8%	24.7%	22.6%	17.2%	20.5%
Infrequent	23.6	18.8	14.1	11.2	11.4	6.9
Light	14.4	16.6	17.4	17.1	20.3	15.1
Moderate	12.7	15.4	16.2	17.3	17.5	16.5
Moderate/ Heavy	7.3	11.7	16.0	17.4	19.0	20.8
Heavy	4.3	9.7	11.5	14.5	14.6	20.2

Source: J. V. Rachel et al., *A National Study of Adolescent Drinking Behavior, Attitudes and Correlates,* Report to the National Institute on Alcohol Abuse and Alcoholism, Department of Health, Education and Welfare (Washington, D.C.: U.S. Government Printing Office, 1975), p. 147.

Figure 11-4 ALCOHOL USE AMONG TEENAGERS IN SAN MATEO COUNTY, CALIFORNIA

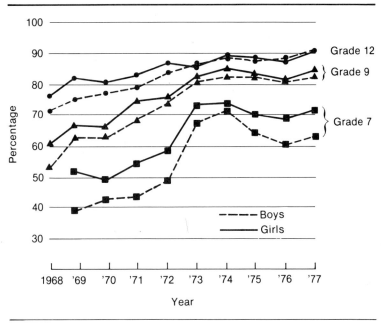

Source: San Mateo County, Department of Public Health, *Summary Report: Surveys of Student Drug Use, San Mateo County, California.*

approval of parents. Thus early in adolescence the parents convey their approval of alcohol consumption, even when later consumption occurs outside the home.

Teens regard drinking as an adult activity. It provides a way for them to act like adults, and in fact getting drunk may be a kind of an initiation rite. Adults usually remember that they too drank as teens and therefore view drinking as innocent or as much less of a problem than "real" drugs.

There are also strong peer pressures to drink and especially to get drunk. Further, a small but significant number of adolescents drink to relieve anxiety and tension. The practitioner can play an important role in helping adolescents cope with the internal and external pressures to consume alcohol and with their own attitudes about drinking. To do this, the practitioner should try to determine the motives behind the drinking and to help the adolescent find other means to deal with those motives. In some cases the practitioner may prefer to help the adolescent to control his or her drinking in the settings that usually lead to drunkenness.

BARBITURATES AND SEDATIVE-HYPNOTICS

Barbiturates and other nonbarbiturate depressants, such as dilantin (Valium), methylqualone (quaaludes, sopors), and others, are medically prescribed as antianxiety or sleep agents. Their effect is to reduce feelings of anxiety, tension, fear, or apprehension, allowing a person to cope more adequately with stress. In larger doses, these drugs lead to an intoxication similar to that of alcohol. It is not uncommon for barbiturates to be used in combination with alcohol.

An adolescent who is using barbiturates may appear drunk but not smell of alcohol. His or her speech may be slurred, coordination impaired, and ability to concentrate on complex problems disrupted. Continued use may lead to distorted perception and heightened anxiety.

Barbiturates are dangerous in high doses, and overdose can lead to death. Regular use of barbiturates leads to increased tolerance plus physical and psychological dependence. Regular users of barbiturates must be withdrawn from the drug slowly; otherwise, the withdrawal symptoms may be too severe.

Barbiturate and tranquilizer use is relatively low among adolescents and is very low among early-adolescents. By late adolescence and young adulthood, however, nonmedical use of sedatives and tranquilizers increases substantially. Among adolescents twelve to thirteen years old, rates of sedative use are less than one-half of one percent and of tranquilizer use, only .1 percent. By ages sixteen and seventeen, however, use rates for those drugs are seven and nine percent, respectively. Over the five-year period from 1972 to 1977, there was little change in the rate of nonmedical usage of sedatives and tranquilizers among adolescents and adults (Abelson et al., 1977).

STIMULANTS

In contrast to depressants, stimulants excite the central nervous system. In small quantities, they increase the level of arousal and help overcome fatigue. The two most commonly used stimulants are caffeine—found in coffee, tea, and cola drinks—and nicotine, found in tobacco. Cocaine, because of its high street-cost, is not a widely used drug among teens and will not be discussed here. The other major group of stimulants, drugs of great concern to those who work with drug-abusing youths, is amphetamines.

AMPHETAMINES

Amphetamine and methamphetamine (speed) abuse usually occur in conjunction with barbiturate abuse. Thus the pattern of nonmedical use of amphetamines among teens is very similar to the pattern of barbiturate usage described previously.

By themselves, amphetamines lead to an increased feeling of power and energy. However, the exhilaration and "high" caused by the stimulant may be followed by a "crash," or a period of profound depression. Chronic users may find that they have trouble "getting down" from an amphetamine high. Thus a pattern of "uppers" in the morning and "downers" at night may emerge.

Adolescents who use amphetamines usually experience a loss of appetite and appear nervous and excitable. Physically, the pupils of their eyes are dilated, they perspire heavily, and their hands may tremble. Emotionally, they are talkative and show rapid mood swings and overreactions to events. Regular users begin to have feelings of fear and apprehension. In extreme cases these fears become severe and may lead to a psychotic breakdown.

As with barbiturates, tolerance and dependence develop rapidly. Chronic abuse and overdose of amphetamines may lead to *toxic psychosis*, in which the user shows behavior very much like an actively psychotic patient. Severe overdose can cause death.

TOBACCO

Smoking has been termed the "largest preventable cause of death in America today" (Pinney, 1979). Despite a general campaign against smoking, and mounting evidence that chronic cigarette smoking is linked to cancer, heart disease, and emphysema, 22 percent of teens and 41 percent of adults do smoke. Of the age group eighteen to twenty-six, nearly half smoke, and most smoke a pack of cigarettes or more each day (Abelson et al., 1977). Among today's adolescents 75 percent have smoked at one time or another (Johnston et al., 1979), and 18 percent admit to smoking half a pack or more per day. Adolescents see smoking, like drinking, as a way of showing their maturity, because they consider smoking an "adult" activity.

In the San Mateo County report, smoking among boys showed an increase until 1974, but since then it has declined. From 1968 to 1977, there has been an overall drop in the percentage of boys who have ever smoked or who smoke heavily. Girls, on the other hand, are smoking more, and there is no indication of any decline in the future. Similarly, the repeated national studies by Johnston and his colleagues found only minor changes in rates of use among high school seniors from 1975 to 1978.

Teenage smokers, like their adult counterparts, are unwilling to admit that they will probably continue their habit. Only 1 percent of high school seniors who are currently smokers definitely expect to be smoking five years in the future. However, 55 percent of the seniors answered that they definitely would not be smoking in five years (Johnston et al., 1979).

HALLUCINOGENS

As with alcohol, the use of hallucinogens is not new. Naturally occurring hallucinogens are found in certain mushrooms, weeds, and cacti. Use of hallucinogenic mushrooms and peyote was recorded as early as 1000 B.C. (Schultes, 1938). Today literally dozens of hallucinogens are available. Some, such as marijuana, are mild hallucinogens, whereas others, such as LSD or PCP, are stronger and potentially toxic.

MARIJUANA

The major drug of choice besides alcohol (excluding cigarettes) among teens seems to be marijuana. Intoxication with marijuana may include

Smoking "grass" has become widespread, and its use is increasing, even among early-adolescents. (© Eric Kroll/Taurus Photos)

feelings of euphoria and of time passing slowly. Although a teen who is intoxicated with marijuana may feel that his words are profound and insightful, to the nonintoxicated observer they may be gibberish.

There is little evidence of any physical dependence associated with marijuana use, although a psychological dependence is very possible. Further, overdose with marijuana is nearly unheard of—the only possible means would be direct intravenous injection. Because smoking is such an easy method for drug taking, there is no reason for injection. Users do not agree on whether the intoxication with marijuana is as deep as with alcohol. Regardless, there is clear intellectual and psychomotor deterioration in both. The more demanding the task attempted under the influence, the more the deterioration. Short-term memory and attention are badly affected.

Nearly one in three youths ages twelve to seventeen admit to ever using marijuana, with about half of them having used it in the previous month

(Abelson et al., 1978). By their senior year over half of American high school students admit to having used marijuana, and nearly 60 percent of college-age youths claim to have ever used it (Abelson et al., 1978; Johnston et al., 1979). Overall, marijuana use has substantially increased. However, after large gains in the early 1970s, the percentage of teens at given age categories who have ever used marijuana has remained relatively stable.

A primary factor in the experimental or casual use of marijuana by adolescents is use by peers (Kandel, 1974). Similarly, continued use is tied to acceptance and use by friends. The impact of friends' use of marijuana on personal use of the drug continues into the young adult years (Jessor, 1979). Further, friendship patterns are based on degree of use. That is, heavy users tend to associate primarily with heavy users.

Users of marijuana tend to rate higher on scales of nonconventionality. They are less likely to feel committed to traditional cultural values and tend to view themselves as nonconformists (Jessor, 1979). In general these nontraditional attitudes tend to prevail across a range of social traditions and values, including sexual morals, religious beliefs, and political beliefs. Users also tend to value and be interested in creativity and novelty more than nonusers. On the other hand, marijuana use is also associated with lower motivation to achieve (Jessor and Jessor, 1977).

One important question that troubles many adults is the relationship of marijuana use to experimentation with other drugs. The evidence is clear that those who have tried marijuana are more likely to try other illegal drugs. The higher the degree of use, the greater the likelihood. However, marijuana is not always the initial drug of experimentation (Blum and Richards, 1979).

LSD AND PCP

Probably the most widely known of the synthetic hallucinogens available to today's young people is lysergic acid diethylamide (LSD). LSD was first synthesized in 1938, and as early as 1943, it was recognized as a hallucinogen. By the late 1960s, LSD had become widely available and was a matter of increasing public concern. Stories of suicides under LSD trips, chromosomal damage, and psychotic reactions of users led the public to view LSD as a seriously dangerous drug.

In a national survey of drug use (Abelson and Fishburne, 1976), only 5 percent of those between the ages of twelve and seventeen report ever having used LSD or another hallucinogen. When asked whether they had used a hallucinogen within the past month, fewer than one percent said that they had. In the age group eighteen to twenty-five, 17 percent admitted to ever using a hallucinogen and only 1 percent to having used one in the previous month (Abelson and Fishburne, 1976). In the ten-year San Mateo study, use of LSD seemed to hit a peak in the early 1970s and has dropped gradually ever since (Blackford, 1978).

Currently, more attention is being focused on the use of phencyclidine

(PCP), or "angel dust." Among American adolescents and youths, the use of PCP is the fastest growing of the potentially dangerous drugs. PCP is used legally as a powerful anesthetic for animals. Its use as an anesthetic for humans was short-lived since patients reported serious psychological disturbances following its use. Regardless, PCP, known as the "peace drug," became a popular drug during the late 1960s. Its use seemed to die off until relatively recently; now it is used much more widely than ever.

VIGNETTE 11-2
Angel Dust

Over the past two decades, a variety of street drugs have appeared and disappeared. For the most part, the drugs that did not survive were found by users to be too dangerous or to have too many side effects. There are, however, some exceptions. PCP first appeared on the drug scene as an additive to LSD and other hallucinogens. For a while use of PCP seemed to be diminishing. However, more recently PCP, or angel dust, has become a highly popular drug. Its popularity is especially alarming because of its real danger. Originally PCP was used as an anaesthetic, but adverse side effects were so great that its use with humans was discontinued. Now its use with animals is also being curtailed. Nonetheless, PCP has found its way into the street market and is currently a problem of serious concern. Under its influence users have been known to inflict serious physical harm on themselves and others without even knowing it. The potential for overdose is high, and the number of overdose cases is increasing.

A 21-year-old Washington, D.C., man stepped out of his shower, climbed naked down the wall of his second-story apartment and started running to New Jersey. The police stopped him several blocks away.

A young California girl and her fiancé decided to go for a swim. While he was changing, she went into the pool. When her fiancé returned, he found her lying dead at the bottom.

A 17-year-old New Jersey boy and his girlfriend decided to rob a nearby summer home at the seashore. Instead, the youth chose to bludgeon to death the elderly woman who lived in the cottage. He awoke the next morning covered with blood and with no recollection of his brutal act.

These bizarre and tragic events have a common thread: three people were high on the latest—and probably most dangerous—street drug to come along since heroin and LSD. The drug is phencyclidine (PCP), but is better known to its users by such colorful names as "angel dust," "super weed," "busy bee," "mist," "goon," "crystal," hog," "tic" and "tac." . . .

Federal officials estimate that nearly 7 million people, most of them from 12 to 25, have tried PCP. Last year alone, the drug sent at least 4,000 of its users to hospital emergency rooms, took 100 lives and triggered an untold number of strange, suicidal or homicidal acts. "It's the most toxic of all the substances I've seen since I started working with street drugs in 1965," says Dr. David Smith, founder of San Francisco's Haight-Ashbury Free Medical Clinic. Adding to PCP's special dangers is the fact that the drug is easy to make and can cause severe reactions with a single dose....

Users rarely inject liquid PCP. More likely, they spray the liquid or sprinkle crystals of PCP on plants such as marijuana, tobacco, mint and parsley and smoke it. The drug can also be snorted, or pressed into tablets or capsules for oral use. Although it was originally used as a booster or additive to other street drugs, in recent months at least half of the users of PCP have been taking the drug as their sole means of attaining a high.

Reactions to PCP are totally unpredictable. According to San Francisco psychologist Steven Lerner, most users report that their first experience was a pleasant one. "I feel wired," "I feel powerful," "I feel superior," are typical testimonies. But there are plenty of bad trips. Angel dust, says Dr. Beatrice Kresky of New York's Jamaica Hospital, can make "Grimm's fairy-tale characters come to life. Parents, nurses and doctors appear as monsters or witches, and police cars take on the form of dragons."

Psychotic reactions to PCP mimic the symptoms of paranoid schizophrenia, with hallucinatory voices and combative or self-destructive impulses. The drug can also give users a distorted sense of their own bodies; people often feel their arms or legs are growing or shriveling. Users may also suffer loss of bowel or bladder control, slurred speech, inability to walk, jerky eye movements and grimacing. Acute toxic reactions can last up to a week after a single dose, and the mental effects can linger for more than a month, often recurring in sudden episodes while the patient is apparently recovering. Taken in larger doses, PCP can induce seizures, coma and death.

The sudden emergence of PCP as a major drug has caught doctors without sure-fire methods of diagnosing and treating its ill effects. The drug tends to lodge in fat and brain tissue, and some poison-control centers are using large doses of vitamin C to acidify the urine and hasten its excretion from the body. Mental disturbances have been treated with tranquilizers such as Valium, but physicians can't agree yet whether these drugs reduce the effects of PCP or may actually accentuate them....

In its liquid form PCP is usually sprayed on parsley or oregano to be eaten or smoked. In some cases it has been sprayed on marijuana to make a "super joint." Usually users report that one experience was so unpleasant, they never tried PCP again. However, some users find the anesthetic and hallucinatory effects much more desirable, and PCP becomes a drug of choice. Chronic users may develop physical tolerance for PCP, but it is unclear whether physical dependence occurs. There is little doubt that psychological dependence may develop.

In extreme cases PCP may lead to bizarre hallucinations and behavior. The PCP user may show symptoms that look very much like severe psychosis. At such times, PCP users have been known to display superhuman strength. One indication of the increased level of abuse of PCP is the number of

Figure 11-5 ADMISSIONS TO EMERGENCY ROOMS FOR HEROIN
AND PCP OVERDOSE

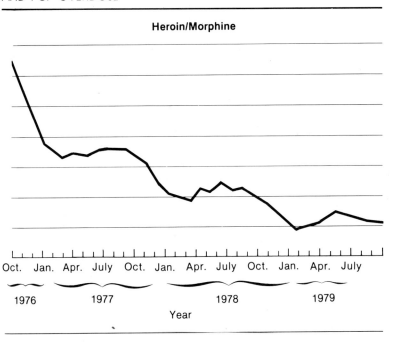

Heroin/Morphine

Oct. Jan. Apr. July Oct. Jan. Apr. July Oct. Jan. Apr. July

1976   1977   1978   1979

Year

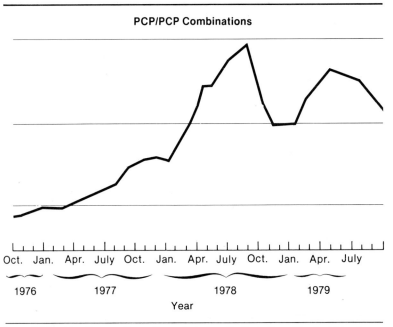

PCP/PCP Combinations

Oct. Jan. Apr. July Oct. Jan. Apr. July Oct. Jan. Apr. July

1976   1977   1978   1979

Year

Source: National Institute on Drug Abuse, *Data from the Drug Abuse Warning Network:*
Quarterly Report, July–September, 1979 (Washington, D.C.: U.S. Government Printing
Office, 1979).

admissions to medical emergency rooms associated with PCP overdose. From 1976 to 1977, there was more than a 100 percent increase in the number of PCP admissions (IMS, 1977, 1978). Looking at the trend of cases from 1975 to 1978 for PCP versus heroin, as shown in Figure 11-5, there was a sharp increase in the cases involving PCP and a decline in cases involving heroin (IMS, 1978b).

INHALANTS

A popular drug use pattern among some adolescents is sniffing glue and using inhalants such as gasoline or aerosols. Chronic inhalant abuse is a problem mainly among young drug users and among the very poor. Inhalants are popular in part because of their ease of availability. A young person can go into any grocery store, buy a tube of airplane glue, get a paper bag, and proceed to get "high." Ease of availability should not, however, be interpreted to mean that such drugs are safe. In one year there were 110 cases of death by inhalants (Bass, 1970), typically by suffocation or heart failure. Inhalation of freon, for example, can freeze the air passages.

Among college-age students, use of nitrous oxide (laughing gas) or chloroform seems more popular, when inhalants are used at all. The effects are the same, however, including giddiness and exhilaration. Chronic use of inhalants increases tolerance, and although no apparent physical dependence has been demonstrated, high toxic levels may cause irreparable harm to the liver and kidneys.

Cocaine, once the drug exclusively of the wealthy because of its high price, is now being used by more people, including adolescents. (© Margaret Thompson)

HEROIN AND OPIATES

Perhaps the class of drugs most frightening to the general public includes heroin and other opiates. In reality, of all the drugs used by adolescents, heroin is used by only a small percentage. Nonetheless, the physically and psychological addictive properties of opiates makes them a source of special concern.

There are four kinds of opiates. First, there are natural derivatives of opium, such as morphine and codeine. These drugs, originally valued as painkillers, also have mood-altering qualities. In some people the drugs produce a feeling of euphoria. Most people, however, achieve only confusion, disorientation, and nausea. It is not unusual for people who experiment with an opiate not to get the euphoric high of regular users.

Heroin, a synthetic derivative of opium, is transformed by the human body into morphine. As with morphine, tolerance levels and physical dependence develop with continued use. In the San Mateo study, about 3 percent of the students admitted to using heroin during 1977; only 1.1 percent used heroin ten or more times. In national surveys, the rates were even lower, with only .6 percent reporting having used heroin in the previous year. These figures are not intended to minimize the problem of heroin use. For even the small proportion of adolescents who use heroin regularly, it is a serious problem. In major metropolitan areas, heroin use often extends to younger drug users and is justifiably a cause of much concern.

The third category of opiates includes the completely synthesized drugs like methadone, which are often used in the treatment of heroin addiction. The use of methadone, however, does not eliminate the physical drug dependence but instead replaces heroin with a less harmful drug. Further, methadone- and heroin-dependent youths are usually polydrug users and may be dependent on other drugs as well.

The fourth category of opiates is probably the least abused; it includes prescriptive drugs that contain minimal quantities of opiates, such as paregoric or codeine cough syrups.

DRUG AND ALCOHOL EDUCATION

When educators are asked to rate their ability to handle alcohol education, they report a general lack of self-confidence (Milgram, 1974). Teachers involved in drug education often lack credibility among the students, because the students think they know more about drugs than the teachers—and they are probably right. There is a real need for teachers to be aware of such attitudes among the student population. Likewise, teachers must have accurate information about the characteristics of various drugs and the symptoms of chronic abuse.

Because so much attention has been directed toward drug and alcohol use among contemporary adolescents, schools and communities have become increasingly involved in drug and alcohol education programs. Many states now require junior and senior high schools to offer drug education in the standard curriculum. Usually such programs have had as an implicit or explicit goal the reduction or elimination of drug and alcohol use among the students. Whether or not abstinence from alcohol or drugs is a reasonable goal is a matter of some debate. There is a general agreement that whenever reduction of drug use has been a goal, drug and alcohol education have been very unsuccessful. Some drug education programs have in fact been credited with an *increase* in drug usage among students.

Martin Wong (1976) has described the more generally used models of drug education. Although Wong directs his comments at drug-education programs, they apply equally to alcohol programs, which are often kept separate from drug education.

The *legal-political model* of drug education is oriented around the premise that drugs are immoral and illegal. Laws are made to protect people from immorality and their stiff enforcement is essential. Confusion sometimes exists in these programs over whether drugs are illegal because they are immoral or whether they are immoral because they are illegal. A legal-political model assumes that informing adolescents of the illegality of a drug will serve as a deterrent.

Programs in this category usually invite police authorities or government officials to describe to large groups the criminal prosecution that may follow if the adolescents are caught breaking the law. As a general approach to discourage experimental or casual use of drugs and alcohol, the legal-political model has not been very effective. It lacks credibility with students, in part because they see the laws as unfair. Further, the programs often include questionable information. The result is that a large population of adolescents choose to ignore the law.

The second major "education" approach to drug education consists of scare tactics. The *fear-induction model* uses films and personal accounts of the devastating effects of alcohol and drugs. Any number of horrors are shown, usually in chilling detail, with the assumption that adolescents will agree that drugs are something to avoid. Some adolescents may. However, most are largely unimpressed by this approach, again because it often confuses truth with fiction. Few controls have been placed on the accuracy of information. Students know, for example, that drugs taken in small quantities will not cause the severe withdrawal effects associated with chronic use.

Many of the films in these programs are so full of inaccuracies that students see them as comical. For example, the 1949 film *Reefer Madness* is very popular in campus movie houses. The film depicts a young girl who smokes one "reefer" and immediately falls prey to all forms of humiliation and degradation. Not only do students view the film as funny, they often report that they like to get high on marijuana while watching the film.

Scare tactics can also take the form of warnings. For example, consider this warning about marijuana use issued by the Federal Bureau of Narcotics:

> Under the influence of this drug marijuana, the will is destroyed and all power of directing and controlling thought is lost... many violent crimes have been committed by persons under the influence of this drug. Not only is marijuana

used by hardened criminals to steel them to commit violent crimes, but it is also being placed in the hands of high school children...Its continued use results many times in impotency and insanity (Testimony to the U.S. Senate Subcommittee on Taxation, 1937, reported in Zinberg and Robertson, 1972).

Many schools and agencies prefer to use what Wong calls the *information-processing, rationality model,* in which educators argue with facts. They are convinced that when drug users or potential users learn all the facts about drugs, they will weigh the evidence and conclude that alcohol or drugs is not worth the risk. Although this type of program has an intrinsic appeal, it is based on the premise that the information is convincing and that the students are able to make weighted decisions. Because much of the information is, by its nature, abstract or remote to the adolescents' immediate experience, those assumptions may not be valid. Also, it may not be the attraction of drugs but instead the influence of peers that is the primary cause of drug experimentation and use (Tolone and Deroff, 1975).

Again, information control is critical with this model. This has been a problem in the past, because much information was misleading. Moreover, there may be an inverse effect. Students may become drug connoisseurs—they know which ones are safer or easier to take, which drugs cause what effects, and so on. This may increase their confidence and their probability of using drugs and alcohol. Information-based drug-education programs often draw upon the testimonials of former addicts to convince young people that the decision to use drugs is a bad one. Although his or her experience makes the former addict an "expert" of sorts, the effectiveness of these speakers in discouraging young people from using drugs has not been encouraging. Students are apparently unconvinced that they can become addicted or that if they become addicted that breaking the habit would be all that difficult.

In some instances, proponents of alcohol and drug education suggest that, rather than dwell on what *not* to do, programs should be geared toward positive adaptive behaviors. In the case of alcohol education, this might include encouraging those who are going to drink to do so responsibly.

As was mentioned earlier, for a variety of reasons adolescents are more vulnerable to the adverse effects of alcohol. Because less than one-third of teens rate themselves as abstainers, it might be appropriate to describe the characteristics of responsible drinking. Dr. Morris Chafetz, who served as the director of the National Institute on Alcoholism and Alcohol Abuse, offers this set of guidelines for adult drinkers that are equally applicable to teen drinkers:

1. *Sip, don't gulp.* Alcohol is processed into the bloodstream almost directly, and drinking large quantities quickly puts more alcohol into the bloodstream. "Chugging," the popular drinking game among high school and college students, can overload the system. There is a safe level of alcohol intake. Individuals who stay within their ability to metabolize alcohol are more likely to remain in control.

2. *Don't drink without eating.* "Never drink on an empty stomach" is an old adage, and, as with many such sayings, it has a grain of truth. Food serves to

slow down the metabolism of alcohol. However, the term *food* does not refer to the typical "munchies" of potato chips and pretzels that are usually eaten while drinking. Carbohydrates are of little help in slowing the transfer of alcohol into the bloodstream. High protein or fatty foods, on the other hand, do help to slow down the process. Thus, a cheeseburger and a glass of milk *before* drinking will do much to slow the rate of metabolism.

3. *Don't drink alone.* Drinking alone because of emotional upset can lead to trouble. It is better to have someone to talk to. Also, drinking in groups has a curious effect. If you are part of a group that expects to act drunk, you will probably feel drunk on less alcohol.

4. *Don't drink to prove yourself.* Unfortunately, adolescents, especially boys, regard alcohol consumption in large quantities as part of being an adult. "How much you can hold" is an index of maturity. This is a very difficult idea to combat without sounding too "preachy" to young people.

5. *If you drink, don't drive.* This guideline needs little elaboration. An enormous number of traffic deaths are related to alcohol consumption. The accident rate for drivers with a BAL of .2 is one hundred times higher than that of nondrinking drivers.

6. *Don't mix drinks.* Switching drinks may lead to faster intoxication, but it also may lead to nausea. Diluting drinks with water slows down absorption, but carbonated beverages and sweet syrups speed it up. Equally as important, do not mix alcohol and other drugs. Alcohol interacts with most drugs to make the effect more potent, but the interaction may be deadly.

Does this position say to adolescents, "You are going to drink anyway—so here's how"? Not really. Rather, the position recognizes that experimental and casual use of alcohol is a normal part of the contemporary adolescent scene, and, that being so, we should at least provide guidelines on how to respond intelligently. Indeed we might tie such an approach with attempts to discourage excessive drinking in teens, much in the same way we should discourage excessive drinking in adults.

Whether or not a given pattern of alcohol or drug education is effective depends, first, on the group of adolescents at which it is being aimed and, second, on the goals that are used to determine success. No single approach has been shown to be effective with all students. Each of the approaches described above may be useful for some subgroups of teenagers. Thus, although fear-induction is not a generally effective approach, it may work for some learners.

SUMMARY

The patterns of drug use and abuse among today's teens are varied. Although the more dangerous drugs receive considerable public attention, the great majority of teens have never tried them. Alcohol, however, is widely used by teens and is the primary drug abused by adolescents. Use of marijuana continues to be the second drug of choice, especially among older adolescents and college-age youths.

Alcohol and drug education programs have been unsuccessful in interrupting drug usage among contemporary adolescents. The major stumbling block to many approaches has been their use of erroneous or misleading information. If a school or public agency is to be at all successful in drug education, it is imperative that the program contain factual information. Warnings of the dangers of drugs are undoubtedly wise, but programs based on scare tactics are unlikely to have any impact.

12 | Juvenile Crime

Each year the FBI issues its Uniform Crime Reports. Those statistics reveal that the greatest proportion of the crimes in the FBI Crime Index are committed by people in the age range fourteen to twenty-four. In the reports for 1975, for example, 51 percent of all criminal arrests were in that age range. In 1975, the fourteen- to twenty-four-year-old group accounted for 76 percent of arrests for auto theft, 72 percent of arrests for burglary, 56 percent of arrests for forcible rape, 71 percent of arrests for robbery, and 44 percent of arrests for murders (Mosher, 1976). Because of these and other statistics, it has been estimated that "one out of every nine children in the United States—one out of every six male children—will be referred to the juvenile court in connection with some delinquent act (other than traffic offenses) before his eighteenth birthday" (Caldwell, 1971, p. 3).

Some, however, argue that the Uniform Crime Index is unfairly biased against crimes that are common to youths and fails to include more "adult" crimes (Jensen and Rojek, 1980). Although the index includes criminal homicide, forcible rape, robbery, aggravated assault, burglary, larceny, and motor vehicle theft, it excludes fraud, embezzlement, counterfeiting, forgery, arson, organized crime, and narcotics traffic. These excluded crimes are committed primarily by adults. The cost to the public of such "white-collar crimes" as consumer fraud and embezzlement far outdistances all the theft-related crimes of the Crime Index (Jensen and Rojek, 1980). Nonetheless, a group that accounts for less than one-quarter of the national population—the youth population—accounts for more than its share of crime. Some writers go so far as to suggest that as the size of the adolescent population diminishes in the next decade, there will be a similar drop in the national crime rate, unemployment, and even venereal disease.

We may reasonably say that the majority of violent crime by adolescents is committed by a small minority of young people, but we must also admit that the great majority of adolescents at one time or another engage in behavior that is delinquent (Gold, 1966; Haney and Gold, 1973). A major study of delinquent behavior among adolescents found that there is a steady increase in the number of delinquent acts among both boys and girls as they move through adolescence. Boys, however, are consistently more likely than girls to admit to having committed serious delinquent acts, and by eighteen they are five times as likely to make such admissions. Further the average seriousness of the delinquent behavior increased for boys but did not increase for girls (Gold and Petronio, 1980). Are we saying that anyone who commits a delinquent act is automatically a juvenile delinquent? No. That would be like calling the drug experimenter a drug abuser.

DEFINING DELINQUENCY

According to one definition, "a delinquent act is one that is illegal and one the individual knows is illegal when he commits it" (Haney and Gold, 1973). Notice that this definition, although precise, skirts the issue of defining a delinquent adolescent. Although the majority of adolescents engage in delinquent behavior, most do not get caught and the overwhelming majority feel they have more than a fifty-fifty chance of never getting caught (Haney and Gold, 1973). However, the more often an adolescent engages in delinquent behavior, the more likely he or she is to get caught. It would be only partly a joke to say that "An adolescent becomes a delinquent only when he gets caught."

The label *juvenile delinquent* arises primarily out of a legal process. Because adolescents who are caught in delinquent behavior and are brought before the courts make up only a minority of those who actually engage in delinquent behavior, our general conclusions about juvenile delinquency and juvenile delinquents may be tainted. The judicial processes that operate in society as a whole also operate in the juvenile justice system. Thus, even among the minority of adolescents who are apprehended for delinquent acts, the likelihood of their case being brought to court and their chance of being sent to a juvenile treatment facility differ for males and females, for blacks and whites, and for lower- and middle-income youths. Hence, any conclusions about the general pattern of adolescent delinquent behavior that are based only on the sample that are caught, are suspect.

One of the primary misconceptions about juvenile crime is that the problem is concentrated in urban, lower-income, black ghettos. Although blacks, and especially black girls, are disproportionately represented in juvenile penal institutions, it does not follow that they are necessarily more delinquent. Indeed the work of Gold (1966) found that neither black males nor black females were more delinquent than their white counterparts. However, because blacks are overrepresented in jails, other factors are apparently operating on the "official" designation of delinquency.

Another myth is that juvenile crime is primarily the activity of established gangs. Gold (1970) also found that most delinquent behavior was *not* well-organized, planned events by a gang. Rather delinquency is more of a "pick-up game," much like playground basketball. Matza (1964) similarly concludes that most delinquent behavior is casual, spontaneous, and loosely organized. Gangs, certainly a real problem, may not account for the majority of youth crime.

There is also a widespread misconception that most violent crime is committed by black offenders on white victims. That is not true. In one survey covering seventeen cities, 90 percent of the homicides and aggravated assaults, and rapes involved victims and offenders of the same race. Further, in two-thirds of the homicides and aggravated assaults and in three-fifths of the rapes in those cities, the victims were black (Moynihan, 1969).

It is true, however, that most violent crime among youths is concentrated in the city and that it is higher in densely populated lower-income areas. As Moynihan (1969) has stated, the poverty and social isolation of the urban poor and minorities are perhaps the single most serious problem facing America today. The poverty of the urban areas breeds not only crime but chronic unemployment and basic deprivation of human rights.

At least some delinquent behavior results from pressures among peer groups to conform. To be accepted by or acceptable to the group, a young person may find it necessary to engage in delinquent behaviors. One young girl, arrested for shoplifting, explained that her friends "dared" her to do it, and she was afraid that, if she did not, her friends would think that she was "chicken." In many ways, delinquent behavior can serve as an initiation rite to prove worthiness of belonging to a group.

This peer expectation of delinquent behavior is not limited to lower-income, inner-city, gang members. The same pressures are found among adolescents from middle- and upper-income families as well as among adolescents from suburban and rural communities. Indeed, in the period 1971 to 1976, the biggest increases in annual crime among youths were in communities with populations less than 25,000 and in rural areas (Alder, Bazemore, and Polk, 1980).

GANGS

The stereotyped model of juvenile crime is built around the concept of the street gang. That stereotype has been nurtured by the media even in the face of evidence that most delinquent acts are not done by gangs. However, street gangs do constitute a major problem, because the crimes they do commit may become excessively violent. In spite of the interest and attention devoted to street gangs, little can be stated with any certainty about their structure. Gang members are typically not willing to be interviewed, and when they are interviewed, one suspects they are telling the interviewer what he or she wants to hear.

Yablonsky (1959) describes the gang as a near-group. The members are bound more by loyalty to the group than to each other. Yablonsky found that a gang typically consisted of a core set of four or five members and a cadre of reasonably regular members who come and go as they are needed and as they desire. On the periphery are other members who occasionally join in gang activities but are not consistent in their allegiance. Yablonsky notes that the size of the gang varies with its sense of security. When the gang's territory, or turf, is endangered, the size of the gang may expand, and it may contract when the territory is secure.

Membership in a gang usually follows ethnic boundaries, and this by itself may provide some degree of commonality. Membership may be presumed of any teenager or preteen who happens to live in the neighborhood. Failure to belong may lead to threats or acts of violence. New members may be recruited

This youth gang from the Bronx includes members from several ethnic groups. Notice that some of them are very young. (J. P. Laffont/Sygma)

or "drafted" as the need arises. The gang leader may have primary responsibility for this function. His "rep," or reputation, may depend on his ability to get a recruit, especially a reluctant one, to "join" (Rubington and Weinberg, 1978).

Because gang membership and identification are fluid, such commitment may be shallow, but it is nonetheless important for the integrity of the gang. Further, although gangs are typically male, females are increasingly being associated with gang activity, either in the form of "female auxiliary" groups or as gangs in their own right. In auxiliary groups, females may be exploited for sexual gratification of gang members, or an individual female may gain status as a result of her primary or sole association with the gang leader. In one recent report (Time, 1977), the arrest rate of females under eighteen for serious offenses climbed 40 percent from 1970 to 1975, whereas the increase for comparable groups of males increased only 24 percent. Because a gang is female does not imply that its crimes are less violent (Time, 1977):

Last month Chicago police finally caught a gang of six girls, ages 14 to 17, after they had terrorized elderly people for months. Their latest crime: the brutal beating of a 68-year-old man. "I was amazed," says Police Lieut. Lawrence Forberg. "They were indignant toward their victims, and none of them shed any tears. This is the first time I've encountered young girls this tough." (p. 19).

VIGNETTE 12-1
Youth Tactics

In the article reprinted below, you will read the testimony of a fifteen-year-old gang member from New York City before a legislative committee on crime. Beyond the description of the tactics used by one gang of youths in robbing elderly people, you will get a sense of the attitudes of this young man about the act. As you read through this interchange, try to get a feeling for those attitudes. What does the young person feel about the crime, about the victim, about the courts?

The Select Committee on Crime of the New York State Legislature held hearings in New York City last December on crimes against the elderly. Among the witnesses was a 15-year-old New York youth who acknowledged participating in gang robberies against the elderly. Here are excerpts from his testimony:

Have you ever been arrested for a crime against an old person?

No, but I have been involved in such—such a crime.

And can you tell us how you got into this?

Well, you know, it's like the neighborhood, coming up. When I was young, coming up, things like that was going on, and as we grew older we started hanging around with these people, getting involved with this and that, hear stories about people, you know, as they say, rushing cribs (robbing elderly persons in their apartments or houses), you know, coming off with big money, you know, so I guess you figure—and they was juveniles under 16, you know. If they got busted they came right

home, so it wasn't nothing as far as a record is concerned, you know.

I guess, you know, every time you get arrested when you are a juvenile they say you have to be 16 or the record doesn't count. That's what they said, so it didn't matter how many times you got busted as long as you was under 16, that you wouldn't be accounted as you got older. So it was easy money, you know, never went nowhere so long as you was a juvenile. So that's why everybody did it.

Was there a plan and did you get together at any particular time and decide who you were going to rob or take from?

Well, we had a little group, you know, around the neighborhood—it was quite a few, you know, elderly people that we felt had a lot of money that was worth, you know, robbing, so like most of the acts—most of the crimes took place in the summertime, you know, during summer vacation from school, and all the group of boys that was going together would meet outside in the morning, you know, early, around 7:30, 8 o'clock, just stand, you know. There was an old ladies' center around our neighborhood where people used to go, old people used to go, go shopping, come from there, go back and eat, stand there, play checkers and stuff. So most of the gang used to stay down there and wait for them to go to the store or bank or whatever, just follow them home.

When you got into the building what would you do?

Usually one of the persons, one of the gang would get on the elevator with the lady, see what button she pressed. Like, if she pressed the fifth floor, he will press the fourth, and the rest of us would be, you know, in the stairway, and he would holler up what floor and we would all just run up to the floor she's getting off on. As soon as she opened the door, just walk behind, push her on in, get the money.

And how many people, how many of you would be on a team doing this?

Well, used to be maybe three or four.

Was there an assignment where one person would hold the old person and the other persons would do the searching of the apartment?

Usually the biggest guy, he'll be the one to hold the old lady. One would be a lookout. Whoever else was left, they would look for the money.

Could you tell us how many crimes you have committed against the elderly without getting caught?

I really couldn't say. It's been quite a few.

During the week, in the summertime, about how many would you commit?

Well, I would say out of a day, you know, however many we would try, we didn't make enough money, we would just go and do maybe five or six a day.

Were you taught how to do this when you first started doing it or did you just pick it up?

Well, when I first did it, you know, I really didn't know too much about it. My brother had did it a few times, you know, so he was having money and I wasn't, and he was not that much older than me, so we was in the same group, hanging out with the same people, so I wanted to get down and do it too, so I just went with him one day and I had never done it before. I just went. We carried it off, so after that I thought it was easy. I just kept doing it.

What was your biggest score?

Oh, a couple of thousand, I guess.

Was there ever a time when you got to Family Court on one of your arrests that there was an adjudication where they found you guilty?

Well, it wasn't on the same kind of charge.

It was a different charge?

Yes. You know, I was found guilty but nothing happened.

Did they place you on probation or anything?

Yes, six-month probation.

What was the charge?

Robbery. Armed robbery.

You had a gun?

Toy.

Toy gun?

Yes.

How old were you when you started picking on the elderly?

Well, I started, I guess, when—I would say I was around 12. My first arrest I was 13, so...

Could you tell us what that crime was?

Well, it was armed robbery in a train station.

Did you go to Family Court on that?

Yes.

What happened to you?

Well, they just dismissed the case and put us on probation for six months.

When you rushed a crib and it was an elderly person, did you threaten them that if they testified against you they would be hurt?

Yes, that was part of it.

And you were told to do that by the other fellows?

Right, in order to keep them from, you know, if anything ever happened, in order to keep them from coming to court. Their being old, you know, they might feel their lives would be endangered, so they were scared.

Have you ever hurt anybody?

Not me.

You have seen them hurt?

Yes. Usually the oldest person is doing it, or the biggest. The biggest guy.

TYPES OF DELINQUENTS

As I have stated, not all delinquent crime is done in gangs, and not all delinquent youths are members of gangs. Gibbons (1970) provides a useful set of categories to describe not only the character of delinquent youths with respect to gang membership but also their motives for delinquent acts and their attitude toward society as a whole. As we noted earlier in the text, our general impression of the delinquent coming from a disorganized or hostile family seems to have validity. Close family ties are strongly related to lower rates of delinquency for both boys and girls (Gold and Petronio, 1980). In most of the cases described by Gibbons, delinquents come from homes characterized by inadequate or careless supervision, overstrict and abusive or erratic discipline, and a general lack of family cohesiveness. Gibbons's categories are the following:

1. The *predatory gang delinquent* is the type of youth that fits the stereotyped image of the gang delinquent. He makes his primary association with the gang and is regularly involved in violent delinquent behavior that will show him to be "cool" or "tough." This individual is antisocial and hostile toward society.

2. The *conflict gang delinquent* identifies with a gang and may join in street fights, "rumbles," or "bopping." Typically, however, his association is less well defined. He is cynical about society rather than hostile, and his commitment to the gang varies.

3. The *casual gang delinquent* is less committed to the gang. His association with the gang is loose, and although he joins in gang activities, his participation is primarily for "kicks." Mostly, this youth sees himself as a nondelinquent and has aspirations of getting an education or at least a well-paying job. His parents are typically blue-collar workers who are themselves law abiding and interested in his welfare. Further, his gang "membership" may not be totally of his own choosing.

4. The *casual delinquent, non-gang member* is what has been termed the "hidden delinquent." His delinquent behavior is intermittent, but he is seldom in trouble with police. Neither he nor adults think of him as delinquent. He is generally committed, in the long run, to the goals of society and describes his delinquent behavior as "having fun."

5. The *auto-theft joyrider* steals cars for joyriding and not for profit. This adolescent typically engages in delinquent behavior in a casual, nonplanned fashion. Like the *casual delinquent*, he usually comes from a middle-class family who gives him close supervision and discipline. He does not see himself as delinquent; however, he likes to think of himself as tough.

6. The *heroin user* thinks of himself more as a drug user than a delinquent. His motives for delinquent behavior are to support his habit. He feels harassed by society and typically rejects it.

7. The *overly aggressive delinquent* is not a member of a gang. He is a loner who engages in seemingly irrational senseless assaults on others. His behavior is sometimes described as sociopathic. He may come from any social

class, he usually was raised in a hostile and rejecting family, and he has rarely had close relationships with peers.

8. The *female delinquent* is typically not a member of a gang, although female gang membership is becoming more common. Her delinquent behavior is usually not violent. She does not consider herself delinquent and may engage in delinquent behavior out of boredom. She typically comes from a dysfunctional family setting.

9. The *behavior-problem delinquent* is, like the overly aggressive delinquent, a loner. His delinquent acts are seemingly senseless, but overall he has conventional attitudes about society. Once again, the family setting is usually dysfunctional.

As with any set of categories, the Gibbons classification system may be oversimplified in some cases, and other cases may not fit neatly. Nonetheless, it helps to underscore the fact that juvenile delinquency is not a simple problem; it is multifaceted.

CAUSES OF DELINQUENCY

The more typical theories of why delinquency occurs involve the breakdown of effective social control as the reason. Generally, when children develop in social or cultural groupings that are well integrated into the mainstream of society, they are socialized by parents, adults, peers, and institutions in those behaviors that are acceptable. Conformity to the mores and values of the dominant society is maintained through use of positive and negative social sanctions. In disenfranchised or segregated subgroups, there is no commitment to that socialization and maintenance process. Children and adolescents from these subcultures feel no allegiance to the conventions of the dominant culture, and their commitment is to the values of the subculture, which may be in opposition to the dominant culture. When this alienation occurs, delinquency and deviance are likely (Weiss, 1977).

When the nonintegration is coupled with poverty, racial and ethnic prejudice, lack of equality in educational and employment opportunities, and family disorganization, the result is—not too surprisingly—frustration and antagonism toward the dominant society. Although youths from these subcultures see and desire the material and social security of middle-class society, they repeatedly are frustrated in their attempts to achieve these goals through legitimate means. Society may assure us of equal opportunity for all, but in reality, most lower-class youths face innumerable stumbling blocks to socially sanctioned success. Ultimately, minority and lower-income youths may recognize that illegitimate means hold the promise of more immediate gratification of their desires. Thus youths learn quickly that because legitimate or socially sanctioned means are not very functional and are at best remote, their better and more immediate recourse is to resort to illegitimate means (Cloward and Ohlin, 1960; Ohlin and Cloward, 1973).

These youths base their hopes that such a route has promise on a variety of immediately available models. The adults—especially young adults—who are close at hand and who have acquired material status may be pimps, pushers, numbers runners, or thieves. They are a symbol that says, in essence, "Look, I got all these good things. You can too. Do what I do!"

In some cases, however, a youth may be unable to achieve desired ends by either legitimate or illegitimate means. Cloward and Ohlin suggest that these cases are "double failures," who may retreat from society to nonfunctional behavior to achieve nonaccepted ends. The drug addict or junkie is a case in point. Cloward and Ohlin note that the addict accounts for a substantial proportion of juvenile crime, but that the motive is not the achievement of traditionally valued outcomes. Rather the motive is maintenance of a drug habit.

Cohen (1955) argues, however, that the limited-opportunities hypothesis fails to account for the senseless crimes of violence that often seem part of the juvenile gang culture. Cohen argues that many such acts are intended not to achieve material gain but rather to establish a reputation, or "rep." Thus what may seem like a senseless, unmotivated act of violence may be an attempt to establish oneself as a "real badass." Beatings of homosexuals by gangs of young teens often fall into this category.

Cohen places his emphasis on establishing a reputation or feeling of power and importance. Adolescents gain status when they are able to excel in the activities that are valued by society. When adolescents live in a subculture with values that are in conflict with the dominant culture, they are oriented toward rewards in their own subculture. In delinquent subcultures, the more daring and brave are put into positions of leadership and are given status according to the degree of danger that is involved in their acts. In New York City, graffiti is a normal, if not pervasive, phenomenon. Often a young artist

False bravado and a desire to establish or maintain a reputation may lead to chance-taking. (Burk Uzzle/Magnum Photos, Inc.)

will leave a trademark in extraordinary places. The more unusual the location and the more danger or skill required in placing the trademark, the more prestige is awarded.

LABELING

An alternative model of delinquency is called the labeling model. In order to follow the argument of the labeling model, suppose you are a judge in a juvenile court. Two cases are brought before you to be decided. Case A involves a fourteen-year-old boy who was arrested for car theft, joyriding, and drunkenness. He appears before the court well dressed and with a recent haircut. He is quiet and subdued. Both his mother and father are present, and the boy is represented by counsel. Both parents tell you, the judge, that they are horrified and distressed over what has happened. They promise that it will not happen again, that they will restrict the boy's privileges, seek professional counseling, and do whatever else you might suggest.

Case B involves another fourteen-year-old boy. He, too, has been arrested for car theft, joyriding, and drunkenness. He, however, is not well dressed— his clothes are dirty and disheveled. When the bailiff tries to direct him to the front of the court, the boy yells, "Keep your hands off me, pig!" The boy's mother is there, his father is not. He is not represented by counsel. His mother complains that she had to take the whole morning off to come down to court, and that, in any case, the boy was never any good. His mother goes on to complain that she cannot control him, that he is simply "no good."

What would you do in those two cases? How would you react? You would probably react as most judges do in these cases. You would be influenced by factors other than the offense itself. The boy in case B is more likely to be labeled "delinquent" even though his crime was no different than case A's. Factors such as race, sex, social class, personal appearance, and family background all have an impact on the chances of being labeled "delinquent"—and that label may itself be the cause of later problems.

One study of two groups of adolescents found that the decision to identify a youth as delinquent was related more to social variables than the severity of the crime (Chambliss, 1974). The first group, the "saints," came from middle-class families and at their court appearance were appropriately submissive and respectful. "Roughnecks," on the other hand, tended to be hostile and belligerent toward the authorities. The "saints" were much more likely to be sent home with a warning or probation. Juvenile justice systems are more likely to use status offenses in dealing with blacks and lower-income youths in their decision to presume delinquency (Waugh, 1977).

Labeling a youth as "delinquent" may have the effect of a self-fulfilling prophecy. If adults and authorities repeatedly tell you that you are a delinquent, you may begin to believe it and act in ways that match the label. The label itself may thus be the cause of additional deviant behavior (Werthman, 1977). A more extreme view argues that the dominant society creates deviance by presuming that its own behavior is normal and ruling that any deviation from that norm is delinquent. The rules can be used to sort out those groups that do not conform and label them as deviant and criminal (Becker, 1969).

DELINQUENTS' VIEWS

When you talk with delinquent youths, you quickly realize that they have developed an elaborate code of rationalization (Sykes and Mazda, 1957). The most frequent type of rationalization they provide is a *denial of responsibility*. They listen to what well-meaning social scientists and social workers say and feed back to these professionals exactly what they expect to hear (Sykes and Mazda, 1957). It is most incongruous to listen to a fourteen-year-old boy who is unable to read and who has been in and out of juvenile detention centers for three years, elaborate on the social consequences of a fatherless home and an abusive environment.

Other common forms of rationalization are *denial of injury* to the victim and *denial of the victim* (Sykes and Mazda, 1957). Adolescents may view lifting of goods in a big store as not making any difference. To them, it is very similar to adult white-collar crime or cheating on income tax. In the second case, the delinquents see the victim as getting what he deserves. Thus they insist that the teacher or storekeeper who is assaulted is being punished for resisting the delinquents or treating them poorly. Alternatively, the youths *condemn the condemner;* that is, they point to the hypocrisy of those in power, such as "cops on the take" or the unfairness of the system.

STATUS OFFENSES

There is a set of "crimes" that are illegal only for juveniles. These crimes, called juvenile status offenses, include behaviors that may be undesirable at all ages but are subject to particularly stern negative sanction when seen in juveniles. Behaviors such as truancy, sexual misbehavior, running away, incorrigibility (unruliness), and disobedience to parents or authority are found in various states' legal statutes. Juvenile courts have jurisdiction over truancy in thirty-nine states and the District of Columbia, for example. In all, status offenses account for up to half of the work load of the entire juvenile justice system (National Institute for Juvenile Justice and Delinquency Prevention, 1977).

Whether juvenile courts should have jurisdiction over status offenses is open to question. Arguments that status offenses reflect predelinquent behavior and that intervention will interrupt the progression toward more severe delinquent acts have not been supported by research. Indeed some researchers have concluded just the opposite. That is, a juvenile offender brought before the courts for status offenses is *more* likely to engage in more serious delinquent behavior later (Werthman, 1969). Another argument for court jurisdiction over status offenses may be even more convincing. In a subset of cases of status offenses, the delinquent behavior represents an acting out of frustrations resulting from an abusive or hostile home environment. Without the legal sanction of the courts, the ability to identify such cases would be seriously impaired.

Because these behaviors are status offenses does not, however, mean that they should be ignored. In some cases, engaging in these behaviors may be a masked plea for help (Weiner, 1980). Likewise, some status offenses may make the adolescent vulnerable to exploitation. This is especially the case with runaways. Each year nearly one million adolescents run away, and over half of all runaways are girls (Walker, 1975).

The highest rate of runaways is found among the fourteen- to sixteen-year-old group, and girls are more likely than boys to run away. Most adolescents who run away do so because they have personal conflicts at home and at school. Either the adolescent becomes so overwhelmed by the conflict that escape is the only recourse, or the adolescent uses running away as a means for drawing attention to the conflict. In the second case, the runaway usually leaves enough clues to assure being readily found.

Not all runaways, however, *choose* to leave home. An unfortunately large percentage of runaways are instead "throwaways," or adolescents who either are directly told to leave by their parents or are coerced out of the house by pressures from the parents. It is estimated that 30 to 60 percent of runaways are actually throwaways (Blare, 1979). Not uncommonly, these young people also have a history of physical or sexual abuse by their parents.

VIGNETTE 12-2
Some Are Throwaways

Each year about one million young people run away from home. If they remain away from home for an extended period of time, they typically end up in major urban areas. In that environment, there is a good chance that young runaways will be lured into a life of prostitution, crime, or drugs. Some are murdered. Although most runaways are attempting to escape what they see as a hostile home environment, a disturbingly large number of cases can more accurately be called "throwaways." That is, the parents "expel" the adolescent from their own home. You might want to discuss the impact of being a "throwaway" on a teenager's feelings of self-worth and competence.

Mike, 17, comes from a middle-class family in Philadelphia. Since he turned 16, his father has kicked him out of the house four times. The first time was when Mike lied about an accident he had while driving the family car. His father found out and began pounding the boy

Source: Excerpted from Julie Raskin and Carolyn Males, "Not All Run Away—Some Are Throwaways," *Parade* (August 13, 1978): 4–5. Reprinted with permission of the authors and the publisher.

with a football helmet, shouting, "Get out of my sight! Leave! Don't come back!"

"I only had one shoe on," Mike remembers. "I went to get the other, but he wouldn't let me. So I stayed at a friend's house for two nights."

Mike was ashamed. "I kept it mostly to myself," he says. He moved in with an aunt and then, after a few weeks, he returned home.

The bad feelings at home continued. Each time his father threw him out, Mike would stay with relatives or friends. When he had finally exhausted all possibilities, he turned to a home for runaways.

Sherry's divorced mother has had a string of boyfriends. In their small New York apartment, 15-year-old Sherry was in the way, so her mother told the child to leave.

She now lives at a runaway house but still misses her mother. "She cries every day," says her counselor there. "She wonders, 'What's wrong with me that my mother doesn't like me?' She has low self-esteem and is self-destructive: 'Why should I care about me since no one else does?' "...

Called trashed kids, pushouts, homeless youth, throwouts and throwaways—they have been rejected by their families and told to "get out," often with no money and only the clothes they are wearing.

A throwaway kid could be the child next door. They come from poor, middle-income and wealthy homes, from rural areas, suburbs, and big cities. They are black, white, girls, boys, and as young as 10, although most are between 15 and 18.

Why do parents kick out kids? "In higher income brackets, throwaway youth are usually the products of family split-ups,"says Loraine Hutchins, an administrator at National Network of Runaway and Youth Services, a coalition of houses for runaways. For example, in a second marriage, a stepparent may not want to deal with a new spouse's child. If a choice has to be made, the natural parent chooses the new spouse over the child. Or, in a remarriage, a tolerable family situation becomes difficult when a child is born to the new couple and the adolescent "gets in the way." Sexual interest by a stepparent can also play a part. If a woman sees that her new husband is attracted to her daughter, she may get rid of the child....

Parents Can't Cope

Adolescent drug abuse, sexual promiscuity, school problems and disagreement over family rules also cause family crises. When parents cannot cope with a child's errant behavior, they may strike out verbally or physically and finally, as a last resort, kick the child out....

No one knows how many throwaways roam the streets or are caught up in a succession of temporary shelters at runaway houses, group residential centers and foster homes. But the number appears to be growing....

Unlike runaways, who may have had time to make plans, throwaways are usually forced out with no place to go. While some stay with friends or relatives, others must make their way in the streets and face rape, starvation, exposure, and exploitation by pimps....

Kids hear about runaway houses from other kids on the streets, from posters or from 24-hour, toll-free hotlines. Runaway houses are informal, comfortable places where adolescents in crisis can get food, clothing and shelter and find someone to talk to. Counselors are there to help them sort out their feelings and obtain legal or medical help....

Runaway houses have a legal obligation to make contact with the parent or guardian soon after a child's arrival. Most shelters also try to involve the parents in family counseling.

Throwing away a child is not easy for parents. In addition to the anger and helplessness they experience, they also feel guilty....

Some parents who throw away their kids never want to see or hear from them again. The feeling is not always mutual, however.

Leslie Ann, from a wealthy Washington, D.C. home, was a good child. When she was 15, her parents divorced and she went to live with her mother, who remarried a year later.

Leslie Ann and her stepfather did not get along, and her mother sided with her new husband. Feeling betrayed, Leslie Ann rebelled by staying out late, smoking marijuana and flouting family rules. Finally, after she spent a night away from home without permission, her mother called the police. Leslie Ann was placed in a group foster home.

The girl still loves her mother and misses her. Each Sunday, visiting day, she and the other girls dress up and look forward to seeing their families.

The visitors arrive. As her friends laugh and talk with their mothers, fathers, brothers and sisters, Leslie Ann sits alone by the window, watching.

Each Sunday it's the same. She sits waiting for the mother who never comes, wondering why she isn't wanted, why she has been thrown away.

Runaways usually suffer a poor self-image and lack interpersonal skills. Typically, they see themselves in conflict with others and are plagued by feelings of self-doubt and anxiety. Although they see themselves as living lives filled with problems, they feel they are victims of fate and are resigned to the idea that their problems will never be solved (Wolk and Brandon, 1977).

Their feelings of low self-worth and lack of security make runaways vulnerable to those who would exploit youths. Too often, runaways are victims of rape or other violent crimes. They may end up working as prostitutes in large cities. New York has so many young prostitutes who come from the Midwest that one area has become known as the "Minnesota Strip." Of the 4,000 young people who contact the shelter home "Under 21" in New York City, 60 percent were engaged in prostitution or pornography (Ritter, 1979).

Runaway youths may seek out assistance from one of the many runaway youth shelters that are found in most cities, or they may choose to make contact with their families through the national runaway youth hotline. Initially, these agencies were established on an informal, local basis by community organizations in response to immediate needs. As the problem of runaways became more widely recognized, more shelters were established with federal funding. Currently runaway shelters provide short-term shelter and counseling for young people who for one reason or another flee from their homes.

One such shelter is Runaway House, a center where young people can receive confidential counseling. To stay in its dormitorylike shelter, runaways must agree to follow rules that prohibit sex, drugs, and alcohol, abide by a curfew, and share responsibilities for cleaning and maintenance. Beyond this the adolescents are expected to try to work on the family problems that led to their running away and attend group and individual counseling. The adolescents have the option of leaving the shelter when they feel ready, usually within three to ten days (Stierlin, 1974).

Although the adolescents in these settings are often ready and even willing to participate in family counseling, the same is not always the case with the parents. When an adolescent runs away from a disruptive or abusive home, the parents may not be willing to admit that they may be part of the problem, preferring to blame their child. For family counseling to be effective, all members must participate.

In some cases the short-term intervention offered by the shelter home is not sufficient. The young person may need longer care. Some may be served by group foster homes, which try to create stable family atmospheres that provide emotional support within relatively well-structured settings. The group foster home operates on the model of a commune, in which each member of the "family" is expected to participate in the upkeep of the home and in decision making. Fundamentally, whether runaways are counseled in a shelter house or a group foster home, the goal is generally to help them to get a better sense of self-worth and to establish a set of personal goals.

SCHOOL VANDALISM AND VIOLENCE

In addition to the serious increases in crimes that compose the Uniform Crime Index, the past twenty years have been marked by a substantial increase in violence and vandalism in the schools. In their 1975 report on school violence and vandalism in the schools, the U.S. Senate Subcommittee on Juvenile Delinquency concluded that the problem had reached crisis proportions (Bayh, 1975). Annual costs for the nation's schools resulting from vandalism now approach $600 million (U.S. Department of Justice, 1980).

In the period 1970 to 1973, there was a general increase in all categories of

Graffiti seems to be a nearly universal phenomenon and ranges from personal to political statements. (© Jim Richardson 1981/Black Star)

crime associated with schools. By far the greatest increases were in the area of assaults on teachers (an increase of 77 percent) and assaults on students (an increase of 85 percent). There was also an 18 percent increase in homicides in schools and a 40 percent increase in rapes. The figures are even more disturbing when one considers that students, teachers, and principals are all reluctant to report assaults. Students fail to report assaults for fear of reprisal. Teachers also fail to report assaults, not only for fear of reprisal but also for fear that they will be blamed for failure to maintain control. Principals are similarly reluctant to report school crimes for fear of negative public reaction (Bayh, 1975).

VIGNETTE 12-3
School Vandalism

The problem of vandalism and violence in American schools has reached alarming proportions. Crimes of violence against students, teachers, and the schools have led to an atmosphere of fear in many schools. In some urban classrooms, teachers are given guidelines on how to avoid being raped or robbed. The cost to our nation's schools detracts from the general level of education available to the students. Nor is the problem unique to large, urban schools in lower-income areas. As you will read in the article below, school vandalism and violence are found in wealthy suburban neighborhoods and rural farm communities. Can you offer some reasonable responses to the situation?

A wave of violence in many of the nation's schools is again playing havoc with American education.

Turmoil and mayhem that terrorized classrooms in the past decade continue to make schools hazardous places in which to work— and to learn.

What is particularly troubling educators and parents is this new development: School violence is moving rapidly to the suburbs—away from the inner-city systems that have actually reduced classroom crime in recent years by tighter security and stricter punishment.

Such cities as Boston, Detroit, Chicago, Kansas City, Miami, Memphis and Portland, Oreg., reported decreases in school crime in the past year after get-tough policies began.

Now, it is the communities noted for good schools and quality education that are being scandalized by physical assaults and threats against teachers and students.

Handguns, ice picks, explosives and other weapons are turning up increasingly at schools in wealthy suburbs of Los Angeles, Denver, Washington, D.C., and New York, as well as in scores of smaller towns across the nation— Humboldt, Iowa; Norfolk, Va.; Bellevue, Wash.; Kittanning, Pa.; New Britain, Conn., and Evansville, Ind.—among them.

"Violence in our schools reflects violence in our society," says Bennie Kelley, president of the National Association of School Security Directors. "As criminal activity increases in suburbs and smaller cities, it follows that this trend will show up in suburban and rural

Source: Reprinted from "Now It's Suburbs Where School Violence Flares," *U.S. News and World Report 86* (May 21, 1979): 63–66. Copyright 1979 U.S. News and World Report, Inc.

schools. That is exactly what is happening."

The National Institute of Education estimates that 5,200 junior- and senior-high-school teachers are physically attacked every month and 6,000 are robbed by force. About 282,000 junior- and senior-high-school students are assaulted and 112,000 are robbed at school every month.

School authorities also emphasize that a high proportion of violent incidents are perpetrated by nonstudent intruders, who have easy street access to many schools.

Most of the violence occurs at the junior-high level, authorities report.

Such violence has produced "a continuous feeling of fear and apprehension among teachers and students, particularly in schools that once were considered safe," asserts an official of the National Association of Secondary School Principals.

Thus, three years after a congressional study declared that "self-preservation rather than education" was the prime concern of students and teachers in many U.S. schools, the threat of violence remains a central preoccupation of hundreds of thousands of teachers and students.

Battle Zone

So perilous have some schools become that psychologists say many teachers suffer from "combat fatigue," with anxiety and neuroses similar to those of soldiers coming out of war zones.

Sara Eisner, who teaches health science at Fairfax High School in Los Angeles, explains how her routine has changed since 1963, her first year as a teacher.

"When I teach my last class of the day, I'm in a far corner on the third floor," she says. "I carry no valuables, and I keep the doors locked. After class, I hurry to a safer area."

Some teachers have begun keeping tear-gas canisters, police whistles and even firearms in their desks to ward off assailants.

Officials of teacher unions—which have been among the leaders in the fight against school violence—say an unsuspecting adult walking into most public schools today would be amazed at what he or she sees.

Students carry blaring portable radios into classes, roughhousing and obscene language are commonplace in hallways, food fights break out in cafeterias, and there is constant noise.

Besides this atmosphere, many schools experience frequent outbreaks of brutal violence, some with deadly results:

- While her second-grade class watched, a California teacher was forced by an intruder to undress at gunpoint, then was sexually assaulted. When he left, the assailant took the woman's clothes and purse. The children covered her with their sweaters and jackets.
- A New Orleans teacher watched while two boys threw a smaller child off a second-floor balcony. She was afraid to interfere because she feared the boys might then attack her.
- High-school girls in Los Angeles, angry over low grades, tossed lighted matches at their teacher, setting her hair on fire. The teacher subsequently suffered an emotional collapse.
- In Alexandria, Va., student vandals slashed tires on a police car in a high school parking lot, painted drug graffiti on library walls, ripped the front gates from the school, smashed windows, ruined a carpet with glue, detonated an explosive in a smoking area, snipped gaping holes in the school's chain-link fence, poured motor oil on a hallway and cut down the school flagpole with a pipe cutter and rammed the pole through a window in the principal's office. The school subsequently was closed after a devastating fire, believed to have been arson.
- In Austin, Tex., while 30 of his classmates watched, the 13-year-old son of former White House Press Secretary George Christian shot and killed his English teacher with a semiautomatic rifle. The teacher had given the boy a failing grade.

Surprisingly, such flagrant examples have occurred during a period when overall school violence has declined slightly, according to law-enforcement officials. One reason for the drop, they say, is that teachers and administrators are increasingly reporting violent acts when they occur. Such quick reporting has increased media exposure and public concern, and thus deterred crime.

"Teachers reached a point where they simply had to fight back," says John Ryor, president of the National Education Association, the nation's biggest teacher organization. "The fear of being mugged or assaulted is so prevalent that teachers haven't been able to perform their basic function of educating children."

Broken Silence

For years, authorities note, teachers were discouraged from reporting serious disruptions because their supervisors did not want trouble exposed.

John Pietrowicz, a member of the New Jersey State Task Force on Reducing Violence and Vandalism in the Schools, observes: "Administrators do intimidate their staffs into forgetting violent incidents. What's unfortunate is that if these acts were performed on the street they would quickly be reported to the police as outright crimes."

Now, teachers in many areas are being encouraged to report every assault, however minor, and demand action from the school board. In addition, teachers are increasingly filing for workers'-compensation benefits, suing for damages and pressing criminal charges for every student-inflicted injury.

Teachers and school are taking measures to deal more forcefully with the threat of violence and disruption.

A major impetus for the new teacher campaign against physical abuse is growing evidence that school mayhem causes severe damage to a teacher's psychological and physical health.

Nervous tension, ulcers, high blood pressure, migraine headaches and coronary stress were listed by teachers surveyed in Chicago on health hazards resulting from teaching.

Psychological stress may be even more serious, says Dr. Alfred Bloch, a Los Angeles psychiatrist who has treated 500 public-school teachers.

"When teachers run into violence that is unprovoked and unwarranted, they often suffer tremendous feelings of failure," Dr. Bloch said. "They believe that if they were good teachers they should have been able to cope with violent acts, or prevent them."

Teachers, he adds, are usually ill-equipped to deal with violence because they tend to be passive, idealistic people who are unable to understand why violence is directed at them.

A single incident of violence in a school can exact a stiff toll, Dr. Bloch adds. "When a teacher in classroom A is raped or assaulted, think what it does to the teacher in classroom B or C or D," he says. "She is living in constant anxiety, always wondering, 'When is it going to be my turn?'"

Teacher Exodus

As the violent trend moves into schools that have traditionally been calm, more teachers are opting to leave the field altogether, educators note. Early retirements and resignations have reduced the number of teachers with 20 years or more experience by half since 1961, with most of that decline in the last five years. What can schools do to prevent disruption and violence, especially those that have not previously had such problems? One solution is to get more parents into the schools to view conditions first hand and consult with officials on corrective actions.

"When I come home from meetings at 2 in the morning, I see 12-year-olds in the street who tell me that their parents don't demand that they be at home," says Robert A. Jordan, a school social worker in Atlanta. "This sort of parental abdication of bringing up children is a root cause of disruption in the schools."

The NEA's Ryor agrees. "The same parents who are demanding that we go back to the basics also want us to teach their children discipline and right from wrong," he says. "Those parents who cry over lack of discipline in the schools are the first to complain or slap a lawsuit on the schools if it is their child who deserves the discipline."

Marjorie Louer, principal at Sterling High School in Brooklyn, also suggests that troublesome students should be given more individual attention.

"Youngsters often will lash out when they are in schools with enrollments of 4,000 or 5,000 students and they are just another number," she notes. "They're handled just like they are in a factory by, in some cases, tired old teachers who don't have much experience or patience in handling troublesome kids."

Further Remedies

Another approach that has worked in many big-city systems is to place unarmed but uniformed guards in schools.

"Trained guards can quickly identify potential troublemakers, where the drug deals are made and which teachers are most vulnerable," says a Chicago School Board official. "The feeling in the schools is more relaxed, and kids feel they can't get away with much."

In some schools, teachers carry small radio transmitters to summon immediate help.

Another method is being tried in Texas that may help smaller schools deal with discipline problems. State officials are issuing a "constitutional, enforceable and understandable" student conduct code that can be voluntarily adopted by each school district. They believe the code will "establish uniform guidelines to curb a much declining respect for authority" in the classroom. Other states are considering such codes.

A statewide code might also make it easier for school boards to operate in the wake of recent court decisions defining broad rights of children. Corporal punishment has also been suggested as a way to quell disruption, but most authorities say the risks are greater than the deterrent.

"Spanking young children can get you in trouble with parents, and trying to spank 17-year-olds can get you a black eye or worse," says a veteran Detroit teacher.

Many large urban schools have shown that classroom crime can be reduced. "The way to combat teacher assaults and other disruptive behavior is to demonstrate to students that these incidents will never be tolerated," says Kenneth Van Spankeren, who has dramatically improved conditions at Chicago's Orr High School on the city's tough West Side since he became principal four years ago.

Students at Orr now know that an assault automatically will bring police action and a 10-day suspension," he observes.

"Most important, everyone understands that the teachers have a right to teach without interference and students have a right to learn," Van Spankeren says. "Once that's made clear, the problems begin to disappear."

Local gangs have found that they can extort money from fellow students for "protection" or threats of assault. Gangs also use the schools as a place to recruit new members or "auxiliary" members who pay dues. Students decide to join one gang or another well before high school; such decisions may be necessary if they are to pass safely through a gang's "turf" going to or from school (Research for Better Schools, 1976).

The causes of school vandalism and violence are many and complex. However, they are probably similar to those related to other forms of alienation. In some cases the school authorities themselves must share some of the blame. Arbitrary and oppressive rules, teachers who do not care about students, and unfair or capricious enforcement of rules lead to frustration and hostility. Also, many former students who are classified as dropouts are really "pushouts" (Bayh, 1975). Although the procedure is illegal, principals will coerce a "troublemaker" or "undesirable" out of school by threatening to press charges on some offense unless the student "voluntarily" drops out of school. Such a procedure gets around the legal requirements for expelling students.

The school, however, is only one of several factors in the social context that contributes to increased school vandalism and violence. Community values, peer groups, personal values of individual students, and community pride all have an effect.

Currently school systems across the country are employing a variety of methods to combat vandalism. The methods range from pride-in-your-school campaigns to armed guards and police dogs patrolling the schools during off hours. Schools in which vandalism has become a serious problem need to institute policy and program changes that address the problem. Among the immediate measures that might be taken are the following:

1. Teachers and students should be encouraged to report all incidents of school crime.
2. Watchdog community committees should be established to ensure that discipline is fair and consistent. Students should be a part of the watchdog committee, with equal standing, because they are as directly affected by violence and vandalism as anyone. They can also provide a positive perspective on the problem.
3. Security and protection of teachers, students, and property must be improved. Often this may require as simple a move as hiring a security guard or installing adequate lighting.

Although increased security measures are useful and most assuredly necessary, they respond only to the immediate problem and fail to address more general issues. Any long-range plan for reversing the pattern of increasing vandalism and violence must involve the whole community. Too often in schools where vandalism is high, the school and local community are at odds.

In one school system, administrators met with local groups to hear their complaints. The principal objection of these groups was that the school administrators and teachers were racist. At first the administrators balked and denied that it was so. Eventually, however, an in-service program was developed for principals and teachers, which increased their awareness of not only blatant forms of racism, but also the subtle and equally demeaning kinds. School atmosphere improved and violence declined.

The number of arrests of youthful offenders, especially for violent crimes, continues at a high level. (© Leonard Freed/Magnum Photos, Inc.)

JUVENILE JUSTICE

What happens when a juvenile offender is caught by police and brought before the courts? The justice system as it applies to young people is not always the same as that for adults. There have been many strides forward in the past few years in providing adolescents who appear before the juvenile courts with the same rights of due process as adults. Nevertheless, in a variety of ways, young people are not afforded the same rights as adults. This is because the juvenile justice system, although it parallels the criminal justice system, is not technically part of it. Rather, its procedures are more in line with civil courts.

When viewed from a historical view, the juvenile courts system emerged as an attempt to treat children differently from adults and to provide some protection for children from adult exploitation. Prior to the seventeenth or eighteenth century, little value was placed on children. They were seen as little more than chattel and were not infrequently sold as servants or prostitutes. In the eighteenth and nineteenth centuries, societal attitudes changed; children were seen as needing not only education but also protection. In addition to the establishment of child labor laws, social activists pressed for a separate system for treating children and adolescents who broke the law.

Most attention was focused on youthful offenders who were being used by adult criminals. Young people were (as they are today) being lured into prostitution and vice. Juvenile courts were established to "protect" young people from exploitation and to provide alternative intervention to the system that judged and punished adults. The juvenile courts assumed a parental role, ensuring proper moral training, discipline, and punishment (Empey, 1980).

Although the original ideals on which the juvenile justice system was based were admirable, the institutionalization of juvenile justice and its growth became less than ideal. By the 1960s, social scientists were claiming that, rather than protecting young people, juvenile courts were themselves an element contributing to juvenile crime. The question became, "Who protects the children from the courts?"

As the juvenile justice system developed, its jurisdiction extended not only to crimes of violence and exploitation but also to a bevy of status offenses. Further, because it was conceived of as independent from the adult justice system, the same legal code did not necessarily apply in both cases.

Until recently the juvenile court was not required to provide juvenile defendents with the same rights of due process as adult defendents. Only in 1966, after a Supreme Court ruling, were some of these rights—including the right to have a lawyer present at all proceedings—extended to young people. However, many of the legal rights of adults are still not afforded juveniles. For example, juveniles are not guaranteed speedy public hearings or protection from unwarranted searches.

As discussed earlier, the system itself may have become a factor in the increase in juvenile crime. The labeling process resulting from court hearings, in and of itself, is associated with increased rates of crimes among juveniles. If the juvenile offender is sentenced to a term in a penal institution, the situation is worse. The institutions to which juvenile courts are prone to send juvenile offenders are credited with being training grounds for criminals. Increasingly, experts are advocating that courts refrain from intervening in the meting out of punishment to juvenile offenders (see Jensen and Rojek, 1980).

One positive indication that the juvenile justice system is becoming less likely to send juvenile offenders to penal institutions automatically is that the number of juveniles held in custody in juvenile facilities decreased from 1971 to 1975, whereas the number of available facilities increased. A large proportion of this reduction was a result of young people being referred to group foster homes or to private treatment centers. Further, most public juvenile facilities have tried to change the jail-like atmosphere that has dominated such institutions in the past (U.S. Department of Justice, 1980).

In attempts to provide other choices for treating the juvenile offender, local, state, and federal agencies have offered such programs as alternative educational settings, work with street gangs, youth shelters, and short-term experiences in jails that are intended only to provide the youthful offender a picture of what life in jail is really like.

One of the common features of chronic juvenile delinquents is their low

Detention in Youth Correction Centers is not always the most effective treatment for youthful offenders but is sometimes the only choice available. (© Jay Paris/Picture Group)

self-esteem, especially their low academic self-esteem. Some authors (for example, Gold, 1979) suggest that traditional educational settings are not responsive to the unique personal needs of these young people. Hence, some argue for treatment programs built around alternative educational modes.

In one way or another, whether the intervention is an educational system or a community-based program, the juvenile system needs to intervene in a positive fashion early in the process. The juvenile system should become involved at the first sign of delinquent behavior rather than after several events, when the youthful offender is already deemed a habitual offender and a delinquent. In my opinion, the last alternative should be institutionalization, but that should be resorted to only after all other possibilities have failed.

SUMMARY

Without question, the problem of juvenile crime is complex. Although statistics indicate that juvenile crime is rampant, the statistics may present a biased picture. What leads a young person to engage in delinquent acts is unclear. Certainly most young people engage in some behavior that is considered delinquent. Only a minority of them persist in delinquent behavior to the extent that they end up in juvenile courts.

Contrary to popular belief, most juvenile crime is not gang crime. Neither is juvenile crime particularly planned; more often juvenile crimes are spur-of-the-moment acts. Peer pressure undoubtedly is an important factor in encouraging of juvenile crime. Youth gangs are not an element in many crimes, but gangs are, nonetheless, a problem of serious concern. Gang crime is often particularly violent. But simply because a young person is a member of a gang does not explain why he or she engages in criminal behavior.

Finally, serious issues surround the treatment of juvenile offenders. Although most people agree that most juvenile delinquents should not be treated in the same way as adult habitual criminals, it remains unclear whether all types of juvenile crime, ranging from status offenses to homicide, should be treated by the same system. At least within the categories of what might be called "lesser crimes," many social scientists are arguing for alternate intervention strategies to those traditionally associated with court referral.

13 | Maladjusted Adolescents

Although most young people pass through adolescence without major trouble, a minority do experience serious adjustment problems. The purpose of this chapter is to provide a brief description of the psychopathology of disturbed adolescents. The chapter is not intended as an extensive overview of the abnormal psychology of adolescence, nor does it discuss in depth those few conditions selected for inclusion. Rather, the chapter is limited to a description of some of the primary forms of psychological maladjustment typically seen by practitioners who work with disturbed adolescents.

The use of the term *psychopathology* in describing maladjusted adolescents reflects the influence of the medical field on this area. Just as *pathology* refers to the nature of a disease, psychopathology refers to the psychological or psychiatric character of a disturbance. Likewise, when psychologists or psychiatrists refer to the "premorbid" personality, they are talking about the personality of the patient prior to the illness.

The most prevalent categories of maladjusted youths that practitioners see in clinical settings are what are broadly labeled as behavioral disorders or character disorders. Such youths are not psychotic—that is, they are not suffering severe personality disorganization. They are, however, coping with environmental stress in ways that are considered maladaptive. These maladaptive behaviors may include some delinquency, violence, or other forms of acting out. Of those adolescents who suffer severe personality disorganizations—that is, who are psychotic—the greatest proportion are schizophrenic. Other categories of psychotic disturbances among adolescents, though recorded, are exceedingly rare.

PSYCHOSOMATIC DISTURBANCES

One of the primary components of a personal sense of identity is an acceptable body image. Any aberration from the "normal" body is thus a source of great concern for the adolescent. As a result of this concern, early- and middle-adolescents may be preoccupied with their bodies and bodily functions and may overemphasize any defect that they notice or imagine, however small.

In some instances, adolescents' concern for their bodies may be converted into real physical discomfort. Pediatricians often report that they "cure" many adolescents who suffer chronic headaches or stomach aches with placebo sugar pills. The pills do not act directly on the discomfort, but the adolescent thinks they do. The effect is the same: the symptoms disappear.

Adolescents who suffer chronic physical discomfort without a clear biological cause, may have some psychological stress that is taking its form as physical distress. The label *psychosomatic* indicates that there is some impact of the state of our mind (the psyche) on our body (the soma). The opposite can also be true. That is, chronic physical disease may lead to an altered self-perception and psychological distress. Adolescents with physical handicaps, diabetes, asthma, or epilepsy may develop self-images in which their physical limitation has influenced their general perception of themselves as adequate. In such cases, the self-perceived physical limit may result in a general negative self-concept. Even youths with minor physical defects may show adjustment problems (Waldrop, 1977).

To say that a symptom is psychosomatic does not mean that the symptom is not real. The symptoms do exist and may be very painful. The asthmatic adolescent girl, for example, who responds to anxiety and stress with wheezing and gasping for breath is in real physical distress. For the physician who responds to the emergency of an acute asthmatic attack, the question of whether the underlying cause of the attack is anxiety, allergies, or some combination of the two may seem only mildly relevant. The most important immediate issue is to relieve the distressful symptoms. In the long run, however, adolescents who respond to stress with somatic symptoms may benefit from counseling. Particularly, these young people often benefit from training in relaxation techniques, in which the individual learns to relax rather than become tense in the presence of stress.

In the case of the asthmatic girl, when the wheezing begins, she has learned to respond by trying to relax. (The initial wheezing may itself be highly anxiety provoking, because she associates it with previous attacks. The anxiety leads to heavier wheezing, which in turn leads to greater anxiety, and so on.) Relaxation interrupts the progression of the attack. The wheezing may not totally dissipate, but it also may get no worse. Eventually she begins to feel that she has some control of her body and over the environment. As these feelings become more well defined, she may also develop confidence in her self-control and a better self-image.

Part of the problem associated with psychosomatic symptoms is that they may lead to *secondary gain*. The adolescent may find that the appearance of the symptoms leads to extra attention and care from others, or the symptoms provide a means to avoid some stressful event. The asthmatic girl may, for example, find the anxiety of participating in a physical education class is circumvented by a wheezing attack before class. The wheezing may be an involuntary response to the stress, but it is reinforced when she is excused from the class. She gains something by the symptom that she may then generalize to other stressful events.

The dilemma of what to do as a teacher or therapist in such a situation is not small. Clearly an adolescent may have a physical impairment that puts him at a disadvantage with "nonimpaired" peers. To reinforce nonparticipation, however, may be a disservice. It may be necessary to provide alternative experiences in lieu of or in addition to those with nonimpaired peers.

Obese adolescents do not participate actively in fast-moving games when they are playing with nonobese peers (Bullen, Reed, and Mayer, 1964). However, when all participants are obese and no one is especially handicapped, activity in such games increases. Alternatively, we should encourage handicapped youths to participate in activities in which they are not at a disadvantage.

ADJUSTMENT REACTIONS

Most young people who are referred for counseling suffer from what may be broadly termed a personality disorder, or *adjustment reaction*. In some sense the coping mechanisms that these young people have developed to deal with stress are either inadequate or inappropriate. Although their behavior is sufficiently unacceptable that they have been brought to the attention of some school or legal authorities, they are not psychotic. The adolescent who suffers from an adjustment reaction may benefit from counseling and therapy in which more appropriate coping behaviors are developed. It is not unusual for those youths who might be considered "delinquent" by one group, to be labeled by another as suffering an adolescent adjustment reaction. Adolescents who fall into this category are usually impulsive, antisocial, and aggressive. Not uncommonly, they come from disorganized and disruptive families. In my experience, there is frequently a background of physical or sexual abuse.

> P was a 16-year-old girl who was referred to a psychiatric treatment facility after several incidents of running away from home. P had been pregnant twice. The first pregnancy had aborted naturally, the second had been aborted therapeutically. P reports that she still does not use contraception although she is still sexually active because, in her words, "I don't give a damn." P was aggressive and attacked attendants three times in the first two weeks at the facility.

> P's first sexual experience was with her father at the age of 8. P's mother reports no knowledge of this, although P contends that she told her mother and that her mother had told her to "shut your dirty mouth." (P also claims that her first pregnancy may have been by her father.) P first ran away from home at age 11. At age 16, after several arrests for running away and after the courts were alerted to the family setting, P was made a ward of the Welfare Department who, in turn, referred P for psychiatric counseling.

Among adolescents who undergo adjustment reactions, girls are more likely to "act out" by running away or through promiscuity. Boys are more apt to act out aggressively, with bullying, robbery, or impulsive violence. *Acting out* is a general term describing the use of unacceptable or unsocialized behaviors in an attempt to respond to built-up frustrations. The behavior is a coping mechanism, but one that is either socially unacceptable or not sanctioned by society.

For some of these young people, being in a safe and supportive, but structured, environment seems to provide them with an opportunity to "get their act together," or develop some behavioral maturity. Basically treatment consists of training these adolescents in behaviors and coping responses that are socially acceptable and in how to channel their aggression into other productive modes.

Treatment programs in institutional settings often involve gradually increasing the amount of freedom with which these adolescents must cope. Part of their difficulty is their inability to handle their anxiety when they are uncertain or when too many alternatives are available. When they become anxious, they strike out. Their inability to deal with uncertainty reflects their general negative self-image. Because they see that they are unable to handle stress, they view themselves as losers and no good. Given freedom they initially seem to try to prove themselves right. One technique, which is sometimes successful, is to gradually increase the number of options available to these young people, rather than to provide too many freedoms too rapidly. If the increase is too great and the adolescent begins to act out, then the treatment is pushed back to an earlier level at which the adolescent experienced success. The critical feature in any treatment program is to train individuals in coping mechanisms and to enhance their feelings of competence through successful use of those behaviors.

A major dilemma in treating these young people arises when they are ready to return to a home environment. If they have not become wards of the court or the welfare department, they may have to be returned to the family. If the family was disruptive to begin with, there may be a rebound effect. That is, the adolescents will return to the treatment facility after a short period of time at home. Although such rebounds are disheartening, they are not always disastrous. Often these failures are opportunities for the adolescents to recognize their own limits; thus they become better prepared to cope with subsequent releases.

Some of these adolescents never make any changes. They seem to thrive on "conning the system." Those who do change must have or acquire a motivation to change. As one young boy said, "I don't want to be a loser all my life."

DEPRESSION

A significant number of young people who seek help report feelings of isolation and depression. *Depression*, in the clinical sense of the term, refers to general feelings of helplessness and despair. The depressed individual may feel out of control or have vague, unclear feelings of dread. In many cases depression does not take the form of sadness, but rather as lethargy, lack of energy, or apathy. In severe cases depression may lead to suicidal thoughts or suicidal behavior.

Depression, however, is not easy to identify in adolescents. Weiner (1980) notes that prior to ages sixteen or seventeen, clinical signs of adult depression are unlikely. The reason, according to Weiner, is that depression is tied to our

Some adolescents suffer marked feelings of depression, despair, and isolation. (© Joel Gordon 1974)

tendency to dwell on some problem or crisis, to give a great deal of thought to it. Early-adolescents do not tend to dwell on thoughts for extended periods of time and are thus less likely to become preoccupied with unclear, abstract problems.

This does not imply that early-adolescents are immune to depression. Instead their depression may be masked by other symptoms, such as fatigue or vague, unspecific illnesses and body problems. As in adults, depression in teens may lead to difficulty in concentrating on or completing a task.

The depressed adolescent may act out the depression in aggressive or delinquent behavior. Such delinquency is different from that of the sociopathic adolescent or the habitually delinquent adolescent, because the behavior usually follows traumatic events like divorce or the death of a parent. The delinquent behavior represents a clear-cut change in behavior. As such, it does not fit the expected behavior pattern of the young person.

Among older adolescents, clinical depression follows much the same pattern as in adults. Depression in middle- to late-adolescents often is tied with excessive alcohol or drug use. Once again, like the early-adolescent, depression often follows some traumatic event. Unlike the early-adolescent, however, the older teen's trauma may be more remote or abstract.

I should make one additional point regarding the relationship of depression to a traumatic event. Depression does not always immediately follow the traumatic event that is later seen to be its cause. M was a boy of fifteen whose father died suddenly. His mother felt some responsibility to "keep a stiff upper lip" for the children, and so she resisted her desire to submit to her grief. M saw that his mother was trying to be strong, and because he was now the "man of the family," he too suppressed his grief and took over the leadership role. M's mother welcomed him as a source of support. Several months later M's school grades went down dramatically. He began to drink heavily and was involved in some serious delinquent activity. M's depression about the loss of his father came to the surface in counseling. Once M was able to work through his grief, he could move forward in a more positive fashion. The point is, the signs of depression did not appear immediately following his father's death but were delayed several months. The clue to the counselor was the suddenness of the shift in behavior.

SCHIZOPHRENIA

A small number of disturbed adolescents are schizophrenic. There is a popular misconception that a schizophrenic has a "split personality" or "multiple personalities," such as the cases popularized in *Three Faces of Eve* or *Sybil*. Actually the "split," if there is one, reflects the fragmentation of the schizophrenic's thinking. A more typical pattern of schizophrenic thought is depicted in Hannah Green's *I Never Promised You a Rose Garden*.

Schizophrenia is a general category of psychotic behavior involving an individual's inability to distinguish between reality and fantasy. Bleuler (1968) lists four general qualities of schizophrenia: Schizophrenics typically react with (l) a loose or disorganized set of associations, (2) flat or inappropriate effect, (3) ambivalence or inability to decide what is real and what is not, and (4) autistic behavior or withdrawal.

VIGNETTE 13-1
The Attack

Working with psychiatrically disturbed adolescents (and patients in general) is an emotionally, and often physically, demanding occupation. It is difficult for many professional and paraprofessional personnel to overcome their own fears of mental illness in order to feel at ease with patients. When we first work with psychiatric patients, we too often expect their behavior to be strange or bizarre. Actually, what we find is that most of the patients' behavior seems relatively normal. When their behavior deteriorates, only in extreme cases

does it become bizarre. Most of the unacceptable behaviors do not seem terribly disturbing, and we may be unnerved that we sometimes see stranger behaviors among untreated people. More than that, however, we often see reflections of ourselves in some of our patients—and that realization is a bit unsettling. It is common, for example, for students taking abnormal psychology to suspect that they suffer from every psychological or psychiatric abnormality from brain disease to schizophrenia. Thus when we face those who have been identified as suffering from a disorder, we may have uncertainties and fears about our own ability to handle stress. On the other hand, when we see patients as people who need

Source: Excerpted from *I Never Promised You a Rose Garden*, pp. 65–66, by Hannah Green (Joanne Greenberg). Copyright © 1964 by Hannah Green. Reprinted by permission of Holt, Rinehart and Winston, Publishers.

help, and when we recognize that there are times when all of us have difficulty in coping, we are more likely to make a positive contribution to their improvement. In this passage from Hannah Green's I Never Promised You a Rose Garden, *the patients "gang up" on an attendant who treats them with disdain. What are the young girl's observations as to why one attendant was attacked but another was not, and probably would not, be attacked?*

Deborah saw one attendant attacked by the patients night after night. The attackers were always the sickest ones on the ward—out of contact, far from "reality." Yet they always chose to go against the same man. On the day after a fight that had been more violent than usual, there was an inquiry. The battle had become a free-for-all; patients and staff were bruised and bleeding and the ward administrator had to ask everyone questions. Deborah had watched the fight from the floor, hoping that an attendant would trip over her foot, so that she might play a little parody of St. Augustine and say later, "Well, the foot was there, but I didn't make him use it. Free will, after all—free will."

The ward administrator spoke to everyone about the fight. The patients were proud of their lack of involvement; even the mutest and most wild-eyed managed a fine disdain and they purposely thwarted all of the questions.

"How did it start?" the doctor asked Deborah, alone and very important for her moment in the empty dayroom.

"Well...Hobbs came down the hall and then there was the fight. It was a good fight, too; not too loud and not too soft. Lucy Martenson's fist intruded into Mr. Hobbs's thought processes, and his foot found some of Lee Miller. I had a foot out, too, but nobody used it."

"Now, Deborah," he said earnestly—and she could see the hope in his eyes, something to do with his own success as a doctor if he could get the answer when another might fail—"I want you to tell me...Why is it always Hobbs and why never McPherson or Kendon? Is Hobbs rough on the patients without our knowing about it?"

Oh, that hope!—not for her, but for her answer; not for the patients, but for a moment in his private dream when he would say matter-of-factly, "Oh, yes, I handled it."

Deborah knew why it was Hobbs and not McPherson, but she could no more say it than she could be sympathetic to that raw, ambitious hope she saw in the doctor's face. Hobbs *was* a little brutal sometimes, but it was more than that. He was frightened of the craziness he saw around him because it was an extension of something inside himself. He wanted people to be crazier and more bizarre than they really were so that he could see the line which separated him, his inclinations and random thoughts, and his half wishes, from the full-bloomed, exploded madness of the patients. McPherson, on the other hand, was a strong man, even a happy one. He wanted the patients to be like him, and the closer they got to being like him the better he felt. He kept calling to the similarity between them, never demanding, but subtly, secretly calling, and when a scrap of it came forth, he welcomed it. The patients had merely continued to give each man what he really wanted. There was no injustice done, and Deborah had realized earlier in the day that Hobbs's broken wrist was only keeping him a while longer from winding up on some mental ward as a patient.

She did wish to say this, so she said, "There is no injustice being done." It seemed to the doctor a cryptic statement—with a patient in bed, another with a broken rib, Hobbs's wrist, another with a broken finger, and two nurses having black eyes and bruised faces....

The inability of schizophrenic youths to distinguish what is real and unreal, especially when they are actively psychotic, results from their thoughts being dominated by distorted perceptions and hallucinations. To the average person, the thought patterns of the schizophrenic have little or no order. The schizophrenic wanders off on irrelevant tangents or in vague or bizarre fantasies. Schizophrenics often believe that they are being controlled or tortured by someone (or something) who has power over their thoughts. Practitioners must be careful, however, about reacting too quickly to the schizophrenic's behavior as "illogical." To the schizophrenic youth, the behavior may be very logical in light of the distorted view of reality.

J was a 15-year-old male who was admitted to a psychiatric treatment facility. He was brought to the facility by the police who picked him up after his mother reported that J had threatened to stab his baby brother with a butcher knife. The police officers reported that when they found J, he was alone in an alley screaming obscenities and "gibberish." His mother said that J had "not been himself"for the last year and a half, following the death of his older brother in an automobile accident. His mother reports, "He had a change in personality. He talked about things that never happened, like talking to B (his dead brother). The last five days he has been very sick. He hasn't eaten and can't sleep. When he threatened the baby, I called the police. J seemed to lose control and ran out of the house. I don't know. One time he likes you, the next he don't. He wants to fight with his dad and me. Wants to burn the house down. . .He uses drugs, you know. He can hardly go a day without using something. But he suffered terribly when we lost B. It upset him for a long time. And right after that his good friend moved out of town. He doesn't have many other friends."

In his interview J denied having any problems but responded to interview questions with flat affect. While J admitted to using LSD and marijuana in the past year, use was apparently not regular, and he denied any use in the last two months because, "I seemed to worry a lot about it." J stopped going to school 4 months prior to his admission. In J's words, "I quit school. I just took off and left. I don't have anything to work for. I question everything I do. I guess I have a lack of confidence. I have a problem with being down, feeling pretty low, as low as you can go. I thought of killing myself one time, but it was just a thought that ran through my head....I hear people talking about me, calling me a two-faced stupid asshole. Even people on TV talk about me sometimes....I'm worrying, worrying. I'm tired of worrying. I wake up in the morning and worry about what the day is going to bring...At night I hear voices, mainly my brother B, but it's only at night. When I wasn't eating, I saw Jesus, but I think it was only in my head. Do you think I'm hopeless?" J asked the meaning of the words "paranoia" and "schizophrenia," which he said he heard while he was in the emergency-room of a local hospital. J reports that since he has been here people on the TV have been calling him a "big drag and a fag and a toad." He denies any homosexual experiences.

J was diagnosed as suffering from an acute episode of schizophrenia. J responded well to drug therapy and psychotherapy, and within a few months was moved to a "middle-way" house before being returned home. In J's case, the schizophrenia followed a series of traumatic events. Prior to that episode, J had not shown any evidence of the psychopathology. The prognosis in such

Planning the treatment of a disturbed youth often takes the form of a team conference that includes the client. (Michael D. Sullivan)

cases is usually better than when the disease unfolds as a gradual, increasingly severe disease. When schizophrenia is a chronic, recurring problem, prognosis is less encouraging.

Whether schizophrenia is a genetic or an environmental disease is not totally clear. Studies of identical twins have showed that if one twin has schizophrenia, the co-twin has a 30 percent chance of having it as well. The family history of schizophrenics commonly includes relatives who were also diagnosed as schizophrenic (Gunderson, 1974).

On the other hand, there is evidence that the family environment of schizophrenic youths may also have an effect. In studies of adopted children who were schizophrenic versus adopted children who were not, it was possible to identify distinct differences in the family interactions of the two groups. Schizophrenic youths often come from parental environments with unclear and disharmonious communication patterns (Singer and Wynne, 1965).

Finally, according to increasing evidence, schizophrenia may be the result of a biochemical imbalance. It appears that the normal metabolism of specific neural chemicals is disrupted in schizophrenics. Rather than being processed into normal by-products, these chemicals are processed into a mescaline-like or LSD-like chemical in schizophrenics. Schizophrenic hallucinations may thus result from an abnormal metabolism of normal body chemicals (Gunderson, 1974).

SUICIDE

The death of a young person is always unnerving; as Zoe Akins says in *The Portrait of Tiero*, "Nothing seems so tragic as the death of someone who is young and this alone proves that life is a good thing." The death of an adolescent as a result of suicide is even more startling and difficult to understand. Yet the number of adolescents who attempt or commit suicide each year is not small, and by all estimates the number is growing. Suicide currently ranks behind accidents and homicide as the leading cause of death among teens and young adults.

Estimates of rates of suicide among adolescents are very likely low because suicides are underreported. It is not uncommon for a physician to report such a death as "accidental" in order to relieve some of the trauma, grief, and social stigma that the family experiences. A large number of vehicular deaths are suspect, and in some instances so are homicides. Inner-city youths, for example, do not see suicide as a noble way of dying. Thus they may set themselves up to be killed by a rival gang. Actual rates of suicide may be two to three times as high as estimated (Duben, 1963).

Since 1957, the rate of adolescent suicide has nearly tripled. Adolescent girls are nine times more likely than boys to *attempt* suicide, whereas adolescent boys are three times as likely to *commit* suicide (NCHS, 1978). When a boy decides to commit suicide, he is more likely to use a violent method with little chance of failure. Girls, on the other hand, are more likely to use a method in which there is no disfigurement. However, attempted suicide is still a serious indicator, because one in ten who attempt suicide will commit suicide within five years, and the majority of those who commit suicide have attempted or threatened suicide in the past (Avery and Winokur, 1978).

VIGNETTE 13-2
Predicting Suicide

*How do you know when someone is seriously considering suicide? No one has yet come up with a foolproof scheme for identifying the suicidal person. However, several scales have been developed to alert the practitioner to warning signals in a patient's presuicidal behav-*ior. The scale presented here is one such attempt, by Dr. Aaron Beck, a psychiatrist who has written widely about suicide.

Dr. Aaron T. Beck, a University of Pennsylvania School of Medicine psychiatrist who has devoted many years to research and development of suicide potential rating scales, devised this "suicidal ideation scale," with the assistance of Kenneth Minkoff, a medical student. It is de-

Source: A. T. Beck, M. Kovacs, and A. Weissman, "Assessment of Suicidal Intention: The Scale for Suicide Ideation." *Journal of Consulting and Clinical Psychology* 47 (1979):343–52.

signed to help the physician-interviewer get an objective overview of a patient's thoughts and emotions about suicide. Says Dr. Beck, "The situations and responses it lists are meant to be guidelines for a very unstructured interview. The physician should cover them all in his questioning, but he shouldn't hew to them at the expense of interreaction with his patient."

The patient responses are presented in increasing order of seriousness—a "0" response is cause for negligible concern, while a "2" is cause for greatest concern. Though Dr. Beck has not as yet set numerical cut-off points for mild, moderate, and severe suicidal risk, he believes a cumulative score of 15 represents a severe risk of suicide.

SCALE FOR SUICIDE IDEATION
(For Ideators)

Name _____ Date _____

Day of Interview

Time of Crisis Most Severe Point of Illness

I. Characteristics of Attitude Toward Living/Dying

( )   1. Wish to Live
       0. Moderate to strong
       1. Weak
       2. None   ( )

( )   2. Wish to Die
       0. None
       1. Weak
       2. Moderate to strong   ( )

( )   3. Reasons for Living/Dying
       0. For living outweigh for dying
       1. About equal
       2. For dying outweigh for living   ( )

( )   4. Desire to Make Active Suicide Attempt
       0. None
       1. Weak
       2. Moderate to strong   ( )

( )   5. Passive Suicidal Attempt
       0. Would take precautions to save life
       1. Would leave life/death to chance (e.g.,
          carelessly crossing a busy street)
       2. Would avoid steps necessary to save or main-
          tain life (e.g., diabetic ceasing to take insulin)   ( )

If all four code entries for Items 4 and 5 are "0," skip sections II, III, and IV, and enter "8" ("Not Applicable") in each of the blank code spaces.

II. Characteristics of Suicide Ideation/Wish

( )   6. Time Dimension: Duration   ( )
        0. Brief, fleeting periods
        1. Longer periods
        2. Continuous (chronic), or almost continuous

( )   7. Time Dimension: Frequency   ( )
        0. Rare, occasional
        1. Intermittent
        2. Persistent or continuous

( )   8. Attitude toward Ideation/Wish   ( )
        0. Rejecting
        1. Ambivalent; indifferent
        2. Accepting

( )   9. Control over Suicidal Action/Acting-out Wish   ( )
        0. Has sense of control
        1. Unsure of control
        2. Has no sense of control

( )   10. Deterrents to Active Attempt (e.g., family, reli-   ( )
        gion; possibility of serious injury if unsuccessful;
        irreversibility)
        0. Would not attempt suicide because of a
           deterrent
        1. Some concern about deterrents
        2. Minimal or no concern about deterrents

        (Indicate deterrents, if any: _____
        _____)

( )   11. Reason for Contemplated Attempt   ( )
        0. To manipulate the environment; get attention,
           revenge
        1. Combination of "0" and "2"
        2. Escape, surcease, solve problems

III. Characteristics of Contemplated Attempt

( )   12. Method: Specificity/Planning   ( )
        0. Not considered
        1. Considered, but details not worked out
        2. Details worked out/well formulated

( )   13. Method: Availability/Opportunity   ( )
                  0. Method not available; no opportunity
                  1. Method would take time/effort; opportunity
                     not readily available
                  2a. Method and opportunity available
                  2b. Future opportunity or availability of method
                     anticipated

( )   14. Sense of "Capability" to Carry out Attempt   ( )
                  0. No courage, too weak, afraid, incompetent
                  1. Unsure of courage, competence
                  2. Sure of competence, courage

( )   15. Expectancy/Anticipation of Actual Attempt   ( )
                  0. No
                  1. Uncertain, not sure
                  2. Yes

IV. Actualization of Contemplated Attempt

( )   16. Actual Preparation   ( )
                  0. None
                  1. Partial (e.g., starting to collect pills)
                  2. Complete (e.g., had pills, razor, loaded gun)

( )   17. Suicide Note   ( )
                  0. None
                  1. Started but not completed; only thought
                     about
                  2. Completed

( )   18. Final Acts in Anticipation of Death (e.g., insur-   ( )
                  ance, will, gifts)
                  0. None
                  1. Thought about or made some arrangements
                  2. Made definite plans or completed
                     arrangements

( )   19. Deception/Concealment of Contemplated Attempt   ( )
                  (Refers to communication of ideation to inter-
                  viewing clinician)
                  0. Revealed ideas openly
                  1. Held back on revealing
                  2. Attempted to deceive, conceal, lie

V. Background Factors

Items 20 and 21 are not included in total score.

( )   20. Previous Suicide Attempts   ( )
        0. None
        1. One
        2. More than one

( )   21. Intent to Die Associated with Last Attempt   ( )
        (if N/A enter "8")
        0. Low
        1. Moderate; ambivalent, unsure
        2. High

In the late 1800s, the French sociologist Emile Durkheim identified three types of suicidal personalities. Durkheim described suicide as a response to social stress and the motive for suicide as altruistic, egoistic, or anomic. *Egoistic* suicides occur among those who are not well integrated into society. They have no close family, social, or religious ties. Single adults who live alone and have no family or no family ties tend to have higher suicide rates. *Altruistic* suicides occur among those who are at the other end of the spectrum. These individuals are so integrated into a group or ideology that they are willing to sacrifice themselves for some perceived greater good. The third type of suicide, *anomic*, occurs in response to a sudden, usually sad, change in an individual's life. Anomic individuals are left with a feeling of confusion and alienation, and they feel unable to cope with their altered life.

A variety of factors influence suicides and suicide attempts among young people. Suicide is more prevalent among college students than among their noncollege peers. There are also differences in rates among college campuses. High-prestige campuses have higher rates than campuses of lesser prestige. Whether college students as a group are more suicidal or more prone to attempt suicide than noncollege students, and whether a college environment generates the stress and feelings of alienation that lead to higher rates of suicide, are open questions.

The commonly held belief that a person who commits suicide "has to be crazy" is not true. Psychopathology, although more likely in suicidal patients (Miller, 1975), is not sufficient to explain away suicide. Neither is suicide an irrational, spur-of-the-moment decision. Suicide attempters usually plan and think about their suicide for some time prior to the actual attempt. In one study of suicidal girls, all had been diagnosed as potentially suicidal well before the event (Peck, 1968). Boys in that same study, however, had no such psychiatric history. When a boy decides to commit suicide, he is more likely to be direct and successful. This is so even though adolescent boys are eight times as likely to be referred for counseling. The percentage of girls who are referred for counseling *and* are considered suicide risks is inordinately high. It may be that the behaviors that lead to referral among boys cover a much broader range of issues than suicide, or it may be that counselors are more likely to presume suicide is a factor in referred girls. Many practitioners have prepared simple scales for rating suicide potential among clients. One particular useful scale was developed by Aaron Beck of the University of Pennsylvania and is reproduced in Vignette 13-3.

Some teens who attempt suicide hold to a strange mythology of death. They sometimes fail to recognize death as a permanent state. A suicidal patient may tell you that he wants to kill himself but does not want to die. In a similar fashion adolescents who attempt suicide in an effort to "get even" with a boyfriend, girlfriend, or parent, often fail to see that they would not be around to "enjoy" the other person's misery. A suicidal girl often envisions a "sleeping beauty" fantasy, in which she sees herself in her coffin and everybody saying how lovely she looks.

SUMMARY

Despite repeated evidence to the contrary, the view that psychological upheaval is a normal part of adolescence remains popular. There are still those who, like Anna Freud, believe that the adolescents who fail to show any deviance or schizoid behavior are the ones who are potentially troublesome Although some overly compliant teens may indeed be a source of concern, the average adolescent is not prone to repeated, antisocial outbursts. Dismissing chronic antisocial or unusual behavior as just a "phase" may be a serious error. Although some adolescents will outgrow their antisocial behavior as they grow older, others will not. An adolescent whose behavior is sufficiently divergent from the norm to draw the attention of practitioners is a candidate for intervention. The abnormal psychological symptoms of adolescence may be the warning signs of more serious disturbance as adults (Masterson, 1967).

Healthy adolescents are able to cope with the normal stresses of adolescence, just as healthy adults are able to cope with the normal stresses of adulthood. Both may have periods of depression or anxiety, but the general pattern is one of positive adjustment.

14 | Counseling Adolescents

Adolescents may be referred to a counselor either in a school setting or in a private setting that may or may not be affiliated with a professional therapist. In either setting the practitioner's task may range from vocational or educational counseling to behavioral counseling. Although the purposes of vocational and behavioral counseling are quite different, there are some similarities.

This chapter will introduce you, as a future practitioner, to some of the major issues in counseling adolescents; it will not train you as a professional therapist. If you are interested, more definitive treatments of the counselor's therapeutic role are presented in John Meek's *The Delicate Alliance* (1971) and Eugene Kennedy's *On Becoming a Counselor* (1977).

Establishing a counseling relationship with an adolescent requires a working alliance between the practitioner and the client. Meeks (1971) describes it well. The relationship is a "delicate alliance" between an adult counselor and an adolescent client. Although the relationship has some characteristics in common with the counselor-adult client relationship, it also has substantial differences because of the unique developmental character of the adolescent client. Many counselors are so uncertain of the nature of that relationship that they avoid adolescent clients.

For many practitioners the prospect of counseling adolescents is a problem best left untouched. The legendary emotionality and obstinacy of adolescent clients are enough to frighten even the most caring of counselors. When the referral problem is behavioral, many practitioners feel uncomfortable about talking frankly about such issues as sexual behavior and drugs with young people. They report that they have difficulty pursuing some areas without seeming to be a prude or a "dirty old man." Often counseling adolescents brings the practitioner face to face with personal unresolved conflicts, which makes the encounter even more stressful. It is, however, possible to establish a professional counseling relationship with adolescents without being too aloof, on the one hand, or so "chummy," on the other, that the professional relationship is hindered.

VOCATIONAL COUNSELING

A central component in the establishment of a personal identity is setting adult vocational goals and expectations. Adolescents need to identify, at least generally, what occupational role they expect to play as adults and to determine some alternative paths toward those goals. Of course, setting vocational goals with high school students should be pursued with the clear understanding by both counselor and client that those goals may be altered with experience. Even among college freshmen, one in eight expects to change the major field of study or the career choice by graduation (Austin, 1978). In reality, the number who end up in other than their expected career as stated in their freshman year is probably considerably greater than 12 percent.

The professional community does not regard guidance toward vocational decision making as very effective (Ryan, 1978). Guidance efforts either have not been systematic or have been based on limited and sometimes inaccurate information.

Career education and guidance should involve experiences that unveil alternative adult work roles and outline the necessary steps for their achievement. Career guidance must also help adolescents to specify their goals and realistically assess their own economic, psychological, and social resources. The counselor should first aid the adolescent to identify his or her strengths, weaknesses, and needs. Unrealistic career goals may do more damage than good to the adolescent's self-esteem. Again, it might be expected that those with low self-esteem might set unrealistically high or low goals. Given a set of alternate career goals, the counselor and adolescent must then map out the educational and economic demands for achieving those goals.

Counselors and schools have a major responsibility to establish career guidance as a continuing process during the high school years. Ryan (1978) has provided a curriculum scheme in which the career guidance process is shifted from career opportunity awareness in grade nine to career preparation in grades 11 and 12. Note that the curriculum emphasizes different aspects of the vocational decision-making process depending on the grade level. A more appropriate guide for counselors might be the level of individual social development, because eleventh-graders are not all at the same point in their emotional or affective development and would not all benefit from the same experiences. Nonetheless, the principal point of the model is accurate: The progression of decision making must be increasingly complex to meet the needs of adolescents as they get closer to adult vocational roles.

Finally, counselors should encourage adolescents to have a backup strategy if their primary occupational choice becomes inaccessible. Economic and social forces may change over time, and those forces may impinge upon an individual's progress toward some goal. The question "What if it does not work out? Then what?" must realistically be faced. The most clear, if overused, example is the exceptional athlete who plans on a career as a professional athlete. These adolescents need to understand that the number of opportunities for professional athletic careers is severely limited, and although it may be a goal worth pursuing, a backup strategy is advisable.

Counselors record progress toward the establishment of vocational goals in the form of individualized plans. Any advancement toward or alteration of goals and skills are thus readily accessible and observable to both counselor and adolescent. The plan specifies short-term and long-term goals, and it can include the achievement or failure to achieve any of those goals. Because progress toward career goals usually takes time, the guidance plan has the advantage of providing evidence, over a long time span, of gain that the adolescent may not have been aware of.

ASSESSING THE PROBLEM

The initial tasks in establishing a counseling relationship with an adolescent are (1) to identify the problem that has led to the need for counseling, and (2) to determine how aware the adolescent is of the problem. Even in routine counseling provided by schools as part of career education, the counselor must determine the adolescent's entering level of career awareness. In areas of behavioral counseling, it is necessary to determine whether the adolescent sees the behavior as a problem and, if so, how much of a problem. Early in the interview process, the counselor must encourage the adolescent client to define the problem areas specifically.

Meeks (1971) suggests the following six questions as guidelines for assessing the adolescent's level of awareness of a behavioral problem and the potential for successful counseling:

1. *What level of psychosocial development has the adolescent achieved?* If the adolescent has already achieved some degree of behavioral and cognitive maturity, the treatment process will be quite different than that for those with lower levels of socialization. Adolescents at higher levels of psychosocial development can reasonably be expected to operate more independently in assessing alternative solutions to the problem. Those at lower levels need more structure and direction in the counseling process. Adolescents who are at a formal-operations level are more able to recognize the multiple aspects of the problem that led to counseling.

2. *What kind of relationship did the adolescent have with his parents prior to adolescence?* If the character of parent-child interaction has been positive through childhood, then any shift in that relationship is probably temporary, and the prognosis for repairing that relationship is good. On the other hand, if parent-child communication has been nonproductive prior to adolescence, the chances of creating a positive pattern of interaction now are reduced.

3. *Did some identifiable event lead up to the problem behavior?* If an adolescent began to show problem behaviors following a divorce or a death of a parent, the therapeutic process will differ from that for a problem behavior with a long history. As with the difference between chronic and acute schizophrenia, described in the previous chapter, delinquent or disruptive behavior suddenly emerging after a crisis has a better prognosis for improvement.

4. *Does the adolescent feel conflict?* If the adolescent shows some concern about the problem and can express that concern, the prognosis for improvement is better than if he or she sees no problem and is hostile and resistant to suggestions that a problem exists. Recognition of the problem may reflect a degree of behavioral maturity.

5. *Is the adolescent able to describe his or her own behavior and feelings with some degree of objectivity?* An adolescent client who is able to clearly recognize and label feelings, emotions, and consequences of behavior is probably at a higher level of behavioral maturity. The client's ability to assess his or her own behavior realistically makes for a more positive therapeutic atmosphere. Conversely, the adolescent who is overly dependent on one or more defenses and is unable to deal with feelings and emotions realistically will need more help and support from the counselor.

6. *Do the parents desire to improve the situation?* Although you would expect most parents to support improved adjustment in their adolescent, a variety of family stresses may work against their support. If the adolescent is acting out as a result of a disruptive home environment, the parents may be unwilling or unable to aid in the therapeutic process, because they fear their own lack of security with each other may be exposed. Cases in which the adolescent sees the parents as concerned and active participants in the counseling process have much better promise.

Finally, Meeks (1971) warns that the counselor should try to determine the adolescent's motives for seeking counseling. Adolescents who initiate counseling on their own are *rare* cases, and self-referral indicates a high level of social maturity. On the other hand, many adolescents who are brought to a counseling setting against their wishes really know they need help but are saving face by projecting the responsibility on someone else. Because an adolescent is coerced by schools, parents, or courts into a counseling relationship does not mean that therapy will not be effective (Marone, 1976). Referred adolescents do quite well. Neither should the counselor expect some form of verbal agreement from the adolescent to improve. Such an agreement may be beyond the limits of his or her social maturity at the time of referral. Ultimately, however, behavioral contracts, in the form of treatment plans with behavioral goals, are a good way to specify what the therapist, the parents, and the schools mean by acceptable behavior.

RESISTANCE TO TREATMENT

Adolescents are often reluctant to cooperate with parents or adult authorities in general. Thus it is not uncommon for adolescents to resist treatment. However, reluctance to participate in a counseling setting does not mean refusal to participate. The hostile, resistant posture that the adolescent brings to the first few interviews may be necessary to save his self-respect, which has already been badly battered by the fact that he was sent to a "shrink," or a counselor. Although many of the patterns of resistance dissipate over several counseling sessions, the adolescent may employ some common defensive maneuvers to protect his psychological self from harm. These mechanisms are used whenever threatening thoughts or emotions arise (Wolman, 1968). The most commonly used defensive mechanism is *repression*. When unwanted or unacceptable thoughts emerge, they are forced back into the unconscious. Repression may be so effective that the anxiety-provoking thoughts may only reappear in disguised fashion. On the other hand, adolescents may deal with unacceptable thoughts through a process of *sublimation*, in which the thoughts or emotions are transformed and expressed in a socially acceptable fashion.

A very popular defense mechanism among middle-adolescents is *intellectualization*. As they begin to explore their powers of formal thought, they resort to intellectualizing and abstracting stress and viewing it in a detached, unemotional fashion. Similarly, adolescents may resort to elaborate explanations of why they behaved in a certain way. The use of such *rationalization* allows the adolescent to reduce feelings of guilt by means of a plausible explanation for some undesirable behavior. The rationalization does not, however, explain the true motive for the action. Sometimes rather than using the intellect to hide motives, the adolescent blames someone else for the unacceptable behavior. In some cases this *projection* involves blaming luck or fate or forces beyond human control.

When faced with information or knowledge that does not match the adolescent's conception of reality, the adolescent may resort to *isolation* or *denial*. Isolation is used when the adolescent views new, unwanted information as somehow distinct from what is already known. The new information is kept separate under the guise of "That's not the same. It's totally different." In Piagetian terms the adolescent refuses to assimilate or accommodate. Adolescents may use isolation when the new information is *too* new or *too* threatening. When new information requires radical restructuring of one's cognitive structure, it may indeed be necessary to hold the new information in abeyance. Over time the need for isolation may diminish, and we can integrate the information into our existing knowledge. *Denial* is a more severe reaction to unwanted information. Unlike isolation, in which the new information is recognized but kept separate, denial is a refusal to admit the information exists. Behind ignoring the problem and denying its existence is the hope that it will go away. Denial may, however, be a necessary defense when certain information is simply too disruptive and the adolescent cannot cope with it. In such cases individuals may be encouraged to return to the problem later, when their ability to cope is greater.

A common defensive mechanism among younger adolescents is *regression*, in which they resort to behaviors that were acceptable when they were younger but that are no longer appropriate. Regression is a particularly frustrating maneuver to adults, who typically respond by telling the adolescent, "Act your age," or "Grow up!" On the other hand, regression can be useful in creative thinking. The individual may try looking at a problem from the naive, uncluttered perspective of a child. Freud, in fact, described creativity as "regression in the service of the ego."

Part of the general portrait of maladjusted youths is that they tend to rely excessively on one or a small number of defense mechanisms. As with other adolescents with low self-esteem, they tend to view themselves as "losers." When placed in settings that exceed their ability to cope, they must revert to the most convenient defensive maneuver. When faced with a frustration born out of an uncertain setting, they often respond with the limited set of coping mechanisms available to them. Typically, they strike out at someone or something. And also typically, the response of those in authority is to remove or expel the disruptive adolescent.

For the maladjusted adolescent, expulsion from an unpleasant setting may be a source of relief. In behavioral terms, expulsion may be negatively reinforcing to the unwanted behavior. The adolescent learns that aggression provides a form of escape from an environment that tests the limits of his ability to cope. Additionally, the action by the authorities may lead to approval by peers. Finally, expulsion may confirm what the adolescent already felt, that he is incapable of succeeding.

Attention-seeking behaviors among adolescents do not, in and of themselves, reflect low self-esteem, or maladaption. "Class clowns" for example tend to rate higher on scales of assertiveness but are also more likely to be seen as leaders and as cheerful. In other dimensions of self-concept, few differences are seen between class clowns and their nonclown peers (Damico and Purkey, 1978). Class clowns, however, tend to view authorities and teachers with less respect than their more conventional peers.

Adolescents' coping behaviors are inextricably tied to their value system. When adolescents face stress, their selection of a given coping maneuver is

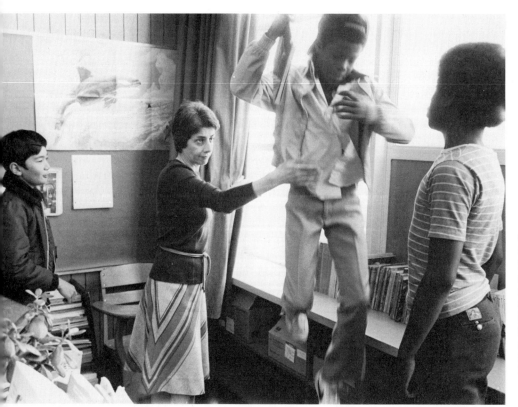

Often, the class clown engages in his disruptive behavior, consciously or unconsciously, because it gains him attention from the teacher and status and popularity from his classmates.(© Elizabeth Crews)

based in part on which coping behaviors are viewed as acceptable and which are not. As adolescents mature, they are exposed to more value systems and acquire alternative coping strategies. The psychologically healthy adolescent can sample from a variety of coping maneuvers rather than depend solely on one or on a small set of behaviors.

In dealing with adolescents who are experiencing emotional or decisional conflict, the practitioner's role is to help them sort through their options. Although a counselor's value structures would dictate one decision, that counselor's responsibility is to help the adolescent explore not only that point of view but others as well. In the end, the adolescent alone must make a choice among the various options that are available. The adolescent who is coerced into a decision that may lead to feelings of guilt afterward may be less able to cope with subsequent decisional stress. The counselor should orient the adolescent toward a posture of *vigilance*, which involves sorting through available information, assessing its value, and making a decision on the basis of all available information rather than responding impulsively (Janis and Mann, 1976). Once the client has made a decision, the practitioner may then need to help the adolescent cope with the ramifications of that decision.

FAMILY COUNSELING

Many counselors of adolescents with behavior difficulties prefer to view the situation as a family problem rather than an individual problem. Their view is that the behavioral problems that caused the adolescent to be referred for counseling inevitably have some impact on, or result at least in part from, the family dynamics at home. Sometimes those family dynamics precede the adolescent's problem behavior, and sometimes they result from it. In either case, counselors argue, to treat one and not the other is futile.

Not all families, however, are ready to submit themselves to counseling. The parents may react by saying, "The family is fine; it is the adolescent who has the problem." Further, parents may be divided on their perceived need for counseling and the value of it. In such cases, a counselor may choose to identify the adolescent as the client of record and explain to the family that their help is needed in establishing a treatment program for the client.

In the initial interviews with parents and, say, an adolescent son, a counselor may get the message from the parents that their son is a destructive ingrate who disrupts and disturbs the entire family. The boy, on the other hand, may present himself as an oppressed martyr who is badgered by uncaring, ignorant reactionaries. The counselor should not be too eager to take sides—the truth usually falls somewhere between the two versions (Meeks, 1976).

Parental reaction to the referral of their adolescent for counseling may range from guilt and grief to unabashed relief. Almost all parents feel some guilt, and the counselor should be empathetic with their feelings. The guilt may take the form of feelings of failure to be a good parent. Those feelings come from a natural tendency of parents to assume everything their child does is their fault. Moreover, those natural feelings are reinforced by articles and books (such as this one) that point to the connection between inadequate

Counseling an adolescent often means counseling the whole family, because it is often the family as a unit, not just the individual, that is troubled. (Peter Vandermark)

parenting and behavior problems. Because their child has behavioral problems, they assume that they have done something wrong. The counselor must never draw that conclusion without evidence that it is so. There are abundant examples of families in which three children have no problems but one does. How can one family yield such different results? Consider, for example, the case of Jack:

> Jack was a twelve-year-old boy who was referred by school officials for counseling and evaluation. His referral sheet described him as habitually truant and a "troublemaker." He was failing most of his courses and was viewed by his teachers and peers as slow. On an individual test of intelligence he was found to be above average in intelligence. Further testing revealed that Jack suffered from *dyslexia*, a learning disability that interferes with learning to read. In other tests of general information, Jack showed considerable knowledge of current events, which he said he learned "just by listening." His acting out was primarily a defense to avoid reading aloud in front of his peers.

Jack's parents were concerned that they had done something wrong in rearing him. They had not had similar problems with his two older brothers or younger sister. They also felt resentment toward Jack's disruptive behavior. Once the problem was adequately diagnosed, both Jack and his parents relaxed a bit and were able to work on a solution. Fortunately for Jack and his family, the counselor recognized the problem as one that was caused by factors other than a "bad home."

Parents may also feel guilty for their resentment and anger toward the adolescent. The parents may rightfully resent the emotional outbursts of their teenage son or daughter, who repeatedly disrupts the family dinner. However, like the new mother who resents losing her sleep to feed an infant, they simultaneously feel guilty for resenting their own child.

In most cases parents are cooperative and motivated to do what will help their child. However, in a minority of cases therapy may turn out to be a matter of helping an adolescent cope with a sick or maladaptive environment. In cases of chronically disruptive adolescents, in which the family is clearly identified as maladaptive, the task for the counselor may be to help the adolescent develop enough positive feelings of self-worth and enough self-reliant behaviors to operate independently of the family.

A problem that occasionally emerges in the treatment of adolescents is an overly dependent relationship between one of the parents and the child. In such a relationship the mother may be totally dependent for support on her teenager, who in turn is totally dependent on the mother. Neither is able to function independently.

> Mary was a 15-year-old girl who was referred for counseling after an attempted suicide. Mary felt at the time that "It was the only way to get free from my Mother!" Every attempt by Mary to assert her own independence from her was met by tears and inferences of some dire illness (usually cancer) by her mother. In group therapy, Mary said that she did not believe her mother had any illness but that she felt terribly guilty about leaving her mother alone.

CONFIDENTIALITY

In counseling adolescents, a practitioner must always wrestle with the issue of confidentiality of information. With adult patients, information revealed to a professional counselor in a clinical setting is considered absolutely confidential and private. When the patient is an adolescent, however, the issue of confidentiality is complicated. Because the adolescent is a minor and still the legal responsibility of the parent, complete confidentiality of information may not be possible, especially as it relates to potentially dangerous behavior. However, to establish a productive relationship, the adolescent must feel reasonably comfortable in divulging information that will not go beyond the confines of the practitioner's office. On the other hand, if the adolescent reveals personal information that the practitioner interprets as possibly harmful to the client's well-being, the counselor may be ethically and legally obligated to relate that information to the parents. Parents are, in the final analysis, directly responsible for the adolescent's welfare.

Early in the counseling process, it may be wise to clarify the limits within which you may reasonably work. You should try to establish a relationship among the parents, the adolescent, and yourself that ensures confidentiality except in those cases in which serious physical or psychological harm may result. If the information involves physical or sexual abuse by the parents, then the issue of confidentiality may be affected by legal statutes. In such instances you may need to serve as an advocate for the adolescent in opposition to the parents. You should, of course, be well informed of your legal position.

In some cases, confidentiality may be strained because informing parents of a serious problem may not appear to be in the best interests of the adolescent. Parental reactions have been known to be counterproductive or even destructive. For example, a pregnant girl may be afraid to inform her parents because of her fear of their reaction. As a counselor, you must try to assess whether her assessment is valid, or whether it is an overdramatization resulting from natural feelings of fear and guilt. You may, in such cases, try to develop a plan through which the adolescent informs her parents in your presence and with your emotional support.

Finally, an adolescent's plea, "Please don't tell my parents," may really be the request, "Please do tell my parents." In such cases it is usually more beneficial for the adolescent to assume the responsibility. As a counselor, you may once again choose to provide your presence and emotional support for the task.

SOME CLOSING THOUGHTS

It was my intention at the outset of this text to introduce to you a body of information about the physical, psychological, emotional, and social development of adolescents. I worked from the assumption that most of you who take a course such as this expect one day to be working with young people. Thus the material that I included reflects my biases about what the professional practitioner should be aware of. There are, however, some leftover thoughts and guidelines that I would like to share with you. These thoughts focus more on my impressions of those who work well with adolescents than on hard data. I believe that you, as future professionals who will work with people, not just adolescents, will find them helpful.

RESPECT THE INTEGRITY OF THE ADOLESCENT

One of the common problems that I observe in adults communicating with adolescents is that they talk down to teenagers. It is important to keep in mind that the adolescent is striving to be an adult. Teenagers are understandably naive about some topics, but to talk to them as though they are children is demeaning. A good rule of thumb is to give the adolescent the same respect you expect the adolescent to give you. This may be more easily said than done when you are faced with a hostile and belligerent teenager and you rapidly reach the limits of your own tolerance. In such cases it is better to break off the interchange than to react by squelching or "putting down" the adolescent. An intellectual or emotional put-down may temporarily "put the adolescent in his place," but the verbal barb may be tough to remove later. In any relationship, "hitting below the belt" is unfair, but in the delicate alliance between the professional and adolescent, the harm may be irreparable. Further, for the adolescent who is already suffering a damaged or poor self-image, a put-down by someone who matters may be devastating.

Throughout the text, I have repeatedly referred to the importance of aiding the adolescent to develop positive feelings of self-worth. The respect that adolescents have for themselves may be the single most important factor in their psychological and social development. If adolescents see important adults as not respecting them as individuals, then their ability to accept themselves may be jeopardized.

As a professional you must always keep in mind that adolescents vary along any number of dimensions. Not only are there differences among adolescents, but there are also differences within individual adolescents. Their reactions to stress differ as a function of their levels of social and intellectual development, their feelings about themselves at a given point in time, and any number of other factors. As practitioners we must avoid the temptation to categorize an adolescent by age, home background, or educational level, in much the same way that we must avoid racial or sexual stereotypes. Among the more popular stereotypes of adolescence is that it is a tumultuous period of development. Granted, some adolescents *do* experience storm and stress during adolescence, but not all do. For some, the transition is rather pleasant and uneventful. It is important not to overgeneralize in any direction.

GIVE A DAMN

Several years ago Mayor John Lindsay of New York City initiated a campaign to raise the level of pride and concern that the residents of New York had for their city and its people. The program was called "Give a Damn." That phrase is a good motto for your future work with adolescents. Perhaps the most important attitude you can convey to the teens with whom you work is that you care about them and care what happens to them. To know that what happens to them matters to you may be a very important force in their own personal growth.

Do not be afraid to go out on a limb and give of yourself. As practitioners you will have the chance to do some things that go beyond the defined responsibilities of your job. You may be able to provide the extra push that some adolescents need to get themselves straightened around and moving forward. In my own life, a high school guidance counselor made just that kind of difference. My high school performance was less than stellar. When I finished high school, I had no intention of going on for further education and proceeded to get a job working on trucks. My counselor's role was officially finished. However, he saw something in me that I did not see in myself. After a year he not only persuaded me to go on to college, but he also arranged for financial assistance. None of these acts were *necessary*. He did them of his own accord. He is, incidentally, one of the three people to whom this text is dedicated.

BE PATIENT—KEEP A SENSE OF HUMOR

Do not expect miracles to happen overnight. Your efforts may not have an immediate impact on the forward progress of an adolescent. Indeed, when we look at progress over short spans of time, we may feel that we are not accomplishing much. However, when we look at the the same adolescents over a longer period of time, we may see definite change.

Similarly, help adolescents see that growth does not suddenly cease at the end of the teen years. So much literature and conversation about adolescence convinces teens that this is the particularly troublesome period of life. It is as though problems and pimples will magically disappear at the age of eighteen. Adolescents do not have a corner on the uncertainty market, and their awareness that you, their parents, and other adults also experience stress may help them gain the perspective that all their problems do not have to be, and will not be, solved immediately. As practitioners we can help adolescents specify what their problems are and seek alternative strategies for resolving those problems. (Those same skills, it can be noted, are useful for problem solving at all stages of life.)

Often the tension of a situation can be relieved by recognizing its complete incongruity. In the same vein, many adult-adolescent interactions can be kept from getting stiff if you can maintain a sense of humor.

DO AS YOU SAY

What you say, what you do, and how you handle stress are important, not only to you, but also to the teenagers who are watching you. As an adult in a position of authority, you will often be identified by adolescents as a model of how adults should behave. You have a responsibility to serve as a model for

Much positive counseling occurs in less-formal settings with a teacher, coach, or principal. (Peter Vandermark)

whatever behaviors and values you profess. Your choices in your use of language, your control of your temper, and your openness will serve as an image of what a mature person acts like. Athletic coaches have an extraordinary responsibility in this area. Because they work very closely with a small group of individuals, coaches are very likely to develop a close personal bond with the adolescents on their teams. When a coach explains the merits of good sportsmanship and then screams at officials in foul language, there is an obvious discrepancy between what is said and what is done. The adolescent is left with the dilemma of whether to behave according to what he sees or what he hears.

BE OPEN AND HONEST

Adults who work with teens sometimes feel obligated to act as if they "have their act completely together." Perfection is a terribly difficult standard to maintain for yourself and for adolescents. Your willingness to admit that you do not have all the answers is not a sign of weakness but a sign of honesty.

Often adolescents will ask practitioners how they feel about certain issues. Adults are sometimes reluctant to share those feelings on the vague fear that they might "convert" the adolescent. In actuality most questions of this form are part of the adolescent's attempts to assess alternate value structures. Your willingness to relate your views also tells the adolescents that you accept them and are able to let them see you as you are.

Do not be afraid to act. Counselors, and even parents, are sometimes reluctant to say, "I think what you are doing is wrong, and I see real problems ahead." If you care, you need to be honest about those feelings. Sometimes you may make mistakes in judgment, but it is better that you make a few mistakes than do nothing.

BE GENTLE WITH YOURSELF

A line from the poem "Desiderata" says, "Beyond a wholesome discipline, be gentle with yourself." When working with young people, especially troubled youths, practitioners tend to blame themselves for the adolescents' failures. Like parents, practitioners may be tempted to ask what they did wrong or what more they could have done. Sometimes there are answers to these questions, sometimes there are none. As a practitioner you will encounter both successes and failures. Recognize both for what they are, and try not to be overly harsh on yourself when you fail to see success. Also, be patient; the results of your counseling or help may not be immediate.

Remember that as a counselor or a practitioner you are first a human being with human emotions and feelings. There will undoubtedly be times when you will be discouraged and feel inadequate in your role. You may be certain an adolescent is on a sure path to trouble and feel frustrated because you cannot reach him or stop the problem. If you choose to work with maladjusted or delinquent adolescents, the chances of this happening increase greatly. It is normal at such times to wonder whether there was more that you could have done. Maybe there was and maybe there was not. It is important to realize that all counselors experience both failures *and* successes.

There is no such thing as the super-counselor who is all things to all people. There will be some adolescents whom, for one reason or another, you will not like. The first time this happens you will inevitably feel guilty, thinking that because you are a professional, you should be above normal interpersonal feelings. That is not so.

Do not expect that as a counselor or practitioner you will always have the ability to say or do just the right thing to guide an adolescent along the way. We see teachers, parents, and doctors on television or in films who seem to know exactly what to say. In the typical scene, the adolescent is in the middle of an immense crisis, and the adult, with calm and dignity, says or does just the right thing to change the adolescent's attitude miraculously and defuse the potentially explosive situation. As I watch those programs I sometimes find myself wishing, "Gosh, I wish I had said that." Well, I could have, if I had a team of writers handing me my dialogue. As people working with adolescents in the "real world," you will not have a team of writers. However, if you are open and honest, you will do well more often than not.

BE HONEST WITH YOURSELF

At this point in your career development, you still have many options. As a future practitioner providing services to adolescents, you should realistically ask yourself the question, "Am I going to feel comfortable working with adolescents?" Quite clearly, for many people the answer to that question is no. The field is not for everybody, and there is nothing wrong in admitting that you are not able to serve all kinds of people.

On the other hand, if the answer to the question is yes, be encouraged that there are many ways in which motivated people can have a significant impact on the lives of young people. There is a need for people who work well with troubled youths; and there are also many other options available for working with normal, well-adjusted adolescents who will benefit from the interaction with adults who care about what happens to them. There is a great deal of personal satisfaction to be gained by working with adolescents. If you see yourself in such a role, I wish you well.

Appendix A | The Study of Adolescents in Laboratory and Natural Settings

What we understand about adolescent growth and development is largely the result of a variety of research studies that differ in format and question but which have as a common element that the group of interest is adolescents. Unlike some areas in the physical sciences, the study of adolescent development is not guided by a single clear-cut theory. Rather, a variety of theories are tested—some with direct relevance to adolescence, some only indirectly related. The methods of research are also many and varied.

The purpose of this appendix is threefold. First, we will review the basic elements of research design as it relates to human and adolescent development. Because it is an overview, the more advanced student who has encountered this information elsewhere may wish to skim for review. The second purpose is to provide some guidelines for evaluating research studies. Third, I will provide some guidance on where to begin research.

RESEARCH METHODS

Research is the systematic analysis of a question through the planned collection, analysis, and interpretation of data. An investigator who wishes to study adolescent behavior and development must start with a clearly stated problem. Usually the problem can be expressed as a question regarding the relationship between two or more variables—for example, "What is the impact of early versus late maturation on self-esteem?" or "What is the relationship of chronic alcohol abuse among early-adolescents to their social adjustment?" Although the statement of the problem appears, on the surface, to be relatively straightforward, it is at this point that many investigators falter. Kerlinger (1973) points out, "It is not always possible for a researcher to formulate his problem simply, clearly, and completely. He may often have only a general, diffuse, even confused notion of the problem" (p. 16). It is the single most common flaw in research proposals.

After stating the problem, the researcher should attempt to incorporate the question within a broader theoretical structure and to relate it to previous research. In the process of delineating the relationship of the question to a broader theoretical and research context, the researcher formulates a specific set of testable hypotheses.

Once the hypotheses are formulated, the researcher must select from the many alternative research designs and methodologies the one that seems most relevant to the question. A wide variety of appropriate methodologies are available to the researcher (see, for example, Campbell and Stanley, 1963; Cook and Campbell, 1979; Festinger and Katz, 1953; Kerlinger, 1973; Webb et al., 1966). However, the principal distinction made in most reviews of research methods is between experimental and nonexperimental research. Both broad categories are then broken down further on the basis of specific designs or methodologies. Although experimental research is clearly the most precise mode of research and allows the researcher the strongest support for a theory, it is often too contrived to ask important questions. In cases in which such a degree of control is not feasible, a nonexperimental approach may be preferable.

EXPERIMENTAL RESEARCH

In the true experimental study, a researcher attempts to measure the impact of some independent variable over which he or she has control on some dependent variable. Independent variables are states that are systematically controlled or that are used as selection criteria. Dependent variables, on the other hand, are the outcomes or criterion measures. For example, if a person were to study the question, "What are the effects of marijuana on driving ability?" marijuana use would be the independent variable and driving ability would be the dependent variable. In this case, a specific amount of marijuana might be provided to a randomly selected *experimental* group, and nothing would be given to another randomly selected *control* group. Each group would then drive in a simulation machine. If differences were found in driving ability between those who had smoked marijuana and those who had not, we would conclude that marijuana smoking affects driving ability.

Certainly such a study would be an oversimplified test of the question of whether marijuana smoking affects behavior. However, another researcher could build on the study by adding more controls and asking additional questions. For example, perhaps just *thinking* you are smoking marijuana alters your behavior. What would happen if larger doses or better grades of marijuana were used? Although the complexity of the question increases, the basic design remains the same. That is, individuals are randomly assigned to treatment groups, and after the experimental or control conditions have been applied, all are given the same outcome test.

Randomization is a very important component of the experimental design, because it is a way of increasing the chances that the groups are similar at the start. In random assignment, every individual has an equal chance of being assigned to one of the experimental groups. This is done to reduce the chances of one group having some characteristics in common that would put them at an unfair advantage over another group. For example, suppose you were studying the effects of giving hints on solving problems. Students from school A are given the "squares problem" from Chapter 4 with the same instructions that you received. Students in school B were given the same problem but were also given hints, such as, "Sometimes we see boxes within boxes," or "Sometimes people stop looking too soon." If, in the end, we found that students in school B were correct more often than those in school A, we could not be sure that our results were not because of differences that already existed between the two schools.

An essential characteristic of the experimental design is that the experimenter tries in every way possible to ensure that all variables other than the variable of interest are controlled or equalized. By doing this, any differences among the groups on the dependent variable are considered to be *caused* by the different treatments.

NONEXPERIMENTAL RESEARCH

In many cases, especially when the population in which the researcher is interested in adolescents, a true experimental design is logically and ethically impossible. We cannot, for example, randomly assign children to rich or poor families when we want to study the impact of family background on some outcome variable. In nonexperimental studies a researcher usually uses a measure of association called the correlation coefficient.

Although historically the correlation coefficient was a major breakthrough for the social sciences, it has today become a less respected tool, perhaps because of an overreaction to its misuses. The coefficient describes a relationship that exists between two variables, ranging from an inverse relationship (negative correlation) through no relationship (zero correlation) to a direct relationship (positive correlation). In any correlation all that is shown is that the scores of two variables tend to correspond in some way. If we have two variables X and Y, and we say that a positive correlation exists between them, then we know that as X scores increase, Y scores also tend to increase. If, on the other hand, we have an inverse relationship between the two variables, as X scores increase, Y scores tend to decrease. Notice that I keep saying "tend to." No cause-and-effect relationship is implied by a correlation coefficient, only a correspondence between sets of scores; that is, a correlation coefficient reflects the amount of common variance, or the extent to which two variables *covary*. For example, suppose you found that there was a negative correlation between self-reported anxiety and performance on the SATs. You might be tempted to conclude that the high anxiety causes the low test performance. However, it could be argued that just the opposite occurred—that is, that low performance on the SAT caused high anxiety. Although correlation coefficients may be used in very strictly defined circumstances to make causal statements (Blalock, 1964), we must be very cautious about such conclusions.

There have traditionally been two primary methodologies for assessing age- or development-related changes. In longitudinal research a group of subjects is identified and studied over a span of several years. In cross-sectional research several groups of subjects, differing in ages, are viewed at one time. Both approaches have advantages and disadvantages, and recently some researchers have combined the two methods into a third methodology, called cohort designs.

In longitudinal research an investigator selects a sample of people and follows their development over a period of time. Thus any characteristic of a subgroup that sets it apart from the total sample may be studied to assess cumulative effects. In one of the more famous longitudinal studies of adolescence, H. Jones (1939a,b) and his associates selected a group of children from the Oakland Bay area that they intended to follow through adolescence. Subsequently the Oakland Growth Study was extended to adulthood (M. Jones, 1965), and still more recently a comprehensive analysis of long-term patterns of personality development has been completed (Block, 1971). Thus in a longitudinal study, stability or instability in patterns of development can be analyzed.

Longitudinal research is not without its problems. First, longitudinal research is exceptionally expensive in both time and money. Sometimes many years may pass before clear results are observed. This passage of time creates another problem. Deaths, moving away, and the simple refusal of subjects to continue participation change the sample over time. In the Oakland Growth Study, for example, Block (1971) managed to study 80 percent of the original sample. However, the 20 percent who were no longer represented may be different in important ways from those who remained in the study. Finally, there is always the problem of 20–20 hindsight. Several years into a longitudinal study, an investigator may regret not having gathered now-important information at an earlier time. This is a problem in all research, but it is particularly frustrating in longitudinal studies.

Cross-sectional designs examine samples of different age groups at one point in time. In contrast to longitudinal studies, the data are collected within a short time span and are available for analysis and synthesis relatively quickly. However, unlike longitudinal research, the investigator has no way of assessing relative developmental status over time, and comparing subjects from one age group to another may not be reasonable. Comparing ten- twenty- thirty- and forty-year-olds may be misleading, because the four groups represent different generations and different cultural effects (Labouvie, 1976). Today's twenty-year-old was an adolescent during the 1970s, whereas the forty-year-old was a teen during the 1950s.

Some of the problems associated with longitudinal and cross-sectional designs are lessened through the use of cohort designs. A cohort is a grouping of subjects selected on the basis of some homogeneous characteristics, such as birth (age). Although there are several versions of cohort designs (Labouvie, 1976; Schaie, 1973; Baltes, 1973; Price, 1974), the most practical and

Table A-1 AGE OF COHORTS AT TIME OF TESTING

Cohort	Age			
	1976	1980	1984	1988
1968	8	12	16	20
1964	12	16	20	24
1960	16	20	24	28
1956	20	24	28	32

widely used is what is called the cross-sequential design (Labouvie, 1976). Thus in the year 1976, we might have selected a 1968 cohort (eight-year-olds), who are to be compared to a 1964 cohort (twelve-year-olds), a 1960 cohort (sixteen-year-olds), and a 1956 cohort (twenty-year-olds). What makes the cohort design different is that we measure our cohort groups four times at four-year intervals, as shown in Table A-l. The advantage of the cohort sequential design is that we can assess both developmental and generational effects. Although the cohort designs are still in the process of clarification, they and other new designs (Nesselroade and Baltes, 1978) are offering new insights into the developmental process.

NATURALISTIC OBSERVATION

As Bronfenbrenner (1977) has cogently argued, research in human development needs to maintain a healthy balance between rigor and relevance. The primary difficulty with most research in human development is that in order to maintain a degree of rigor, children and adolescents are asked to respond to unusual tasks in an unnatural setting—the laboratory. Consequently, most behavior reported in research studies is artificial and measured over very short periods of time. Bronfenbrenner calls for increased use of observation in natural settings, guided by some of the same demands for precision and rigor that dominate experimental research.

In the study of human behaviors, we do not have the degree of control that is available in the physical sciences. Ethics preclude the use of experimental treatments that could lead to physical or psychological damage of the subject. Thus we are often left with nonexperimental settings from which we must make inferences. Increasingly, researchers in human development (for example, Barker, 1965; Altman, 1975; Scott, 1978) are calling for an ecology of human behavior—that is, the scientific study of human behavior in its natural surroundings. In using an ecological approach for the study of adolescents, we would need to specify carefully the observable elements of a person's environment.

Suppose you were to try to identify the impact of an environment on some behavior of a target adolescent under a variety of settings. The adolescent's behavior may differ when in school, at church, at home, at a drive-in theater, and so on. Thus, when speaking of a person interacting with his or her environment, we must specify *which* environment.

Bronfenbrenner suggests that an ecosystem (the composite of environmental forces affecting an individual) can be broken down into at least four levels of influence on the behavior of a person at a given point in time. The first level, the immediate environment, is called a *microsystem*. You are reading this text in a specific setting, perhaps a dormitory room. That room is really a composite of stimuli that affect you. The air may be stuffy or pleasant, the radio may be playing, the view from your window may be attractive. Your reaction to these components of your environment may aid or hinder your studying behavior (Rothkopf, 1968). Further, the radio in the background may serve to help you study but may have the opposite effect on your roommate.

At another level, Bronfenbrenner proposes you operate within a *mesosystem*. Not only is your present behavior affected by your immediate environment, you are affected by your friends' attitudes about studying, the "atmosphere" of the college at which you are studying, and your parents' attitudes about work in general. Although this part of your ecosystem is less tangible, it does nonetheless have an impact on your present studying behavior. Your peers, for example, do not have to be physically present to influence you. Elements of your mesosystem help define the roles you specify for yourself.

At a still more remote level, you operate in an *exosystem,* which is composed of formal and informal agencies of society that help shape our attitudes and behavior. These agencies may also shape the character of the elements of our mesosystem. The mass media and the government are examples of agencies in our exosystem. The effect of such agencies, though remote or less direct, is real and continuous.

At the most remote level of influence is what Bronfenbrenner calls the *macrosystem,* which includes general societal ideologies. The system of government, current social values, ethnic or national heritage, and educational models influence attitudes and behaviors at a general level. The macrosystem gives organization and meaning to the roles defined by the other levels of our ecosystem.

Using naturalistic observation requires that the observer be well schooled in the category system to be used. The researcher must be able to demonstrate that, given a coding scheme, a variety of observers would agree, at some reasonable level, on what is being observed. Naturalistic observation, if it is done well, may be the most demanding of research methodologies.

OBSERVER INTERFERENCE

In the scientific study of adolescents, a researcher has to be aware that the behavior observed or measured may not be totally natural. The fact that someone is observing or measuring another person's behavior is *obtrusive*—that is, measuring and observing behavior alters it (Webb, Campbell, Schwartz, and Sechrist, 1966). For example, suppose you are driving along and suddenly see a state police car in your rearview mirror. Irrespective of whether you were speeding or not, you are likely to monitor your speed and become much more aware of your driving behavior. In much the same way, a subject in a psychological experiment is aware of being watched and does not want to "act badly." Actually any of three elements in an experiment can alter the natural behavior being studied: (1) the person being observed or measured; (2) the observer or the instrument; or (3) the demand of the task. Although the intrusiveness of observers or testing situations diminishes over time, we suspect that the impact is never totally eliminated.

A person participating in an experiment typically knows it. (Ethics preclude imposing experimental treatments without the subjects knowing about it.) Thus we are apt to see what might be called a guinea-pig effect (Webb et al., 1966). When people realize that they are part of an experiment, very often they will try to figure out what the experimenter is "trying to prove." Once they determine this, correctly or incorrectly, they are likely to start playing roles. Most often the roles assumed by the subjects are intended to be helpful to the researcher. Every so often, however, a subject will assume a role that is meant to be disruptive. In either case, the results are altered.

An additional source of error from a person being observed is called a *response set*. People often respond to a test with patterns that have little to do with what is supposedly being measured. Most people have filled out attitude surveys with statements like "Cats are nice animals," and five alternatives: strongly agree, agree, uncertain, disagree, strongly disagree. Some people are reluctant to mark either extreme even though they may despise cats. Alternately, some people are most apt to *strongly* agree or disagree with nearly everything. A third group has a tendency to mark uncertain very often. A researcher's interpretation of the attitudes of such individuals will therefore be clouded by factors other than those supposedly being measured.

The researcher may unknowingly bias the results. Perhaps one of the cleverest demonstrations of obtrusiveness in experimental research was by Robert Rosenthal. The phenomenon has become known as the Rosenthal effect. Rosenthal demonstrated that an experimenter enters a laboratory with some advance knowledge of how the results should come out. The net result is that the experimenter may unwittingly convey expectations to the subject and thereby bias the outcome. In Rosenthal's classic study, students in a psychology rat lab were given rats and were told that their rat was either a genetically superior or inferior rat. Actually, the assignment of rats to students was random. Nonetheless, the learning performance of the two sets of rats was in accord with what would be expected of the two "genetic groupings." Apparently the students' expectations influenced the rats' behavior.

Finally, the task itself or the setting may be obtrusive. When you walk into a church, a temple, or a library, your behavior differs from your behavior in a football stadium, a sorority or fraternity house, or a tavern. In effect, your surroundings dictate appropriate and inappropriate behavior. Likewise, as you enter a medical or psychological laboratory your behavior changes. You take stock of the behavior that is appropriate and act as expected, or in ways that run counter to what is expected, depending on your personality.

THE ETHICS OF RESEARCH

The history of research with children and adolescents includes several studies in which an investigator has placed the importance of the research question ahead of the rights of the individual who served as the *subject* of study. Research subjects have been deceived and manipulated in the name of science in ways that could possibly lead to their physical or psychological harm with little or no apparent regard on the researcher's part for the rights of the people involved.

Although such studies make up a minority of research, their existence has motivated many professional societies and government agencies to take a strong stand on such procedures. Their position is that an individual who agrees to participate in a study should not, as a result of the study, be subject to any physical or psychological harm.

Physical harm is, of course, easier to define than psychological harm. Psychological stress and anxiety may occur as a result of some experimental manipulation, and an investigator must try to assess whether the stress is a necessary outcome of the study, and, if so, whether the study is necessary. As an example, in the "classic" Watson and Raynor (1920) study of Albert, an infant was placed in a room with a white rat. Initially Albert liked the rat. However, every time Albert approached the rat or the rat approached Albert, the experimenter struck a loud gong. In a short time Albert was terrified by the rat as well as by other objects that reminded him of the original source of the fear. Although Watson and Raynor claimed to have deconditioned Albert from his fear, did they have the right to submit the child to the study in the first place?

Because of studies like this one and others, there have been attempts to clarify what rights people have when serving as research subjects. Organizations such as the Society for Research in Child Development (1977) have provided detailed guidelines for the ethical use of human subjects, which are briefly summarized here. The net impact of these guidelines is that anyone who participates in a research study will be adequately informed of what is going to happen in the study, why the study is being done, and, most of all, of his or her right to agree or refuse to participate.

The demand that adolescents who are asked to participate in a study be informed of what is to happen and what they are expected to do before they agree to participate, creates some problems for researchers. *Informed consent,* the name applied to this demand, requires that the investigator explain to the adolescent in clear terms what is happening, without biasing the subject by creating expectancies of how he or she is supposed to behave. This is no easy task. However, an honest review of the procedures and the general purpose of the study, without explaining specific expectations, usually suffices. However, the individual must be fully informed of any risks.

Because adolescents are still minors, researchers have a responsibility to get informed consent not only from the adolescents but also from their parents. Once again the procedures, purposes, and risks of the study must be stated in clear terms, and the parents must provide permission (preferably in writing) for their child to participate.

Any data that is collected from an adolescent subject must be held in confidence. Although an investigator may and should provide a summary of general results of the study, individual data should not be made available. In rare circumstances, information may surface during a study that you, as a researcher, see as an indicator of serious risk to the adolescent subjects. If that occurs, you may wish to get guidance from your professor as to how to handle such information.

Often in studies using adolescents, information regarding school achievement or school performance may be useful. Such information is protected by law as confidential, and it is not generally available unless written consent is obtained from both the adolescent and the parents.

Most universities and colleges now have a review committee to evaluate whether research violates the rights of a human subject. Members of such a committee might be consulted early in the development of a research problem to see what guidelines might be followed. Ultimately, however, the responsibility for ensuring that the rights of the adolescent subjects are preserved rests with the researcher. In any event the rights of the adolescent override the needs of the researcher. You should evaluate any research study that you might pursue in light of the adolescent's rights to privacy and freedom from physical or psychological harm.

WHERE TO BEGIN

When students in a course such as this are asked to write a term paper or conduct research, they often rightfully complain that they are just becoming familiar with the area and that they are at a loss as to where to begin beyond the index at the end of this book. How do you go about finding information about adolescents when you've just begun to learn about the area? A wide variety of disciplines directly or indirectly study adolescents. Where do you begin? Fortunately most libraries have indexes that abstract reference journals and books in specific areas. Also, most disciplines have regular publications that provide a current review of the relevant literature on a specific topic. Presented below is a limited selection of such resources that you may find helpful in pursuing a topic in adolescent behavior and development.

Probably the first index that you should study is the *Child Development Abstracts and Bibliography*. It is published three times a year by the Society for Research in Child Development and indexes journals and books that focus on children (including adolescents) and development. Other indexes that are less *specifically* related to child and adolescent development but that have references to studies in adolescence are *Psychological Abstracts, Sociological Abstracts, Current Index to Journals in Education (CIJE), Language Behavior Abstracts, Index Medicus*, and *Education Index*.

Leading researchers and writers on a specific topic in child or adolescent development are often asked to write reviews of current literature and provide an overview of current thought. *The Annual Review of Psychology* has an update on research in developmental psychology every other year. However, that review is usually limited in value for those interested in adolescence. Volumes such as the *Review of Child Development Research, Advances in Child Development and Behavior, Review of Research in Education, Yearbooks of the National Society for the Study of Education* (especially 1976), or Gallagher's *Medical Care of the Adolescent* (3rd ed., 1976) contain useful and current summaries of research in specific content areas. The two-volume *Carmichael's Manual of Child Psychology*, edited by Paul Mussen (1970), remains an excellent summary of many areas in child and adolescent development.

You should ask a series of basic questions about the article you are reviewing:

1. Does the author clearly state the research question and the hypotheses to be tested? You should be able to identify with reasonable ease the problem to which the researcher is attending.
2. Is the study worth including in your review? This doesn't mean that all research studies need to be profound—few are. Rather, you, as a person evaluating research, must decide whether the study is worth including in *your* review.
3. Is the research designed to answer the question? Unfortunately, many studies use designs and procedures that are not necessarily the best for, or even appropriate to, the question asked. Quite often, research studies need to be so controlled that they lose the element of reality that exists outside the laboratory.
4. How well does the study control other variables? In the elementary study we described earlier in this chapter, the answer was, "Not too well." One must be careful, however, not to get carried away with looking for other variables. An investigator simply cannot control everything. Rather, it is necessary to look at questions covered by series of studies that complement each other. Also, hindsight is often much better than foresight; the investigator, too, may now recognize the same limitations.
5. Is the sample of subjects for the study appropriate? Sometimes researchers make mistakes in their selection of people, which in turn casts doubt on the degree to which we can generalize to the population as a whole. If the subjects in our study were all heavy users of marijuana, can we say anything about nonusers? Very often a number of questions arise about randomization, an important control procedure.
6. Do the conclusions follow from the results? Are the author's conclusions and generalizations justified on the basis of the reported study?
7. Finally—for those with enough expertise—is the statistical analysis appropriate? Are the data and results presented accurately and in an understandable form?

SUMMARY

Our understanding of adolsescent growth and development is a result of the types of research designs that are used to study adolescents. The methods we use influence the interpretations we make. However, when we make inferences about any group of humans, and especially about adolescents, we need to temper our conclusions by the knowledge that there are wide variations among individuals and even within individuals.

To review, research in adolescent behavior starts with the statement of a question. Once the question is stated the researcher must then determine which among many research methodologies is most appropriate for providing an answer to the question. In some cases, research questions are answerable through true experimental designs. In other cases, a researcher cannot establish the degree of control needed for an experimental design and must depend on nonexperimental or observational studies. In either case the researcher must be alert to the influence of various levels of the adolescent's ecosystem. Finally, any researcher must pay close attention to the ethical issues associated with using adolescents as research subjects.

Appendix B | Teaching Adolescents

> The most important thing in teaching is that you practice what you teach and not always yell at the students like it is their fault or something. And understand each and every student.
>
> Eighth-grade student

> The teacher has to be understanding and really make the class foremost. Teachers do not understand kids and the class is absolutely awful. The teacher has to do different things, not always the same procedure. If the teacher is fun and nice but still teaches and makes the kids learn, the kids will like him or her and they will make better grades. There aren't enough teachers who are like that.
>
> Tenth-grade student

What makes a good teacher? We have all had instructors we thought were really excellent. On the other hand, not all of us would agree on the same teachers. You have probably had the experience of having friends tell you how great teacher X is, only to find that you and that teacher have a personality conflict.

Basically an instructor is responsible for establishing conditions that facilitate learning among students. Learning in the classroom is neither automatic nor inevitable. An instructor who wishes to achieve specific outcomes must ensure that conditions are appropriate for learning to take place. Although some learning may occur in unorganized, unplanned instruction, there is no guarantee that what is learned is productive or beneficial.

Instruction may be provided by a classroom teacher, or by a computer, a teaching machine, a film, a text, and so on; the same principle holds. Effective instruction demands organization to achieve outcomes, which must be specified in advance. The instructor must have a clear understanding of the structure of the material and the characteristics of the learners, in advance. This does not mean that instruction is teacher-centered, autocratic monologues that lead the student in lock-step fashion. Even so-called open classrooms, when they are effective, have structure. The structure, however, differs. Similarly, problem-based discovery learning may offer room for increased student flexibility, but all the elements of the solution to the problem, including relevant background knowledge, must be available if the learner is to resolve the problem successfully (Gagne, 1978; Suchman, 1959). Although the primary focus in this chapter is on classroom learning, the same premise holds in other settings: If you designated a behavioral outcome, you need to organize the environment to aid the adolescent in achieving that behavior.

THE STRUCTURE OF LEARNING

Gagne (1977) defines learning as "a change in human disposition or capability which persists over a period of time, and which is not simply ascribable to processes of growth" (p. 3). Our best indication that learning has occurred is the appearance of a specific outcome behavior by the learner. It is not enough to assume that a learner who has been exposed to instruction, even carefully planned instruction, automatically gains the information or skills intended. The instructor must be able to specify in clear terms how the students can demonstrate the new knowledge.

Instructors should state in *precise behavioral terms* what constitutes successful learning. An instructor who intends to raise learners to an acceptable level of performance must be prepared to specify what "acceptable performance" means. Note that this is very similar to the assumptions underlying the competency-testing movement described in Chapter 4.

Outcomes may be categorized as intellectual skills, verbal information, cognitive strategies, motor skills, or attitudes. An important aspect of Gagne's model is the presumption that higher-level skills and outcomes depend on satisfactory completion of lower-level skills. A learner cannot enter problem-solving activities in the absence of prerequisite factual knowledge and concepts. Thus in organizing instruction the teacher must understand the structure of knowledge that underlies the desired outcomes.

Further, students should be informed of the types of outcome behaviors that are expected. How students study and try to learn depends on their understanding of the demands of the task at hand. Learners do what they are expected to do or what they *think* they are expected to do. Much of a student's time is directed toward "psyching out" the teacher to see what is expected. If instructors do not make their expectations clear, students are left to guess at what is demanded. The trouble, of course, is that what the students think the teacher desires may be way off the mark.

ASSOCIATIVE LEARNING

At the lowest skill level, the learner may feel that the task is one that demands rote memorization of facts. Although educators often scorn rote memorization, certain areas of information have no intrinsically meaningful organization; the learner must use rote memory. The names of bones in the human body, the color code for resistors, and other arbitrary sets of labels are examples of this kind of information. Learners often find mnemonic, or memory-aid, devices helpful for rote recall. For example, the relationship of the sides of a right triangle to sine, cosine, and tangent can be remembered by memorizing SOH-CAH-TOA, pronounced "soke-a-toa"—sine = *o*pposite over *h*ypotenuse, *c*osine = *a*djacent over *h*ypotenuse, and *t*angent = *o*pposite over *a*djacent.

CONCEPTUAL LEARNING

At an intermediate skill level, the learner may feel that the task demands categorization or organization of information. In this case the learner will study and learn in ways that allow, for example, inferences of how things go together or how to apply a principle.

As adult learners we take for granted a fairly sophisticated and wide-ranging set of concepts. That conceptual network is the result of considerable learning and experience. One only has to compare the concepts of adults and children to appreciate how refined those of adults are. For example, think about the concept of "dog." Although there is an almost infinite variety of dogs, we have little difficulty identifying dogs as such. We seldom confuse dogs with cats, even though some of their characteristics are strikingly similar. In contrast, children, particularly very young children, are notorious for confusing "cat" or "dog" with any variety of animal. Those of you who have any experience with deer hunting may be tempted to think that some adults who shoot cows have a very inadequate concept of "deer." In a sense they overgeneralize an already very rudimentary concept.

What, then, is a concept? If the term is to be of use to teachers, then we should be able to identify the concept of "concept." That task, however, is not as easy as it sounds. In general when we speak of concepts, we tend to think of a common label for some variety of examples or objects. Thus we classify a variety of dishes under the broad category "dish," or "china." Likewise, "china" and "China" are different concepts, even though they are phonetically the same. An example of a word with a variety of uses is "pitch," which is associated with at least a dozen different concepts. For purposes of this chapter, however, concepts are categories of a variety of stimuli, which are seen as belonging together because of some definable and identifiable relationship between or among a set of *attributes*. The extent to which we have a clear definition of a concept depends on how well we know its critical features. An attribute refers to any *quality, subcategory, feature,* or *characteristic* that can be used to describe a concept—for example, size, color, mass, shape, and so on. A given attribute may not be unique to one concept. The attribute "stripes," for example, is common to tiger, barber pole, candy cane, zebra, and others. Stripes, in each case, are insufficient to define the concept. They need to be joined with some other attributes. The more unique (or the more precise) the definition, the greater the differentiation of the intended concept from other similar concepts.

Consider the concept "scrim." Unless you have had experience in theatre, the concept is probably unfamiliar. A scrim is a special stage curtain that is transparent when lighted from behind. When lighted from the front, it appears opaque. Thus special stage effects can be achieved by having one or more actors on each side of the scrim. For a learner to possess the concept of "scrim," then, requires a clear understanding of its attributes. The learner needs to be able to differentiate "scrim" from other stage curtains.

The ability of adolescents to recognize or generate abstract or concrete attributes may be limited if they have not yet made the transition to formal thought. When asked to respond to the question "Who am I?" younger children and adolescents are likely to list their physical traits, whereas older adolescents are likely to relate abstract attitudes and personality characteristics (Montemayor and Eisen, 1977).

Likewise, some curricula are loaded with abstract concepts. Adolescents who have not yet made the transition to formal thought may have difficulty in grasping concepts with no concrete referents. In some cases instructors may need to develop concrete analogs, or demonstrations. Biology teachers, for example, often use concrete schematic representations of a double helix to convey the structure of DNA, which cannot be seen.

To learn a concept means that we are able to generalize across several different cases and abstract some commonality. Glaser (1968) proposes that concept formation proceeds through a series of three stages: (1) the learner identifies the attributes of a variety of events; (2) the learner abstracts the common characteristics of the events and groups them; and (3) the learner applies a categorization label.

If we define a concept by its attributes and the relationship among those attributes, then the instructor who wishes to teach about a given concept should have a clear, precise definition available. Very often you will find, however, that some attributes are much more obvious than others. It may be the less-obvious attributes that distinguish one concept from another. For example, to the untrained, baroque and gothic architecture may seem to be the same.

PROBLEM SOLVING

At the highest skill level, the learner understands the task to require creative thinking or problem solving. At this level the learner needs to use strategies for pulling together different pieces of information in new ways (new for the learner, at least) to resolve some dilemma. Figure B-1 (p. 339) presents a problem that demands this kind of thinking; please try to solve it now.

Some critics of contemporary education claim that schools are biased toward emphasizing critical thinking to the exclusion of original thinking, creativity, or curiosity. Silverman (1970) writes:

> It is not possible to spend any prolonged period of time visiting public school classrooms without being appalled by the mutilation visible everywhere—mutilation of spontaneity, of joy in learning, of pleasure in creating, of sense of self. (p. 10)

That is to say, students and teachers alike are compelled to be certain in their

Figure B-1 THE SQUARE PROBLEM

How many squares are in this figure?

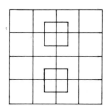

Answer: _____

How sure of your answer are you?

Totally
Sure   Sure   Unsure   Totally
Unsure

knowledge, as if all current knowledge were permanent. Uncertainty and doubt are not acceptable states of knowledge.

Berlyne (1960, 1965) has presented a model of productive thinking based on the assumption that when learners are uncertain or, as Berlyne prefers, suffer cognitive conflict, the uncertainty gives rise to curiosity. Curiosity then impels the learner to seek out information to resolve the dilemma that aroused the uncertainty. Repeated success at resolving dilemmas leads to the development of epistemic curiosity, or curiosity about knowledge itself. Epistemic curiosity reflects an attitude of simple pleasure in learning for learning's sake. Day and Langevin (1969) state that encouraging curiosity is fundmental to developing creative behavior.

Learners in the schools are not in the habit of allowing themselves to be uncertain. Seiber (1969) describes the behavior of school-age children responding to a relatively simple problem. Given a question, they had to answer and also indicate how certain or uncertain they were of their answer. Irrespective of the correctness or incorrectness of their answers, the children were uniformly certain that they were right. They seemed unwilling or unable to allow themselves the luxury of admitting they were not sure. Seiber has labeled this attitude secondary ignorance—they don't know that they don't know.

You were asked to solve the problem in Figure B-1 at the beginning of this section. I find a similar pattern of secondary ignorance among high school and college-age students, as well as among most adults, in this problem. The problem is stated in reasonably simple terms: "How many squares are there?" To solve the problem you must break set and look for squares that extend boundaries across other lines. What is interesting is not the number of people who come up with the right answer (only about 15 percent) but the number of people who are wrong but rate themselves as sure or totally sure that they are right. In one test, of the ninety-nine who were in error, only fourteen rated themselves as uncertain. How sure of your answer are you now? Learning that others have not done well probably shakes your confidence. Therein lies one of the most useful techniques for inducing uncertainty in learners. The teacher may offer new information that does not agree with what the learner believes or thinks is true. (The correct total of squares is forty.)

Secondary ignorance is particularly dysfunctional to original thinking and problem solving. If you are certain that you have the "truth," you stop searching and stop asking questions. To maintain a moderate degree of uncertainty is psychologically beneficial. Uncertainty motivates you to gather more information and thereby to create a more elaborate cognitive structure. Instructors should capitalize on the motivating effects of uncertainty.

Once again, adolescence is a particularly prime time for using this motivation. Adolescents are often enamored of potential incongruities and eager to reorganize them. Often this takes the form of challenging authority as inconsistent or hypocritical. Religion is frequently a target of this questioning. Adolescents begin to reorganize the abstract nature of many of the concepts they have been taught. Often they note seeming inconsistencies in biblical writings and point them out with the question, "How do you explain *that*?" An effective instructor would capitalize on the uncertainty and develop the dilemma into a useful teaching lesson.

The dilemma and the motivation to resolve it are the fundamental elements of discovery learning, or problem-based instruction. The principle is reasonably straightforward: The instructor capitalizes on the intrinsic desire of learners to reduce the uncertainty aroused by a dilemma. Once a learner resolves a dilemma, the principle that emerges is not easily forgotten. In addition, uncertainty, in moderate amounts, seems to be pleasant. I have used the problem in Figure B-2 as a source of discussion not only in algebra classes but also in classes much like the one you are now attending.

In creating a problem for discovery learning, or problem-based instruction, the teacher presents learners with information that has a certain degree of ambiguity. That ambiguity may result from omitting some pieces of information. The omitted information becomes crucial to reducing the ambiguity. The

Figure B-2 DISCUSSION-STARTER FOR DISCOVERY LEARNING

$A = B$	A statement of equality.
$A^2 = AB$	Equals multiplied by equals are equal.
$A^2 - B^2 = AB - B^2$	Equals subtracted from equals are equal.
$(A+B)(A-B) = B(A-B)$	Both sides are factored.
$(A+B)\,\cancel{(A-B)} = B\cancel{(A-B)}$	Equals divided by equals are equal.
$(A+B) = B$	
$B + B = B$	
$2B = B$	Substitution ——————→ Statement 1
$2 = 1$	

teacher *leads* the learner to realize this lack of knowledge, and the student is motivated to reduce the uncertainty by searching out that information. As long as the uncertainty is not overwhelming, learners will be motivated to reduce the gap between what they *know* and what they *need* to know.

Berlyne (1960, 1965) has suggested that uncertainty and curiosity are aroused by particularly qualitative characteristics of a dilemma. These characteristics are grouped according to the effect they have. For present purposes, we will restate some of the variables in terms of teacher behaviors.

1. *Generate doubt.* The teacher creates uncertainty by introducing evidence that forces learners into a situation in which they have a tendency to disbelieve what they previously believed.
2. *Generate perplexity.* The teacher leads the students to accept alternative, but mutually exclusive, beliefs.
3. *Introduce contradiction.* The teacher introduces new information that is incongruent with the learners' present belief. (This really is a special case of doubt.)
4. *Generate conceptual incongruity.* The teacher creates a situation in which two or more events that normally do not occur together now apparently do.
5. *Create confusion.* The teacher creates a situation in which learners (with their present level of knowledge) are not capable of accepting new information incongruent with their existing beliefs. The information is such that the learners are unable to suggest alternative hypotheses.
6. *Create response irrelevance.* Although Berlyne offers this as a source of uncertainty, it appears that it is a special case that leads to inefficient behavior. That is, learners may be presented with a problem to which they can offer no plausible response, and they thus generate irrelevant responses. Such a situation may lead to overwhelming frustration and thwart future information-seeking behavior.

Crucial to the whole concept of uncertainty and discovery learning is the notion that a gap exists between what the learner knows and what he or she needs to know to respond to a dilemma. Once this gap is reorganized, the learner can act to obtain the necessary knowledge. Uncertainty occurs when the learner is left with the question "Who?", "What?", "Where?", "When?", or "How?"

RECEPTION LEARNING

A common myth in education and psychology is that meaningful instruction occurs only with discovery learning techniques and that learning by listening to lectures or by reading is inherently second class. David Ausubel (1963, 1967; Ausubel, Novak, and Honesian, 1978) points out that instruction based on lecture or reading can be meaningful if it is appropriately structured or organized.

For information to be meaningful, the learner must be able to relate it to an existing knowledge base (cognitive structures) in a "nonarbitrary, substantive fashion" (Ausubel, Novak, and Honesian, 1978, p. 27). Rote learning is characterized by an arbitrary association of labels and stimuli. We can acquire rote information with little knowledge of why labels and stimuli go together. As we noted earlier, some knowledge is by nature rote or arbitrary and nonsubstantive. However, most learning that has any transfer value is not, and therefore should not be taught by rote methods.

When the instructor is introducing new information and the learner has no useful knowledge base within which to subsume (incorporate) the new concepts, the instructor may desire to use an *advance organizer*. An advance organizer is a paragraph-length presentation that charts the general organization of the concepts of concern. Although Ausubel maintains that the advance organizer is not an overview, the structure of most advance organizers seems to serve that function. The advance organizer provides the learner with a rudimentary working schema.

Ausubel warns instructors that the logical organization of concepts may or may not correspond with the psychological organization imposed by the learner. The learner's ability to generate a logical structure is a function of his or her existing knowledge base, developmental status, intellectual ability, motives, and personality factors. Ausubel presumes that for meaningful learning to occur, the learner must not only interpret the task as requiring meaningful, rather than rote, learning but must also have a motive to try to learn meaningfully.

Instruction should relate new concepts and information to the learners' existing knowledge base. Instructors should aid learners to reconcile each new concept with existing knowledge, at the same time they identify the key characteristics that differentiate it from other similar concepts. Failure to maintain some degree of uniqueness of new concepts may later lead to the learners' inability to separate the new information from the old cognitive structures.

ENCOURAGING CLASSROOM DISCUSSION

Teachers often enter a classroom intending to lead their class in lively discussion of a timely topic. After introducing the topic and setting the stage for a heated discussion, the teacher is met with total silence. Fearing that the class does not understand the issue, the teacher goes on to elaborate. Eventually, the teacher throws in the towel and reverts to lecture. Later the teacher may grumble to colleagues about the students' unwillingness to participate.

Most often the mistake that teachers make in this situation occurs right at the beginning. After you have made your opening remarks, be quiet. If you have said what you wanted to say, close your mouth and give the students a chance to respond or to formulate a response. The silence may seem endless; however, it also has its effects on the students. Sooner or later, one of the students will break the silence. If that student's contribution does not elicit reactions from other students, react to the student with a follow-up question that probes the depth of his or her understanding. *Probing* is a teacher response to the student's statement that is intended to force the student to extend the boundaries of the original response (Gliessman, 1977). In another case the teacher may wish to probe another student in the class on the basis of the first response—for example, "Harold, how do you feel about what Jane said?"

The teacher may also use a student's response as an opportunity to *inform* the class of relevant information that they may not possess. Once again, when you have finished providing the needed information and have redirected the discussion, remain quiet. Your function in classroom discussion is to facilitate rather than to dominate. An effective discussion leader guides and encourages interchange, inserting relevant information where appropriate.

Gliessman (1977) suggests that in addition to *probing* and *informing*, the teacher may vary the type of questions, asking for *productive* or *reproductive* responses. Reproductive questioning requires the student to reproduce specific information (for example, "What does the First Amendment to the U.S. Constitution guarantee?" or "What is the largest city in Nova Scotia?"). Reproductive questioning requires lower-level transformations of the type described earlier (DiVesta, 1971). Productive questioning, however, requires the student to manipulate the information and generate a response (for example, "What impact would the secession of Quebec from Canada have on the U.S. or Canadian economy?" or "How would you measure the volume of an ashtray?"). Productive questioning requires middle- or upper-level responses from Bloom's taxonomy (Bloom, 1956).

In facilitating classroom (or other) discussion, the teacher may offer feedback. In some cases you may wish to be directive (for example, "No, that's wrong. You probably made a mistake in. . . ."), or you may wish to be less direct (for example, "How do you account for. . .?"). A teacher often needs to maintain a delicate balance between encouraging student responding behavior without directly accepting specific responses.

It is important to remember that as adolescents are making the transition to formal operational thought, they may be unable to express their thoughts clearly. Their verbal ability may not be adequate to relate their thoughts. A discussion leader can help with judicious rewording, such as "Now let me see if I understand you. Are you saying. . .?" or "Tell me if I'm following your line of thought." If you have misunderstood, the adolescent will be only too glad to correct you. If, however, you offer a clearer statement of what the individual was trying to express, he or she will likely appreciate the help, as long as it is not patronizing. Note that reformulation should be separated from informing. Rewording also provides the student with an example of an effective statement of the thought. Again, once the student's position is clarified, be silent and let the discussion progress.

The important feature to remember is that as a facilitator you are in charge of the discussion without dominating it. You should have some idea of where the discussion is likely to lead and what outcomes should emerge. Because the expected and desired outcomes sometimes fail to emerge, be sure to have a backup strategy in mind.

SUMMARY

Teaching is a demanding profession. Effectively transmitting a body of knowledge to learners with a variety of backgrounds, abilities, and motives tests the wisdom of the best of us. However, teaching adolescents is not impossible, and indeed most teachers do quite well. I often ask my students to think of the high school teachers that they felt had the most positive impact on them. I then ask them why those teachers were the most important. The answers range from the way a teacher treated students to the teacher's enthusiasm for the subject matter. You might benefit from asking yourself those questions. What does your conclusion about that teacher mean to you in terms of your own future activities with adolescents?

I have argued here that effective teachers need to specify what learning outcomes they wish to achieve. Teachers must analyze the content, determine the learners' entering abilities, and then sequence the instruction in accordance with that information. Teachers should attempt to explain to the students what kinds of outcomes they expect. If higher-level thinking is desired, then instruction must be meaningfully related to the learner's existing knowledge base, and the learner must be given an opportunity to apply a principle in testlike settings.

One last comment: The primary focus in this appendix has been teaching as it relates to cognitive achievement. To separate the affective or emotional domain as I have done, however, is misleading. The impact of a teacher on a learner's feelings of self-worth can be pervasive. Perhaps your answer to the question I just asked had little to do with content areas but instead related to how the teacher made you feel about yourself. As I have emphasized repeatedly in this text, the importance of our feelings of self-worth cannot be overstated.

Glossary

abortion The natural or therapeutic expulsion of a fetus.

accommodation Piaget's term for the process of altering existing schema to meet the demands of new information.

achievement In schooling, the attainment of specified levels of knowledge.

achievement motivation Hypothetical motive to excel or to compete against a standard of excellence in an achievement-oriented setting.

achievement tests Standardized instruments designed to assess levels of academic accomplishment in specific or general areas.

acne (acne vulgaris) A common skin problem of adolescence, characterized by an excessive eruption of blackheads and whiteheads.

addiction Physiological or psychological dependence on a drug.

adolescence A period of personal development during which a young person develops a sense of individual identity and feelings of self-worth, including adaptation to an altered body image, improved intellectual ability, demands for behavioral maturity, and preparation for adult roles.

adolescent An individual going through adolescence.

adolescent society A term used by James Coleman to refer to the demands for common language, behavior, values, and dress codes that dominate the youth population.

adolescent transition See **adolescence.**

advance organizer A paragraph-length presentation occurring before a lecture or reading passage, which charts the general organization of the concepts of concern.

affect An individual's feelings or attitudes.

alcohol A depressant drug, called ethanol.

amphetamines A class of stimulant drugs.

anorexia nervosa A disease, most often occurring in young women, in which the patient loses appetite and excessive amounts of weight. The disease usually has a psychological base and takes the form of a food phobia.

aptitudes General or specific abilities related to the potential to succeed in some domain.

assimilation Piaget's term for the act of altering information to meet the existing structure of an individual's schema.

authoritarian parents Parents who offer little emotional support but exert strong, dogmatic control.

authoritative parents Parents who offer high emotional support and exert strong control.

barbiturates A class of depressant drugs.

blood-alcohol level The percent of alcohol in an individual's bloodstream.

body image An individual's perception of how adequate his or her body is in relation to some idealized body.

capitalization strategy A strategy for intervention that takes advantage of the individual's strengths.

career education An organized set of experiences to introduce a young person to career alternatives and to aid in the development of career goals.

child abuse The physical or mental injury, sexual abuse, negligent treatment, or mistreatment of a child under the age of eighteen by a person who is responsible for the child's welfare.

cliques Closely knit groups of peers who typically exclude others from group membership.

cognitive development Changes in intellectual ability that occur as an individual progresses from infancy through adulthood.

cognitive theory Psychological theories that emphasize active, purposeful, conceptual thinking.

cohort A group of persons who share a common experience.

coitus Sexual intercourse.

compensatory intervention Intervention strategies that are intended to provide some mechanisms or skills to compensate for the individual's limitations.

concrete operations Thought processes, especially among elementary-school-age children and young adolescents, that are tied to concrete examples. The third stage of Piaget's theory of cognitive development.

contraception Use of birth control procedures or devices.

conventional morality The middle stages of moral development described by Kohlberg. The motive for morality is primarily social approval, and morality is seen in arbitrary, concrete terms.

conversion experience An intellectual and/or emotional religious experience that deepens religious faith.

correlation A measure of the degree to which two variables are related.

creativity The ability to offer unique and divergent responses to common events.

cross-sectional research Developmental research in which differences in age groups are assessed by measuring individuals grouped at different ages.

cultural bias A test structure that benefits individuals from one group but not another.

defense mechanisms Coping strategies used by an individual to reduce or avoid anxiety.

delinquent behavior Criminal or illegal activity, typically associated with juvenile offenders.

denial A defense mechanism in which unwanted information is ignored. It is a refusal to admit that the information exists.

dependent variable In an experiment, the outcome variable to be studied.

depressants Drugs that serve to slow down nervous system activity.

depression A psychological state of despondency and dejection that may lead to lack of motivation.

developmental goals Skills and objectives that need to be attained in order to adapt at one stage of life and prepare for the next.

disequilibrium A state of uncertainty in which an individual's schema fails to account for a perceived reality.

drug abuse The use of any drug that interferes with the normal functioning of an individual at home, work, or school.

early maturation Significantly premature emergence of primary and secondary sexual characteristics.

ecological research The study of human (or animal) behavior in natural, unaltered settings.

ectomorph A body type characterized by leanness.

egocentrism The assumption that one's own view of reality is the only true perspective.

ego ideal An idealized system of moral values.

ejaculation Emission of seminal fluid.

endomorph A body type characterized by excessive fat tissue.

equilibrium A state of balance. In cognitive theory, it refers to a balance achieved between new information and existing schema.

experiment A controlled pattern of observation in which a researcher systematically manipulates one or more characteristics of the environment and records the outcome.

experimenter bias The intentional or unintentional influencing of the results of an experiment to conform to the experimenter's expectations.

extinction A behavioral term referring to the elimination of behavior by withholding reinforcers.

faith development Changes in religious or faith concepts that occur as an individual matures.

fear of failure A general motive in which an individual's achievement is affected by the degree to which he or she is anxious about not succeeding.

fear of success A hypothetical motive in which achievement is affected by an individual's anxiety about being excluded for being overly successful.

formal operations (formal thinking) Thought patterns that allow for abstract, hypothetico-deductive thinking. Piaget's fourth stage of cognitive development.

functional illiteracy The inability to read well enough to perform the basic skills necessary to get along in society.

gangs Highly structured groups that may be organized around illegal or delinquent activities.

gender roles Expectations of behaviors that are based solely on one's sex.

generation gap A widely held belief in extreme differences in attitudes between adults and adolescents.

genius Exceptional talent and creativity in a given area.

gonorrhea An epidemic venereal disease caused by the bacteria gonococci; treatable with antibiotics.

hallucinogens (psychedelics) Drugs capable of producing alterations in perceptions, such as illusions, hallucinations, and distortions of reality.

herpes simplex virus II A venereal disease caused by the herpes simplex virus. There is no currently available cure.

heterosexuality Sexual behavior involving individuals of both sexes.

homosexuality Sexual behavior between individuals of the same sex.

identity crisis A major reorganization of the adolescent's self-concept, which emerges from a desire to establish oneself as a unique person.

identity foreclosure The avoidance of an identity crisis by the early commitment to an intact identity, usually provided by parents.

identity formation The lifelong process of developing a personal conception of oneself.

identity moratorium The period in which the adolescent delays fixing upon a final identity and experiments with alternative identities.

independent variables In an experiment, those variables that are under the direct or indirect control of the researcher.

individualized treatment plan (ITP) A specific plan of therapy or intervention based on an individual's strengths, weaknesses, and long-term and short-term goals.

inhalants A class of psychoactive chemicals that produce intoxication or altered perception when their fumes are inhaled.

intellectualization A defense mechanism in which unwanted feelings are analyzed in a detached, rational fashion.

intelligence The general ability to solve problems and to act in a purposeful manner.

intelligence quotient (IQ) The ratio created by dividing an individual's chronological age (CA) by his or her mental age (MA) and multiplying by 100. No longer in general use but now often used as a generic term to refer to intelligence.

invisible audience An imaginary group of people that an adolescent feels is watching every move and is concerned with his or her behavior and appearance.

isolation A defense mechanism in which unwanted information is seen as somehow distinct from what is already known.

juvenile delinquent A young person who has committed a crime and has been labeled by the courts as a juvenile offender.

late maturation Significantly delayed emergence of primary and secondary sexual characteristics.

locus of control The source of an individual's perceived control of events, either internal (self) or external (others).

longitudinal research Studies of maturation and development in which changes in behavior with age are measured on a single group of people over an extended period of time.

mainstreaming The integration of handicapped youngsters into regular classrooms.

masturbation Sexual self-, or autoerotic, stimulation.

maturation Developmental changes that result from genetic predispositions or age rather than from experience.

menarche First menses, the onset of menstruation.

menses The normal expulsion of blood and unused ova during the woman's menstrual cycle.

mental retardation Impaired intellectual ability ranging from moderate to profound restriction of ability.

modeling The learning of behaviors by imitation, or copying the behaviors of a significant other person.

moral development Changes in concepts of morality that occur as an individual matures.

mnemonics Memory aids or devices useful for rote recall.

narcotic Medically, a drug used to inhibit pain; more generally, any illegal drug.

naturalistic observation Studying and recording behavior as it occurs in the natural environment, without any manipulation or interference by the researcher.

negative identity The acceptance of a socially disapproved identity as one's own.

negative reinforcement A behavioral term referring to the removal of an aversive stimulus following a desired behavior.

neglectful parents A parenting style in which parents offer little emotional support and exert little or no control.

nocturnal emission Ejaculation of semen by the male during sleep; also called a "wet dream."

obesity Excessive accumulation of body fat.

obtrusiveness Alteration of normal behavior by the mere presence of an observer, experimenter, or unusual device.

occupational prestige The general status afforded a given occupational category.

opiates A general class of drugs derived from real or synthetic opium.

peers Individuals who share some common attribute(s), such as age, sex, race, socioeconomic level, and so on.

percentile Relative standing in a population indicating the percentage who score lower than a given point.

permissive parents Parents who offer high emotional support but exert little control.

personal fable A form of adolescent egocentrism described by Elkind, in which the person sees himself or herself as totally unique in thoughts and feelings.

PL 94-142 (Education of all Handicapped Children Act) Federal legislation requiring that all handicapped children be educated in the least restrictive environment.

positive reinforcement A behavioral term referring to the presentation of a pleasant stimulus following a desired behavior.

postconventional morality The advanced stages of moral development described by Kohlberg, in which morality is seen in abstract, relativistic, and universal terms.

preconventional morality The early stages of moral development described by Kohlberg, in which motives for morality are primarily defined by self-gratification.

primary sexual characteristics The genitals, which at puberty reach adult status and are essential for sexual reproduction.

projection A defense mechanism in which the blame for unacceptable thoughts or behaviors is directed at someone else.

pseudostupidity Apparent but not real inability of adolescents to solve complex problems, in which a discrepancy exists between real knowledge and the ability to display the knowledge.

psychoanalytic theory Theories of personality development rooted in Sigmund Freud's writings. Personality development is seen in light of satisfactory or unsatisfactory resolution of psychosexual stages.

psychopathology Diseases that are psychological in origin and that result in severe distortion of reality.

psychosomatic illness Illness that results when psychological factors influence bodily functions.

puberty The stage of maturation at which an individual becomes physically capable of sexual reproduction.

pubescence The onset of the transition to adult sexual maturity; the coming of puberty.

rationalization A defense mechanism in which the individual offers a plausible explanation to justify otherwise unacceptable behavior.

reception learning The acquisition of knowledge through meaningful prose.

reinforcement A behavioral term referring to any event that increases the likelihood of the behavior that immediately preceded it being repeated.

religiosity Degree of commitment to a set of religious values.

repression A defense mechanism in which unwanted or unacceptable thoughts are forced back into the unconscious.

rites of passage Initiation ceremonies that mark the entry of a young person into adult status.

role diffusion The failure to achieve a clear personal identity.

schema A collection of bits of knowledge organized into a pattern that aids our interpretation of our environment.

schizophrenia A psychotic disturbance characterized by severe distortion of perceptions of reality, especially the inability to distinguish fact from fantasy.

secondary gain Social or psychological advantages that result from others responding to features of a disease or disability.

secondary ignorance Not knowing that you do not know.

secondary sexual characteristics Physical features of maleness or femaleness that emerge at pubescence but that are not essential for sexual reproduction; for example, pubic hair and breasts.

secular trend Changes in physical maturation patterns seen over successive generations.

self-concept The set of attributes an individual uses to describe himself or herself.

self-esteem The net value or worth that an individual places on the elements of his or her self-concept.

self-fulfilling prophesy An event occurring because it is *expected* to occur.

self-image The set of perceptions that an individual has about himself or herself.

sex education The systematic instruction in the elements of human and nonhuman sexuality.

socialization The learning of the values, attitudes, and skills of the society within which an individual must function.

socioeconomic status Relative social status, related to family income, education, and prestige.

sociogram A technique for measuring the relative popularity of individuals in an existing group.

sociometric status The relative popularity of an individual in a group.

sociopathic Chronically using illegal or immoral behavior without any feelings of guilt or concern for the victims.

somatotypes Body or physique types described by Sheldon, which are associated with specific personality characteristics.

status offenses Offenses that are defined as illegal only for specific subgroups of society on the basis of some characteristic—for example, age or sex.

stimulants Drugs that excite or speed up the activity of the central nervous system.

storm and stress A phrase used by G. Stanley Hall and some other social scientists to describe the tumultuous characteristics of adolescence.

sublimation A defense mechanism in which unacceptable thoughts are disguised and expressed in socially acceptable forms.

syphilis A sexually transmitted disease caused by spirochetes. It is usually treated effectively with antibiotics.

teenager A general term, usually used by adults, to refer to an adolescent. The term implies that adolescence is tied to the "teen" years.

tolerance The increased ability of the body to

withstand the effects of a given drug, so that increased doses of the drug are needed to achieve a desired effect.

unsocialized aggressive reaction Impulsive, uncontrolled expression of hostility and aggression. Typically, this impulsiveness dissipates with maturity and improved socialization, in contrast to sociopathy.

vandalism Willful, malicious destruction of property.

variable A measurable trait that may have different states or values—for example, sex, achievement, age, race.

variance The spread of a group of scores around the average score.

venereal disease (VD) A disease that is transmitted sexually.

vocational development Changes in concepts of vocational goals that occur as an individual matures.

References

ABEL, D. Can a student sue the schools for educational malpractice? *Harvard Educational Review*, 1974, *44*, 416–436.

ABELSON, H. I., and FISHBURNE, P.M. *Nonmedical use of psychoactive substances: 1975–6 nationwide study among youths and adults. Part 1: Main findings.* Princeton, N.J.: Response Analysis, 1976.

ABELSON, H. I., FISHBURNE, P. M., and CISIN, I. *National survey on drug abuse, 1977: A nationwide study of youth, young adults and older people, vol. 1, Main findings.* National Institute on Drug Abuse. Washington, D.C.: U.S. Government Printing Office, 1978.

ADELSON, J. The myth of a generation gap. *Psychology Today*, 1979, *12*(9), 33–34, 37.

ADLER, N. J. Emotional responses of women following therapeutic abortion. *American Journal of Orthopsychiatry*, 1975, *45*, 446–454.

ADLER, C., BAZEMORE, G., and POLK, K. Delinquency in nonmetropolitan areas. In D. Shichor and D. H. Kelly (eds.), *Critical issues in juvenile delinquency*. Lexington, Mass.: Lexington Books, 1980.

ALEXANDER, K. L., and ECKLAND, B. K. School experience and status attainment. In S. E. Dragastian and G. H. Elder (eds.), *Adolescence in the life cycle*. New York: John Wiley, 1975.

ALLEN, R. O., and SPILKA, B. Committed and consensual religion: A specification of religion-prejudice relationships. *Journal of the Scientific Study of Religion*, 1967, *6*, 191–206.

ALTMAN, I. Environmental psychology: At the start of something big. *Contemporary Psychology*, 1975, *20*, 205–207.

ANASTASION, N. J.; GRIMMETT, S. A.; EGGLESTON, P. J.; and O'SHAUGHNESSY, T. E. Educational implications of earlier sexual maturation. *Phi Delta Kappan*, 1974, *56*, 198–200.

ANDRISANI, P. J. The establishment of stable and successful employment careers: The role of work attitudes and labor market knowledge. Conference report on youth unemployment: Its measurement and meaning. U.S. Department of Labor. Washington, D.C.: U.S. Government Printing Office, 1978.

ANSELL, E. M., and HANSEN, J. C. Patterns in vocational development of urban youth. *Journal of Counseling Psychology*, 1971, *18*, 505–508.

ARNOLD, C. B. The sexual behavior of inner city adolescent condom users. *Journal of Sex Research*, 1972, *8*, 298–309.

AUSUBEL, D. P. *The psychology of meaningful verbal learning.* New York: Grune and Stratton, 1963.

AUSUBEL, D. P. A cognitive-structure theory of school learning. In L. Siegal (ed.), *Instruction: Some contemporary viewpoints*. San Francisco: Chandler, 1967.

AUSUBEL, D. P., MONTEMAYOR, R., and SVAJIAN, P. *Theory and problems of adolescent development.* 2nd ed. New York: Grune and Stratton, 1977.

AUSUBEL, D. P., NOVAK, J. D., and HANESIAN, H. *Educational psychology: A cognitive view.* 2nd ed. New York: Holt, Rinehart and Winston, 1978.

AVERY, D., and WINOKUR, G. Suicide, attempted suicide and relapse rates in depression. *Archives of General Psychiatry*, 1978, *35*, 749–753.

BABIN, P. *Adolescents in search of a new church.* New York: Herder and Herder, 1969.

BACHMAN, J. G., GREEN, S., and WIRTANEN, I. *Dropping-out—Problem or symptom? Youth in transition, vol. 3.* Ann Arbor, Mich.: Institute for Social Research, 1971.

BACHMAN, J. G., O'MALLEY, P. M., and JOHNSTON, J. *Adolescence to adulthood—Change and stability in the lives of young men. Youth in transition, vol. 6.* Ann Arbor, Michigan: Institute for Social Behavior, 1978.

BACKMAN, M. E. Patterns of mental abilities: Ethnic, socioeconomic and sex differences. *American Educational Research Journal,* 1972, *9,* 1–12.

BAIN, R. K., and ANDERSON, J. G. School context and peer influences on educational plans of adolescents. *Review of Educational Research,* 1974, *44,* 429–445.

BAKER, O. V., DRUCKMAN, J. N., and FLAGLE, J. E. The identification and development of community-based approaches for meeting the social and therapeutic needs of youth in variant family configurations characterized by divorce, separation and family separation. Executive summary. Palo Alto: American Institutes for Research, 1980.

BALDWIN, B. T. *A measuring scale for physical growth and physiological age.* Fifteenth Annual Yearbook of the National Society for the Study of Education, pt. 1. Chicago: University of Chicago Press, 1916.

BALDWIN, W. H. Adolescent pregnancy and childbearing: Growing concern for Americans. *Population Bulletin,* 1976, *31*(2).

BALDWIN, W. H. Testimony before the House Select Committee on Population. vol. 2, Washington, D.C.: U.S. Government Printing Office, 1978.

BALTES, P. B. Prototypical paradigms and questions in life-span research on development and aging. *Gerontologist,* 1973, *13,* 458–467.

BANDURA, A. The stormy decade: Fact or fiction. *Psychology in the Schools,* 1964, *1,* 224–231.

BANDURA, A. Behavior theory and the models of man. *American Psychologist,* 1974, *29,* 859–869.

BANDURA, A., and MCDONALD, F. J. Influence of social reinforcement and the behavior of models in shaping children's moral judgments. *Journal of Abnormal and Social Psychology,* 1963, *67,* 274–281.

BANDURA, A., and WALTERS, R. H. *Adolescent aggression: A study of child-training practices and family interactions.* New York: Ronald Press, 1959.

BARDWICK, J. M. and DOUVAN, E. Ambivalence: The socialization of women. In K. Gornick and B. K. Moran (eds.), *Woman in sexist society.* New York: Basic Books, 1971.

BARKER, R. G. Explorations in ecological psychology. *American Psychologist,* 1965, *20,* 1–14.

BARNES, H. V. Physical growth and development. In H. V. Barnes (ed.), *The Medical Clinics of North America,* 1975, *59,* 1305–1317.

BARNES, H. V., and BERGER, R. An approach to the obese adolescent. In H. V. Barnes (ed.), *The Medical Clinics of North America,* 1975, *59,* 1507–1516.

BARRY, H. III, BACON, M. K., and CHILD, I. L. Cultural survey of some sex differences in socialization. *Journal of Abnormal and Social Psychology,* 1957, *3,* 327–332.

BAUMRIND, D. Authoritarian vs. authoritative control. *Adolescence,* 1968, *3,* 255–272.

BAUMRIND, D. Early socialization and adolescent competence. In S. E. Dragastian and G. H. Elder (eds.), *Adolescence in the life cycle.* New York: John Wiley, 1975.

BAYH, B. (chairman). Our nation's schools—A report card: "A" in school violence and vandalism. Report of the U.S. Senate Committee on the Judiciary. Washington, D.C.: U.S. Government Printing Office, 1975.

BAYH, B. (chairman). Challenge for the third century: Education in a safe environment. Final report on the nature and prevention of school violence and vandalism. Report of the U.S. Senate Committee on the Judiciary. Washington, D.C.: U.S. Government Printing Office, 1977.

BAYLEY, N. Research in child development: A longitudinal perspective. *Merrill-Palmer Quarterly of Behavior and Development,* 1965, *11,* 183–208.

BECKER, H. Deviance and the response of others. In D. R. Cressey and D. A. Ward (eds.), *Delinquency, crime and social process.* New York: Harper and Row, 1969.

BECKER, W. C. Consequences of different kinds of parental discipline. In M. L. Hoffman and L. W. Hoffman (eds.), *Review of child development research.* vol. 1. New York: Russell Sage, 1964.

BEIT-HALLAHMI, B. Self-reported religious concerns of university underclassmen. *Adolescence,* 1974, *9,* 333–338.

BELL, A. P., BRODERICK, C. B., and GOLDSMITH, S. "Adolescent sexuality in contemporary America": Three reviews. *SIECUS Report,* 1973, *2*(1), 1, 3, 11, 12.

BEREITER, C. The morality of moral education. *The Hastings Center Report,* 1978, *8*(2), 20–25.

BERLYNE, D. E. *Conflict, arousal and curiosity.* New York: McGraw-Hill, 1960.

BERLYNE, D. E. *Structure and direction in thinking.* New York: John Wiley, 1965.

BERSCHEID, E., and DION, K. Physical attractiveness and dating choice: A test of the matching hypothesis. *Journal of Experimental Social Psychology*, 1971, *7*, 173–189.

BHANJI, S., and THOMPSON, J. Operant conditioning in the treatment of anorexia nervosa: A review and retrospective study of 11 cases. *British Journal of Psychiatry*, 1974, *124*, 166–172.

BLACKFORD, L. Summary report—Surveys of student drug use, San Mateo County, California. San Mateo County Department of Public Health and Welfare, 1977.

BLALOCK, H. M. *Causal inferences from nonexperimental research*. Chapel Hill, N.C.: University of North Carolina Press, 1964.

BLASI, A., and HOEFFEL, E. C. Adolescence and formal operations. *Human Development*, 1974, *17*, 344–363.

BLAU, M. Why parents kick their children out. *Parents Magazine*, 1979, *54*, (Apr.), 64–69.

BLEULER, M. *The schizophrenic disorders: Long-term patient and family studies*. Trans. Siegfried M. Clemens. New Haven: Yale University Press, 1978.

BLITZER, P. H., BLITZER, E. C., and RIMM, A. A. Association between teenage obesity and cancer in 56,111 women: All cancers and endometrial carcinoma. *Preventive Medicine*, 1976, *5*, 20–31.

BLOCK, J. *Lives through time*. Berkeley, Calif.: Bancroft, 1971.

BLOOM, B. S. *Stability and change in human characteristics*. New York: John Wiley, 1964.

BLOOM, B. S.; ENGELHART, M. B.; FURST, E. J.; HILL, W. H.; and KRATHWOHL, D. R. *The cognitive domain*. Taxonomy of educational objectives: The classification of educational goals, handbook 1. New York: Longmans Green, 1956.

BLOS, P. *On adolescence*. New York: Free Press, 1952.

BLOS, P. The function of the ego ideal in adolescence. *The Psychoanalytic Study of the Child*, 1972, *27*, 43–97.

BLUM, R. H. *Horatio Alger's children: Role of the family in the origin and prevention of drug risk*. San Francisco: Jossey-Bass, 1972.

BLUM, R. H., and RICHARDS, L. Youthful drug use. In R. L. Dupont, D. Goldstein, and J. O'Donnell (eds.), *Handbook of drug abuse*. Washington, D.C.: U.S. Government Printing Office, 1979.

BORING, E. G. Intelligence as the tests test it. *New Republic*, 1923, *35* (June 6), 35–36.

BOROW, H. Career development. In J. F. Adams (ed.), *Understanding adolescence*. 3rd ed. Boston: Allyn and Bacon, 1976.

BRACHT, G. N.; FOLLINGSTAD, D.; BRAKASH, D.; and BERRY, K. L. Deviant drug use in adolescence: A review of psychological correlates. *Psychological Bulletin*, 1973, *79*, 92–106.

BRAUN, J., and BAYER, F. Social desirability of occupations: Revisited. *Vocational Guidance Quarterly*, 1973, *21*, 202–205.

BRICKELL, H. Seven key notes on minimum competency testing. *Phi Delta Kappan*, 1978, *59*, 589–592.

BRONFENBRENNER, U. Toward an experimental ecology of human development. *American Psychologist*, 1977, *32*, 513–531.

BROWN, J. K. Adolescent initiation rites: Recent interpretations. In R. E. Grinder (ed.), *Studies in adolescence*. 3rd ed. New York: Macmillan, 1975.

BRUCHE, H. Perceptual and conceptual disturbance in anorexia. *Psychosomatic Medicine*, 1962, *24*, 189–194.

BRUCHE, H. Perils of behavior modification in treatment of anorexia nervosa. *Journal of the American Medical Association*, 1974, *230*, 1419–1422.

BULLEN, B. A., REED, R. B., and MAYER, J. Physical activity of obese and nonobese adolescent girls appraised by motion picture sampling. *American Journal of Clinical Nutrition*, 1964, *14*, 211–223.

BURLINGAME, W. V. An investigation of the correlations of adherence to the adolescent peer culture. U.S. Office of Education. Washington, D.C.: U.S. Government Printing Office, 1967.

BURTON, R. V. Generality of honesty reconsidered. *Psychological Review*, 1963, *70*, 481–499.

BYRNE, D. *The attraction paradigm*. New York: Academic Press, 1971.

CALDWELL, R. G. *Juvenile delinquency*. New York: Ronald Press, 1971.

CALLAHAN, D., CISIN, I. H., and CROSSLEY, H. M. *American drinking practices. A national study of drinking behavior and attitudes*. Monograph No. 6. New Brunswick, N.J.: Rutgers Center on Alcohol Studies, 1974.

CAMPBELL, D. T., and STANLEY, J. C. *Experimental and quasi-experimental designs for research*. Chicago: Rand-McNally, 1966.

CANNING, H., and MAYER, J. Obesity: An influence on high school performance. *American Journal of Clinical Nutrition*, 1967, *20*, 352–354.

CASTANZO, P. R., and SHAW, M. E. Conformity as a function of age level. *Child Development*, 1966, *37*, 967–975.

CASTER, J. Share our own specialty: What is mainstreaming? *Exceptional Children*, 1975, *42*, 174.

CATTELL, R. B. *Abilities: Their structure, growth and action.* Boston: Houghton Mifflin, 1971.

CATTELL, R. B., and CATTELL, A. K. S. *Handbook for the Culture Fair Intelligence Test.* Champagne, Ill.: Institute for Personality Testing, 1960.

CAVIOR, N., and DOKECKI, P. R. Physical attractiveness, perceived similarity and academic achievement as potential contributors to interpersonal attraction among adolescents. *Developmental Psychology*, 1973, 9, 44–54.

CENTER FOR DISEASE CONTROL. *VD fact sheet, 1976.* 33rd ed. Atlanta, Georgia, 1977.

CHAMBLISS, W. The saints and the roughnecks. *Society*, 1973, 11 (Nov.–Dec.), 24–31.

CHAND, I. P., CRIDER, D. M. K., and WILTIS, F. K. Parent-youth disagreement as perceived by youth: A longitudinal study. *Youth and Society*, 1975, 6, 365–375.

CLOWARD, R. A., and OHLIN, L. E. *Delinquency and opportunity: A theory of delinquent gangs.* Glencoe, Illinois: Free Press, 1957.

COCHRANE, P. V., and WESTLING, D. L. The principal and mainstreaming: Ten suggestions for success. *Educational Leadership*, 1977, 34, 506–510.

COHEN, A. *Delinquent boys.* Glencoe, Illinois: Free Press, 1955.

COLEMAN, J. C. Friendships and the peer group in adolescence. In J. Adelson (ed.), *Handbook of adolescent psychology.* New York: John Wiley, 1980.

COLEMAN, J. S. *The adolescent society.* New York: The Free Press, 1961.

COLEMAN, J. S. Equal schools or equal students? In D. M. Gordon (ed.), *Problems in political economy: An urban perspective.* Lexington, Mass.: D. C. Heath, 1971.

COLEMAN, J. S. *Youth: Transition to adulthood.* Chicago: University of Chicago Press, 1975.

COLES, R. The children of affluence. *Atlantic Monthly*, 1977, 240, 52–60.

COMBS, J., and COOLEY, W. W. Dropouts in high school and after school. *American Educational Research Journal*, 1968, 5, 343–363.

CONGER, J. J. Sexual attitudes and behavior among contemporary adolescents. In J. J. Conger (ed.), *Contemporary issues in adolescent development.* New York: Harper and Row, 1975.

CONGER, J. J. *Adolescence and youth.* New York: Harper and Row, 1977.

COOK, T. D., and CAMPBELL, D. T. *Quasi-experimentation.* Chicago: Rand-McNally, 1979.

CORNWELL, G. How dangerous are religious cults? *Reader's Digest*, 1976, 108 (Feb.), 96–100.

COVINGTON, M. V., and BEERY, R. G. Self-worth and school learning. New York: Holt, Rinehart and Winston, 1976.

COWAN, E. L., and ZOX, M. Early detection and prevention of emotional disorder: Conceptualizations and programming. In J. W. Carter (ed.), *Research contributions from psychology to community mental health.* New York: Academic Press, 1970.

COWAN, E. L., DORR, D. A., and ORGEL, A. R. Interrelations among screening measures for early detection of school dysfunction. *Psychology in the Schools*, 1971, 8, 135–139.

CRISP, A. H.; DOUGLAS, J. W.; ROSS, J. M.; and TONEHILL, E. Some developmental aspects of disorders of weight. *Journal of Psychosomatic Research*, 1970, 14, 313–320.

CROCKENBERG, S. B. Creativity tests: A boon or boondoggle for education? *Review of Educational Research*, 1972, 42, 27–46.

CSAPO, M. G. Utilization of normal peers as behavior change agents for reducing the inappropriate behavior of emotionally disturbed children in regular classroom environments. Unpublished doctoral dissertation, University of Kansas, 1971.

CUTRIGHT, P. Illegitimacy in the United States, 1920–1968. In C. F. Westoff and R. Parks, Jr. (eds.), *Demographic and social aspects of population growth.* Report of the Commission on Population and the American Future, research reports, vol. 1. Washington, D.C.: U.S. Government Printing Office, 1971.(a)

CUTRIGHT, P. Illegitimacy: Myths, causes and cures. *Family Planning Perspectives*, 1971, 3(1), 26–48.(b)

CUTRIGHT, P. The teenage sexual revolution and the myth of an abstinate past. *Family Planning Perspectives*, 1972, 4, 24–31.

CVETKOVITCH, G.; GROTE, B.; BJORSETH, A.; and SARKISSIAN, J. On the psychology of adolescents' use of contraceptives. *Journal of Sex Research*, 1975, 11, 256–270.

DAMICO, S. B., and PURKEY, W. W. Class clowns: A study of middle-school students. *American Educational Research Journal*, 1978, 15, 391–398.

DAVIDSON, M. A., McINNES, R. G., and PARNELL, R. W. The distribution of personality traits in seven-year-old children: A combined psychological, psychiatric and somatotype study. *British Journal of Educational Psychology*, 1957, 27, 48–61.

DAY, H. I., and LANGEVIN, R. Curiosity and intelligence: Two necessary conditions for a high level of creativity. *Journal of Special Education*, 1969, 3, 263–268.

DIEPOLD, J., JR., and YOUNG, R. D. Empirical studies of adolescent sexual behavior: A critical review. *Adolescence*, 1979, *53*, 45–64.

DITTES, J. E. Psychology of religion. In G. Lindsey and E. Aronsen (eds.), *The handbook of social psychology*. 2nd ed. Vol. 5. Reading, Mass.: Addison-Wesley, 1969.

DION, K., and BERSCHIED, E. Physical attractiveness and peer perception among children. *Sociometry*, 1974, *37*, 1–12.

DION, K., BERSCHIED, E., and WALSTER, E. What is beautiful is good. *Journal of Personality and Social Psychology*, 1972, *24*, 285–290.

DI VESTA, F. J. An evolving theory of instruction. *Educational Technology*, 1972, *12*(12), 34–39.

DOUVAN, E., and ADELSON, J. *The adolescent experience*. New York: John Wiley, 1966.

DUNCAN, O. D., FEATHERMAN, D. L., and DUNCAN, B. *Socioeconomic background and achievement*. New York: Seminar Press, 1972.

DUNPHY, D. C. The social structure of urban adolescent peer groups. *Sociometry*, 1963, *26*, 230–246.

DUNPHY, D. C. *Cliques, crowds, and gangs*. Melbourne: Cheshire, 1969.

DWYER, J., and MAYER, J. Effects of variations in physical appearance during adolescence. *Adolescence*, 1968, *3*, 353–368.

EBEL, R. L. What are schools for? *Phi Delta Kappan*, 1972, *54*, 3–7.

ELDER, G. H., JR. Parental power legitimation and its effect on the adolescent. *Sociometry*, 1963, *26*, 50–65.

ELDER, G. H., JR. *Children of the Great Depression*. Chicago: University of Chicago Press, 1974.

ELIAS, J., and GEBHARD, P. Sexuality and sexual learning in childhood. *Phi Delta Kappan*, 1969, *7*, 401–405.

ELKIND, D. Egocentrism in adolescence. *Child Development*, 1967, *38*, 1025–1034.

ELKIND, D. Understanding the young adolescent. *Adolescence*, 1978, *49*, 127–134.

ELLIOTT, D. S. Delinquency, school attendance and dropouts. *Social Problems*, 1966, *13*, 306–318.

ELLIOTT, D. S., and VOSS, H. L. *Delinquency and dropout*. Lexington, Mass.: D. C. Heath, 1974.

ELMER, E. *Children in jeopardy*. Pittsburgh: University of Pittsburgh Press, 1967.

ELMER, E., and GREGG, G. Developmental characteristics of abused children. *Pediatrics*, 1967, *40*, 596–602.

EMPEY, L. T. Revolution and counter-revolution: Current trends in juvenile justice. In D. Shehor and D.

H. Kelly (eds.), *Critical issues in juvenile delinquency*. Lexington, Mass.: Lexington Books, 1980.

ERIKSON, E. H. Identity and the life cycle. *Psychological issues, monograph no. 1*, 1959, 1.

ERIKSON, E. H. *Identity, youth and crisis*. New York: W. W. Norton, 1968.(a)

ERIKSON, E. H. *Young man Luther*. New York: W. W. Norton, 1968.(b)

ERIKSON, E. H. *Gandhi's truth*. New York: W. W. Norton, 1969.

ESKIN, B. When do nocturnal emissions begin in adolescence? Does the date coincide with or resemble first menstruation in girls? *Medical Tribune*, 1977.

FARR, R., FAY, L., and NEGLEY, H. *Then and now: Reading achievement in Indiana (1944–45 and 1976)*. Bloomington, Indiana: Indiana University Press, 1978.

FARR, R., and TUINMAN, J. J. *Reading achievement in the United States: Then and now*. Bloomington, Indiana: Indiana University Press, 1974.

FARRINGTON, D. C. The family background of aggressive youths. In L. A. Hershov, M. Berger, and D. Shaffer (eds.), *Aggression and anti-social behavior in children and adolescents*. Oxford: Pergammon Press, 1978.

FAUST, M. S. Developmental maturity as a determinant of prestige in adolescent girls. *Child Development*, 1960, *31*, 173–184.

FAUST, M. S. Somatic development of adolescent girls. *Monographs for the Society for Research in Child Development, series no. 169*, 1977, *42*(1).

FEATHER, N., and RAPHELSON, A. Fear of success in Australian and American student groups: Motive or sex-role stereotype. *Journal of Personality*, 1974, *42*, 190–201.

FEIGHNER, J. P.; ROBINS, E.; GUZE, S. B.; WOODRUFF, R.; WINOKER, G.; and MUNOZ, R. Diagnostic criteria for use in psychiatric research. *Archives of General Psychiatry*, 1972, *26*, 57–63.

FESTINGER, L., and KATZ, D. (eds.). *Research methods in the social sciences*. New York: Holt, Rinehart and Winston, 1953.

FEUER, L. *The conflict of generations: The character and significance of student movements*. New York: Basic Books, 1969.

FLAVELL, J. *Cognitive development*. Englewood Cliffs, N.J.: Prentice-Hall, 1977.

FLORA, R. R. The effect of self-concept upon adolescent's communication with parents. *Journal of School Health*, 1978, *48* (Feb.), 100–102.

FORBES, G. B. Biological implications of the adolescent

growth process: Body composition. In J. I. McKigney and H. M. Munroe (eds.), *Nutrient requirements in adolescence*. Cambridge, Mass.: M.I.T. Press, 1976.

FOWLER, J. W. Stages in faith: The structural developmental approach. In T. C. Hennessy (ed.), *Values and moral development*. New York: Paulist Press, 1976.

FOX, L. H. Identification and program planning: Models and methods. In D. P. Keating (ed.), *Intellectual talent: Research and development*. Baltimore: Johns Hopkins University Press, 1976.

FRENCH, E. G. Effects of the interaction of motivation and feedback on task performance. In J. W. Atkinson (ed.), *Motives in fantasy, action and society*. Princeton, N.J.: Van Nostrand, 1958.

FREUD, A. *The ego and the mechanisms of defense*. Rev. ed. The writings of Anna Freud, vol. 2. New York: International Universities Press, 1968.

FRISCH, R. F., and MCARTHUR, J. W. Menstrual cycles: Fatness as a determinant of minimum height for weight necessary for their maintenance or onset. *Science*, 1974, *185*, 949.

GAGNE, R. M. *The conditions of learning*. 3rd ed. New York: Holt, Rinehart and Winston, 1977.

GALLAGHER, J. R. *Medical care of the adolescent*. 2nd ed. New York: Appleton-Century Crofts, 1960.

GALLAGHER, J. R., HEALD, F. P., and GARELL, D. C. *Medical care of the adolescent*. 3rd ed. New York: Appleton-Century-Crofts, 1976.

GALLUP OPINION INDEX. American public leans to pessimism on job outlook in their communities. Report No. 174, 1979, pp. 10–12.

GECAS, V., and NYE, F. I. Sex and class differences in parent-child interaction: A test of Kohn's hypothesis. *Journal of Marriage and the Family*, 1974, *36*, 742–749.

GENERAL ACCOUNTING OFFICE. *Preventing mental retardation—More can be done*. Washington, D.C.: U.S. Government Printing Office, 1977.

GIBBONS, D. C. *Delinquent behavior*. Englewood Cliffs, N.J.: Prentice-Hall, 1970.

GINSBERG, E.; GINSBERG, S. W.; AXELROD, S.; and HERMAN, J. L. *Occupational choice: An approach to a general theory*. New York: Columbia University Press, 1951.

GLASER, R. Concept learning and concept teaching. In R. M. Gagne and W. J. Gebhart (eds.), *Learning research and school subjects*. Itaska, Ill.: F. E. Peacock, 1968.

GLIESSMAN, D., PUGH, R. C., and BIELAT, B. Acquiring teaching skills through concept-based training.

Paper presented to the annual meeting of the American Association of Colleges of Teacher Education, 1978.

GLOCK, C. Y., and STARK, R. *Religion and society in tension*. Chicago: Rand-McNally, 1965.

GOERTZEL, V., and GOERTZEL, M. G. *Cradles of eminence*. Boston: Little, Brown, 1962.

GOLD, M. Undetected delinquent behavior. *Journal of Research in Crime and Delinquency*, 1966, *3*, 27–46.

GOLD, M. *Crime in an American city*. Belmont, Calif.: Wadsworth, 1970.

GOLD, M. Scholastic experiences, self-esteem and delinquent behavior: A theory for alienated schools. *Crime and Delinquency*, 1978, *24*, 290–308.

GOLD, M., and DOUVAN, E. *Adolescent development*. Boston: Allyn and Bacon, 1970.

GOLD, M., and PETRONIO, R. J. Delinquent behavior in adolescence. In J. Adelson (ed.), *Handbook of adolescent psychology*. New York: John Wiley, 1980.

GOLLADAY, M. A. *The condition of education, 1977*. National Center for Educational Statistics. Washington, D.C.: U.S. Government Printing Office, 1977.

GOLLADAY, M. A. *The condition of education, 1978*. National Center for Educational Statistics. Washington, D.C.: U.S. Government Printing Office, 1978.

GORDON, E. W. Methodological problems and pseudoissues in the nature-nurture controversy. In R. Cancro (ed.), *Intelligence: Genetic and environmental influence*. New York: Grune and Stratton, 1973.

GOSLIN, D. A. Accuracy of self-perception and social acceptance. *Sociometry*, 1962, *25*, 283–296.

GOTTLIEB, J., and BUDOFF, M. Social acceptability of retarded children in nongraded schools differing in architecture. *American Journal of Mental Deficiency*, 1973, *78*, 15–19.

GOTTLIEB, J., SEMMEL, M. I., and VELDMAN, D. Correlates of social status among mainstreamed mentally retarded children. *Journal of Educational Psychology*, 1978, *70*, 396–405.

GRIBBONS, W. D., and LOHNES, P. R. Shifts in adolescents' vocational values. *Personnel and Guidance Journal*, 1965, *44*, 248–252.

GUILFORD, J. P. Three faces of intellect. *American Psychologist*, 1959, *14*, 469–479.

GUNDERSON, J. G. Special report: Schizophrenia, 1974. *Schizophrenia Bulletin*, 1974, *9*, 16–18.

GUTTMACHER, ALAN, INSTITUTE. *11 million teenagers: What can be done about the epidemic of adolescent pregnancies in the United States?* New York: Planned Parenthood Federation, 1976.

GUTTMACHER, ALAN, INSTITUTE. *Teenage pregnancy: The problem that hasn't gone away.* New York: The Alan Guttmacher Institute, 1981.

HAAN, N., SMITH, M. B., and BLOCK, J. Moral reasoning of young adults: Political social behavior, family background and personality correlates. *Journal of Personality and Social Psychology,* 1968, *10,* 183–201.

HAIER, R. J., and DENHAM, S. A. A summary profile of nonintellectual correlates of mathematical precocity in boys and girls. In D. P. Keating (ed.), *Intellectual talent: Research and development.* Baltimore: Johns Hopkins University Press, 1976.

HAIER, R. J., and SALANO, C. H. Educators' stereotypes of mathematically gifted boys. In D. P. Keating (ed.), *Intellectual talent: Research and development.* Baltimore: Johns Hopkins University Press, 1976.

HAKEL, M. D., HOLLMANN, T. D., and DUNNETTE, M. D. Stability and change in the social status of occupations over 21- and 42-year periods. *Personnel and Guidance Journal,* 1968, *46,* 762–764.

HALL, G. S. *Adolescence: Its psychology and relations to physiology, anthropology, sociology, sex, crime, religion and education.* New York: Appleton, 1916.

HAMMILL, P. V. V.; DRIZD, T. A.; JOHNSON, C. L.; REED, R. B.; and ROCHE, A. F. *NCHS growth curves for children birth–18 years.* Vital and Health Statistics, series 11, no. 165. National Center for Health Statistics. Washington, D.C.: U.S. Government Printing Office, 1977.

HAMMOND, W. H. The status of physical types. *Human Biology,* 1957, *29,* 223–241.

HANEY, B., and GOLD, M. The juvenile delinquent nobody knows. *Psychology Today,* 1973, *7*(4), 49–51,55.

HANLEY, C. Physique and reputation of junior high school boys. *Child Development,* 1951, *22,* 247–260.

HANNERZ, U. *Soulside: Inquiries into ghetto culture.* New York: Columbia University Press, 1969.

HARTSHORNE, H., and MAY, M. A. *Studies in deceit: General methods and results.* New York: Macmillan, 1924.

HARTUP, W. W. Peers, play and pathology: A new look at the social behavior of children. *Newsletter of the Society for Research in Child Development,* 1977, (Fall). 1–3.

HARVEY, A. L. Goal setting as compensation for fear of success. *Adolescence,* 1975, *10,* 137–142.

HARVEY, O. J., HUNT, D. E., and SCHRODER, H. M. *Conceptual systems and personality organization.* New York: John Wiley, 1961.

HAVIGHURST, R. J. *Developmental tasks and education.* 3rd ed. New York: David McKay, 1972.

HAVIGHURST, R. J., and GOTTLIEB, D. Youth and the meaning of work. In R. J. Havighurst and P. H. Dreyer (eds.), *Youth.* Seventy-fourth Yearbook of the National Society for the Study of Education, pt. 1. Chicago: University of Chicago Press, 1975.

HEALD, F.; LEVY, P. S.; HAMMILL, P. V. V.; and ROWLAND, M. *Hemocrit values of youths 12–17 years.* Vital and Health Statistics, series 11, no. 146. Washington, D.C.: U.S. Government Printing Office, 1974.

HEATHERINGTON, E. M. Effects of father absence on personality development in adolescent daughters. *Developmental Psychology,* 1972, *7,* 313–326.

HEBER, R. F., and DEVER, R. B. Research on education and habituation of the mentally retarded. In H. C. Haywood (ed.), *Social-cultural aspects of mental retardation.* New York: Appleton-Century-Crofts, 1970.

HERRNSTEIN, R. IQ. *The Atlantic Monthly,* 1971, *228* (Sept.), 43–64.

HERRON, J. D. Piaget for chemists. *Journal of Chemical Education,* 1975, *52,* 146–150.

HERRON, J. D. Piaget applied: Suggestions for inaction. Paper presented at the national meeting of the American Chemical Society, 1977.

HERZOG, E., and SUDIA, C. E. Children in fatherless families. In B. M. Caldwell and H. N. Ricciuti (eds.), *Review of child development research, vol. 3.* Chicago: University of Chicago Press, 1973.

HERZOG, A. R., BACHMAN, J. G., and JOHNSTON, J. Young people look at changing sex roles. *Newsletter of the Institute for Social Research,* 1979, *7* (Spring), 3, 5.

HESS, R. D., and GOLDBLATT, I. The status of adolescents in American society: A problem of social identity. *Child Development,* 1957, *28,* 459–468.

HODGE, R. W.; SIEGAL, P. M.; and ROSSI, P. H. Occupational prestige in the United States 1925–63. *American Journal of Sociology,* 1964, *70,* 286–302.

HOFFMAN, L. Fear of success in males and females: 1965 and 1971. *Journal of Consulting and Clinical Psychology,* 1974, *42,* 353–358.

HOLLAND, J. L. A theory of vocational choice. *Journal of Counseling Psychology,* 1959, *6,* 35–45.

HOLLAND, J. L. *Making vocational choices: A theory of careers.* Englewood Cliffs, N.J.: Prentice-Hall, 1973.

HOLLAND, J. L.; WHITNEY, D. R.; COLE, N. S.; and RICHARDS, M. J., JR. *An empirical occupational classification derived from a theory of personality and intended for practice and research.* ACT Report No. 29. Iowa City: American College Testing Program, 1969.

HOLTZMAN, W. H., and MOORE, B. M. Family structure and youth attitudes. In M. Sherif and C. W. Sherif (eds.), *Problems of youth: Transition to adulthood in a changing world*. Chicago: Aldine, 1965.

HOOKER, E., and CHANCE, P. Facts that liberated the gay community. *Psychology Today*, 1975, 9(7), 52–55, 101.

HORNER, M. Femininity and successful achievement: A basic inconsistency. In J. M. Bardwick (ed.), *Feminine personality and conflict*. Belmont, Calif.: Brooks/Cole, 1970.

HORROCKS, J. E. *The psychology of adolescence*. Boston: Houghton Mifflin, 1976.

HUMPHREY, L. G. Characteristics of type concepts with special reference to Sheldon's typology. *Psychological Bulletin*, 1957, 54, 218–228.

HUNT, D. E. *Matching models in education: The coordination of teaching methods with student characteristics*. Toronto, Ontario: Ontario Institute for Studies in Education, 1971.

HUNT, D. E. BPE: A challenge found wanting before it was tried. *Review of Educational Research*, 1975, 45, 209–230.

HUNT, D. E., and SULLIVAN, E. V. *Between psychology and education*. Hinsdale, Ill.: Dryden Press, 1974.

IACOVETTA, R. G. Adolescent-adult interaction and peer group involvement. *Adolescence*, 1975, 10, 327–336.

IMS AMERICA, INC. *Drug abuse warning network reports*. Drug Enforcement Administration and National Institute on Drug Abuse. Washington, D.C.: U.S. Government Printing Office, 1979.

INGERSOLL, G. M. On the use of height/weight indices as an index of obesity. Bloomington, Ind.: Institute for Child Study, 1979.

INGERSOLL, G. M., and FEREN-STEGER, S. Birthweight and childhood intelligence: A reconsideration. Unpublished manuscript, Indiana University School of Education, 1979.

INHELDER, B., and PIAGET, J. *The growth of logical thinking from childhood to adolescence*. New York: Basic Books, 1958.

INKELES, A., and ROSSI, P. H. National comparisons of occupational prestige. *American Journal of Sociology*, 1956, 61, 329–399.

JACKSON, J. The pregnancy epidemic. *Washington Post*, 1977 (March 3), C7.

JANIS, I. L., and MANN, L. Coping with decisional conflict. *American Scientist*, 1976, 64, 657–667.

JENSEN, A. R. How much can we boost IQ and scholastic achievement. *Harvard Educational Review*, 1969, 39, 1–123.

JENSEN, A. R. *Genetics and education*. New York: Harper and Row, 1972.

JENSEN, G. F., and ROJEK, D. G. *Delinquency: A sociological view*. Lexington, Mass.: D. C. Heath, 1980.

JESSOR, R. Marihuana: A review of recent psychological research. In R. L. Dupont, A. Goldstein, and J. O'Connell (eds.), *Handbook on drug abuse*. Washington, D.C.: U.S. Government Printing Office, 1979.

JESSOR, S. L. On becoming a drinker: Social-psychological aspects of an adolescent transition. *Annals of the New York Academy of Sciences*, 1972, 197, 199–213.

JESSOR, S. L., and JESSOR, R. *Problem behavior and psychosocial development*. New York: Academic Press, 1977.

JOHNSTON, L. D., and BACHMAN, J. G. Educational institutions. In J. F. Adams (ed.), *Understanding adolescence*. Boston: Allyn and Bacon, 1976.

JOHNSTON, L. D., BACHMAN, J. G., and O'MALLEY, P. M. Drug use among American high school students, 1975–1977. National Institute on Drug Abuse. Washington, D.C.: U.S. Government Printing Office, 1977.

JOHNSTON, L. D., BACHMAN, J. G., and O'MALLEY, P.M. Drugs and the class of '78: Behaviors, attitudes and recent national trends. National Institute on Drug Abuse. Washington, D.C.: U.S. Government Printing Office, 1979.

JONES, H. E. The adolescent growth study: 1. Principles and methods. *Journal of Consulting Psychology*, 1939, 3, 157–159. (a)

JONES, H. E. The adolescent growth study: 2. Procedures. *Journal of Consulting Psychology*, 1939, 3, 177–180. (b)

JONES, M. C. The later careers of boys who were early- or late-maturing. *Child Development*, 1957, 28, 113–128.

JONES, M. C. Psychological correlates of somatic development. *Child Development*, 1965, 36, 899–911.

JONES, M. C., and BAYLEY, N. Physical maturing among boys as related to behavior. *Journal of Educational Psychology*, 1950, 41, 129–133.

KAGAN, J., SONTAG, L. W., BAKER, C. T., and NELSON, V. L. Personality and IQ change. *Journal of Social Psychology*, 1958, 56, 261–266.

KALACHEK, E. *The youth labor market*. National Manpower Task Force Policy Papers in Human Resources and Industrial Relations, no. 12. Washington, D.C.: U.S. Government Printing Office, 1969.

KANDEL, D. B. Similarity in real-life friendship pairs. *Journal of Personality and Social Psychology*, 1978, *36*, 306–312. (a)

KANDEL, D. B. Homophily, selection and socialization in adolescent friendships. *American Journal of Sociology*, 1978, *84*, 427–436. (b)

KATCHADORIAN, H. A. *The biology of adolescence.* San Francisco: W. H. Freeman, 1977.

KATZ, I. The socialization of academic motivation in minority group children. Nebraska Symposium on Motivation, University of Nebraska Press, 1967.

KEATING, D. P. (ed.) *Intellectual talent: Research and development.* Baltimore: Johns Hopkins University Press, 1976.

KENISTON, K. *The uncommitted.* New York: Harcourt Brace Jovanovich, 1965.

KENISTON, K. Heads and seekers: Drugs on campus, counterculture and American society. *American Scholar*, 1968, *36*, 97–112.

KENISTON, K. Youth: A "new" stage of life. *The American Scholar*, 1970, *39*, 631–641.

KENNEDY, E. *On becoming a counselor.* New York: Seabury Press, 1977.

KERLINGER, F. N. *Foundations for behavioral research.* 2nd ed. New York: Holt, Rinehart and Winston, 1973.

KETT, J. F. *Rites of passage: Adolescence in America 1790 to the present.* New York: Basic Books, 1977.

KING, K., BALSWICK, J. O., and ROBINSON, I. E. Sexual revolution among college females. *Journal of Marriage and the Family*, 1977, *39*, 455–459.

KINSEY, A. C., POMEROY, W. B., and MARTIN, E. E. *Sexual behavior in the human male.* Philadelphia: W. B. Saunders, 1948.

KINSEY, A. C.; POMEROY, W. B.; MARTIN, E. E.; and GEPHART, P. H. *Sexual behavior in the human female.* Philadelphia: W. B. Saunders, 1953.

KLECK, R. E., RICHARDSON, S. A., and RONALD, L. Physical appearance cues and interpersonal attraction in children. *Child Development*, 1974, *45*, 305–310.

KLOOS, P. Maroni River Caribs of Surinam. Atlantic Highlands, N.J.: Humanities Press Inc., 1971.

KOHLBERG, L. The development of modes of moral thinking and choice in years ten to sixteen. Unpublished doctoral dissertation, University of Chicago, 1958.

KOHLBERG, L. Development of moral character and moral ideology. In M. L. Hoffman and L. W. Hoffman (eds.), *Review of child development research.* vol. 1. New York: Russell Sage Foundation, 1964.

KOHLBERG, L. Moral education in the schools: A developmental view. *School Review*, 1966, *74*, 1–29.

KOHLBERG, L. The cognitive developmental approach to moral education. *Phi Delta Kappan*, 1975, *10*, 670–677.

KOHLBERG, L., and GILLIGAN, C. The adolescent as philosopher: The discovery of self in a post-conventional world. *Daedalus*, 1971, *100*, 1051–1086.

KOHN, M. I. *Class and conformity: A study in values.* Homewood, Cal.: Dorsey, 1969.

KOLATA, G. B. Gonorrhea: More of a problem but less of a mystery. *Science*, 1976, *192*(April 16), 244–247.

KOVAR, M. G. Some indicators of health related behavior among adolescents in the United States. *Public Health Reports*, 1979, *94*, 109–118.

KUDER, F. *Occupational interest survey, Form D D.* Chicago: Science Research Associates, 1974.

KUHLEN, R. G., and ARNOLD, M. Age differences in religious beliefs and problems in adolescence. *Journal of Genetic Psychology*, 1944, *65*, 291–300.

LABOUVIE, E. W. Longitudinal designs. In P. M. Bentler, D. J. Lettieri, and G. A. Austin (eds.), *Data analysis strategies and designs for substance abuse research.* Research Issues, no. 13. National Institute on Drug Abuse. Washington, D.C.: U.S. Government Printing Office, 1976.

LANZETTA, J. T., and HANNAH, T. E. Reinforcing behavior of "naive" trainers. *Journal of Personality and Social Psychology*, 1969, *11*, 245–252.

LEE, G. R. Age at marriage and marital satisfaction: A multivariate analysis with implications for marital stability. *Journal of Marriage and the Family*, 1977, *39*, 493–504.

LEON, G. R. Current directions in the treatment of obesity. *Psychological Bulletin*, 1976, *83*, 557–578.

LEON, G. R., and ROTH, L. Obesity: Psychological causes, correlations, and speculations. *Psychological Bulletin*, 1977, *84*, 117–139.

LERNER, R. M., and SPANIER, G. B. *Adolescent development: A life-cycle perspective.* New York: McGraw-Hill, 1980.

LIBERTY, B. E., JONES, H. C., and MCGUIRE, J. E. Age-mate perceptions of intelligence, creativity and achievement. *Perceptual and Motor Skills*, 1963, *16*, 194.

LIPSITZ, J. *Growing up forgotten.* Lexington, Mass.: Lexington Books, 1977.

LIPSITZ, J. Adolescent development: Myths and realities. *Children Today*, 1979, *8*(5), 2–7.

MACMAHON, B. *Age at menarche.* Vital and Health Statistics, series 11, no. 133. Washington, D.C.:

U.S. Government Printing Office, 1973.

MARCIA, J. E. Development and validation of ego identity status. *Journal of Personality and Social Psychology.* 1966, *3,* 551–555.

MARCIA, J. E. Identity in adolescence. In J. Adelson (ed.), *Handbook of adolescent psychology.* New York: John Wiley, 1980.

MARONE, R. C. Adolescent behavior problems. *Audio-Digest Pediatrics,* 1977, *22,* (16).

MASLOW, A. H., and SAKODA, J. M. Volunteer-error in the Kinsey study. *Journal of Abnormal and Social Psychology,* 1952, *47,* 259–262.

MASTERSON, J. F. The symptomatic adolescent five years later: He didn't grow out of it. *American Journal of Psychiatry,* 1967, *123,* 1338–1345.

MCCREARY-JUHASZ, A. Sexual decision-making: The crux of the adolescent problem. In R. E. Grinder (ed.), *Studies in adolescence.* New York: Macmillan, 1975.

MCCREARY-JUHASZ, A. A cognitive approach to sex education. In J. F. Adams (ed.), *Understanding adolescents.* Boston: Allyn and Bacon, 1976.

MCKEACHIE, W. J. Psychology in America's bicentennial year. *American Psychologist,* 1976, *31,* 819–833.

MCQUEEN, R. The token economy and a target behavior. *Psychological Reports,* 1973, *32,* 599–602.

MEAD, M. *Coming of age in Samoa.* New York: Morrow, 1928.

MEAD, M. *Culture and commitment: A study of the generation gap.* New York: Basic Books, 1969.

MEEKS, J. E. *The fragile alliance.* Baltimore: Williams and Wilkins, 1971.

MEEKS, J. E. Counseling adolescents. *Audio-Digest Pediatrics,* 1978.

MILGRAM, G. G. Alcohol education in the schools perceived by educators and students. *Journal of Alcohol and Drug Education,* 1974, *20,* 4–12.

MILLER, J. Suicide in adolescence. *Adolescence,* 1975, *8,* 11–24.

MISCHEL, W. Sex-typing and socialization. In P. H. Mussen (ed.), *Carmichael's manual of child psychology.* New York: John Wiley, 1970.

MITCHELL, J. C. The differences in an English and American rating of the prestige of occupations. *British Journal of Sociology,* 1964, *15,* 166–173.

MITCHELL, M. Attitudes of adolescent girls toward vocational education. Final report. Bloomington, Ind.: School of Education, Indiana University, 1977.

MONEY, J. Sex education for normal and hypopituitary patients. In S. Raiti (ed.), *Advances in human growth hormone research.* Washington, D.C.: U.S. Govern-ment Printing Office, 1973.

MONTEMAYOR, R., and EISEN, M. The development of self-conceptions from childhood to adolescence. *Developmental Psychology,* 1977, *13,* 314–319.

MOORE, K. A., and CALDWELL, S. B. The effects of government policies on out-of-wedlock sex and pregnancy. *Family Planning Perspectives,* 1977, *9,* 164–169.

MORENO, J. L. *Who shall survive? Foundations of sociometry, group psychotherapy and sociodrama.* 3rd ed. Beacon, N.Y.: Beacon House, 1953.

MOYNIHAN, D. P. *Maximum feasible misunderstanding.* New York: Free Press, 1969.

MUSON, H. Teenage violence and the telly. *Psychology Today,* 1978, *11*(Mar.), 50–54.

MUSSEN, P. (ed.). *Carmichael's manual of child development.* New York: John Wiley, 1970.

National Assessment of Educational Progress. *Education for citizenship: A bicentennial survey.* Washington, D.C.: U.S. Government Printing Office, 1976.

National Assessment of Educational Progress. *Changes in political knowledge and attitudes, 1969–1976.* Washington, D.C.: U.S. Government Printing Office, 1978.

National Assessment of Educational Progress. *Reading achievement.* Washington, D.C.: U.S. Government Printing Office, 1976.

National Center for Health Statistics. *Facts of life and death, 1978.* Washington, D.C.: U.S. Government Printing Office, 1978.

National Institute for Juvenile Justice and Delinquency Prevention. *Jurisdiction–Status offenses.* Vol. 5. Washington, D.C.: U.S. Government Printing Office, 1977.

NESSELROADE, J. R., and BALTES, P. B. Longitudinal research in the behavioral sciences. Final report, National Institute on Education. University Park, Penn.: Pennsylvania State University Press, 1977.

NEWCOMB, T. M. The general nature of peer group influence. In T. M. Newcomb and E. K. Wilson (eds.), *College peer groups.* Chicago: Aldine, 1966.

O'CONNOR, R. D. Relative efficacy of modeling, shaping, and the combined procedures for modification of social withdrawal. *Journal of Abnormal Psychology,* 1972, *79,* 327–334.

OHLIN, L., and CLOWARD, R. The prevention of delinquent subcultures. In M. S. Weinberg and E. Rubington (eds.), *The solution of social problems.* Glencoe, Ill.: Free Press, 1973.

OLDHAM, D. G. Adolescent turmoil: A myth revisited. *Journal of Continuing Education in Psychiatry,* 1978,

39, 23–32.

O'LEARY, V. E. Some attitudinal barriers to occupational aspirations in women. *Psychological Bulletin,* 1974, *81*, 809–826.

OLSEN, N. J., and WILLEMSEN, E. W. Fear of success: Fact or artifact. *Journal of Psychology,* 1978, *98*, 65–70.

ORIEL, J. D. Chlamydia trachomatis infections. *Medical Aspects of Human Sexuality,* 1977, *14*, 54, 58–60.

ORNSTEIN, M. D. *Entry into the American labor force.* New York: Academic Press, 1975.

OSIPOW, S. H. The relevance of theories of career development to special groups: Problems, needed data and implications. In J. S. Picon and R. E. Campbell (eds.), *Career education of special groups.* Columbus, Ohio: Charles E. Merrill, 1975.

OWENS, W. A. Age and mental abilities: A longitudinal study. *Genetic Psychology Monographs,* 1953, *48*, 3–54.

OWENS, W. A. Age and mental abilities: A second follow-up. *Journal of Educational Psychology,* 1966, *57*, 311–325.

PASAMANICK, B., and KNOBLOCK, H. Epidemiologic studies on the complications of pregnancy and the birth process. In G. Caplan (ed.), *Prevention of mental disorders in children.* New York: Basic Books, 1961.

PASANELLA, A. L., and VOLKMAR, C. B. *Coming back ...or never leaving.* Columbus, Ohio: Charles E. Merrill, 1977.

PECK, M. Suicide motivations in adolescence. *Adolescence,* 1968, *3*, 109–118.

PERVIN, L. A. Performance and satisfaction as a function of individual-environment fit. *Psychological Bulletin,* 1968, *69*, 56–68.

PIAGET, J. *The moral development of the child.* New York: Free Press, 1965 (originally published, 1932).

PIAGET, J. *Six psychological studies.* New York: Random House, 1967.

PIAGET, J. Piaget's theory. In P. H. Mussen (ed.), *Carmichael's manual of child psychology.* New York: John Wiley, 1970.

PINNEY, J. M. The largest preventable cause of death in the United States. *Public Health Reports,* 1979, *94*, 107–108.

PRICE, D. O. Constructing cohort data from discrepant age intervals and irregular reporting periods. *Social Science Quarterly,* 1974, *24*, 167–174.

RACHEL, J. V.; WILLIAMS, J. R.; BREHM, M. L.; CAVANAUGH, B.; MOORE, R. P.; and ECKERMAN, N. C. A national study of adolescent drinking behavior, attitudes and correlates. Final report, National

Institute on Alcohol Abuse and Alcoholism. Washington, D.C.: U.S. Government Printing Office, 1975.

RAUH, J. L., BURKET, R. L., and BROOKMAN, R. R. Contraception for the teenager. In H. V. Barnes (ed.), *The medical clinics of North America,* 1975, *59*, 1407–1418.

RAVEN, J. C. *Guide to the Standard Progressive Matrice.* London: H. K. Lewis, 1960.

REHBERG, R. A., and ROSENTHAL, E. R. *Class and merit in the American high school: An assessment of the revisionist and meritocratic arguments.* New York: Longman, 1978.

REISNER, R. M. Acne vulgaris. In D. C. Garrell (ed.), *The Pediatrics Clinic of North America,* 1973, *20*(4), 851–864.

Research for Better Schools, Inc. *Planning assistance program to reduce school violence and disruption.* Philadelphia, 1976.

REST, J. R., DAVISON, M. L., and ROBBINS, S. Age trends in judging moral issues: A review of cross-sectional, longitudinal, and sequential studies of the Defining Issues Test. *Child Development,* 1978, *49*, 263–279.

RITTER, B. The adolescent runaway: A national problem. *USA Today,* 1979, *107*(Mar.), 30–32.

ROBBINS, J. Even a Moonie has civil rights. *Nation,* 1977, *224*(Feb. 26), 238–242.

ROFF, M., SELLS, S. B., and GOLDEN, M. M. *Social adjustment and personality development.* Minneapolis: University of Minnesota Press, 1972.

ROGERS, E. Group influence on student drinking. In G. L. Maddox (ed.), *The domestic drug: Drinking among collegians.* New Haven: College and University Press, 1970.

ROMER, N. The motive to avoid success and its effect on performance in school age males and females. *Developmental Psychology,* 1975, *11*, 689–699.

ROSENBERG, M. *Society and the adolescent self-image.* Princeton, N.J.: Princeton University Press, 1965.

ROSENBERG, M. The dissonant context and adolescent self-concept. In S. E. Dragastian and G. H. Elder (eds.), *Adolescence in the life cycle.* New York: Halstead, 1976.

ROSZAK, T. *The making of a counterculture.* New York: Doubleday, 1969.

ROTHKOPF, E. Z. Two scientific approaches to the management of instruction. In R. M. Gagne and W. J. Gephart (eds.), *Learning research and school subjects.* Itaska, Ill.: F. E. Peacock, 1968.

ROTTER, J. B. Generalized expectancies for internal vs. external control of reinforcement. *Psychological*

Monographs, whole no. 609. 1966, *80*, 1.

RUBINGTON, E. and WEINBERG, M. S. *Deviance: The interactionist perspective.* 3rd ed. New York: Macmillan, 1978.

RUTTER, M. Family, area and school influence in the genesis of conduct disorders. In L. A. Hershov, M. Berger, and D. Shaffer (eds.), *Aggression and antisocial behavior in children and adolescents.* Oxford: Pergammon Press, 1978.

RYAN, C. W. Practical linkages between career guidance and career education. *Viewpoints in Teaching and Learning*, 1978, *54*(1), 10–19.

SAARIO, T. N., JACKLIN, C. N., and TUTTLE, C. K. Sex-role stereotyping in the schools. *Harvard Educational Review*, 1973, *43*, 366–416.

SADKER, M., and SADKER, D. Sexism in the schools: An issue for the 70's. *Journal of the National Association of Women Deans, Administrators, and Counselors*, 1974, *37*, 69–78.

SAGHIR, R. C., and ROBINS, E. *Male and female homosexuality: A comprehensive investigation.* Baltimore: Williams and Wilkins, 1973.

San Mateo County (See BLACKFORD.)

SARETSKY, G. The strangely significant case of Peter Doe. *Phi Delta Kappan*, 1973, *54*, 589–592.

SCANLON, J. *Intellectual development of youths.* Vital and Health Statistics, series 11, no. 128. Washington, D.C.: U.S. Government Printing Office, 1973.

SCANLON, J. *Self-reported health behavior and attitudes of youths 12-17 years.* Vital and Health Statistics, series 11, no. 147. Washington, D.C.: U.S. Government Printing Office, 1975.

SCHACHTER, S., and RODIN, J. *Obese humans and rats.* New York: Academic Press, 1971.

SCHAIE, K. W. A general model for the study of developmental problems. *Psychological Bulletin*, 1965, *64*, 92–107.

SCHAIE, K. W., and STROTHER, C. R. A cross-sequential study of age changes in cognitive behavior. *Psychological Bulletin*, 1968, *70*, 671–680.

SCHALMO, G. B., and LEVIN, B. H. Presence of the double standard in a college population. *Psychological Reports*, 1974, *34*, 227–230.

SCOTT, M. Ecoenvironmental psychology: A critical period. Unpublished manuscript, Bloomington, Indiana, 1978.

SEARS, R. R., MACCOBY, E., and LEVIN, H. *Patterns of child rearing.* New York: Harper and Row, 1957.

SELTZER, C. C., and MAYER, J. A simple criterion of obesity. *Postgraduate Medicine*, 1965, *38*(2), a:101-a:107.

SHAH, F., ZELNICK, M., and KANTNER, J. F. Unprotected intercourse among unwed teenagers. *Family Planning Perspectives*, 1975, *7*(1), 39–44.

SHELDON, W. H. Constitutional factors in personality. In J. McV. Hunt (ed.), *Personality and the behavioral disorders.* New York: Ronald Press, 1944.

SHUEY, A. M. *The testing of Negro intelligence.* 2nd ed. New York: Social Science Press, 1966.

SIEBER, J. Lessons in uncertainty. *Elementary School Journal*, 1969, *69*, 304–312.

SIEGAL, C. L. F. Sex differences in the occupational choices of second graders. *Journal of Vocational Behavior*, 1976, *3*, 15–19.

SIEGLER, R. S., and LIEBERT, R. M. Acquisition of formal scientific reasoning by 10- and 13-year olds: Designing a factorial experiment. *Developmental Psychology*, 1975, *11*, 401–402.

SIGAL, H., and ARONSON, E. Liking as a function of physical attractiveness and nature of the evaluations. *Journal of Experimental Social Psychology*, 1969, *5*, 93–100.

SIGAL, H., and MICHELA, J. I'll bet you say that to all the girls: Physical attractiveness and reaction to praise. *Journal of Personality*, 1976, *44*, 611–626.

SIGUSCH, V., and SCHMIDT, G. Teenage boys and girls in West Germany. *Journal of Sex Research*, 1973, *9*, 107–123.

SILBERMAN, C. E. *Crisis in the classroom: The remaking of American education.* New York: Random House, 1970.

SIMAN, M. L. Application of a new model of peer group influence to naturally existing adolescent friendship groups. *Child Development*, 1977, *48*, 270–274.

SINGELL, L. D. Some private and social aspects of the labor mobility of young workers. *The Quarterly Review of Economics and Business*, 1966, *6*(1).

SINGER, J. J., and WYNNE, L. C. Thought disorder and family relations of schizophrenics IV: Results and implications. *Archives of General Psychiatry*, 1965, *12*, 281.

SMITH, S. M. *The battered child.* London: Butterworths, 1975.

SMITH, T. E. Foundations of parental influence upon adolescents: An application of social power theory. *American Sociological Review*, 1970, *35*, 860–873.

SMITH, T. E. Push versus pull: Intra-family versus peer-group variables as possible determinants of adolescent orientations toward parents. *Youth and Society*, 1976, *8*, 5–28.

Society for Research in Child Development. Ethical

standards for research with children. *Newsletter for the Society for Research in Child Development*, 1974 (Fall), 3–4.

SOLOMON, T. History and demography of child abuse. *Pediatrics*, 1973, *51*, 1152–1156.

SORENSEN, R. *Adolescent sexuality in contemporary America*. New York: World, 1973.

South Carolina State Department of Education. Curriculum model for preventing dropouts, grades 9-12. Columbia, South Carolina (ERIC ED 084 474), 1972.

SPANIER, G. B. Formal and informal sex education as determinants of premarital sexual behavior. *Archives of Sexual Behavior*, 1976, *5*, 39–67.

STAFFIERI, J. R. A study of social stereotype of body image in children. *Journal of Personality and Social Psychology*, 1967, *1*, 101–104.

STAFFIERI, J. R. Body build and behavioral expectancies in young females. *Developmental Psychology*, 1972, *6*, 125–127.

STANLEY, J. C. Use of tests to discover talent. In D. P. Keating (ed.), *Intellectual talent: Research and development*. Baltimore: Johns Hopkins University Press, 1976.

STANLEY, J. C., KEATING, D. P., and FOX, L. H. *Mathematical talent, research and development*. Baltimore: Johns Hopkins University Press, 1974.

STARBUCK, E. D. *The psychology of religion*. London: Walter Scott, Ltd., 1899.

STEELE, B. F., and POLLOCK, C. B. A psychiatric study of parents who abuse infants and small children. In R. E. Helfer and C. H. Kempe (eds.), *The battered child*. Chicago: University of Chicago Press, 1968.

STEEN, E. B., and PRICE, J. H. *Human sex and sexuality*. New York: John Wiley, 1977.

STEPHANSON, S. P., JR. The transition from school to work with job search implications. Conference report on youth unemployment: Its measurement and meaning. U.S. Department of Labor. Washington, D.C.: U.S. Government Printing Office, 1978.

STERN, M. S., and MACKENZIE, R. G. Venereal disease in adolescents. In H. V. Barnes (ed.), *The medical clinics of North America*, 1975, *59*(Nov.), 1395–1405.

STICKLE, G., and MA, P. Pregnancy in adolescents: Scope of the problem. *Contemporary Obstetrics and Gynecology*, 1975 (June). McGraw-Hill reprints.

STIERLIN, H. *Separating parents and adolescents*. New York: New York Times Books, 1974.

STRANG, R. *The adolescent views himself*. New York: McGraw-Hill, 1957.

STRONG, E. K. *Vocational interests of men and women*. Stanford: Stanford University Press, 1943.

STRONG, E. K. *Vocational interests 18 years after college*. Minneapolis: University of Minnesota Press, 1955.

SUCHMAN, J. R. Training children in scientific inquiry. Paper presented at the annual meeting of the Society for Research in Child Development, 1959.

SUGARMAN, A. A., and HAROONIAN, F. Body type and sophistication of body concept. *Journal of Personality*, 1964, *32*, 380–394.

SUPER, D. E. A theory of vocational development. *American Psychologist*, 1953, *8*, 185–190.

SUPER, D. E. *The psychology of careers*. New York: Harper and Row, 1957.

SUPER, D. E.; STARISHEVSKY, R.; MATLIN, N.; JORDAAN, J. P. *Career development: Self-concept theory*. New York: College Entrance Examination Board, 1963.

SYKES, G., and MATZA, D. Techniques of neutralization: A theory of delinquency. *American Sociological Review*, 1957, *22*, 664–670.

TANNENBAUM, A. J. *Adolescent attitudes about academic brilliance*. New York: Columbia University Press, 1962.

TANNER, J. M. *Growth at adolescence*. London: Blackwell, 1962.

TANNER, J. M. Physical growth. In P. H. Mussen (ed.), *Carmichael's manual of child psychology*. New York: John Wiley, 1970.

TANNER, J. M., WHITEHOUSE, R. H., and TAKAISHI, M. Standards from birth to maturity for height, weight, height velocity and weight velocity: British children. *Archives of Diseases of Childhood*, 1966, *41*, 454–471, 613–635.

TERMAN, L. M. *Mental and physical traits of a thousand gifted children*. Genetic studies of genius, vol. 1. Stanford: Stanford University Press, 1925.

TERMAN, L. M. *The promise of youth*. Genetic studies of genius, vol. 3. Stanford: Stanford University Press, 1930.

TERMAN, L. M., and ODEN, M. H. *The gifted child at midlife*. Genetic studies of genius, vol. 5. Stanford: Stanford University Press, 1959.

THELEN, H. A. *Classroom grouping for teachability*. New York: John Wiley, 1967.

THOMAS, D. L., GECAS, V., WEIGERT, A., and ROONEY, E. *Family socialization and the adolescent*. Lexington, Mass.: D. C. Heath, 1974.

THOMAS, L. E. Generational discontinuity in beliefs: An exploration of the generation gap. *Journal of Social Issues*, 1974, *30*, 1–22.

THURSTONE, L. L. Primary mental abilities. *Psychological Monographs*, no. 1. 1938.

TIME. The youth crime plague. *Time Magazine*, 1977, *110*(July 11), 18–20, 25, 26, 28.

TOMLINSON-KEASEY, C. Formal operations in females ages 11 to 54 years of age. *Developmental Psychology*, 1972, *6*, 364.

TORRANCE, E. P. *Torrance Tests of Creative Thinking: Directions manual*. Princeton, N.J.: Personnel Press, 1966.

TORRANCE, E. P. Can we teach children to think creatively? *Journal of Creative Behavior*, 1972, *6*, 114–143.

TRESEMER, D. Fear of success: Popular but unproven. *Psychology Today*, 1974, *7*(Mar.), 82–85.

U.S. BUREAU OF THE CENSUS. *Statistical abstract of the United states., 1977*. 98th ed. Washington, D.C.: U.S. Government Printing Office, 1977.

UROLOGY TIMES SYMPOSIUM. NGU: Today's most prevalent venereal disease. *Urology Times*, 1977, *5*(5).

U.S. BUREAU OF THE CENSUS. *School enrollment—Social and economic characteristics of students: October, 1976.* Current Population Reports, series P-20, no. 319. Washington, D.C.: U.S. Government Printing Office, 1978.

U.S. DEPARTMENT OF LABOR. Students, graduates and dropouts in the labor market. Special Labor Force Report, no. 215. Washington, D.C.: U.S. Government Printing Office, 1978.

U.S. DEPARTMENT OF LABOR. Employment and unemployment during 1978: An analysis. Special Labor Force Report. no. 218. Washington, D.C.: U.S. Government Printing Office, 1979.

VANDERMYN, G. *National assessment: Achievements, findings, interpretations and uses.* Denver: Educational Commission of the States, 1974.

VENER, A. M., and STEWART, C. S. Adolescent sexual behavior in Middle-America revisited. *Journal of Marriage and the Family*, 1974, *36*, 728–735.

VENER, A., STEWART, C. S., and HAGEN, D. L. The sexual behavior of adolescents in Middle-America: Generational and American-British comparisons. *Journal of Marriage and the Family*, 1972, *34*, 696–705.

VENEZKY, R. L. NAEP—Should we kill the messenger who brings the bad news? *Reading Teacher*, 1977, *30*, 455–463.

VERNON, P. E., ADAMSON, G., and VERNON, D. F. *The psychology and education of the gifted children*. Boulder: Westview Press, 1977.

VOGT, D. K. *Literacy among youths 12-17 years.* Vital and Health Statistics, series 11, no. 131. Washington, D.C.: U.S. Government Printing Office, 1973.

VOSS, H. L., WENDLING, A., and ELLIOTT, D. S. Some types of high-school dropouts. *Journal of Educational Research*, 1966, *59*, 363–368.

WADSWORTH, B. J. *Piaget for the classroom teacher*. New York: Longman, 1978.

WAGNER, H. The increasing importance of the peer group during adolescence. *Adolescence*, 1971, *6*(21), 53–58.

WALDROP, M. F., and HALVERSON, C. F., JR. Minor physical deficits and hyperactivity in young children. In J. Hellmuth (ed.), *Exceptional infant*. New York: Bruner/Mazel, 1971.

WALKER, R. N. Body build and behavior in young children: II. Body build and parents ratings. *Child Development*, 1963, *34*, 1–23.

WALLACH, M. A., and WING, C. W. Faulty construction. *Contemporary Psychology*, 1970, *15*, 3–4.

WALSTER, E., ARONSON, V., ABRAHAMS, D., and ROTTMANN, L. Importance of physical attractiveness in dating behavior. *Journal of Personality and Social Psychology*, 1966, *4*, 508–516.

WALTERS, D. R. *Physical and sexual abuse of children*. Bloomington, Ind.:. Indiana University Press, 1975.

WATSON, J. B., and RAYNOR, R. Conditioned emotional responses. *Journal of Experimental Psychology*, 1920, *3*, 1–14.

WAUGH, I. Labeling theory. In *Preventing Delinquency. A comparative analysis of delinquency prevention theory*, vol. 1. National Institute for Juvenile Justice and Delinquency Prevention. Washington, D.C.: U.S. Government Printing Office, 1977.

WEBB, E. B., CAMPBELL, D. T., SCHWART, R. D., and SECHREST, L. *Unobtrusive measures: Nonreactive research in the social sciences*. Chicago: Rand-McNally, 1966.

WECHSLER, D. *The measurement and appraisal of adult intelligence*. 4th ed. Baltimore: Williams and Wilkins, 1958.

WEINER, B. Attribution theory, achievement motivation and the educational process. *Review of Educational Research*, 1972, *42*, 203–216.

WEINER, B., and KUKLA, A. An attribute analysis of achievement motivation. *Journal of Personality and Social Psychology*, 1970, *15*, 1–20.

WEINER, I. B. The adolescent and his society. In J. R. Gallagher, F. P. Heald, and Garell, D. C. (eds.), *Medical care of the adolescent*. 3rd ed. New York: Appleton-Century-Crofts, 1976.

WEINER, I. B. Psychopathology in adolescence. In J. Adelson (ed.), *Handbook of adolescent psychology.*

New York: John Wiley, 1980.

WEIS, J. Comparative analysis of social control theories of delinquency—The breakdown of adequate social controls. In *Preventing Delinquency*. A comparative analysis of delinquency prevention theory, vol. 1. National Institute for Juvenile Justice and Delinquency. Washington, D.C.: U.S Government Printing Office, 1977.

WERNER, E., and SMITH, R. S. *Kauai's children come of age*. Honolulu: University of Hawaii Press, 1977.

WERTHMAN, C. Delinquency and moral character. In D. R. Cressey and D. A. Ward (eds.), *Delinquency, crime and social process*. New York: Harper and Row, 1969.

WERTHMAN, C. Status offenses. In *Preventing Delinquency*. A comparative analysis of delinquency prevention theory, vol. 1. National Institute for Juvenile Justice and Delinquency Prevention. Washington, D.C.: U.S. Government Printing Office, 1977.

WILSON, A. B. Residential segregation of social class and aspirations of high school boys. *American Sociological Review*, 1959, 24, 836–845.

WISE, H. D. In defense of teachers. *School Review, 83* (Nov.), 113–118.

WOLKS, S., and BRANDON, J. Runaway adolescents' perceptions of parents and self. *Adolescence*, 1977, 12, 175–186.

WOLMAN, B. B. *The unconscious mind*. Englewood Cliffs, N.J.: Prentice-Hall, 1968.

WONG, M. Different strokes: Models of drug abuse education. *Contemporary Educational Psychology*, 1976, 1, 1–20.

WONG, M. R., and ALLEN, T. A three-dimensional structure of drug attitudes. *Journal of Drug Education*, 1976, 6, 181–191.

WUNDERLICH, R. A., and JOHNSON, W. G. Some personality correlates of obese persons. *Psychological Reports*, 1973, 32, 1267–1277.

YABLONSKY, L. *The violent gang*. New York: Macmillan, 1962.

YANKELOVICH, D. *The new morality: A profile of American youth in the 70's*. New York: McGraw-Hill, 1974.

ZACKER, J., ANDELMAN, S. L., and BAUER, F. The young adolescent as an obstetrical risk. *American Journal of Obstetrics and Gynecology*, 1969, 103, 305–312.

ZARETSKY, I. I. Cult participation in America. *Intellect*, 1977, 105(Mar.), 299–300.

ZARETSKY, I. I., and LEONE, M. P. *Religious movements in contemporary America*. Princeton, N.J.: Princeton University Press, 1975.

ZELNICK, M., and KANTNER, J. F. Sexuality, contraception and pregnancy among young, unwed females in the United States. In C. F. Westoff and R. Parker, Jr. (eds.), *Commission on population growth and the American future: Demographic and social aspects of population growth*. Vol. 1. Washington, D.C.: U.S. Government Printing Office, 1972.

ZELNICK, M., and KANTNER, J. F. Sexual and contraceptive experience of young unmarried women in the United States: 1970 and 1976. *Family Planning Perspectives*, 1977, 9, 55–71.

ZIGLER, E. Developmental versus difference theories of mental retardation and the problem of motivation. *American Journal of Mental Deficiency*, 1969, 73, 536–556.

ZINBERG, N. E. and ROBERTSON, J. A. *Drugs and the public*. New York: Simon and Schuster, 1972.

Index of Names

Strong, E., 133
Strother, C., 61
Suchman, J., 336
Sugarman, A., 37
Super, D., 133–35
Svajian, P., 5, 146
Sykes, G., 279

Tannenbaum, A., 175
Tanner, J., 29
Terman, L., 53, 73
Thelen, H., 98
Thomas, D., 151–52, 158
Thompson, J., 48
Thurstone, L., 56
Tomlinson-Keasey, C., 68
Torrance, E., 76
Tresemer, D., 118
Tuinman, J., 87
Tuttle, C., 119

Vandermyn, G., 87
Veldman, D., 23

Vener, A., 184, 190, 193
Venezky, R., 87
Vernon, P., 73
Vogt, D., 84
Volkmor, C., 21
Voss, H., 93

Wadsworth, B., 65
Wagner, H., 169
Waldrop, M., 294
Walker, R., 37, 280
Wallach, M., 75
Walters, D., 163–64
Walters, R., 154, 216
Walster, E., 40
Watson, J., 330
Waugh, I., 278
Wechsler, D., 56, 61
Webb, E., 324, 328
Weinberg, M., 272
Weiner, B., 117
Weiner, I., 179, 280, 296
Weis, J., 276

Werner, E., 199
Werthman, C., 278–79
Westling, D., 81
Willemsen, E., 118
Wilson, A., 114, 178
Winokur, G., 302
Wise, H., 98
Wolks, S., 282
Wolman, B., 313
Wong, M., 265
Wunderlich, R., 42
Wynne, L., 301

Yablonsky, D., 271
Yankelovich, D., 189, 233
Young, R., 163, 183

Zabik, J., 250
Zacker, J., 194
Zaretsky, I., 235
Zelnick, M., 192–93, 202
Zigler, E., 69
Zinberg, N., 266

Index of Concepts

1 2 3 4 5 6 7 8 9 0